# Essentials of Microservices Architecture

## Paradigms, Applications, and Techniques

# Essentials of Microservices Architecture

## Paradigms, Applications, and Techniques

by
Chellammal Surianarayanan
Gopinath Ganapathy
Pethuru Raj

CRC Press
Taylor & Francis Group
Boca Raton London New York

CRC Press is an imprint of the
Taylor & Francis Group, an **informa** business

CRC Press
Taylor & Francis Group
6000 Broken Sound Parkway NW, Suite 300
Boca Raton, FL 33487-2742



Printed on acid-free paper

International Standard Book Number-13: 978-0-367-24995-3 (Hardback)



**Visit the Taylor & Francis Web site at**
**http://www.taylorandfrancis.com**

**and the CRC Press Web site at**
**http://www.crcpress.com**

# Contents

# Foreword

Microservices Architecture (MSA) is being positioned as the most influential and insightful architectural style and pattern for designing, developing, and deploying mission-critical software applications across multiple verticals. MSA is innately blessed with several unique competencies that strengthen and speed up software construction and usage. Microservices are being touted as the most optimal block and unit not only for application realization but also for application delivery and deployment.

Microservices are publicly discoverable, self-defined, interoperable, network-accessible, etc. Microservices are easily and effectively composed through the application of service orchestration and choreography techniques and tools. The authors of this book reiterate that microservices have emerged as the most viable entity for bringing forth a litany of smart and sophisticated software solutions and services for society.

A quick glance at the contents of this book: first, we commence with a simple introduction to the functions and context of MSA—the humble and simple origin of the unique MSA style; the steady and speedy growth of MSA across business verticals; the communication style of microservices; how data consistency and management are being tackled efficiently; the various design, composition, and reliability patterns; how monolithic applications get modernized and migrated as a dynamic collection of microservices; the security aspect of microservices; and how Java microservices are being developed through the Spring Boot platform, etc.

I am sure readers will immensely and immeasurably benefit from the information herein, and this book will answer all the lingering doubts of software architects, consultants, and engineers, DevOps professionals, site reliability engineers, and academicians. Further, research students and scholars will richly benefit from this book, which is written by people with education, experience, and expertise in MSA.

I wish all the success to this book and its readers.

**Prof. S. Ponnusamy, F. N. A. Sc.**
*Department of Mathematics, IIT Madras, Chennai-600036.*
*Guest Professor of Hengyang Normal University, China.*

# Preface

The Microservices Architecture (MSA) style is currently gaining a lot of momentum among software architects and engineers. MSA is accelerating software solution design, development, and deployment in a risk-free manner. Taking any software system into production is elegantly simplified and sped up through the smart application of the various competencies of MSA (development platforms, runtime environments such as Docker containers, acceleration engines, design patterns, integrated frameworks, a variety of tools, etc.). Toward next-generation software engineering, the MSA ecosystem is rapidly growing through a bevy of third-party product vendors in order to automate as many tasks as possible. Precisely speaking, MSA is being positioned as an enterprise-grade and agile application design method. This book is specially written with the aim of clearly rendering the distinct features and facilities offered through MSA to our esteemed readers.

The objective of the first chapter is to introduce the concepts of Service-Oriented Architecture (SOA) by presenting different co-existing object-oriented distributed computing technologies, such as Common Object Request Broker Architecture (CORBA), the Distributed Component Object Model (DCOM), and Remote Method Invocation (RMI) and by contrasting how SOA differs from object-oriented models. From this chapter, the reader will understand the purpose of SOA, the technologies and protocols (web services) used for SOA, and the typical use cases of SOA. Ultimately, the reader will get to know the deployment difficulties associated with SOA applications.

The second chapter demystifies Microservices Architecture (MSA). Requirements of modern applications are very dynamic due to frequently changing customer needs. Such requirements are needed for the continuous delivery to customers. This requires an appropriate application architecture which supports frequent deployment and delivery. In this context, the objective of this chapter is to introduce the essentials of MSA as an architecture that breaks down an application into microservices, each of which can be independently, as well as frequently, deployed and thus facilitate continuous delivery of the application to customers. By the end of the chapter, the reader will understand the need for MSA, how MSA meets the modern business requirements, and typical use cases, benefits, and drawbacks.

The third chapter explains the various current and emerging communication models for microservices. There are various key architectural elements involved in developing an MSA-based application. The objective of this chapter is to introduce one of the key architectural elements: the communication models of MSA. By the end of this chapter, the reader will understand how services interact with one another synchronously and asynchronously using standard architectures, protocols, and message brokers.

The fourth chapter describes how microservice Application Programming Interfaces (APIs) are designed in an efficient manner as well as also describing the various MSA middleware platforms. The prime objective is to describe the three major architectural elements related to communication, namely (i) designing APIs for microservices, (ii) developing middleware platforms, and (iii) data formats for communication. By the end of this chapter, the reader will understand why microservices require APIs, how to design APIs for microservices, and how to establish middleware platforms with existing standards and frameworks such as REST, SOAP, Apache Thrift, and gRPC. Further, the reader will understand different data formats of communication. By the end of this chapter, the reader will be able to visualize how different concepts, namely APIs, data formats, communication models, and middleware platforms, fit with one another to enable inter-service interaction and hence integration.

The fifth chapter illustrates microservice discovery and the role of the API gateway in discovery. The objective of this chapter is to introduce two related concepts, namely service discovery and the API gateway. By the end of this chapter, the reader will understand how clients discover and access different services using service discovery mechanisms and the API gateway

The sixth chapter introduces two service integration/composition techniques, namely service orchestration and choreography for composing individual services so as to achieve useful business processes. By the end of this chapter, the reader will come to know about the basic concepts of orchestration and choreography, with traditional orchestration and choreography languages, as well as how microservices are integrated flexibly and easily with the help of readily available orchestration platforms and workflow engines.

The seventh chapter depicts how database transactions happen in microservices-centric applications. The objective of this chapter is to introduce the concept of database transactions in MSA. By the end of this chapter, the reader will understand how data is decentralized between different microservices, and how transactions in such as a decentralized environment can be carried out with high availability and eventual consistency.

The eighth chapter is dedicated to listing and explaining all the relevant MSA patterns. There are design, composition, security, and deployment patterns for using microservices for producing and sustaining enterprise-grade, service-oriented, event-driven, cloud-hosted, business-critical, people-centric applications. The objective of this chapter is to present popular design patterns that are useful for the design, development, and deployment of microservices. By the end of the chapter, the reader will understand how different categories of patterns, such as decomposition patterns, composition patterns, observability patterns, database architecture patterns, cross-cutting concern patterns, and deployment patterns, are useful for MSA

The ninth chapter is allocated to how microservices security is enabled and how legacy applications are modernized and migrated to optimized IT environments, such as cloud centers. The objective of this chapter is to handle two complementary concepts: MSA security and MSA migration. By the end of the chapter, the reader will understand how security in MSA differs from that of conventional systems and how different security mechanisms are implemented in MSA applications using reference architecture. The reader will also understand the basic concepts of MSA migration, the motivating factors for MSA migration, issues associated with MSA migration, the migration process, and candidate applications for MSA migration.

The tenth chapter is specially dedicated to software architects and engineers for building powerful microservices and how their composition results in pioneering software applications for businesses and people. With the exponential growth of IoT devices (smartphones, wearables, portables, consumer electronics, drones, robots, instruments, appliances, equipment, machines, etc.), microservices are being developed and deployed on resource-constrained as well as resource-intensive devices in order to construct people-centric applications. Thus, the role of microservices is continuously expanding in order to set up smarter environments (smart homes, hotels, hospitals, etc.). We have chosen Spring Boot as the integrated development environment in order to build Java microservices. There are other development environments and rapid application builders for different programming languages and hence the days are not too far off for ubiquitous yet disappearing microservices.

# Acknowledgments

**Chellammal Surianarayanan**

First, I thank the Almighty with whom I always realize a lot of blessings, confidence, bliss, and peace. He has given me the opportunity for writing this book. I thank Him as He helped me to complete the book with success.

I send my deepest gratitude to Mr. John Wyzalek, Senior Acquisitions Editor, at CRC Press/Taylor & Francis Group, who gave me the chance to dive and swim into the deep seas of Microservices Architecture and come out with this book.

I convey my sincere gratitude to one of my co-authors, Dr. Pethuru Raj, Chief Architect and Vice President, Site Reliability Engineering Division, Reliance Jio Infocomm. Ltd. (RJIL), Bangalore, India, who cared so much about the work, and responded to my questions and queries so promptly. He took special effort in attending to my doubts. Like microservices, he is very quick and agile while discussing the technical and technological aspects related to MSA. He provided insightful comments and feedback on the chapters which encouraged me to cover Microservices Architecture from various perspectives. He is the sole inspiration for writing this book. His simplicity, readiness, and help motivated me to work with gigantic force and momentum so that I could complete the book on time. He has consistently proposed excellent improvements for this book. Through this note, I convey my sincere gratitude to him from my heart, brain, and soul.

I express my sincere thanks to another of my co-authors, Dr. G. Gopinath, Registrar of Bharathidasan University, Tiruchirappalli, India, for being an exemplary mentor of my academic and professional life. He provided me with a positive spirit and energy to complete this book. I am also thankful to him as, without his generosity and selfless support, this work would have never seen the light as it has now. Through this note, I convey my heartfelt gratitude to him.

I convey my sincere thanks to Dr. T. Unnamalai, Principal, Bharathidasan University Constituent Arts and Science College, Tiruchirappalli, India, for her support.

I have great pleasure in expressing my deep sense of thanks to my parents, my husband, R. Ganesan, and my lovely son, G. Srimurugan, for their kindness, support, and care.

I sincerely convey my thanks to everyone on the editing, proof reading, and publishing team of CRC Press/Taylor & Francis Group.

**Gopinath Ganapathy**
I place on record my gratitude to Dr. P. Manisankar, Vice-Chancellor, Bharathidasan University, Tiruchirappalli, India, for his support and encouragement.

I profusely acknowledge the tireless effort, energy, and time spent by Chellammal and Pethru Raj on writing this book. I thank CRC Press/Taylor & Francis Group for their choosing us to be part of their prestigious family. I thank John Wyzalek for his constant follow ups and extraction of quality work from us, from time to time.

I express my thanks to the School of Computer Science and Engineering, Bharathidasan University, Tiruchirappalli, India, for their ecology and Kalaivani Sridhar for the infra and software support. I thank Vikram, PhD scholar, for preparing the table of contents and index for this book.

I recall the tremendous faith and dreams of the parents of Chellammal being realized as the true outcome of completing this highly enriched book. I thank my parents, my wife, Renuka, and daughter, Grisha, too, for their understanding and love.

**Pethuru Raj**
I extend my sincere gratitude to John Wyzalek, Senior Acquisitions Editor, CRC Press/Taylor & Francis Group, for the opportunity rendered to us to bring forth this book. I thank Prof. Chellammal Surianarayanan, PhD, for her unwavering zeal in putting together her vast and varied technical competency in producing this prestigious book. I appreciate her unflinching determination and discipline in completing this book with all the right and relevant details. Her expertise and experience in crafting this textbook on Microservices Architecture in a precise and concise manner for a larger audience is really laudable. Let God appropriately reward her for all her hard work.

I solemnly submit here my profound gratitude to my managers, Mr. Anish Shah and Mr. Kiran Thomas, the President at Reliance Industries Limited, Bombay, for their moral support. I also appreciate my former manager, Mr. Sreekrishnan Venkateswaran, Distinguished Engineer (DE), IBM Cloud, for all the enchanting technical discussions. I appreciate my colleagues, Senthil Arunachalam and Vidya Hungud, for their cooperation.

At this moment, I reflect upon the selfless sacrifices of my parents during my formative days. I thank my wife (Sweetlin Reena) and my sons (Darren Samuel and Darresh Bernie) for their extreme patience. Above all, I give all the glory and honor to my Lord and Savior Jesus Christ for granting the physical strength and the knowledge required toward contributing to this book.

# About the Authors

**Chellammal Surianarayanan** is an Assistant Professor of Computer Science at Bharathidasan University Constituent Arts and Science College, Tiruchirappalli, Tamil Nadu, India. She earned a doctorate in Computer Science by developing optimization techniques for the discovery and selection of semantic services. She has published research papers in *Springer Service-Oriented Computing and Applications*, *IEEE Transactions on Services Computing*, *International Journal of Computational Science*, *Inderscience*, and the *SCIT Journal of the Symbiosis Centre for Information Technology*, etc. She has produced book chapters with IGI Global and CRC Press. She has been a life member of several professional bodies such as the Computer Society of India, IAENG, etc.

Before coming to academic service, Chellammal Surianarayanan served as Scientific Officer in the Indira Gandhi Centre for Atomic Research, Department of Atomic Energy, Government of India, Kalpakkam, Tamil Nadu, India. She was involved in the research and development of various embedded systems and software applications. Her remarkable contributions include the development of an embedded system for lead shield integrity assessment, portable automatic air sampling equipment, the embedded system of detection of lymphatic filariasis in its early stage, and the development of data logging software applications for atmospheric dispersion studies. In all she has more than 20 years of academic and industrial experience.

**Gopinath Ganapathy** is the Registrar of Bharathidasan University, Tiruchirappalli, Tamil Nadu, India. He has 30 years of experience in academia, industry, research, and consultancy services. He has around 8 years of international experience in the US and UK. He served as a consultant for a few Fortune 500 companies that include IBM, Lucent-Bell Labs, Merrill Lynch, Toyota, etc. He specializes in the design of Multi-Tier and Enterprise Application Integration (EAI) technologies. He received the Young Scientist Fellow award for the year 1994 from the Govt. of Tamil Nadu. His areas of research are semantic web, AI, auto-programming, ontology, and text mining. He has published and presented almost 100 research papers in international journals and at conferences. He has acted as an academic advisor for mediating off-campus programs at the University of Valley Creek, North Dakota.

He is a member of several academic and technology councils in various universities in India. He has convened many international conferences/workshops/seminars. He is a referee and editorial member for a few international journals. He has guided 12 PhD scholars. He is a Professional Member of the IEEE, ACM, and IAENG. He is a life member of the Indian Science Congress, Indian Society for Technical Education, and Computer Society of India. He has visited the London Business School, UK; the University of Birmingham, UK; Rutgers University, New Jersey; the Stephan Institute, New Jersey; Imperial College, London; Oxford University, UK; the University of Valley Creek, North Dakota; the University of Utara, Malaysia; and the University of West Australia.

**Pethuru Raj** is the Chief Architect and Vice President of the Site Reliability Engineering Center of Excellence (CoE) Division, Reliance Jio Infocomm Ltd. (RJIL), Bangalore. His has had previous stints with the IBM Cloud CoE, Wipro Consulting Services (WCS), and Robert Bosch Corporate Research (CR). In total, he has gained more than 17 years of IT industry experience and 8 years of research experience. He completed a CSIR-sponsored PhD degree at Anna University, Chennai, and continued with UGC-sponsored postdoctoral research in the Department of Computer Science and Automation, Indian Institute of Science, Bangalore. Thereafter, he was granted a couple of international research fellowships (JSPS and JST) to work as a research scientist for 3.5 years in two leading Japanese universities. He has published more than 30 research papers in peer-reviewed journals from IEEE, ACM, Springer-Verlag, Inderscience, etc. He has authored ten books thus far which focus on some of the emerging technologies such as IoT, cognitive analytics, blockchain, digital twin, Docker containerization, data science, microservices architecture, fog/edge computing, etc. He has contributed 30 book chapters thus far for various technology books edited by highly acclaimed and accomplished professors and professionals.

# Chapter 1

# An Introduction to Service-Oriented Architecture

***Objective***

The objective of this chapter is to introduce the concepts of Service-Oriented Architecture (SOA) by presenting different co-existing object-oriented distributed computing technologies such as Common Object Request Broker Architecture (CORBA), Distributed Component Object Model (DCOM), and Remote Method Invocation (RMI), and by contrasting SOA from object-oriented models. From this chapter, the reader will understand the purpose of SOA, the technologies and protocols (web services) used for SOA, and the typical use cases of SOA. Ultimately, the reader will grasp the deployment difficulties associated with SOA applications.

***Preface***

There are two service-based architectures, namely, SOA and Microservices Architecture (MSA). An overview of SOA and its purpose, its implementing technologies, such as web services, and its typical use cases, will help the reader to distinguish the recent MSA from SOA. With this thought in mind, this chapter introduces different distributed object-oriented computer programming models, namely CORBA, DCOM, and RMI. It highlights that these technologies are tightly coupled technologies. The chapter discusses the need for an enterprise to integrate various applications but in a loosely coupled manner to fulfill the dynamic needs of customers. This need is addressed by Service-Oriented Architecture.

SOA, as an architectural style, emphasizes that applications should be developed in such a way so that they can interact with one another using standard communication protocols. The chapter presents why SOA has been developed, its purpose, and its implementing technologies with the help of typical use cases. Ultimately, the chapter discusses that, though SOA applications have been in use over a decade, the way an SOA application integrates more and more elements with SOA, the size of an SOA application itself has been turned as a bottleneck, which prevents quicker development, deployment, and delivery. The chapter closes with the idea that there is yet another concept that is still needed, which is capable of supporting frequent deployment and continuous delivery as modern applications have to deliver on customer demands quickly and frequently.

### *Motivating Questions*

1. There are already proven distributed technologies such as CORBA, RMI, and DCOM in place. Why do we need SOA? Are we re-inventing the wheel?
2. What is the purpose for which SOA has been developed?
3. What is SOA? How does SOA differ from distributed computing technologies?
4. Can SOA replace distributed technologies?
5. How is SOA implemented? What are web services?
6. Why did web services become popular?
7. What are the risks of web services?
8. What is an Enterprise Service Bus?
9. Do you think SOA/web services are currently in use?
10. Why may SOA/web services become obsolete?

## Introduction

The various requirements of business applications greatly influence the evolution of different computing technologies. Conventionally, applications have been developed in a monolithic style where an application resides in a single machine and is typically run by a single user. The growth of networking technologies has brought about the concept of sharing various computing resources (both hardware and software resources) among different users over a network. This led to the development of splitting an application into identifiable tiers, clients, and servers in which a client tier is typically a physical machine which runs the client or interface part of the application and the service tier (physical machine) which runs the core application. Users access the application running on a server over the network. This is the so-called "two-tier client-server programming" which has brought about a shift from monolithic computing to network-based computing, and thus has enabled many people to access an application simultaneously over a network. In the earlier stage of two-tier client-server programming, applications are typically accessed over a Local Area Network (LAN) and around only ten users can access an application.

When there is an increase in the number of users, the LAN-based two-tier model becomes insufficient to give the required scalability (in terms of users) and availability of the application. Hence, toward providing higher scalability and availability, the two-tier model is enhanced into a three-tier architecture where business logic is separated from databases. Three distinguished logical modules of the application, namely the client/presentation module, business logic module, and data access and database modules, are deployed in different machines. This kind of three-tier architecture model stood as the standard business architecture for over two decades.

The evolution of the internet has brought tremendous changes in the needs of business applications. Customers wanted to access business applications over the internet, which led to the development of web applications. This means that the presentation layer of an application is typically accessed using a browser over the internet. This not only changes the way how an application is being accessed but greatly increases the number of users of typical commercial applications such as online shopping, online travel booking, online banking, online financial applications, and online e-governance applications such as online electricity bill payment, online public distribution, etc.

The above trends demand that business applications are readily available and highly scalable. This again produced changes in the way applications are being developed. The scale of the network means the application is distributed over long-range networks. Typically, enterprise branches all over the globe started developing distributed applications. This means that different components of an application get distributed to different locations, and they are accessed over private enterprise networks. Similar to the growth of networking technologies, corresponding to the development of distributed applications, various object-oriented distributed programming specifications, standards, and frameworks have been invented. Such common technologies include CORBA, DCOM, and RMI. These technologies focus on how to distribute objects, invoke their methods from a remote machine, and handle the interaction between two applications, but in an object-oriented tightly coupled manner.

The growing, dynamic needs of customers compel business organizations to integrate their individual applications so that overall processes and information can be effectively used to draw aggregated information which is necessary to meet the needs of customers. This has been addressed by an architectural style called Service-Oriented Architecture. SOA is commonly implemented using a suite of XML-based open communication protocols called web services.

## 1.1 Common Object Request Broker Architecture (CORBA)

*CORBA is a specification developed by the Object Management Group (OMG) which defines the technical standard for invoking methods of a remote object over a network.*

CORBA [1] enables communication between object-oriented applications (i.e., Object Remote Procedure Call) running on computers which have different operating systems in a TCP/IP network. The main objectives of CORBA are to provide:

(i) Cross-platform support for client and server
(ii) Cross-language support for clients and server
(iii) Common services for application development

The core components of CORBA architecture include:

(i) Object Request Broker (ORB)
(ii) CORBA Interface Definition Language (IDL)
(iii) IDL Compiler, Stub, and Skeleton
(iv) Internet Inter-ORB Protocol (IIOP)
(v) CORBA common services

Core CORBA architecture is shown in Figure 1.1.

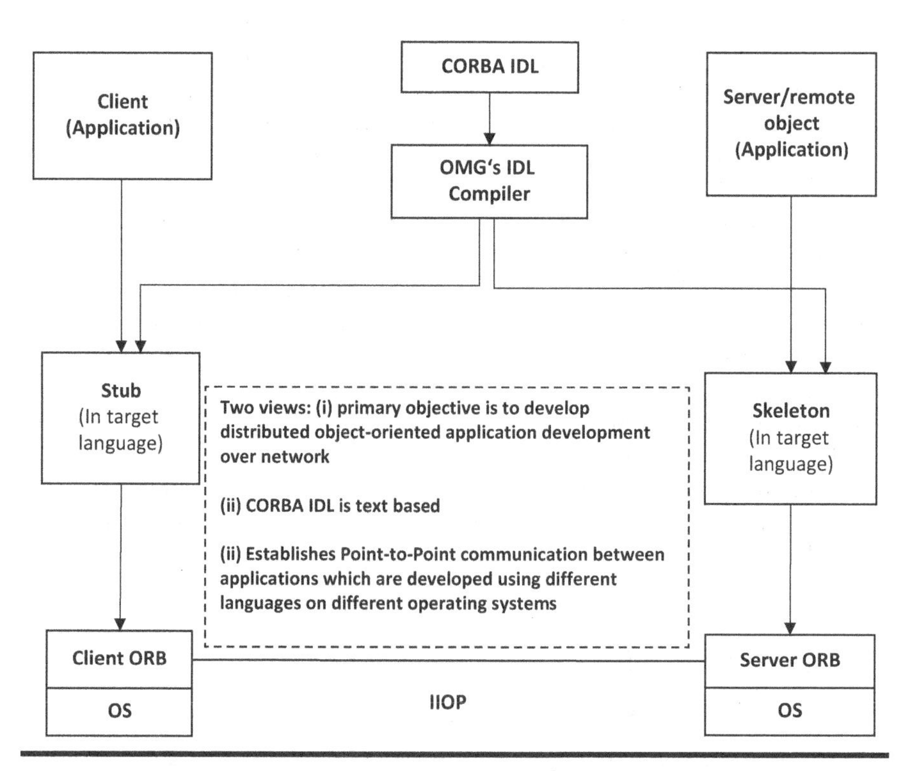


**Figure 1.1 The core of CORBA architecture.**

***Interface Definition Language (IDL)***

In the CORBA model, the remote object is the server whose method is invoked by a client from a remote location. In order to invoke the remote method, a client should know:

(i) The location of the server object
(ii) The call semantics of the required methods

To enable communication between client and server, the server should expose its interface. CORBA defines a platform-independent standard method for a server object to expose its methods and interface called *CORBA Interface Definition Language* (IDL). CORBA IDL is a text-based platform-independent specification for describing the interface for the server object. It is the key feature that makes CORBA platform-independent. After the implementation of the server object, the developer has to develop a *CORBA IDL interface* for the object according to the specification of CORBA IDL specification.

***IDL Compiler, Stub and Skeleton***

In order to support cross-language support, CORBA provides IDL-targeted language mapping for different languages such as C++, Ada, Java, etc. After developing CORBA IDL for a server object, the interface file is given as input to an *IDL compiler*, and *it generates skeleton and stub in the required targeted languages with the necessary IDL-language mapping*. A stub is the client version of the server object, and it stays on the client's computer. When a client makes a request to the server, it actually submits its request to a stub as in Figure 1.1. Then the request is passed to the ORB layer which performs the marshaling of the request and sends it to the server. On the server side, the ORB performs the unmarshalling and hands over the request to the skeleton. Skeleton stays on the server and handles the requests received from clients.

***Object Request Broker***

ORB *establishes communication between two applications*. Also, it locates the server object and performs the marshaling (conversion of method arguments and return values from language-specific formats to network-specific formats) and unmarshalling (conversion of data from network-specific formats to language-specific formats).

***Internet Inter-ORB Protocol***

According to CORBA specifications, applications should use the standard protocol, Internet Inter-ORB Protocol, for communication

***CORBA Common Services***

CORBA offers a rich set of common services, such as naming and directory, security, transaction, persistence, event, messaging, concurrency, etc., and availability of these common services enables developers to focus on core application development.

***Typical Steps in CORBA Model***

The following are the typical steps in the CORBA model with a prerequisite that ORB is installed on both computers which are going to communicate.

- Develop the CORBA server object which supports remote references.
- Develop the CORBA IDL for the server object.
- Develop the appropriate stub and skeleton by giving the developed IDL to the IDL Compiler (the IDL compiler will generate a language-specific stub and skeleton).
- Distribute stub to the client.
- Develop a client application to create a remote reference for a server object by specifying the unique name of the server to the context and naming services.
- After obtaining a reference, the client can invoke methods (please keep it in mind that it uses IIOP protocol on top of the TCP/IP network).

Thus, a CORBA-based program from any vendor, on almost any computer, operating system, programming language, and network, can interoperate with a another CORBA-based program, from the same or another vendor, on almost any other computer, operating system, programming language, and network using ORB, CORBA IDL, IDL Compiler, Stub, Skeleton, and IIOP.

## 1.2 Distributed Component Object Model (DCOM)

Microsoft's Distributed Component Object Model (DCOM) allows object-oriented applications and systems of different languages to interact as long as the applications adhere to use the binary standard specified by Microsoft [2]; i.e., DCOM is a proprietary standard from Microsoft for distributed, object-oriented computing which brings interoperability between Microsoft applications.

In the Microsoft DCOM model, which is shown in Figure 1.2, Microsoft Interface Definition Language (MIDL) defines the interface of the remote object. MIDL is a proprietary, and Microsoft defined binary interface standard, and hence DCOM achieves interoperability among programming languages over Microsoft's Operating System, typically Windows. The chief focus of DCOM is to provide object-oriented communication over Microsoft Windows applications. It uses the Microsoft Object Remote Procedure Call (Microsoft ORPC) for communication.

## 1.3 Remote Method Invocation

RMI technology is used to invoke methods from a remote Java object from another java application. The RMI model of communication is shown in Figure 1.3.

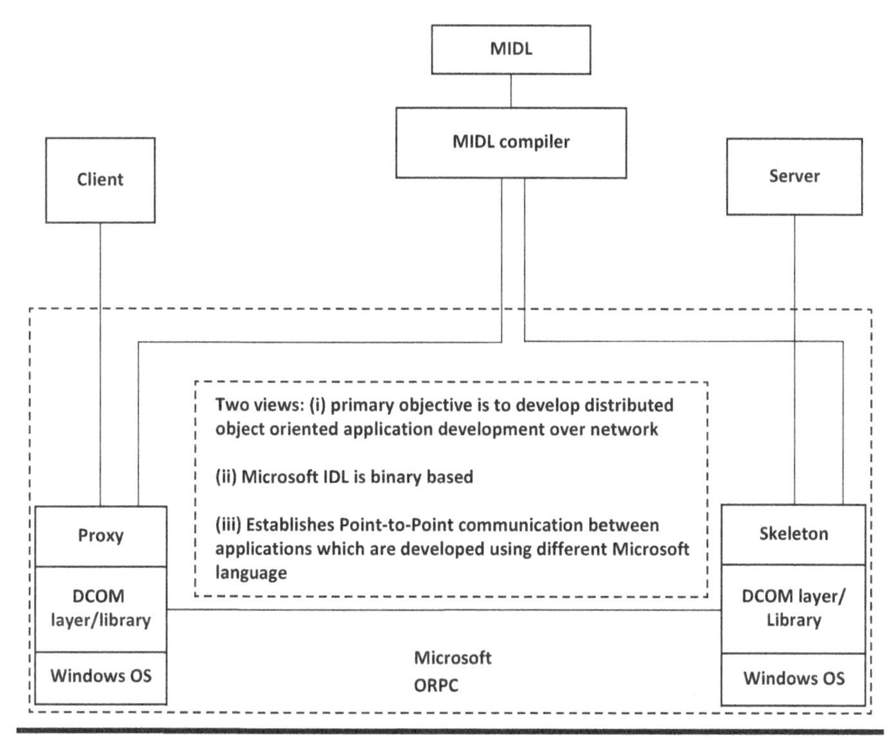


**Figure 1.2 The Microsoft model.**

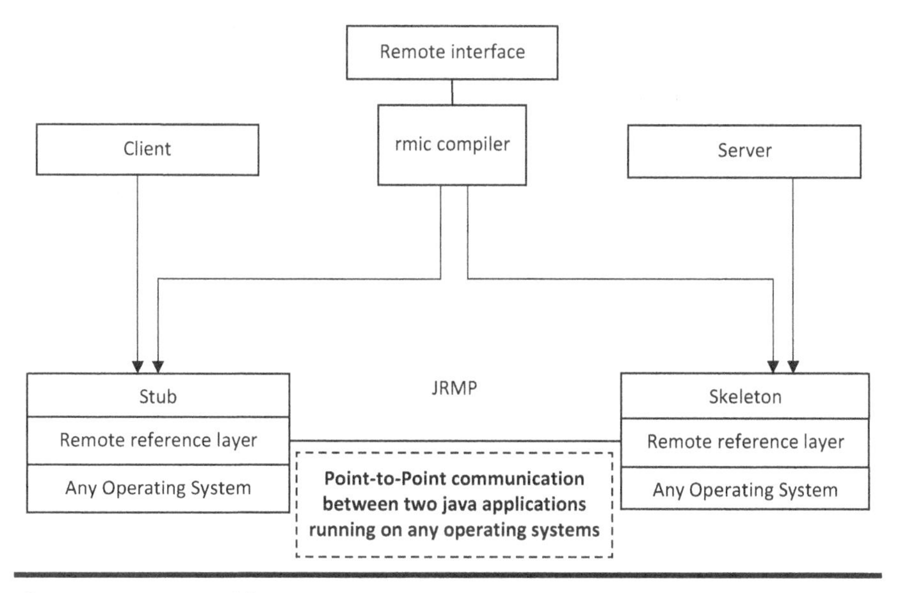


**Figure 1.3 RMI architecture.**

As RMI is based on Java, it implicitly achieves cross-platform features, but it only supports Java. In RMI, the remote object exposes its capabilities through the remote interface which then is compiled using a rmic compiler to produce stub and skeleton. The stub and skeleton interact via the remote reference layer using Java Remote Method Protocol (JRMP).

## 1.4 Prerequisites for CORBA, DCOM, and RMI

*Mandatory prerequisites for CORBA*—CORBA aims to achieve application to application communication with cross-platform and cross-language support as well as to provide the common services to applications, such as naming and directory services, security, transaction, concurrency, messaging, fault tolerance, etc. This facilitates the developers to focus on the actual core application functionality rather than on the common services.

Server and client should install ORB. The server should expose its interface only through CORBA IDL. Client and server should keep the corresponding language-mapped stub and skeleton, respectively. Client and server applications should interact according to IIOP or any other OMG compliant communication standard on which both server and client should be agreed upon.

In addition, the interfaces of server objects should be stored with a unique name (which must include the location of the object) in a registry (i.e., in "interface repository"/"implementation repository") and it should be accessible to the client. This enables a client to search and find its required interfaces, which it creates using the remote reference of the server object.

*Mandatory prerequisites for DCOM*—DCOM aims to achieve object-oriented communication among Windows-based applications with cross-language support as well as to provide naming, directory, transaction, load balancing, and transaction services. The scope of DCOM is windows-based operating systems and Microsoft-based languages.

Server and client should install the Microsoft DCOM layer. The server object should expose its capabilities using a Microsoft IDL, but it is a binary and proprietary interface. The objective of DCOM is to provide an application to application interaction over the network using Microsoft Object Remote Procedure Call (RPC) on the top of TCP/IP. Similar to CORBA, server objects should store their interfaces in the Windows registry, and clients will look into it by mentioning the unique name of the object.

*Mandatory prerequisites for RMI*—Applications should be in Java. They should have installed the Remote Reference Layer, rmic compiler, and JRMP which come as part of the Java Development Kit (JDK). In RMI, the interfaces of server objects are also archived in the RMI registry using a client which will look for its required server object.

## 1.5 Typical Use Cases and Confined Focuses of CORBA, DCOM, and RMI

From the above section, it is understood that, though CORBA, DCOM, and RMI provide an application to application interaction, the elements will work as long as the applications adhere to the prerequisites. In other words, meeting the prerequisites may not be a flexible way of communicating on a global scale. This is illustrated with a few examples as given below:

**Example—1 (CORBA Typical Use Case)**

Consider two business partners, *Partner-A* and *Partner-B*. These partners are in collaboration on a project using the CORBA model. Obviously, they would have established a private network (maybe a private WAN or Virtual Private Network (VPN) tunnel over the internet) and fulfilled all the prerequisites of CORBA. Everything goes well as far as the partners communicate goes. But what would happen if the server object had to be available to all clients on a global scale over the internet? Is it possible to compel all the clients to install ORB and compel them to use IIOP? Even if they agree, will the firewall of the enterprises allow IIOP traffic freely without any issues?

The answer is as follows. CORBA is a proven solution for object-oriented communication between applications, and it provides very good performance, reliability, fault tolerance, security, transaction support, etc. for an enterprise business. If an enterprise really wants to go for distributed object-oriented computing with cross-platform and cross-language support (CORBA supports interoperability among languages as long as an IDL that uses language mapping is available), CORBA is an appropriate choice. It is not a global scale solution. Its purpose is not to provide a global level solution as obviously performance would be negatively affected. CORBA was not developed to simply provide simple message-based communication among different servers and clients over the internet. The sole purpose of CORBA is to provide enterprises with a robust distributed object-oriented computing model along with a wide range of common services so that they can confine their focus to core application development without worrying about common services. Enterprises can distribute their core applications over different machines at different locations.

**Example—2: Typical use case for DCOM**

Imagine that the business partners, *Partner-A* and *Partner-B* are working in an environment with a Windows platform. Imagine that they want to develop a collaborative project using an object-oriented paradigm.

Now the appropriate technology to use is the DCOM model. The reader should understand that DCOM is a proven object-oriented solution for distributed enterprise application development over a network of Windows-based systems. Here, also, DCOM provides support for common services so that programmers can concentrate on core application development.

Similarly, this argument goes for Java RMI. RMI is used to establish interaction between any two Java applications running on different Java Virtual Machines (JVMs) equipped with the elements of RMI, i.e., remote interface, remote reference layer, rmic, rmi registry, and JRMP.

From the above aspects, all three technologies have the same broad objective—establishing communication between two object-oriented applications. But each method has its own confined focus. CORBA aims to provide an application to application interaction with cross-platform support, and IDL-target language mapping is available for languages such as C++, Java, Smalltalk, Ada, Python, Lisp, (also, in the case of C, COBOL provides RPC communication), etc. DCOM has its confined focus as providing cross-language support among Microsoft applications. It implies that it brings interoperability among Visual C++, C#, VB.Net, and ASP. Net. Similarly, RMI has its confined focus as providing interaction between two java applications.

Overall, the emphasis here is to convey that one technology is not meant to replace the other one. Enterprises have to choose the appropriate technology according to the environment in which it is working, i.e., the reason why all the technologies are co-existing.

## 1.6 Concept of Service-Oriented Architecture

Though object-oriented distributed communication facilitated the development of enterprise applications significantly, not all the needs of enterprises are fulfilled by these technologies. Consider a scenario. In practice, business organizations tend to have a well-defined organizational structure which typically includes different departments such as payroll, accounts, administration, manufacturing, production, purchase, sales, stock, inventory, etc. This kind of organizational structure helps in identifying people with relevant expertise and allotting them to the relevant department. The needs and operations of each department can be performed efficiently. In this organizational structure, every department has been given sufficient freedom to decide its facilities. Information technology is being used by almost all sections/departments. In general, a department tends to choose its technological solution based on (i) the technical needs of the department, (ii) budget and time constraints, and (iii) the available technologies to meet the needs under budget constraints. The key point here is that every department independently decides its technological solutions, keeping the local objectives of that department in mind. These types of enterprise solution have resulted in the following situations.

(i) Independent applications are being implemented using different technologies, different programming languages, different database solutions, different interfaces/APIs, different operating systems, etc.

(ii) Though the above applications can help the concerned departments, on a global scale throughout the enterprise, it becomes difficult to execute overall business processes between different applications.
(iii) As the applications are independently developed, duplication of the same data in different departments arises.
(iv) In a nutshell, it becomes a challenge to execute an integrated business process and to draw enterprise-level data due to the heterogeneity of the technologies of individual applications.

One might ask: Why do we need to integrate individual applications?

The main motivation behind integrating all applications is to effectively use the data that is generated by different applications. The main benefits include:

(i) Data can be shared among different applications. For example, consider the Customer Relations Management (CRM) application of an enterprise. This application maintains customer data. Now the marketing department can initiate marketing and send advertisements to the targeted customers suggested by the CRM. This ultimately improves the sales of products, which in turn increases production. The whole process can even be automated.
(ii) Integration of applications provides a single point of access to global data. When applications are integrated, an employee can access any of his required data via a single point of access. Both data and business processes can be efficiently managed.
(iii) Integration of applications increases a business organization's ability to look for new business opportunities.
(iv) With an integrated environment, an enterprise can deliver responses to customers quickly; it improves customer satisfaction significantly.

Thus, the basic need for integration is driven by the dynamic needs of customers and a single point of access to global data. With modern technologies, such as the internet and smartphones, customers have become very choosy and discerning in selecting their business providers. For example, if a customer chooses a shipment of his goods from one location to another location with shipment services, he closely watches and tracks the status of his shipment. The customers need both quality and quick services from business organizations. Customers want to be informed about their needs.

In simple words, it becomes very difficult to deliver on the dynamic needs of customers. One of the major issues that exist with business applications is heterogeneity among applications. Due to the heterogeneity of applications, they stand as *information silos*, and drawing useful information and taking business decisions is tedious. Heterogeneity in applications prevents them (i) from interacting with one another and hence sharing or reusing already developed functional modules, (ii) from integrating various applications which actually contain complete, enterprise-level information which is very much needed to respond to the customer's needs quickly. Now the critical challenge is: *How to bring in interactions among applications in spite of their heterogeneity?*

The challenge is addressed by Service-Oriented Architecture. SOA is an architectural style or architectural concept (it is an not implemented one) that emphasizes the development of applications in the form of independent software components with well-defined interfaces (called services) which should be accessible over a network with a standard communication protocol; i.e., The primary purpose of SOA [3] is to *bring interoperability among business applications and establish application to application communication*. Interacting applications might have been developed using different languages and might have been deployed on different operating systems. SOA emphasizes that the applications should be able to communicate with one another over the network with standardized communication protocols so that a component of one application can be shared by the component of other application. The concept of SOA can be seen in Figure 1.4

The concept of SOA is not new. There are some distributed computing models which have already established the interactions among heterogeneous applications. Examples include Common Object Request Broker Architecture (CORBA), Distributed Component Object Model (DCOM), Remote Method Invocation, and web services. The key point is that the origin of CORBA/DCOM/RMI is not to implement SOA. These technologies focus on the development of distributed object-oriented applications, and hence they implicitly have to handle the application to application interaction. More important is that CORBA/DCOM/RMI are tightly coupled technologies that aim at developing robust enterprise applications distributed over a network, whereas SOA aims at loose coupling among applications in order to establish an application to application interaction so that integrated business processes can be achieved.

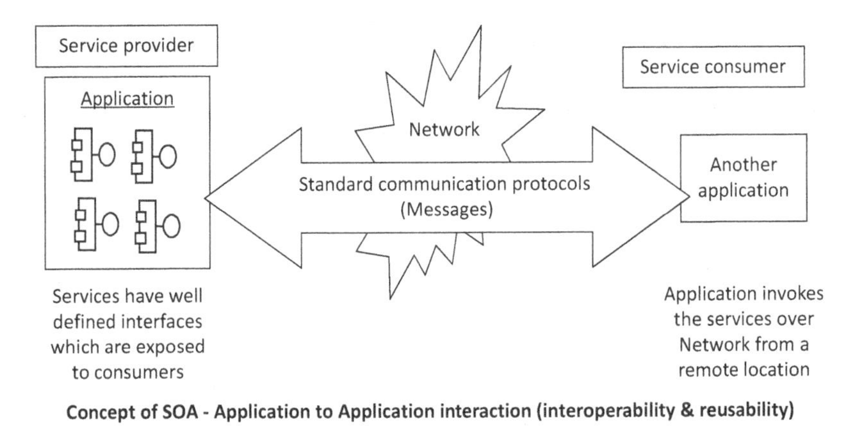


**Figure 1.4 The concept of SOA.**

## 1.7 Web Services

In line with previous technologies, namely CORBA, DCOM, RMI, web services are a suite of XML-based open communication protocols which were developed to implement SOA [4]. Its primary objective is to provide application to application interaction in a message-based loosely coupled manner using standard communication protocols. Web services refer to a stack of XML-based open protocols. This technology stack includes the Simple Object Access Protocol (SOAP), Universal Description, Discovery and Integration (UDDI) and Web Service Description Language (WSDL). This technology stack typically uses HTTP as its transport protocol. This is shown in Figure 1.5.

**Web Service Description Language**

Web Service Description Language (WSDL) is an XML-based protocol used to describe the interface of services. The functional capabilities of a service are exposed to clients through WSDL. WSDL consists of two parts, an abstract part, and a concrete part. The abstract part defines various operations of a service, their input and output messages, and data types of messages. The concrete part of WSDL gives the URL address of the service, port details, and transport mechanism to invoke the service.

**Universal Description, Discovery, and Integration**

The service descriptions should be published in a registry so that clients can search and find the required services. In order to publish the interfaces and to search the interfaces, web services define a protocol called Universal Description, Discovery, and Integration.

UDDI is an XML-based open protocol which is used to (i) publish service details & WSDL and (ii) search and find the required WSDL. From this, one should know that a developer cannot publish his services as he wishes but has to follow the specification of UDDI. Basically, UDDI specification has a data structure

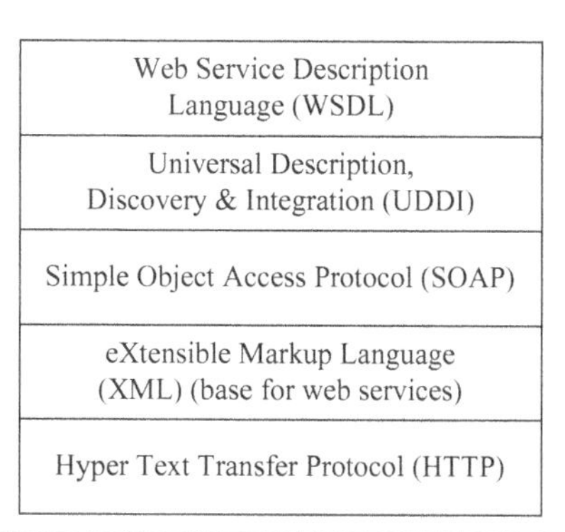


**Figure 1.5 Web services technology stack.**

which consists of three elements, namely businessEntity, businessService, and tModel. businessEntity gives the details of service providers; businessService gives the details of services provided by a businessEntity, and tModel gives the technical description of the services (i.e., WSDL). In addition, the service description and service details as per UDDI are archived in registries of corporate. (Please note: conventionally, there was a registry called the Universal Business UDDI Registry, UBR. It was maintained by service providers such as IBM, SAP, and Microsoft, but was closed in 2006 due to maintenance issues).

**Simple Object Access Protocol**

A web services stack defines a protocol called SOAP for communication between server and client. SOAP is an XML-based open messaging protocol with which the client will invoke the method of service. Further, SOAP defines two types of messages, namely SOAP literal or document style which is used for communicating one-way messages such as posting a purchase order and SOAP RPC style which is a request–response type or two-way communication, typically used to invoke a function of a service.

Overall, the above protocols are based on XML. XML is a text-based protocol, and it can be interpreted only in the same or similar way by all operating systems. Hence web services inherently acquire the property of platform independence. XML serves as the key in achieving platform neutrality.

The relationship between the three protocols can be understood using Figure 1.6. As in Figure 1.6, *Currencyconvert* is the server object which publishes its WSDL through any one of the mechanisms such as the UDDI corporate registry of provider's facility, marketplace, point of sale, or service portal. A consumer searches through any one of the above ways and finds his required service. After obtaining the WSDL of the required service, a consumer will construct a SOAP request according to the calling semantics specified in the WSDL. Then he invokes the required function using a SOAP call. (Please note: the service will get executed in the remote server and the SOAP response is sent to the consumer.)

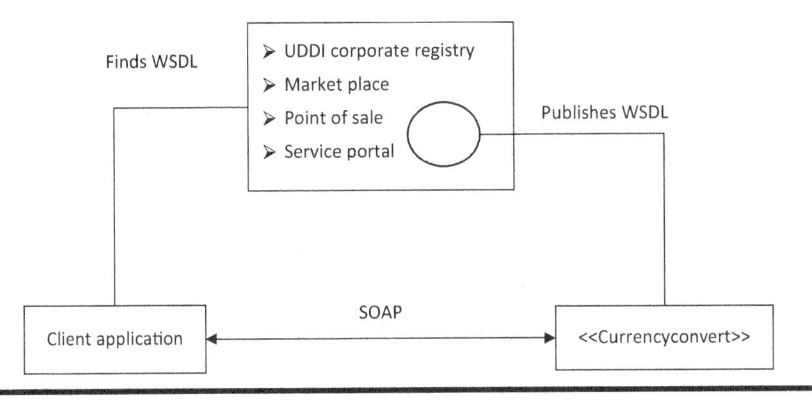


**Figure 1.6 The relationship between WSDL, UDDI, and SOAP.**

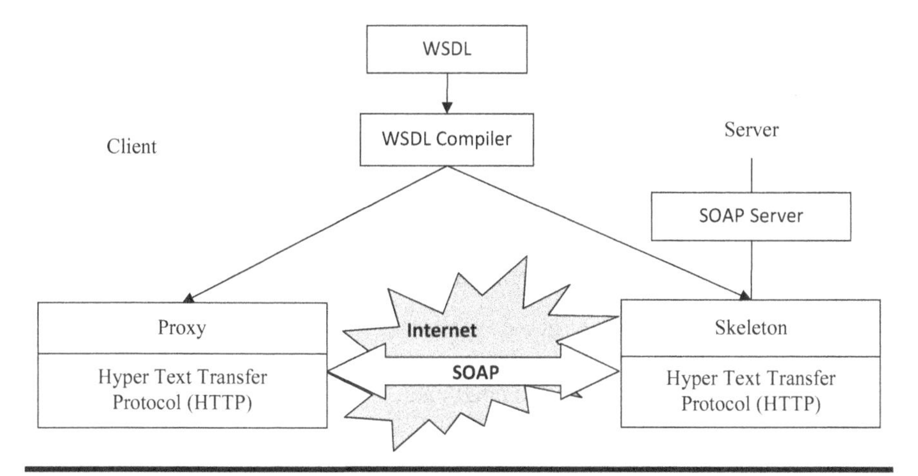


**Figure 1.7 An application to application interaction using web services (high-level architecture).**

### *1.7.1 High-Level Architecture of Application to Application Interaction Using Web Services*

Figure 1.7 shows the interaction between two applications using web services technology. As in Figure 1.7, a server object exposes its capabilities through an XML-based protocol called Web Service Description Language (WSDL). A WSDL compiler is used to generate a proxy and a skeleton. The server and client should understand that a WSDL-concerned language-mapped compiler should be used to generate stub and skeleton in the concerned target languages. For example, WSDL-Java compiler will be used to generate stub and skeleton in java. After generating stub and skeleton, the client-side proxy and server-side skeleton communicate using SOAP.

### *1.7.2 Unique Capabilities of Web Services*

Above the reader has been exposed to different technologies that enable application to application interaction. From the core web services architecture, one can find out about the attractive and unique capabilities of web services.

The characteristic which distinguishes web services from other previous technologies is that it uses HTTP as its main transport protocol. Since HTTP is the primary protocol used on the internet, there is no extra infrastructure required to establish web services based communication. Please recall that, in the case of CORBA, one should have ORB. In the case of DCOM, one should have a COM layer. In the case of RMI, one should have RRL. But in the case of web services, no extra infrastructure is required as they use HTTP.

Another inherent advantage is that HTTP traffic is not blocked by firewalls. This makes interaction on a global scale very easy.

### 1.7.3 Can Web Services Replace CORBA/DCOM/RMI?

There are some misconceptions about web services that they play a significant role in distributed computing by bringing interoperability among heterogeneous applications irrespective of platforms and languages.

Though web services are useful in bringing about the interaction between heterogeneous applications, web services are not a real object-oriented distributed computing technology. There is no object concept in web services (except for the name in SOAP!!).

Web services provide a simple message-based communication. In addition, it is text-based. It takes a longer time to send and receive messages when compared to object protocols.

*CORBA is an object-oriented distributed computing model.* It provides a complete solution for developing distributed, object-oriented enterprise applications. It provides a rich set of common services such as naming and directory, transaction, security, concurrency, persistence, etc. which are essential for developing distributed enterprise applications. These services enable developers to focus on their core competence. CORBA has been used in many industries such as defense, banking, finance, e-commerce, manufacturing, healthcare, etc.

Overall CORBA/DCOM/RMI has been developed primarily for meeting the requirements of distributed object-oriented interaction, whereas web services are used for providing message-based interactions between applications. Thus, web services cannot replace CORBA/DCOM/RMI.

### 1.7.4 Why Do We Need Web Services?

One might have a question in mind: If web services are simply offering message-based communication between applications, why should we use web services? The answer lies in the fact that there are many interactions that occur over the web. The central strength of web services is that it uses HTTP as its transport protocol. So, it makes it easy to send and receive messages on top of HTTP over the internet. The applications do not require any extra infrastructure at all. As mentioned earlier, HTTP is firewall friendly

Another big advantage of web services are that they are based on XML. It is a text-based open protocol mainly used to structure data, describe data with schema, and transport data. It brings portability for data. Web services can define namespaces and data types using XML namespace and XML schema, respectively. The XML schema facilitates the portability of data among applications. Usage of XML brought platform independence to web services.

In addition, web services have strong support from the open source community. Another advantage and disadvantage of web services are that there is no defined standard either top or bottom of the SOAP layer. SOAP becomes the de facto standard for performing RPC over the web. SOAP is very simple to implement, and hence it becomes ubiquitous.

Thus, web services fit as a natural choice primarily for integrating applications running on different languages or platforms with simple XML-based messaging over HTTP.

### 1.7.5 Typical Use Cases of Web Services

*Use Case—1: application to application interaction with a lightweight communication model.*

Very frequently, enterprises want to share their applications with the applications of a partner organization. The following is a real example: Consider a travel package company (i.e., trip advisor) that offers a complete travel package to customers by internally performing the following functions:

(i) It takes the source and destination of travel, the date of travel for an onward journey, and the date of the return journey.
(ii) It interacts with different flight booking companies and books tickets.
(iii) It interacts with different hotels and books rooms.
(iv) It interacts with cab services and books cabs for taking customers to sightseeing locations.

How web services facilitate communication among four different businesses (travel agency, flight booking agencies, hotels, and cab providers) is shown with a high-level schematic in Figure 1.8.

From Figure 1.8, it is understood that business processes (here flight booking, hotel booking, and cab booking) expose their business functions through WSDL while hiding the implementation of their functions. So other partners like travel agencies can use the WSDL to construct a SOAP message and invoke the required services. The emphasis goes to web services as follows: Compared to previous technologies which require separate a communication medium and heavyweight protocol, here web services are found as a more suitable choice as it uses the internet

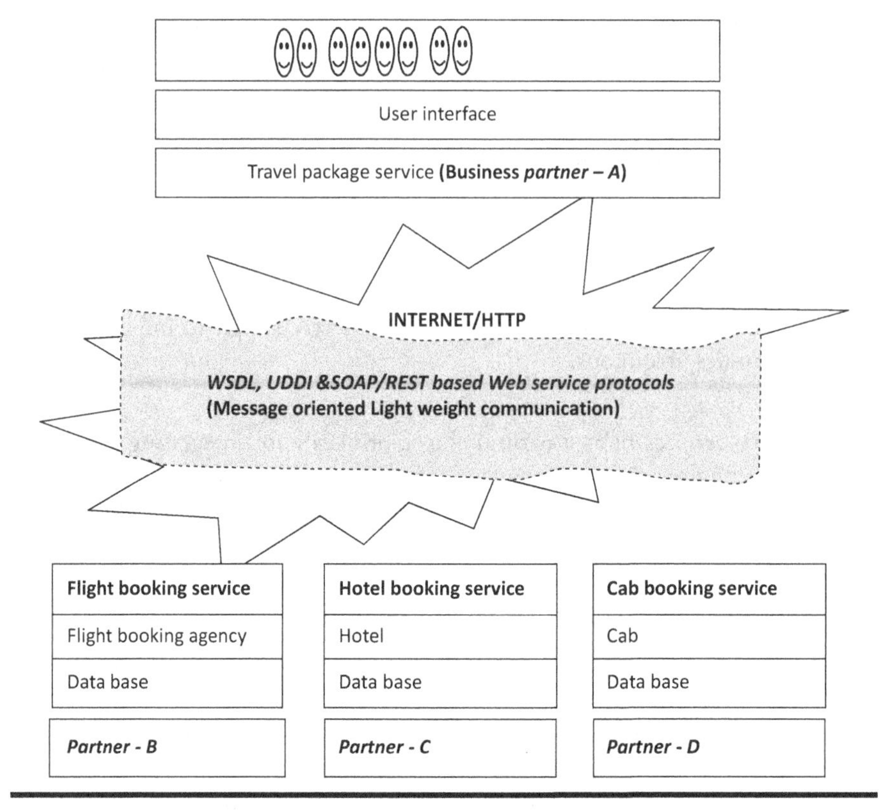


**Figure 1.8 An application to application interaction using web service protocols.**

and HTTP as its base. The client can simply invoke services using a SOAP request. Only on the business application side, i.e., service provider's side, should SOAP handlers handle or process the request and invoke the respective operation. The purpose of web services is to provide message-based and loosely coupled communication among applications which are running on different operating systems within a different language runtime environment. Its purpose is to establish interactions among different applications, and it is not meant for pure object-oriented elements.

*Use Case—2: Web services are used to implement web interfaces*

Business enterprises can expose their services through web services rather than a web application. The advantage of this is that web applications can only be used by human users, whereas web services can be used by machines, processes, or applications; i.e., web services enable business to business interaction. For example, Amazon provides all its services using Amazon Web Service (AWS). So, it's business partners can consume Amazon services seamlessly, and it facilitates quick business to business collaboration, as shown in Figure 1.9. Amazon Associates, the marketing affiliates of Amazon (i.e., business partners of Amazon), which markets the products of Amazon by providing the product catalog to the users, access the

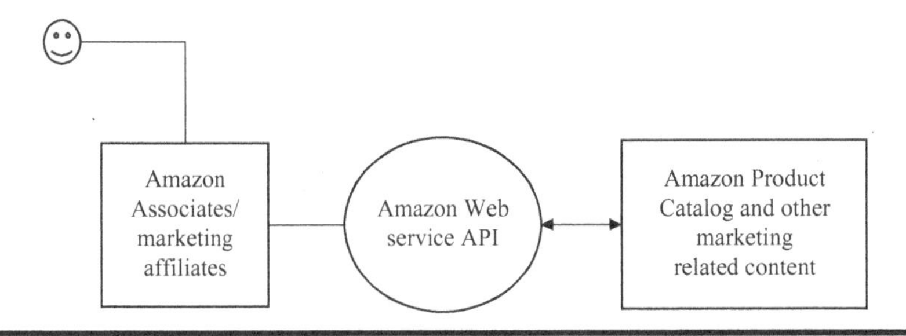


**Figure 1.9 Implementing a web interface using web services.**

catalog and other related content through the Amazon web service API without any difficulty. This results in improved business.

*Use Case—3: Turning legacy applications into services using web service wrappers*

In most of the enterprises, the existing applications would have been built a couple of decades before. The applications might have been developed using old technologies such as COBOL, CGI script, etc. They also would have used many other third-party software (even if those vendors had gone out of business). The heterogeneity in applications creates several challenges in achieving communication and interoperability among applications, reusability, performance, and security. So, enterprises should somehow enable flexible communication between applications. The applications and systems should communicate regardless of their language, platform, and network configurations. So, legacy applications are converted into service-oriented applications by developing web service wrappers. How a legacy application interacts with a service-oriented environment is shown in Figure 1.10

A wrapper is a program which converts a legacy application into a service without disturbing its internal behavior. The wrapper provides two-way communication support to a legacy application. This means that external clients can access a legacy application as a service. Also, the legacy application can access other services using this wrapper.

*Use Case—4: Converting CORBA applications to web-aware or mobile aware applications*

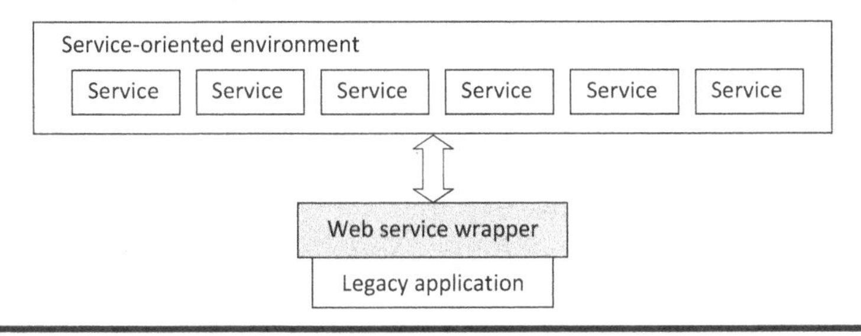


**Figure 1.10 A legacy application interacts with other services using a web service wrapper.**

Consider a scenario where a CORBA application wants to provide a web interface to its core application. By convention, any client who wants to interact with CORBA has to have an ORB interface, which is not only expensive but an extra burden to web clients. In such situations, the CORBA application can opt for a web services wrapper, which can accept the data entered by the user and return it to the core application, as shown in Figure 1.11.

From Figure 1.10, one can understand that the CORBA application can be accessed even from a mobile phone via the internet. In CORBA, there is no readily available concept to deal with mobility. But in web services, the mobility of users can be dealt with by forwarding the client interactions to the concerned proxy servers as per the mobility of users. Thus, web services support any thin or ubiquitous client.

*Use Case—5: Web services promote data sharing with XML*

Web services can facilitate data sharing among different applications, as shown in Figure 1.12.

This unique feature of XML provides platform independence and language independence. In web services, SOAP messages can be represented using, XML and sent over the internet. This kind of data sharing over the internet enhances business collaboration irrespective of technologies.

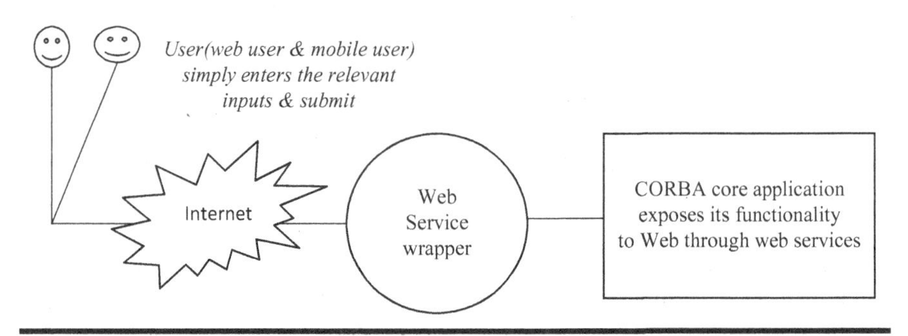


**Figure 1.11 A CORBA application adds a web interface through web services.**

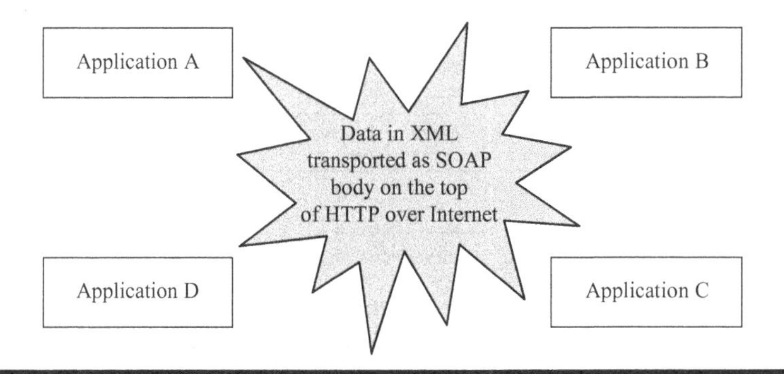


**Figure 1.12 Transporting data in XML among collaborating applications.**

*Use Case—6: Enterprise Application Integration (EAI) using Web Services*
Before how web services are used in EAI is discussed, the need for EAI is highlighted.

***Need for EAI***
As emphasized earlier, the typical use of web services is to integrate disparate applications of an enterprise. In fact, web services gained its popularity by its use in EAI [5].

Typically, in an enterprise, different departments deal with different kinds of operations and tasks. For example, consider a product manufacturing company. The sales department deals with customers. According to demands and sales, the planning department prepares a plan for producing products. The purchase departments deal with the purchase of raw materials. Inventory deals with the storage of the purchased raw materials. The production department manufactures the product as per the plan. The transportation department delivers the goods to the customer. Each department independently chooses appropriate technologies and programming languages to develop its applications. For example, sales representatives may use a Sales Force Automation application developed in.NET. The purchase department may use a Supply Chain Management application developed using J2EE. In addition, the core applications of the enterprise might have been developed using COBOL. Here, the key point is that an enterprise by nature consists of many independent systems and applications, which provide various services to the company for carrying out daily business tasks.

Though enterprises may perform their routine activities using these individual applications without any issues, the overall efficiency of the enterprise is very low. The main reason for this is that the systems and applications stay independent. They are not connected with one another. Systems cannot communicate with one another due to the heterogeneity in their operating systems, languages and communication protocols, etc. Due to the lack of communication, the applications cannot share data and processes with one another. The applications and systems of enterprises stand as information silos. This difficulty leads to the maintenance of identical data in many places, which obviously in turn leads to data consistency and integrity issues. Lack of communication also prevents the automation of different processes. Overall the business processes become inefficient, and the enterprise as a whole cannot keep up with the rest of the market, which is the very first objective of any business. So, enterprises need to integrate their data and processes. Different data, applications, and processes of an enterprise are integrated using the EAI technique. EAI enables existing data to flow between different applications by supplying different interfaces for managing different data flows [6, 7]. EAI gives many remarkable benefits, such as:

(i) EAI enables the smooth flow of data across the enterprise. The flow of any data of any complexity can be simplified to a large extent, and any data can be flown smoothly through various applications, departments, and users who are in need of that data. Different applications can share their respective data from a single point of access.

(ii) EAI provides a solid understanding of how applications work together in an organization and bring a strong project management discipline.

(iii) Enterprise Application Integration helps with the more effective and efficient collaboration among applications and employees of the enterprise.

(iv) EAI ensures that critical applications perform seamlessly and flawlessly at all times.

(v) The organization can serve its customers with the highest level of satisfaction.

(vi) EAI provides an integrated solution which is highly robust, stable, and scalable.

*Integration types of EAI*

There are different types of integration, as shown in Figure 1.13.

- ***Point-to-Point integration***

  In a point-to-point integration model, each application is connected to every other application using a connector component. This connector handles all data transformation, integration, and any other messaging-related services that must take place between only the specific pair of components it is designed to integrate. This kind of integration works well for only a limited number of applications. Even for say ten applications to be connected using point-to-point integration, it needs $(n(n-1))/2$ number of connections; i.e., $((10\times9)/2)=45$ number of connections. Hence, with respect to the increase in the number of applications, the number of connections becomes too large, and the maintenance of applications will become very tough. Hence this model is not used for medium or large enterprises.
- ***Central integration***

  In a central integration approach, there are two methods. They are broker-based central integration and Enterprise Service Bus based integration.

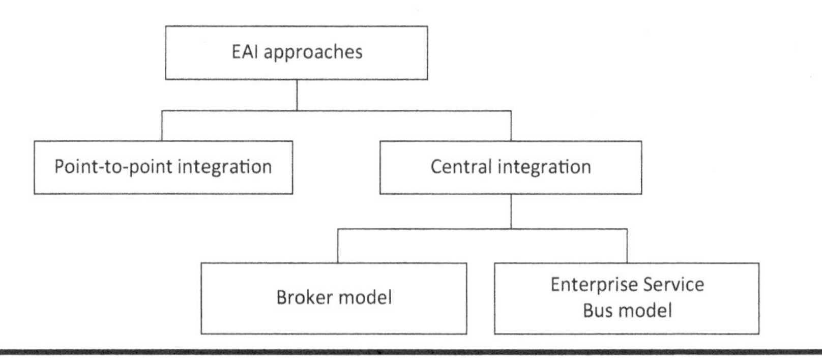


**Figure 1.13 Different EAI approaches.**

- ***Broker method***

  In this method, all the applications are connected to a central broker in a master–slave model, as given in Figure 1.14.

  Each application notifies the broker about any change in the data. The broker in turn notifies all other applications connected to it about the change. In this way, if there are *n* applications, this model simply requires only one connection from each application to the broker. This means that for ten applications, the broker model requires only ten connections.

  *Advantages*—The broker model allows loose coupling between applications. This means that applications are able to communicate asynchronously, sending messages and continuing work without waiting for a response from the recipient, knowing exactly how the message will get to its endpoint, or in some cases even knowing the endpoint of the message.

  *Disadvantages*—The broker suffers from a single point of failure.
- ***Enterprise Service Bus Model***

  Basically, an Enterprise Service Bus is a bus connecting all the applications of an enterprise using appropriate adapters. Unlike hub, ESB is more intelligent and performs various functions such as (i) decoupling client from service providers, (ii) performing conversion of transport protocol, (iii) performing message transformation (for example, converting an XML message to JSON), (iv) routing a request to the concerned service, (v) performing security-related functions such as authentication and authorization, (vi) performing Process Choreography and Service Orchestration, and (vii) performing transaction management. Thus, compared to the hub, ESB is very intelligent.

**Web Services and ESB**

One should understand that ESB [8] is a bus infrastructure, and web services can be used in ESB for integrating applications. Consider different applications such as Supply Chain Management, Customer Relationship Management, Human Resource Management, Sales Force Automation, Financial application, and

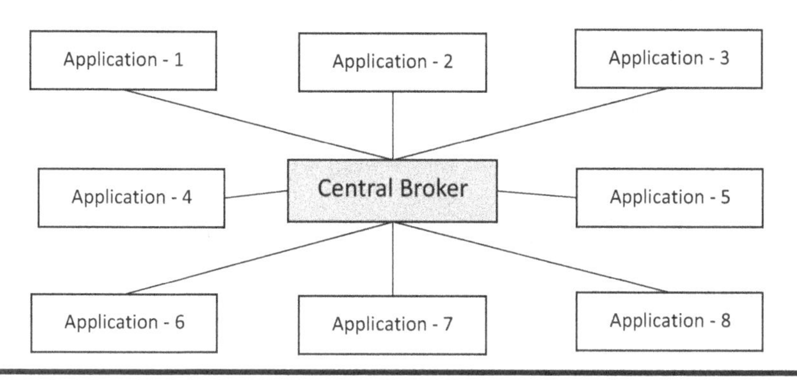


**Figure 1.14 Central broker-based integration.**

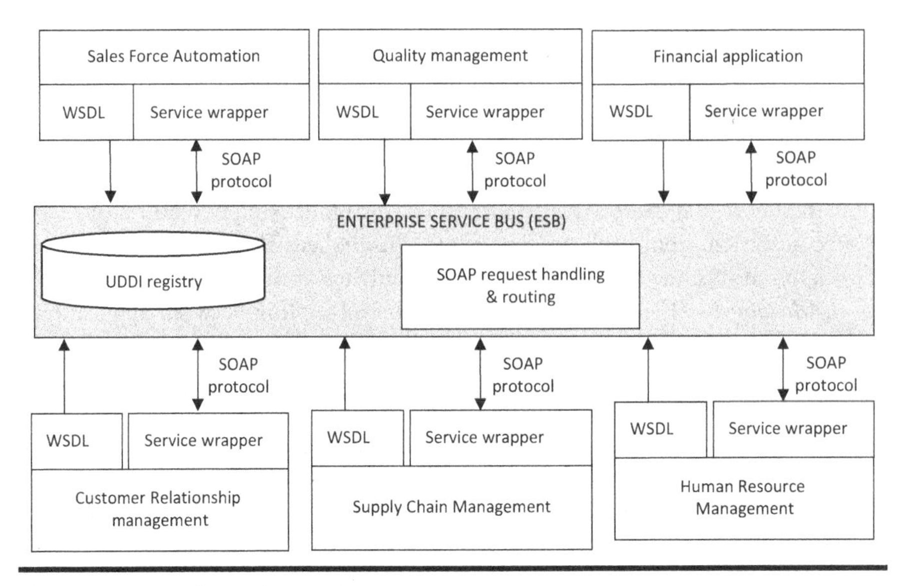


**Figure 1.15 Web services and EAI.**

Quality Management, as shown in Figure 1.15. Consider that these applications are running on different operating systems and using different language environment. In order to bring about interactions or communication among applications, these applications are connected to ESB through a WSDL wrapper. A short code is developed to expose the functions of applications through WSDL. All applications are exposed using WSDL. The ESB bus maintains a registry of all WSDLs according to UDDI specification. It provides a search mechanism for client applications. Any client who wants to access a particular application, can search through the registry and choose the required service. The request is sent to the concerned application using SOAP protocol. A simple adapter is developed which converts the SOAP and calls the respective application's protocol. Similarly, the response of the application is returned as XML to the client.

### *1.7.6 Distinction between Web Services and CORBA/DCOM/RMI*

This section describes the distinction between web services/SOA and CORBA/DCOM/RMI.

A couple of decades ago, at the beginning of the e-commerce and internet era, a great shift was required in the way enterprise applications were developed. Internet technologies and e-commerce support made customers expect better and quicker solutions from enterprises. However, most of the enterprises were had a traditional setup, and their applications were developed with old technologies such as COBOL, CGI Script, etc. Most of the business applications were running in mainframes systems with a master–slave configuration. Even within a single organization, the applications are highly heterogeneous. Each department of the organization has its applications developed independently with its appropriate technologies and languages. Ultimately, enterprises were unable to use their traditional applications in the world of the internet.

To address the above challenges to the development of enterprise applications, SOA as an architectural style demanded the developers to develop applications in such a way that it should be interoperable and reusable among different applications. So, whenever a requirement comes, it need not be developed from scratch, but rather it can be assembled using existing services. This will enable the business to meet the dynamic demands of customers. Hence, the purpose of SOA is to bring interoperability between applications which are tied up with disparate operating systems and languages. With this purpose, it promotes the development of applications as network-accessible services with well-defined interfaces so that consumers can invoke the services using their interface over a network according to the Service Level Agreement between provider and consumer. Hence,the focus of SOA is the interoperability and reusability of software components.

The purpose of SOA is reflected in the technologies which were developed at the time of SOA, namely CORBA, DCOM, and RMI. Though CORBA, DCOM, and RMI indirectly meet the SOA requirements to some extent, they are not especially meant for bringing loosely coupled technologies for application to application interaction, because those technologies were developed to distribute object-oriented stuff over the network and to access remote server objects from the client. So, they have their confined focus as distributed object-oriented stuff over enterprise-level networks (not for the internet). Also, they are tightly coupled technologies. Since their focus is to develop enterprise applications in a distributed manner, they have provided robust specifications along with a special emphasis on common services, such as naming and director services, database connectivity services, persistence services, transactions support, security support, load-balancing support, fault tolerance, etc.

Whereas web services were developed to provide loosely coupled message-oriented communication between disparate applications over the internet. It is not meant for individual enterprise-level applications or object-oriented applications. It enables application to application interaction in a loosely coupled manner without requiring any extra infrastructure over the global scale of the internet with omnipresent HTTP as the transport protocol. The main strengths of web services are XML, HTTP, and the openness of protocols.

Both the technologies, i.e., CORBA, DCOM, and RMI on one hand and web services on the other hand coexist as the purpose and focus of these technologies are different. For example, DCOM becomes the right choice for fulfilling the need of distributed object-oriented interactions among Windows-based applications. CORBA fits well to fulfill the need for distributed object-oriented interactions over cross-platform with well-defined security. Similarly, RMI works well to bring distributed computing among Java applications. These technologies have been developed with specific but different purposes, and hence they coexist.

In contrast to the distributed computing technologies mentioned above, a web services technology stack does not deal with objects at all. It does not provide any rich set of functions or common services which are essential for distributed computing. For example, web services do not have a transaction service, security service, concurrency service, event or notification service, persistence service, state maintenance, etc. However, using web services means any two applications can interact and interoperate irrespective of their languages or platforms via a simple XML-based messaging protocol. There are always many critical needs such as Enterprise Application Integration, Provision of the web interface to existing legacy or any application to make it net-aware, message-based communication between two heterogeneous applications (which don't need to be object-oriented in nature), say COBOL to J2EE, and also to enable interaction between any two evenly distributed object-oriented applications. These needs are very flexible as well as readily and universally implemented with web services. Another important aspect of web services is that they perform well with communication over the internet as the XML messages are sent as a payload of HTTP, which is firewall friendly.

### 1.7.7 Why Have Web Services Become Obsolete? What Are the Issues with Web Services? Are We Still in Need of Yet Another Architecture to Meet Business Requirements?

Web services enabled business applications to interact and interoperate seamlessly in a loosely coupled manner with an Enterprise Service Bus. ESB is the key enabler that hides all the heterogeneity among applications. This means that it provides the necessary protocol conversion or data format conversion. It is the main element in establishing service orchestration and choreography. As more and more applications are connected via ESB, ESB itself becomes too bulky to deploy and maintain. Since the application is growing larger and larger, deployment becomes time-consuming. Not only that, as the application grows in size, several developers need to work on different parts of the same application. Also, developers are inherently and implicitly compelled to wait for one another to finish their work; for deployment, the business organizations have to deliver their applications and products quickly and dynamically so as to fulfill customer needs, customer satisfaction, and ultimately achieve business agility. Another problem is the maintenance of the ESB itself. It has to be deployed with sufficient scalability to cater to the needs of many users, and it has to provide the required availability. The above limitations of SOA motivated software engineers and experts to discover yet another architecture that supports the frequent deployment and continuous delivery of applications.

***Summary***

This chapter has presented an overview of how different distributed computing technologies, such as CORBA, DCOM, and RMI, facilitated the invocation of methods on the remote objects of applications. It pointed out that the primary purpose of these technologies is to hide the heterogeneity in development platforms or programming languages and to provide common services to enterprise applications so that the developers can focus only on the core development of the concerned applications. It has highlighted how customer needs are growing fast and dynamically with the internet and how such needs can be addressed by SOA. This chapter has described SOA as a loosely coupled architectural style with a standard communication style, which is very frequently implemented using web services protocols. It has emphasized how web services can resolve the difficulty in integrating various applications of an enterprise with many examples. Thus, the chapter has explained that either object-oriented technologies or web services will not replace one another; rather, each has its own problems to be solved. The distinction between CORBA/DCOM/RMI and web services has been clearly illustrated. In the last section, the chapter discussed how SOA or web services have become obsolete. Ultimately, the chapter has clearly explained how an SOA application becomes thick and large in size with the concept of an Enterprise Service Bus, which itself prevents the frequent deployment and continuous delivery of the application.

***Exercises***

1. Have you ever thought about why one talks about CORBA/DCOM/RMI in the context of SOA? Is there any direct link between SOA and CORBA/DCOM/RMI? What is the real origin of CORBA/DCOM/RMI? How do they fit into the context of SOA? Explain your thoughts with examples.
2. Explain the purpose of SOA? Why are web services considered as the right choice for implementing SOA?
3. How do you visualize SOA? Would you prefer it as an architecture for developing enterprise applications? Or would you support other technologies? Justify your answer with an explanation.
4. Consider the situation: A company has its core application logic developed in CORBA, and it is distributed over two branches. Now there is a need for the company to support web clients and mobile clients all over the globe. Draw the required architecture and explain how it achieves this need.
5. Where do you have to deal with continuous delivery? Is frequent deployment necessary? Do you think the three-tiered architecture used so far has flaws?
6. You would have gone through an ESB. Where exactly would you use the ESB?
7. Can we throw the proven and matured distributed object-oriented technologies out just because SOA came along? Explain when an enterprise should go for SOA? (compulsory assignment question)
8. Why did web services/SOA become obsolete?

## References

1. Ciaran McHale. CORBA Explained Simply. 2005. Available at http://docenti.ing.unipi.it/~a009435/issw/extra/CORBAbook.pdf.
2. Markus Horstmann and Mary Kirtland. DCOM Architecture. 2003. Available at: http://cs.hadassah.ac.il/staff/martin/Seminar/middleware/DCOM_arch.pdf.
3. Jeff Davies, David Schorow, Samrat Ray, and David Rieber, "*The Definitive Guide to SOA—Oracle Service Bus,*" Second Edition, A Press, 2008, ISBN-13 (pbk): 978-1-4302-1057-3, ISBN-13 (electronic): 978-1-4302-1058-0.
4. Mark Endrei, Jenny Ang, Ali Arsanjani, Sook Chua, Philippe Comte, Pål Krogdahl, Min Luo, and Tony Newling, "*Patterns: Service Oriented Architecture and Web Services,*" ibm.com/redbooks, First Edition, April 2004, https://www.redbooks.ibm.com/redbooks/pdfs/sg246303.pdf
5. Oldooz Karimi, and Nasser Modiri, "Enterprise Integration using Service-Oriented Architecture," *Advanced Computing: An International Journal (ACIJ)*, Vol. 2, No. 5, September 2011, pp. 41–47.
6. Pierre de Leusse, Panos Periorellis, and Paul Watson, "Enterprise Service Bus: An Overview," *Technical Report Series*, 2007.
7. Stephen Todd, senior technical staff member, WebSphere MQ Strategy, IBM Hursley Park laboratory, "Understanding Web Services in an Enterprise Service Bus Environment," IBM, March 2005.
8. Stephen Todd. Understanding Web Services in anEnterprise Service Bus Environment. 2005. Available at: https://www-05.ibm.com/si/soa/att/understanding_web_services_in_an_enterprise_service_business_context_.pdf.

# Chapter 2

# Demystifying MSA

***Objective***

The requirements of modern applications are very dynamic due to frequently changing customer needs. Such requirements are necessary for services to be continuously delivered to customers. This requires an appropriate application architecture which supports frequent deployment and delivery. In this context, the objective of this chapter is to introduce the essentials of Microservices Architecture (MSA), as an architecture that breaks down an application into microservices, each of which can be independently as well as frequently deployed and thus facilitate the continuous delivery of the application to the customers. By the end of the chapter, the reader will understand the need for MSA, how MSA meets modern business requirements, and its typical use cases, benefits, and drawbacks.

***Preface***

There are two service-based architectures, namely, SOA and MSA. In the previous chapter, the reader learned about how SOA enables interaction among heterogeneous applications using standard open communication protocols in a loosely coupled manner. In this chapter, the reader will learn MSA as an architectural style that breaks an application into small, functionally independent, deployable software modules with well-defined interfaces called microservices which ultimately lead to the continuous delivery of applications. SOA is an architecture that enables communication between heterogeneous applications and brings interoperability, whereas MSA is an architectural style for an individual application that facilitates frequent deployment and continuous delivery. The chapter discusses the issues of monolithic applications, the need for MSA, how MSA alleviates issues with a monolithic application, core MSA architecture, key enablers of MSA, and typical use cases, benefits, and drawbacks in detail.

***Motivating Questions***

1. Why do we need the frequent deployment of applications?
2. What are the driving forces of MSA?
3. What are the technological foundations or key enablers of MSA?
4. Is there any other architecture other than MSA for frequent deployment?
5. Should we need MSA for all applications?
6. What will happen to the proven three-tiered enterprise application architecture? Does MSA replace all such applications?

## 2.1 Need for Microservices Architecture

Martin Fowler documented "microservices" as a term used in a software architects' workshop in 2011. According to Martin Fowler, Microservices Architecture consists of "suites of independently deployable services" organized "around business capability, automated deployment, intelligence in the endpoints, and decentralized control of languages and data." The main idea behind MSA is that an application becomes simpler to build and maintain if it is broken down into small microservices that work seamlessly together to achieve the same unified application level goal [1]. *The first key point with MSA is that it deals with the architecture of a single enterprise application and is in no way related to SOA, which deals with application to application interaction, but both the architectures are service-based.*

One might ask: Three-tiered architectures such as the Java Two Enterprise Edition (J2EE) and the .NET framework for developing enterprise applications are already well proven. Why then do we need another architecture for enterprise applications? In addition, breaking up an application into independent modules is also not new. So why do we need MSA?

Typically, an enterprise application is divided into three tiers: the presentation tier, business logic tier, and data access tier. *Here the modularization of applications is based on the expertise development teams; for example, the user interface (UI) team will work with presentation logic, developers with specific domain knowledge will work with core business logic, and database developers will work with data access tier. With these partitions, each team can independently work with its respective module.* They are physically deployed in different machines. Here the breaking up of an application into different tiers is over a big scale. The granularity of modularization is coarse-grained. With this kind of modularization, the presentation logic stays in the web server; business and data access logic stay in the application server; and the database server will be centrally located in another machine.

*The key point is that all application-related features and functions are handled by a single monolithic server-side application*, as shown in Figure 2.1. All the presentation-related code is built as a *web archive file (.war file)* and deployed in a web server such as Apache Tomcat. Similarly, the business logic and data access logic modules are

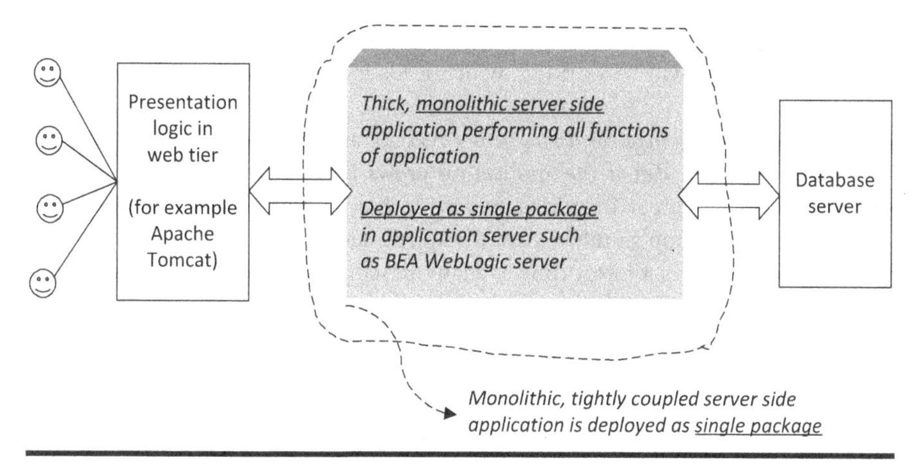


**Figure 2.1 A tightly coupled, Monolithic server-side application.**

tightly coupled, and the modules are combined as a *single package* say for example, as a *single .jar file* and deployed in application servers such as BEA Weblogic/IBM Websphere/Sun's JBoss server. Emphasis should be given to the way we deploy the tiers. Typically, each tier is deployed as a single package. The development of any large enterprise application involves several developers of around 100 in number working on different modules of the same application, i.e., different people working on different code blocks.

It becomes difficult to deploy as soon as a team completes its task for two main reasons (i) the size of project is big, and it takes a long time for deployment and (ii) as many teams are simultaneously working on different portions of same application, a team needs to wait for others to finish their ongoing work.

Hence, this architecture becomes unsuitable for applications that need to be frequently deployed for continuous delivery.

Thus, as Gartner stated, "To deal with the rapidly changing demands of digital business and scale systems up—or down—rapidly, computing has to move away from static to dynamic models," i.e., models that can dynamically assemble and configure individual elements of an application as required.

## 2.2 Issues with Traditional Enterprise Applications

Large monolithic enterprise applications which were developed using traditional architectures have the following issues.

*1. Tightly coupled and single large executable*—The modules of monolithic applications are tightly coupled. Though there may be different class modules performing the different functions of the application, the application as a whole is deployed as a single executable file. When more and more features are added to the application, the package size of the application itself will become larger in size. When the size grows, many teams will be working, which leads to dependency issues among the teams [2].

2. *Difficulties with frequent deployment*—As long as the application remains small, there is no problem. But if the application grows in size, and since there is tight coupling among different functions, and with many development teams working on the same application simultaneously, frequent deployment becomes very tough. Release planning takes a lot of time as many developers from various groups need to be coordinated. Frequent release is discouraged to make sure that the application doesn't become faulty due to the newly released feature. But frequent deployment is essential for an enterprise to stay on par with customer's expectations.

3. *Problems with continuous delivery*—Large tightly coupled applications prevent frequent deployment because (i) the deployment time is very long and (ii) the different development teams will be working with large-sized applications. Due to tight coupling, only the application as a whole can be deployed. Even small changes performed in the application need a frustratingly long time for deployment. So continuous delivery (CD) becomes unfeasible in the case of large-sized tightly coupled applications, but continuous delivery plays a crucial role in meeting the customer demands quickly.

4. *Difficulty in maintenance and management*—As the size of the application grows, maintenance, monitoring, and management of the application become tedious.

5. *Lack of technology diversity*—As traditional applications have many interdependencies and tightly coupled modules, almost the same and balanced technology will be chosen, keeping all the functional and non-functional requirements of the application in mind.

6. *Less reliable and long development cycle*—In large traditional somewhat tiered applications, many development teams will be working on the same project. Though the teams may work independently on different functions, they are not actually very independent. They have to work very closely with the other teams. Obviously, if a team makes a change, it cannot simply go for deployment as it has to consult with the other teams. This makes the development schedule a longer one. In addition, since many teams are working simultaneously with the application, the changes made by different teams may make the application code less reliable.

7. *Scalability at an expensive cost*—In a tightly coupled monolithic application, if an enterprise needs scalability for a particular function, say, for example, scalability for database access is heavy with around 3000 user requests, the scalability can be introduced only for the entire application as a whole and not just for a single function. Hence, high scalability ends up with a high cost.

8. *Bug tracking and fixing becomes difficult*—Once the application becomes big, bug tracking and fixing become too difficult and time-consuming.

*9. Overloaded web container*—Since the application package itself is very large, it takes a long time for the web server to start up.

*10. Overloaded integrated development environments (IDE)*—With larger sized applications, the IDE gets overloaded, and it takes a long time for the IDE to start up. This reduces the productivity of developers.

*11. Limited reuse*—Monolithic applications often provide only limited reuse across applications.

## 2.3 How Does MSA Handle the Issues with Monolithic Applications?

Microservices Architecture addresses the challenges associated with monolithic server-side applications by breaking them up into several *single-purpose, self-deployable, self-contained, independent modules called microservices. In MSA, the modularization is not based on the expertise of development teams; rather, it is based on single-purpose or single functional capability. As in the name "microservices," MSA is little concerned with the size of the service, but it depends on the nature of the application.*

The major limitations of monolithic applications are their size and the tight coupling among modules which prevents frequent deployment and continuous delivery of the application. This limitation is alleviated by decomposing the application into loosely coupled independent, self-deployable software modules. This core feature of MSA is illustrated using an example as follows.

Consider a simple online shopping cart example. A shopping cart is a piece of software which shows the product catalog to the customers; customers can select their required products from the catalog and can place an order for the selected products. A shopping cart enables consumers to select products, review what they selected, make modifications or add extra items if needed, and purchase the products. Typically, the shopping cart deals with customers, the product catalog, and orders to purchase products.

Now, the online shopping cart application is broken into three functional modules. They are:

1. Customer management
2. Product catalog management
3. Order management

Typically, these modules can be developed and deployed independently as microservices. A better understanding of how the application would have been developed and deployed in the monolithic server and how it would be for a MSA is shown in Figures 2.2 and 2.3, respectively.

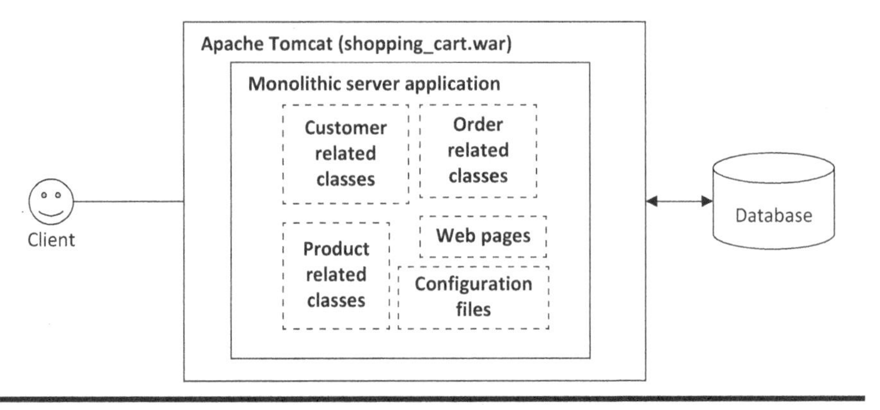


**Figure 2.2 A monolithic shopping cart.**

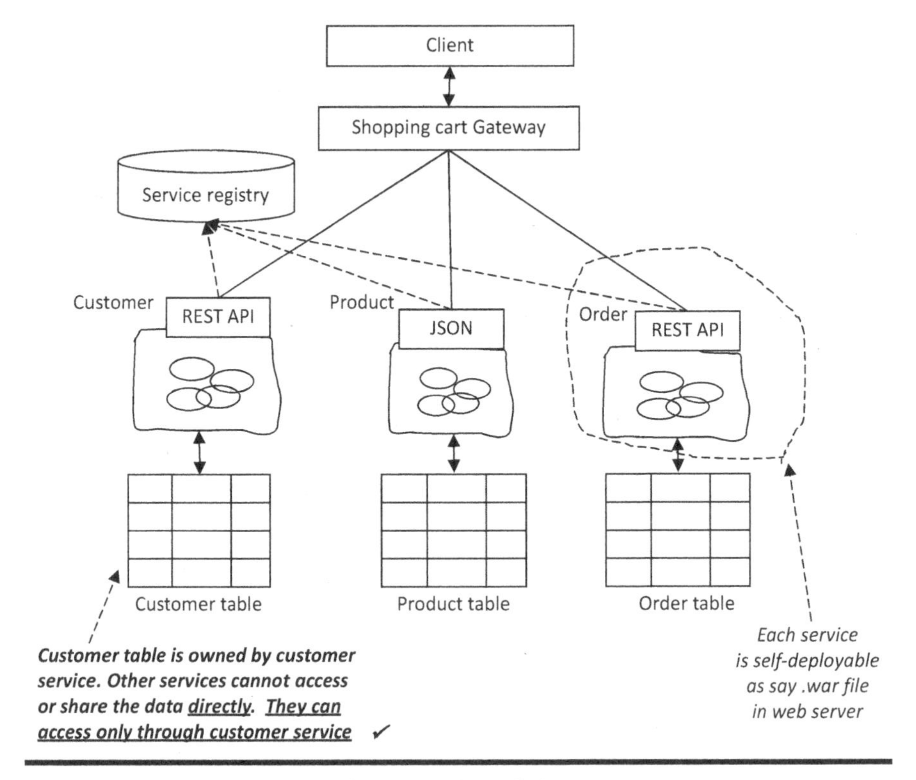


**Figure 2.3 Microservices Architecture-based shopping cart.**

- *Consider the monolithic model*

Assume that Java Server Pages (JSP) is used to implement the required web pages. Core shopping cart modules and data access logic are developed using different classes. Configuration files are created. All class files, web pages, and configuration files are packaged into a single web archive file (*.war*) and deployed into the Apache Tomcat server. The application as a whole has database connectivity with the concerned database server, as shown in Figure 2.2.

- *Consider the microservices-based model*

Let us consider that the application is divided into three independent microservices, say *customer*, *product*, and *order*. Decomposition of the application should be based on the *Single Responsibility Principle. Each microservice should perform a single function only.* The granularity of the microservices is based on its functional capability. All the code related to a single function is combined as a microservice. *Combine all the modules which work for a single function together as one microservice. Decomposition of applications should be done very carefully because the very purpose of MSA is to develop and deploy services as independent applications.* If decomposition is not performed correctly, then, as with the monolithic model, dependencies will occur which will certainly prohibit frequent deployment. Another key point is that a single microservice offers only limited functionality. It cannot deliver any useful business processes. In order to deliver a useful process, there should be *some loosely coupled provision* through which one microservice is able to interact with another.

As in Figure 2.3, the three microservices, customer, product, and order, can be developed using their own individual technologies. For example, customer service might be developed using Python; order service might be developed using J2EE. The product service might be developed using say Ruby or PHP; i.e., each service can be developed using the technology which is more appropriate to its functionality. Each service is deployed as a single package. For example, if the services are developed using say J2EE; then, three individual packages will be deployed along with the concerned libraries and dependencies. The services can be deployed on web servers, physical servers, Virtual Machines, or containers in the cloud environment. Container fits as the right choice for the deployment of microservices, as containers share the same underlying host operating system for their operation whereas VMs require a guest OS on the top of the hypervisor. Dockers make the creation and management of containers very easy. (This will be discussed in detail in Section 2.5.) In addition, each microservice has its own data [3]. For example, customer service works with the customer table. Either it can have a customer database itself, or it can have a customer table, or the service can take a copy of a customer table from the master database at the start-up of the service. Irrespective of the way it owns the data, as long as the service holds the data, no other service can directly access the data that is owned by the customer service. If any other service requires that data, it has to access customer service through its REST API and get the required data. Thus, the careful planning of microservices design is a must for utilizing the full benefits of the architecture.

As in Figure 2.3, each service exposes its functionality through the API so that other services can access it through the gateway. There is a service registry in which instances of the services have to register themselves and their locations. A client who wants to access any of the available services has to look into the service registry to get the location of the service, and then they can access it. An important part of a microservices-based application is the API gateway. The API gateway should not be confused with the APIs of individual microservices. Each microservice has its own API interface so that other services can access it by determining the location of service from the service registry directly. Within an application, this kind of direct communication probably seems like a good performance, but when an external user accesses a microservices-based application which is composed of several microservices, it will be tough for an external client to invoke the application with many requests sent over the public network/external network. So, in practice, an API gateway is used to create a single entry point for a microservices-based application through which a client can access it. The API gateway encapsulates the internal system architecture. It is tailored according to the needs of each client. It might have responsibilities such as:

- Request routing
- Composition
- Protocol translation
- Authentication
- Monitoring
- Load balancing
- Caching
- Request shaping and management
- Static response handling

Though the API gateway can provide all the above functions to a client, it is also a component that should be developed, deployed, and managed properly. If the API gateway becomes too thick, then it will turn into a bottleneck for MSA. It should be designed as a lightweight component with the required core functions only.

The capabilities, features, and benefits of microservices are summarized in the following subsection.

## 2.4 Capabilities, Features, and Benefits of MSA

*The goal of MSA*—The main goal of MSA is to achieve easy maintenance, quick software development with frequent deployment, short development cycles, and continuous delivery. MSA achieves its goal by breaking up the application into functionally independent fine-grained services which are typically developed by a small team of around 6–10 developers.

*Support for a decentralized approach for software development*—In MSA, each service runs a unique process and usually manages its own database. This offers a more decentralized approach to developers for building applications. MSA also allows each service to be deployed, rebuilt, redeployed, and managed independently.

*MSA provides loosely coupled and individual deployment*—As each microservice is a single-purpose service, it does not interfere with other microservices. Each service is deployed independently. MSA implements a *separation of concerns*. The code or modules related to a single purpose are combined together as a microservice, and the modules or code that work for different purposes are kept as different services. This makes each service independent and facilitates an individual deployment of services. Precisely speaking, one microservice does not depend on other services. But in case of need, one service can invoke another service using its API. Within an application, the services are loosely coupled with one another through lightweight API calls, and the services are individually deployed.

*MSA facilitates frequent deployment, and continuous delivery*—When compared to a monolithic environment where several developers work on a large application, in MSA few developers are engaged with individual services, and they need not depend on or wait for other development teams. As soon as a microservice is ready for deployment, it can be implemented without any constraints or time delay. Since the size of a microservice is small, the time taken for deployment is less. This enables the frequent redeployment of services as well as continuous delivery of the project.

*High scalability at individual service level and at low cost*—In a monolithic application, scalability is achieved for the entire application as a whole, whereas in MSA each service can scale on its own without disturbing other services. Since the required scalability is implemented at the service level, the cost involved in obtaining high scalability is less.

*Support for easy extension of features*—In MSA, new features can be added very easily without affecting the other services. Consider the shopping cart example. In this application, adding new features such as *payment service* and *shipping service* is easier.

*Support for diverse technologies (polyglot)*—MSA does not put any constraints on the technologies used for developing microservices. It is not mandatory that all services of an application should adopt the same technology. Each service of an application can choose its own technology according to its need. Languages such as Python, Java, Ruby, C, C++, etc. are commonly used for developing microservices. Here one should note that microservices are preferably used to develop native cloud applications with containerization and an open source technology stack. This feature of developing a single application using different technologies is called polyglot.

*Reliable and support for short development cycle*—In a monolithic development, several developers *simultaneously* work with larger code and hence the code becomes less reliable. In MSA, only a few developers are engaged in the development of microservices and the code remains more reliable. In addition, MSA is always implemented along with *Development Operations* (DevOps) practice. According to DevOps practice, there is a strong collaboration among the different teams of software development. That is, different teams such as the development team, testing team, deployment team, database team, etc. work together in collaboration. It is not like the development team will simply stop with the development job alone. Precisely speaking if a team of people is allotted to the development of a microservice, then that team has to work with the service throughout all the stages, namely development, testing, deployment, release, maintenance, and further extension or update. Thus, the practice of different teams being involved at all stages of software development makes the code more reliable. In addition, the size of the services and their ability of self-deployment facilitates shorter development cycles.

*Support of code reuse*—As microservices expose their functionality via APIs, one service can be invoked by another service of the same application or another application. This enhances reusability.

*Better fault isolation*—In MSA, even if one service fails, the other services will continue functioning without any issues. Services with a flaw can be isolated without affecting the entire application.

*Increased freedom to developers and increased developers' productivity*—MSA gives increased freedom to developers as each service is independent. In addition, MSA facilitates frequent deployment with less time, which enhances the productivity of developers.

*Eliminate vendor or technology lock-in*—MSA does not put any constraint on the way services are implemented; i.e., services can be implemented using any technology. Services can also interoperate with one another.

*Easy to understand*—With added simplicity, developers can better understand the functionality of a service.

Ultimately the above capabilities, features, and benefits of MSA alleviate maintenance, scalability, and other inter-dependency issues in monolithic applications.

## 2.5 Key Enablers for MSA

Microservices Architecture is growing rapidly due to its key enabling technologies shown in Figure 2.4.

The key enablers for MSA include:

(i) Availability of containers, container orchestration, and management platforms

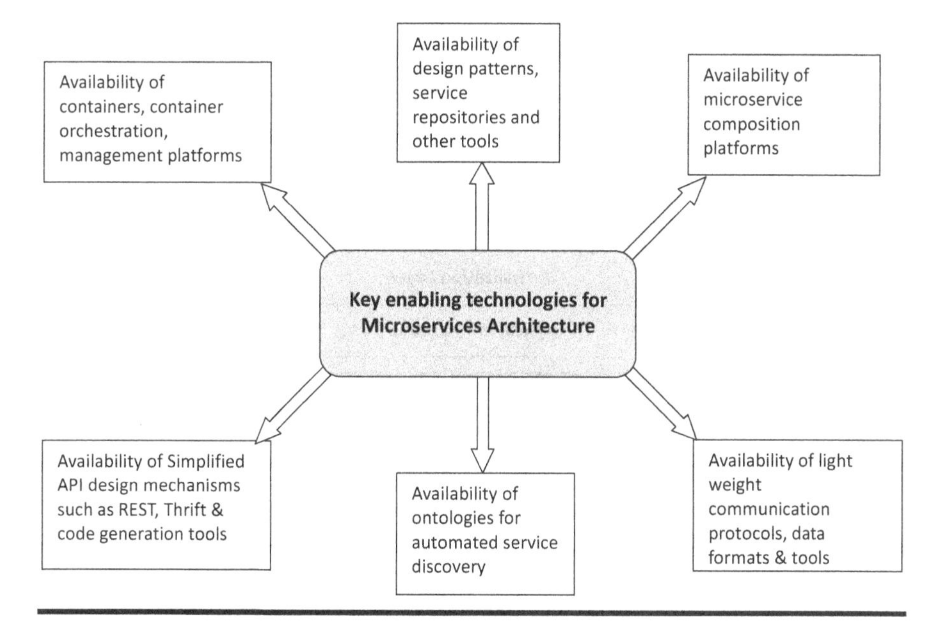


**Figure 2.4 Key enablers for MSA.**

(ii) Availability of communication protocols and implemented communication infrastructure
(iii) Availability of simplified API design mechanisms and automatic code generation tools
(iv) Availability of microservice composition platforms
(v) Availability of design patterns, service repositories, and tools
(vi) Availability of ontologies for automated discovery

**(i) Availability of containers, container orchestration, and management platforms**

MSA is an architectural style for developing agile applications that need to be frequently deployed and delivered continuously. MSA has become the basis for many applications as it enables businesses to develop new digital offerings faster. The chief objective of MSA is to provide a frequent and quick deployment of a microservice. So, the obvious question is: Which execution environment will facilitate the frequent deployment of microservices?

With conventional technologies, the answer would be running many microservices on a single machine or bare metal server. But with the advent of cloud computing technologies, the available physical infrastructure is shared among multiple Virtual Machines (VM) as in Figure 2.5.

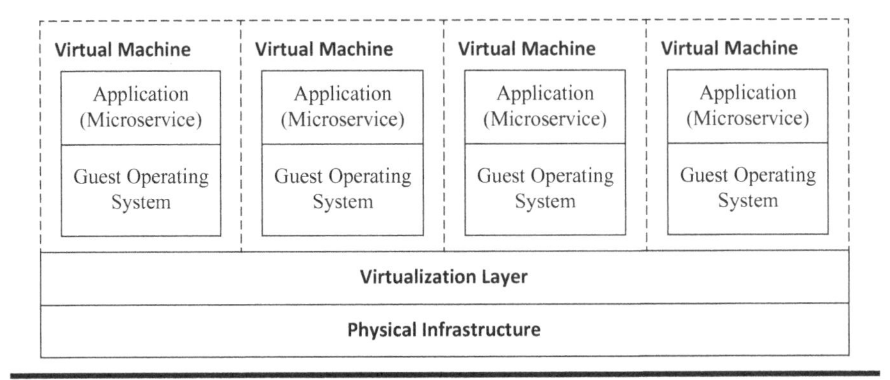


**Figure 2.5 The concept of virtualization.**

*A Virtual Machine is not a real physical machine. It is a software implemented machine having software-based CPU, chipset, RAM, standard peripheral access cards, etc. Hence, an operating system and other applications can be installed on the Virtual Machine. An operating system and applications cannot differentiate a Virtual Machine from a real machine. It is the virtualization layer that provides virtualized hardware to its upper layers. The primary advantage of virtualization is the same physical hardware is shared by many Virtual Machines, and each Virtual Machine can have its own operating system. So, different operating systems can be deployed in Virtual Machines but with the same underlying hardware.*

With the evolution of the virtualization technique, earlier microservices were deployed in Virtual Machines. This is shown in Figure 2.5. However, currently, microservices are not deployed in VMs due to the following reason. In VM-based deployment, each service is typically deployed in a VM, i.e., each microservice has its own VM. Though VMs make it easy to partition the execution environment, a VM is heavy as it contains a guest operating system. Guest operating systems themselves are large. For example, Linux contains over 25 million lines of code; Windows contains over 50 million lines of code; MacOS contains over 85 million lines of code. So, *deploying the operating system itself will consume several minutes.* In addition, guest operating systems consume much of the physical server. Hence the Virtual Machine is not a suitable choice for deploying a microservice.

Alternatively, containers are used for deploying microservices.

Containers, by contrast, perform execution isolation at the operating system level, as shown in Figure 2.6.

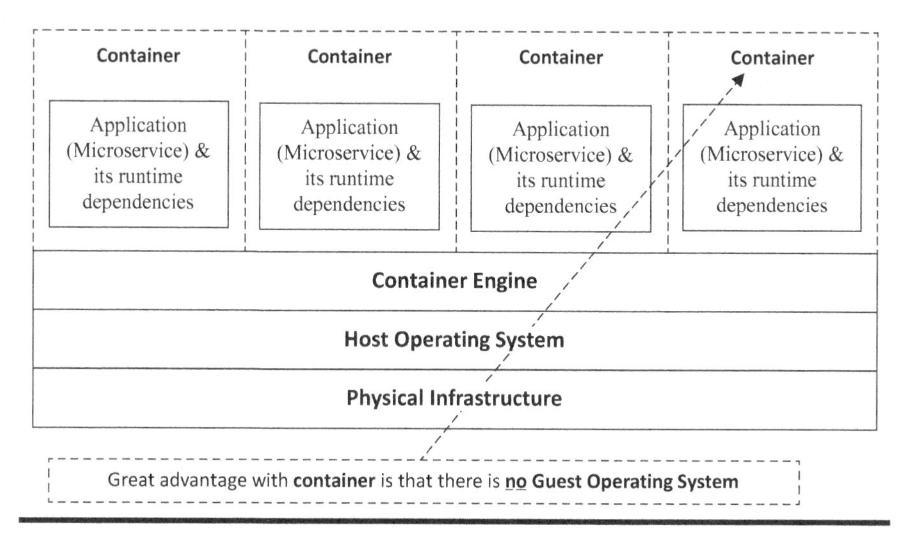


**Figure 2.6 Microservices deployed in containers.**

A single operating system instance can support multiple containers, each running within its own and separate execution environment. Containers are independent, isolated runtime environments which typically consist of an application along with it all its runtime dependencies. Since containers are independent environments, they do not depend on the software of physical machines and hence provide portability. That is, containers provide a consistent software environment for an application from the developer's desktop from testing to final production deployment. Containers can run on physical or Virtual Machines.

Thus, compared to Virtual Machines, containers consume fewer resources. The key point is that containers are small in size. Hence, containers become appropriate for deploying microservices [4]. In addition, when microservices are deployed with a guideline of *one microservice per container,* since both container image and microservice are small in size, the deployment of a service will take only a few seconds (rather than several minutes as in the case of the Virtual Machine). Since containers are small in size, several containers can be deployed over cloud resources. For example, Google is launching around 2 million containers per week over its cloud resources. It should be realized that the combination of microservices and containers are more appropriate for developing agile applications

**Microservices + containers = appropriate style for developing agile applications**

Containers provide enhanced isolation and a required resource allotment through two basic techniques of the Linux kernel, namely:

- *Namespace concept*—With namespace, a container achieves isolation. That is that an application run within a container is isolated from other containers and hence from other applications.
- *Cgroup* or *Control group*—Control group (Cgroup) is a Linux kernel feature which limits, isolates, and measures the resource usage of a group of processes. At first, a group is created. Then, the required resources are assigned to that group. Then, applications are added to that group. Now an application can avail of the set of resources that are assigned to the Cgroup to which it belongs to.

Consider that a Cgroup is created with a name *group#1.* Now, the required resources can be assigned to a Cgroup. For example, *"60% of the CPU and 40% of available memory"* is allotted to *group#1.* Also, as a guideline, each microservice is deployed in a separate container. A container can be added to a Cgroup through its *namespace*. Thus, each container has its own resource allotment through its Cgroup. The resources that are assigned for a Cgroup can be dynamically changed to scale up/down/out. In addition, containers can be created and destroyed quickly. Containers are portable across a range of platforms (development, test, and operations environments). Containers provide several mechanisms for interfacing with the outside world. Containers can be obtained from a registry which archives templates for container images. When an application consists of multiple services deployed in multiple containers with clear interfaces, it becomes very easy to upgrade and update individual containers, and application can be delivered continuously with the required versions of microservices. Similarly, the required scalability for each service can be independently achieved by increasing its number of container instances alone without affecting other services.

***Tools for containerization***

*Docker* is the most popular containerization platform. It was developed by Docker Inc., in 2013. It packages an application and all its dependencies together in the form of a *Docker container* to ensure that an application works seamlessly in any environment. A *Docker container* is a standardized unit which can be created on the fly to deploy a particular application or environment. For example, an Ubuntu container, CentOs container, etc. are used as operating system containers, whereas a CakePHP container is an application container. Containers are created from images, whereas the image is the setup of the virtual computer.

The Docker platform consists of three components, namely, (i) Docker software, (ii) Docker objects, and (iii) the registry, as shown in Figure 2.7.

**Software**—The Software Component Of The Docker Platform Primarily Refers To The Docker Daemon (Docker Engine) That Manages Docker Containers And Docker Objects. Users Can Interact With The Docker Engine Via A Command Line Interface Using The Docker Engine's API.

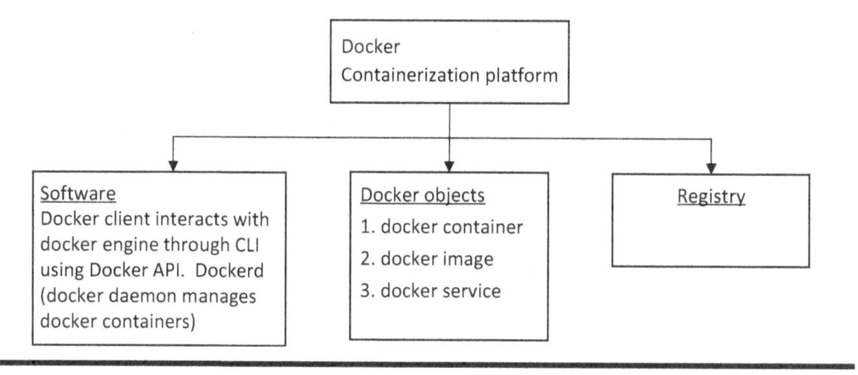


**Figure 2.7 Components of the Docker platform.**

**Objects**—There are three Docker objects, namely Docker container, Docker image, and Docker services. A *Docker container* is an isolated and independent runtime environment which runs an application. A Docker image is a read-only template used to create Docker containers. A Docker file is a simple text file that contains the commands a user could call to assemble an image. A Docker service allows containers to be scaled across multiple Docker daemons.

**Registry**—A Docker registry is a repository for Docker images. A Docker client can download and upload images from/into the registry. The registry can be public or private. Two popular public registries are Docker hub and Docker cloud. Docker hub is the default registry where the Docker looks for images

*Docker compose* is a tool for defining and running applications which consist of multiple containers. Typically, the services which comprise an application are defined in a *.yml* file and all the services run together in an isolated environment.

Docker swarm is an open source container orchestration platform which is used to manage a cluster of Docker nodes as a single virtual system.

**(ii) Availability of communication models and implemented communication infrastructure**

With MSA, an application typically consists of multiple, independent microservices, each with its own data. A service can communicate with another service basically in two ways, (i) synchronous communication and (ii) asynchronous communication. Communication protocols have been developed and are available to meet out both types of communication. In general, the REST protocol is used for synchronous communication. REST is very simple, and it is an HTTP based protocol. Message-Oriented Middleware tools such as RabbitMQ and Apache Kafka are used for asynchronous communication models. Hence the availability of protocols and messaging middleware ease the development of MSA-based applications. In addition, there are standard data formats such as JavaScript Object Notation (JSON), eXtensible Markup Language (XML), Google Protocol Buffer, etc. which are used to serialize the data during communication.

**(iii) Availability of simplified API mechanisms and automatic code generation tools**

Each microservice exposes its functionality through its API so that other applications or services can invoke it. Please note, when two applications are communicating with one another, a stub and skeleton need to be generated. So, there are two essential things to be done in order to enable the interaction between two microservices: (i) Through a well-defined method, a service has to expose its API from which the client understands the calling semantics of the services and (ii) to facilitate the interaction, stub and skeleton have to be generated. As mentioned earlier, microservices support a polyglot feature. So, each service can be developed using its own languages or operating system. This polyglot nature should be taken into account while developing stub and skeleton. There are tools which support both the design of API as well as the generation of stub and skeleton in the required targeted languages. Tools such as *Apache Thrift* can help not only for designing a Thrift API Interface but also can generate stub and skeleton in the required target languages. Developers need to write only the handlers.

**(iv) Availability of microservice composition platforms**

In MSA, an application is split up into many small-sized microservices, in order to realize the whole application, the individual services need to be invoked with a specific pattern so that the planned business process can be completed. There are two major approaches to combine or compose the services. They are (i) service orchestration and (ii) service choreography. In service orchestration, business logic/logic of the business process is developed using languages such as Business Process Execution Logic and deployed in a centralized coordinator which performs the invocation of different services as per the logic. In general, for small applications, the API gateway is designed to serve as a coordinator for orchestration. In service choreography, the logic is incorporated within the individual services either using (i) languages, such as web service Choreography Description Language (WS-CDL) or (ii) using event-based commands and actions which can be realized using tools such as Apache Kafka.

In practice, during service composition, operational failures, errors, and time outs are likely to occur. In order to facilitate monitoring and management of service composition, various service composition platforms such as Camunda, Zeebe, RockScript, Conductor, JOLIE, Jexia, etc. are available.

**(v) Availability of design patterns, service repositories, and other tools**

Each microservice registers itself with service repositories where a service client will search for the required service. Different service discovery mechanisms are already in place. Either the client can discover and invoke directly, or the API gateway/load balancer can perform server-side service discovery and invocation for the client.

**(vi) Availability of ontologies for automated microservice discovery and composition**

When service interfaces are enhanced with ontologies, service discovery can be performed automatically by matching a service request with all the service interfaces available. That is that ontologies help with the automation of the discovery process.

## 2.6 Drawbacks of MSA

*Complexity in managing a large number of services*—In MSA, an application is partitioned into services based on the Single Responsibility Principle (SRP). This causes the application to consist of several services. Now managing a huge number of microservices can become more complex.

*Decomposing an application takes time*—The success of MSA solely depends on the successful decomposition of an application. The very purpose of MSA is individual deployment and speedy development for continuous delivery. If the application is not broken down with independence, the very purpose of MSA will end in failure. So, decomposing an application into independent services is not an easy task. It needs careful planning, deep analysis of requirements, and partitioning the application into individual features. Designing individual services is not only difficult but consumes time.

*Microservices are likely to be less stable*—As an individual service, a microservice would probably behave well, but when it is combined with other services, there may be a chance that it interacts in an unforeseen way because it is practically impossible to test all possible configurations with all possible services.

*Microservices are likely to have more security vulnerabilities*—Since MSA supports diversified technologies for application development, different services may use different technologies, and the application is likely to have many vulnerabilities. This gives hackers more opportunities to penetrate the system.

*Multiple databases make management and transaction difficult*—In MSA, each microservice should have its own related tables or databases. As there are many services in an application, there will be many tables and databases that are tied up with individual services. These kind of multiple databases make both database design and management difficult. In addition, implementing transactions over distributed tables or databases is tedious and involves many operations. Also, microservices frequently use NoSQL databases which do not support Two-Phase-Commit Protocol for implementing transactions.

*More documentation overhead*—Each service should have a well-documented description of its functionality. Otherwise, other services/clients will not understand how a service behaves. Hence, MSA involves with heavy documentation overhead

*Operations overhead and huge upfront costs*—Though each service is independently deployable, in order to deliver the intended purpose of the complete application, individual services have to be tested, deployed, monitored, and composed. Operating and orchestrating all these services is obviously an overwhelming task. Monitoring and orchestrating several services need a high-quality infrastructure.

*Significant effort is required* to manage all processes and operations. So, MSA involves a heavy operations overhead.

*Testing an MSA application is tough*—As each service of an MSA application has its own technology and its own configuration setting, testing an MSA application is tough. In addition, since the services in MSA are likely to be distributed over different locations, a special set of testing tools are needed to test them.

*Increased Resource usage*—In MSA since the services are independently and individually running in their own containers, the resource usage, such as in containers, CPUs, memory, network, database, etc. is very high.

*Increased Network communication*—Independently running microservices need to interact with each other over a network. So, an MSA application requires a high bandwidth/fast network infrastructure.

*DevOps complexity*—Implementation of MSA requires a mature, high-level Development Operations team to handle the complexity involved in maintaining a microservice-based application. It requires skilled software professionals and a huge amount of time.

*Reduced performance*—In a monolithic application, the modules are tightly coupled, and hence it gives a better performance. But in MSA, the services are running as separate processes, and an application is assembled by invoking the required services over the network. The calls made over the network are slower than the calls made over memory. Hence, in MSA, the performance of an application gets affected.

*Refactoring is difficult*—Refactoring an application across multiple services is very hard. For example, MSA allows the use of heterogeneous technologies among services. If one wants to port the functionality of one service to another, then the heterogeneity in services makes the refactoring tough.

*The need for a service registry and service discovery infrastructure*—An MSA application requires a service registry infrastructure where each service has to register itself and its location. Service search and discovery mechanisms have to be established so that the client can find and invoke its required service; i.e., MSA requires an infrastructure for service registry and discovery. In addition, in cloud-based infrastructures where microservices are heavily used for implementing native cloud applications, the location of service instances keep on changing. Hence, a continuous update of service locations is to be performed in the registry.

## 2.7 Differences between SOA and MSA

MSA is compared against SOA as in Table 2.1.

From the sections presented so far, the reader is expected to understand that both SOA and MSA are service-based architectures. They share platform independence, language independence, and location independence. Both the architectures are composed of services. But their purpose and confined focuses are different.

**Table 2.1 Differences between SOA and MSA**

| *Aspect* | *Service-Oriented Architecture* | *Microservices Architecture* |
|---|---|---|
| *Origin* | In general, an enterprise is likely to have its IT applications developed over a couple of decades. So, they have been developed with different platforms, languages, and technologies. But about a decade ago, businesses were compelled to *integrate their individual applications* in order to *address dynamic customer needs, single point of enterprise-level access to global data and business agility*.<br>*Thus, SOA has its origins in Enterprise Application Integration or application to application interaction using standard communication protocols.* | Nowadays, customers are likely to want their products and services with all modern features and capabilities; more specifically, the services are expected to be accessed over a wide range of customer devices. This means businesses must release their products as quickly as possible with a short development cycle as well as with customer involvement. So, enterprises need to adopt an agile software model which promotes the continuous delivery of the product in an incremental fashion. MSA has come out as an enabler for frequent deployment and continuous delivery of products.<br>*Thus, MSA has its origins in agile software development, or it is an enabler for a continuous delivery with frequent deployment.* |
| *Purpose* | • To provide an *application to application interaction*<br>• *It deals with communication between applications* | • To provide frequent and quick deployment<br>• *It deals with the architecture or structure of a single application* |
| *Vision* | • Exposes enterprise-level solutions to other enterprises | • Exposes functional operations of an application |
| *Confined scope* | • Reusability<br>• To support business to business collaboration | • Decoupling among services with the Single Responsibility Principle<br>• To support agile application development |

(Continued)

**Table 2.1 (Continued) Differences Between SOA and MSA**

| *Aspect* | *Service-Oriented Architecture* | *Microservices Architecture* |
|---|---|---|
| *Final outcome* | • Interoperability among applications | • Continuous delivery of product with increased maintenance and scalability |
| *Service granularity* | • Coarse-grained services<br>• Typically, a complete subsystem is implemented as service | • Fine-grained services<br>• Typically, a single function or a business operation is implemented as a microservice |
| *Nature of sharing* | • Promotes the sharing of services as much as possible | • Supports little sharing. MSA works within a *bounded context, which refers to a service coupled to its data*. But one service can access another service through its API |
| *Protocols* | • WSDL, SOAP, and UDDI | • JavaScript Object Notation (JSON), REST API |
| *Communication infrastructure* | • Typically using Enterprise Service Bus (ESB) | • A simple messaging system such as JMS, MSMQ |
| *Messaging type* | • Synchronous messaging model | • Asynchronous messaging model |
| *Databases* | • The database is shared by all services | • Each microservice has its own database |
| *Type of databases* | • Uses traditional relational databases more often | • Uses modern, non-relational or NoSQL databases |

*(Continued)*

**Table 2.1 (Continued) Differences Between SOA and MSA**

| *Aspect* | *Service-Oriented Architecture* | *Microservices Architecture* |
|---|---|---|
| *Service taxonomy* | • SOA offers a wide range of services as:<br>• Application services— Fine-grained services perform specific operations of an application. These services invoked by the user interface<br>• Business services— Coarse-grained services that define core business functions. Used in B2B communication through WSDL<br>• Enterprise services— Represent business processes. Usually implemented by combining business services with specific workflow patterns<br>• Infrastructure services— These services are common to all applications such as security service, transaction service, naming service, event service, persistence service, etc. | • MSA provides two types of services:<br>• Functional services— Fine-grained services of an application which perform a complete but single operation of an application<br>• Infrastructure services— As in SOA, these services represent services that are common to many applications such as security, transaction, persistence, etc. |
| *Runtime environment* | • Typically run in application servers | • Typically run in containers |
| *Attributes* | • Reusability<br>• Business context<br>• Composition | • Productivity<br>• Resilience<br>• Scalability |
| *Constraints on protocols* | • Businesses have to use standardized common protocols (WSDL, SOAP, and UDDI) | • There is no standardization of protocols. REST and asynchronous message brokers are used |
| *Development life cycles* | • Longer development cycles | • Shorter development cycles |

(i) SOA addresses the heterogeneity among enterprise-level applications. It does not look into small application level aspects. It achieves automated, orchestrated business processes by composing heterogeneous coarse-grained services. SOA is an enabler for application to application interaction, and it enhances reusability to the greatest extent possible. SOA composes the individual applications so as to complete a higher-level business process with reduced calls and higher performance.

(ii) MSA addresses frequent deployment and continuous delivery of individual applications by breaking the application into a collection of microservices. MSA is an enabler for agile software development. It provides the architecture of a single application.

## 2.8 Where Do SOA and MSA Fit into Business Enterprises?

Both SOA and MSA have their origins in facilitating business enterprises. Where exactly these architectures play crucial roles is highlighted in Figure 2.8. As in Figure 2.8, when an enterprise deals with higher-level business to business

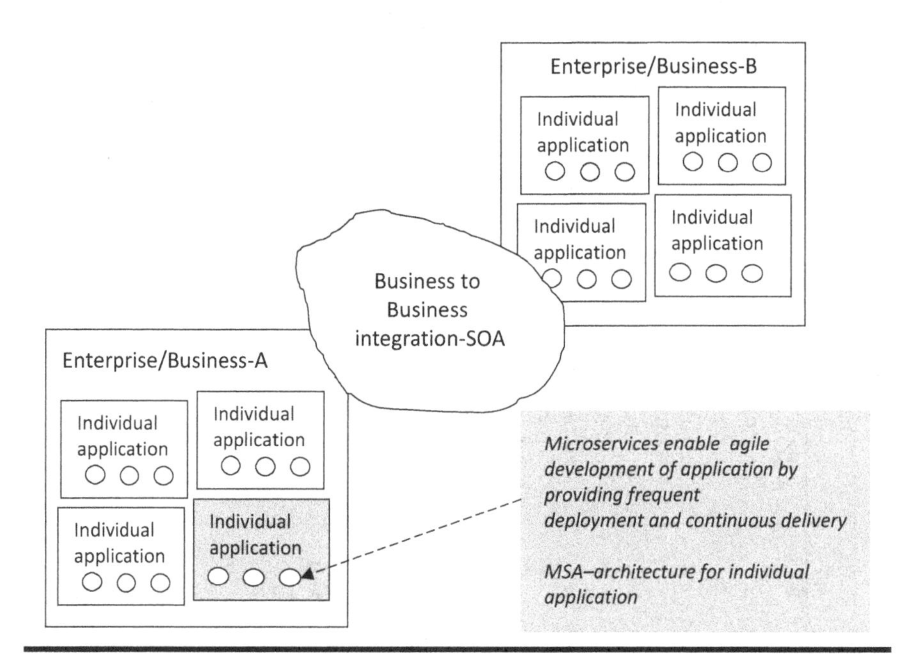


**Figure 2.8 Where SOA and MSA fit into business enterprises.**

interaction, SOA plays a major role. If one looks for an application architecture which facilitates the quick release of products, MSA plays a major role. Since both SOA and MSA are service-based architectures, they share many characteristics in common. Both the architectures consist of independent, autonomous, interoperable, reusable services having well-defined interfaces which can be invoked over the network. In both the architectures, the services have the following characteristics in common.

(i) Abstraction—A service should expose its capability while hiding its implementation.
(ii) Service contract/interface—The capabilities of a service are described in the service contract or interface.
(iii) Service discoverability—The client must know the location of service in order to access it. So, services should be discoverable.
(iv) Service independence/autonomy—Services should be independent and autonomous.
(v) Services must be loosely coupled.
(vi) Services should be composable in order to deliver a higher level of business goal.
(vii) Services should be reusable.
(viii) Services should be resilient.
(ix) Services should be stateless and scalable.
(x) Services should encourage open source technologies, modernization, containerization, and cloud environments as enterprises are moving to the cloud.

One can view MSA as the logical evolution of SOA, and as a subset it stays inside SOA to address modern business use cases.

## 2.9 Applicability of MSA in Contrast to SOA

*SOA*

- SOA is well suited for large and complex business application environments that involve the integration of many heterogeneous applications.
- When businesses need to deal with the orchestration of different tasks to generate a big business process, SOA is the ideal choice.

***MSA***

Some of the companies which employ MSA for their services include (i) Netflix, (ii) eBay, (iii) Amazon, (iv) the UK Government Digital Service, (v) Twitter, (vi) PayPal, (vii), *The Guardian*, and many other large-scale enterprises.

MSA fits as an ideal choice when:

- Applications are developed using an agile software process model.
- Large applications require a high release velocity.
- Complex applications need to be highly scalable.
- Applications have rich domains or many subdomains.
- An organization consists of small development teams.

## 2.9.1 Typical Use Cases of MSA

### 2.9.1.1 How Amazon Uses MSA and the Cloud

According to Werner Vogels (CTO, Amazon), it is understood that Amazon was facing a lot of technical challenges in the early 2000s. The major drawback was that the Amazon e-commerce web site was developed using conventional tiered architecture. Due to the thick and large nature of the monolithic server-side application, it took a long time to compile and deploy the required changes. Backend databases were massive, and it was tough to manage them.

Technical architects at Amazon decided to shift to MSA. At present, the home page_*amazon.com is launched using a few hundred microservices.* One of the primary reasons for the success of Amazon is that it followed the idea of the *two-pizza team* concept. This means that the team size should be small enough to contain a small number of people who can share two pizzas. In practice, Amazon implemented a team size of a maximum of ten people. Amazon has hundreds of such teams working for its website. At a later stage, again, there was a notable decrease in productivity. Again, Amazon realized that developers were forced to look after the operations, monitoring, and management of a huge number of microservices, which is why productivity decreased. Hence, Amazon established its own cloud infrastructure. In this manner, the Amazon e-commerce site was implemented using MSA from the cloud. Ultimately, Microservice Architecture enabled Amazon to implement continuous deployment. Now Amazon engineers could deploy code once every 11.7 seconds.

### 2.9.1.2 How Netflix Uses Microservices

Netflix began to move its monolithic architecture to cloud-based Microservices Architecture in 2009. When operating on a monolithic architecture, Netflix had constant server outages. Microservices Architecture and modern UI technology helped Netflix engineers to deploy their code thousands of times per day. Today Netflix can serve 93.8 million users globally while streaming more than 10 billion hours of movies and shows without any issues.

#### 2.9.1.3 How Capital One Uses Microservices

According to Irakli Nadareishivili, Director of Technology, Capital One, the DevOps team of Capital One manage the businesses' conflicts effectively and efficiently by implementing MSA. In a cloud computing environment, the available physical infrastructure is shared by multiple processes with the concept of containerization. The underlying layer of the cloud computing infrastructure is a physical infrastructure, which is governed by a Linux host operating system. On top of the OS, one can have many containers. Containers offer various scheduling and orchestration solutions for managing the microservices deployed in it. Containers consume fewer resources when compared to Virtual Machines. In addition, containers offer monitoring, security, and standardization solutions. *The primary driver for using microservices is the containerization of applications for deployment benefit. Due to the nature of containers, putting a large monolithic architecture into containers is not useful. If an entire monolithic architecture is deployed in a container, again it is going to be a point of a single failure. So, containerizing the application into microservices and deploying them in containers will give the expected benefit.* In addition, conventional centralized databases are also posing many issues. Alternately *technique of event sourcing* ensures that all changes to the application are stored as a sequence of events. Event sourcing gives a log of all changes that occur in the application. Ultimately, the availability of tools such as *pods in Kubernetes, Apache Kafka (an event sourcing system) facilitate the combination of containers and microservices as a better choice for Capital One's services.*

#### 2.9.1.4 Microservices Are the Perfect Choice for Developing Cloud-Native/Optimized Applications

Recently enterprises have begun migrating to a cloud computing environment in order to avail both business level and technical level benefits such as (i) reduced capital and operational costs, (ii) quick delivery of their product, (iii) dynamic resource provisioning capabilities, (iv) almost infinite resource capacity, (v) dynamic and rapid scale up and scale out provisioning of required resources on demand, and (vi) a pay-as-per-usage pricing model. Cloud computing offers three major kinds of services, namely Infrastructure as a Service (IaaS), Platform as a Service (PaaS) and Software as a Service (SaaS). In addition to the above major factors, the cloud offers high scalability, and it supports a wide range of customers. Customers are interested in availing their services with any kind of connected device including:

- Laptops
- Smartphones
- Any connected device (i.e., cloud computing supports *Bring Your Own Device* (BYOD) for getting connected to the cloud to use the services)

Also, user interfaces of cloud services are very much responsive and reactive to meeting customer's expectations. The above features of the cloud make it the right choice for enterprises. Cloud providers encourage microservices-based application development due to the following:

(i) If the application adopts MSA, then new or up to date features can be very quickly developed and launched within the application. Customer demands can be satisfied in almost no time.
(ii) In MSA, each service can scale independently without affecting other services. As far as the scalability is concerned, the resources have to be provisioned only to the concerned microservice, which requires high scalability but not to the entire application as a whole. Thus, scalability is achieved at low cost. In addition, when applications are migrated to the cloud, if they are refactored or re-engineered, then they can avail the utmost benefits of the cloud. MSA is the ideal choice for cloud-optimized/cloud-native or SaaS applications.

#### *2.9.1.5 Microservices for E-Commerce Applications*

Traditionally retailers have used three-tier architecture-based applications to manage e-commerce applications. In this model, applications are componentized according to layers, namely presentation, business logic, and data access logic, and not by functionality. But nowadays, customers are very smart in analyzing the features of the products. For example, a customer goes through the specification and features of many products using his mobile; he makes an order based on his interests. He will be closely watching the status of his order. Once the product is shipped to the customer, he shares his feedback about both the product and service provided by the retailers. So, retailers cannot stick with their old technologies. *They have to modernize their applications so that they can meet the Omni-channel demands from customers, i.e., through different channels such as web, mobile, social channels, offline store, etc. Customers always want their services to be readily available. So, enterprises have to relay the right information to the right place at the right time so that they can have the competitive edge.*

E-commerce retailers are shifting from monolithic application architecture to MSA to get the following benefits:

(iii) Quick implementation changes and the ability to address customer needs quickly
(iv) Faster User Interface responses
(v) Personalized services over an Omni-channel facility
(vi) Increased sales

Thus, in the above example, e-commerce retailers begin with refactoring the presentation layer with new reactive UI layer and proceed with the partitioning of e-commerce applications in functionality based microservices such as (i) search service, (ii) catalog service, (iii), order (iv), inventory, (v) shipping, (vi) cart, (vii) payment, and (viii) promotion.

#### 2.9.1.6 Microservices for Developing Web Applications

MSA finds its application in developing web applications where there may be some modules which need to have high scalability whereas some other modules may not require high scalability. Consider a web application. Assume that the application has different modules like (i) login modules, (ii) new registration modules, and (iii) location modules with GPS service, etc. In these services, the location module with GPS has to continuously update the location of the user, whereas registration data of a user remains almost the same. Here employing MSA facilitates the design of the location module as an individual microservice and allows it to scale independently. In addition to the above benefit, MSA provides fast page reloads for any web application.

#### 2.9.1.7 Microservices for CPU/RAM Intensive Parts of Applications

Another scenario where microservices are the ideal choice is in handling the CPU/RAM intensive functions of applications. Consider a text analytics application. It handles many models and natural language processing algorithms to process and analyze the text contents. In this application, database related processing will be less. There will be modules related to the presentation, such as graphing and user related interactions. It is better to isolate the processing part, which involves large CPU/memory related computations from other presentation or user interactions. If the computation intensive part is isolated as microservices, the required level of performance can be implemented for those services. In case of need, these services can interact with other modules through their APIs. Similarly, business intelligence or business analytics applications can get benefits by implementing MSA.

#### 2.9.1.8 Applications Having Multiple Teams Working on the Same Product

One of the major strengths of MSA is that it provides increased freedom and flexibility to developers. Consider a traditional, large application such as Facebook or Twitter. In these examples, multiple teams work simultaneously on the same project. In such large projects even though one team completes a change and wants to go for deployment, it may not be that easy as the project is a large one and obviously dependences arise among the teams. Typically, large applications prefer to go for long development cycles. In these situations, it takes time to see the updated changes. If large applications having multiple teams are partitioned into microservices with separate teams of only a few people, then the team can individually decide the deployment. The team will get increased freedom and flexibility. Thus, MSA enhances the developers' productivity significantly.

#### 2.9.1.9 Microservices as Enablers for Cloud Adoption

Though microservices and cloud computing are different technologies, the combination of microservices and cloud computing naturally fit as a good IT match for satisfying customer demands quickly. For example, containers make everything from deployment to monitoring, scheduling, orchestration, and management of microservices very easy and at the same time microservices have the capacity to scale up/scale down at a service level rather than an application level. This provides optimized resource usage. Another attractive part of microservices is that it uses *event-driven computing*. How the cloud and microservices can play a crucial role in meeting business needs are realized as follows. Amazon can provision its computer resources according to the demands *that arise through events*. Since microservices support event-driven computing, it can invoke Amazon's API, which generates appropriate events which further lead to the provisioning of the required resources; i.e., when the API call occurs, the concerned routine needs to execute. Required resources for that routine are provisioned. After the execution of that routine, the resources are automatically decommissioned. Thus, the combination of containers, appropriate tools, event-driven computing, and the cloud works very effectively to meet the modern needs of customers.

#### 2.9.1.10 Identifying Microservices Use Cases from Classic SOA

As mentioned earlier, SOA operates at a higher level where one business interacts with other businesses. Usually, SOA is handled by enterprise-level technical architects whereas microservices are developed and handled by application-level technical architects. Now, one of the most interesting aspects is when application-level architects interact with enterprise-level architects; this means it will become easy to identify which functions or services will be heavily used across different applications. Such services can be separated out from the application as microservices, and they can scale independently to serve the customers with stateless behavior.

Thus, from the above use cases, one would have got when switching to MSA is desirable as *MSA involves a huge upfront cost and a long time to implement.*

To summarize, MSA is desirable when:

- (i) There is a need for frequent deployment of an application, and if the size of the application is prohibitively large to consume a long time for deployment.
- (ii) If individual parts of applications can be isolated for scaling.
- (iii) If an application deals with multiple teams and communication among the teams becomes a headache in deploying the application.

(iv) If an enterprise has already decided to reengineer its workloads for cloud migration.
(v) If an application deals with too many user interactions and if responsive and reactive UI is required.

## 2.10 Trade-Offs in MSA

Like any other computing technology, MSA also comes not only with benefits but also with costs and operational complexity [5]. So, an enterprise should think about the cost and operational complexity involved in implementing MSA, and then it should adopt MSA.

### 2.10.1 Gain the Benefit of Strong Service Boundaries at the Cost of Distribution

In MSA, the application is broken down into single-purpose services with strong boundaries defined by context. MSA discourages dependency with other services. It is based on the concept of *doing one thing and doing the thing well*. So, it establishes a strong boundary between services. Here, the services are distributed among various hosts. In order to avail the benefit or overall outcome of the application, the services are invoked using their APIs. Now this involves more cost. Since the microservices are invoked over the network, the performance of applications may get reduced. If the application remains monolithic, it gives a better performance as many of the functions are tightly coupled. So MSA needs a high-speed network or low latency and high bandwidth to maintain the expected performance of the application. This can be achieved at a higher cost and more resource usage.

### 2.10.2 Gain the Benefit of Individual Deployment at the Cost of Eventual Consistency

When an application is partitioned into many small independent microservices according to functionality, the services can be deployed individually without waiting or affecting other services of the applications. This gives the benefit of both frequent deployment and continuous delivery. But independence and strong boundary separation can be achieved only with *decentralized databases*. The nature of decentralized databases brings another problem of data consistency. With a monolith application, one can update a bunch of things together in a single transaction. This means that monolithic applications have strong consistency. Whenever an update is made, it reaches to all the required places immediately without any delay. Whereas microservices require multiple resources to be updated and distributed transactions are to be carried out. MSA is capable of providing eventual consistency where, for any data update, it takes some time to reach its required places to be updated. With MSA, developers need to be aware of consistency issues and figure out how to detect when things are out of sync.

### 2.10.3 Avail Independent Deployment at the Cost of Operational Complexity

In MSA, since the application is partitioned into many microservices, monitoring and managing the services becomes an issue. There is no way of monitoring microservices without automation, orchestration, and a huge set of tools. Testing and debugging microservices in a distributed environment make the operational activities complex. Handling this operational complexity requires a host *of new skills and tools*. Along with the need for better skills and tools, *an enterprise also needs to introduce a DevOps culture*: greater collaboration between developers, operations, and everyone else involved in software delivery. *Cultural change is difficult*, especially in larger and older organizations.

### 2.10.4 Avail the Benefit of Technology Diversity at the Cost of Interface Issues

With MSA, there are no constraints on the technologies that are used for developing services. Developers can mix multiple languages, frameworks, and databases to implement the required function. Though each service may be simple to understand, when there is an interconnection needed, it becomes a little complex. Though developers can flexibly choose their technologies, when one service needs to be composed with another in order to produce business outcomes/processes/decisions, then integration consumes both cost and time.

***Summary***

This chapter illustrates how monolithic server-side applications of a typical three-tiered architecture suffers from long deployment, multiple or huge teams of people, a huge centralized database, lack of technology diversity, dependency among teams, decreased flexibility, decreased developers' productivity, etc. Out of these drawbacks, the major bottleneck which prevents continuous delivery and an agile software process model is the large project size and its long deployment time. In this context, the chapter introduces MSA. It describes how MSA alleviates the difficulties of monolithic application with its unique capabilities and features. The chapter explains the various key enablers for MSA, such as containers, the availability of tools and platforms, etc. Then it describes the differences between SOA and MSA. Ultimately, to give a better insight to MSA, various use cases of MSA were highlighted. Trade-offs in MSA were also presented.

***Exercises***

1. Why do we need MSA?
2. Discuss in detail the typical use cases of MSA.
3. How does MSA differ from SOA?
4. How does containerization help for MSA?
5. List the different key enablers for MSA
6. Can we follow MSA for developing all applications? Or under what circumstances do we go for MSA?

## References


1. Irakli Nadareishvili, Ronnie Mitra, Matt McLarty, and Mike Amundsen, "*Microservice Architecture, Aligning Principles, Practices, and Culture*," O'Reilly Media, Inc., 2016.
2. Lee Atchison. Microservice Architectures: What They Are and Why You Should Use Them. 2018. Available at: https://blog.newrelic.com/technology/microservices-what-they-are-why-to-use-them/
3. Smartbear. What Is Microservice? Available at: https://smartbear.com/learn/api-design/what-are-microservices/
4. Imanol Urra Ruiz and Félix Freitag. Distributed Microservice Architecture with Docker. 2016. Available at: http://openaccess.uoc.edu/webapps/o2/bitstream/10609/56264/7/iurraTFM0616mem%C3%B2ria.pdf
5. Adam Bertram. Seven Reasons to Switch to Microservices—And Five Reasons You Might Not Succeed. 2017. Available at: https://www.cio.com/article/3201193/it-strategy/7-reasons-to-switch-to-microservices-and-5-reasons-you-might-not-succeed.html

# Chapter 3

# Communication Models for Microservices

***Objective***

There are various key architectural elements when developing an MSA-based application. The objective of this chapter is to give an overview of various architectural elements that constitute MSA, and introduce one of the most important architectural elements: communication models for MSA. By the end of this chapter, the reader will understand how services interact with one another synchronously and asynchronously using standard architectures, protocols, and message brokers.

***Preface***

In the previous chapter, the reader learned that the purpose of MSA was to enable the frequent deployment and continuous delivery of applications, which are typically developed using an agile software process model. From this chapter onwards, various architectural elements of MSA are gradually introduced so as to facilitate reader understanding of the significance of each architectural element. First, this chapter presents an overview of the various architectural elements of MSA and design principles of microservices. Then the chapter describes two major communication models, namely the synchronous communication model and the asynchronous communication model. It gives special emphasis to three commonly used communication protocols, namely Representational State Transfer (REST) for synchronous communication; Advanced Message Queuing Protocol (AMQP) and its open source implementation, RabbitMQ, for asynchronous message-based communication; and an asynchronous message broker with high scalability and high throughput, namely Apache Kafka. Thus, the chapter answers questions such as:

1. How do different architectural elements constitute MSA?
2. How do we design microservices?
3. How can we establish communications in MSA?
4. Do microservices need to fulfill any prerequisites for communication?
5. How do services interact with one another?
6. What protocols are being used?
7. Do we have any standardized protocols?
8. Are there any readily available architectures for inter-service communication?
9. What are RabbitMQ and Apache Kafka?
10. Can we use JMS in microservices?

## 3.1 Key Architectural Elements of MSA

Typically large monolithic applications have a long deployment time and prohibit the frequent deployment of applications. With the monolithic type of architecture, it is tough to adapt to business innovations and new trends of computing. As mentioned earlier, nowadays, the expectations of customers are high and dynamic. For example, a customer wants to purchase something online. He is likely to go through various web sites. According to his interest, he places an order for a product. The customer then wants to know the progress of the order, tracks the order, and even wants to add personalized features to the ordered product. In addition, he wants to work very closely with the vendor. Ultimately, he shares his feedback about the product and the vendor's services with his friends over social networking. Another key point is that commercial web sites such as eBay, Flip Cart, Snap Deal, etc., and social networking web sites such as Facebook, LinkedIn, etc. are continuously updated by several people. In this scenario, *the conventional architecture turns out to be a bottleneck due to its tight coupling between the modules and its prohibitively larger package size, whereas MSA is a perfect choice for this. In addition, MSA-based application development is facilitated by containerization and other tool/platforms.*

Since MSA is an evolving architecture, a proper understanding of various elements of the architecture becomes essential, and is a prerequisite for the successful development of an MSA-based application. The key elements of the MSA are shown in Figure 3.1.

The key elements of MSA include:

- Design principles for microservices
- Communication models for microservices
- Data formats for microservices
- API design and middleware for microservices
- Service registration

(Communication models, data formats, and API design and middleware: } Essential prerequisites to enable communication among services)

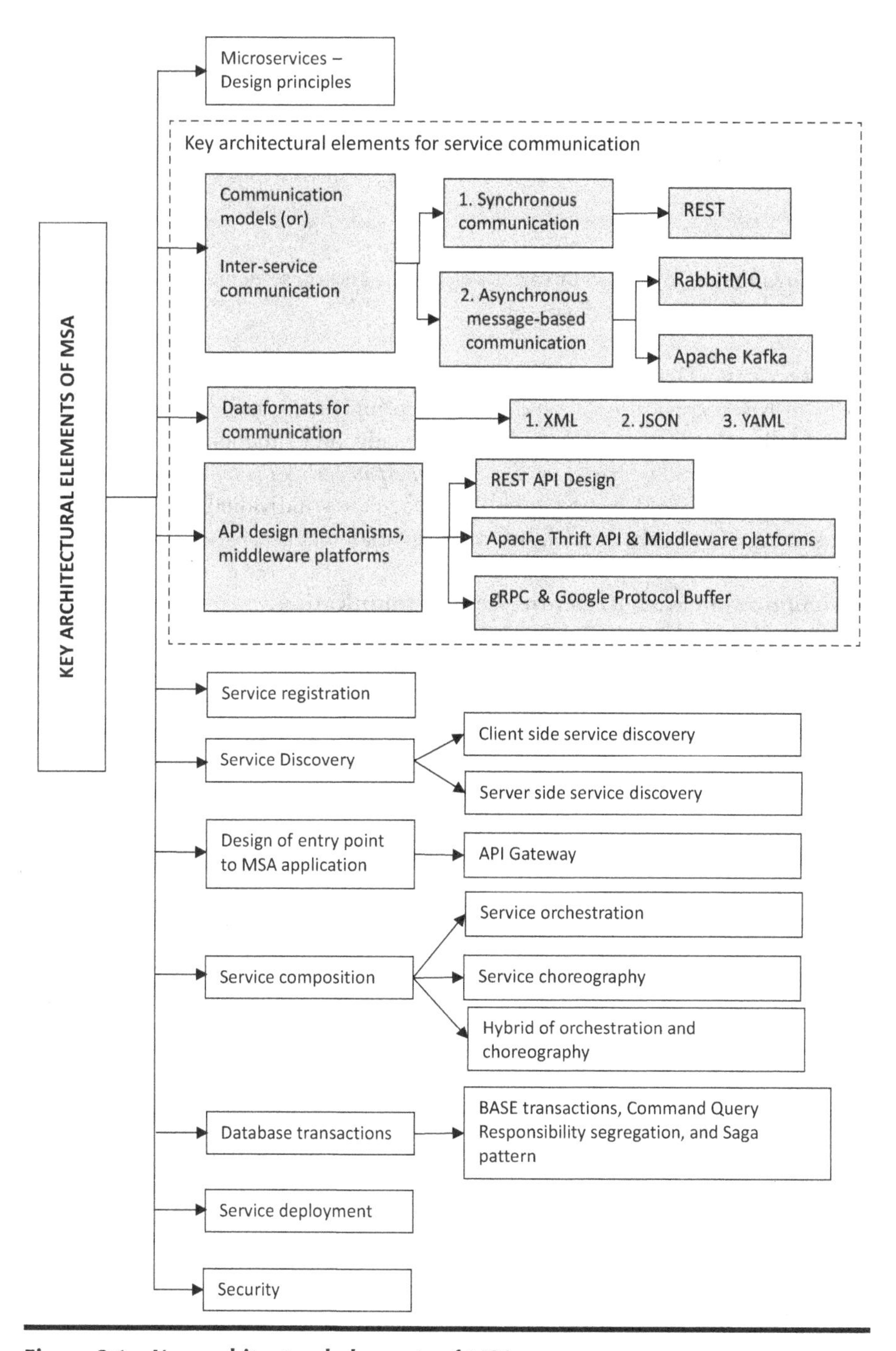


**Figure 3.1 Key architectural elements of MSA.**

- Service discovery
- Design of entry points to the MSA application–API gateway
- Service composition
- Database transactions
- Service deployment
- Security

The following is an overview of various elements, and these elements are covered in the subsequent chapters in detail.

**Microservices—Design Principles**

An MSA-based application should be split up into many services based on their functionality. Each service should perform only one function. The Design of microservices should be based on the *Single Responsibility Principle*. This keeps the services both independent and small. This facilitates individual deployment, the provisioning of individual scalability, and easy maintenance.

**Communication Model/Inter-Service Communication**

Since services are designed with *Single Responsibility Principle*, frequent situations will arise where one service needs to communicate with another service. For example, a service called shipment service will seek the payment service to check whether payment has been made or not. So, interaction among services is a common requirement in MSA. It is achieved in two ways, namely synchronous and asynchronous. In synchronous communication, both the sender and receiver are online. The REST protocol is extensively used to implement synchronous communication between services. In asynchronous communication, the sender and receiver are offline, and it is messaged based. AMQP is commonly used for message-oriented asynchronous communication. The RabbitMQ tool is a message-oriented middleware which implements AMQP. In order to have a high message throughput, message brokers such as Apache Kafka may be used.

**Data Formats for Communication**

Microservices communicate with one another by sending messages. The messages are constructed using standard data formats, i.e., messages represented in higher-level languages are serialized to a format that can be sent over the network. Commonly used data serialization formats for MSA are:

- eXtensible Markup Language (XML)
- JavaScript Object Notation (JSON)
- Yet Another Markup Language
- Google Protocol Buffer, etc.

**API Design and Middleware for Microservices**

Any microservice should expose its method signatures to other applications/services through its Application Programming Interface (API). The other applications will interpret the calling semantics of the methods specified in the API and invoke their desired methods. So, the way in which APIs are developed becomes very important. There are standard mechanisms for developing the APIs of microservices. The most commonly used API design mechanisms are:

1. REST API design
2. Apache Thrift API design
3. Google Protocol Buffer

Along with API design, the following key aspect, or middleware platform, has to be developed to enable client–service interaction. That is, a service exposes its functionality through its API. Client and microservice might use different operating systems and different programming languages, etc. In order to hide the heterogeneity and to facilitate communication between client and service, it is essential to generate stub and skeleton. Modern tools like Apache Thrift not only provides standard Interface Description Language (Thrift IDL) to expose the interface/API of a service but also provides tools that automatically generate stub and skeleton (i.e., a middleware platform) in the targeted languages.

**Service Registration**

Once a service is developed and deployed, each service instance has to register its location in a service registry. A service registry is a database with which all services should register their locations and update their healthiness. In addition, if there is any change in the location of the service instance, the location information has to be updated. The service registry provides APIs for service providers and clients to publish service locations and discover their required services, respectively

**Service Discovery**

Service clients should know about the location and API of a service in order to consume it. Service discovery is the process of finding a matched or suitable service for fulfilling the client's request. Service discovery can be performed in two ways, client-based service discovery and server-based service discovery. In client-based service discovery, the client itself directly searches the service registry, finds the required service, and then makes a request to the concerned service. In server-side discovery, an element called a load balancer or API gateway (which serves as the entry point to an MSA application) searches the registry and discovers the service which matches a client's request. Then, the API gateway/load balancer places the request to the concerned service.

**API Gateway—Entry Point to an MSA Application**

In MSA, an application is split into many microservices according to functional capabilities. Even a small application will consist of a considerable number of microservices. In this situation, if a client directly communicates with the application, then it has to invoke each and every service over an external network, such as the internet. This kind of direct communication between the client and an MSA-based application involves huge network traffic, and thus it is not considered as a good practice. An architectural element called an API gateway is used as a single entry point to the client. It receives requests from all clients and makes the required subsequent requests to the concerned services within an internal network. This kind of accessing an application not only hides direct exposure of the services to the client but also provider better performance as the requests are made within an internal network.

**Service Composition**

There are situations where a client request may not be fulfilled by a single service and the request is fulfilled by composing more than one service in a particular execution pattern. The process of combining more than one service in a particular execution pattern called workflow in order to achieve a given business process is called *service composition*. Service composition can be done in two ways, service orchestration and service choreography. In service orchestration, a central coordinator component which contains the logic to achieve the given business process is used to invoke the individual services according to the logic. In service choreography, the processing logic is distributed among the participating services themselves. For example, the client may invoke the first service, and at the end of the first service the first service then invokes the subsequent service, and this continues until the desired process returns the results to the client.

**Database Transactions**

According to the design principles of microservices, each service should possess its own database/table. Also, services may be distributed. In database management systems, transactions are used as a technique to implement the Atomicity, Consistency, Isolation, and Durability (ACID) properties of a database. A database transaction generally consists of more than one atomic task, and according to conventional database principles in order to preserve the consistency and logical validity of database, *a transaction should happen in its entirety, or it should not happen at all.* If a transaction happens in its entirety, the change will be permanently committed to the database. If a transaction happens to occur only partiality due to failure, then all the changes will not be committed to the permanent store. The transaction will be rolled back to preserve the consistency of the data. Conventionally a Two-Phase-Commit protocol (2PC protocol) is used to implement transactions in distributed databases.

But in microservices, since the databases are decentralized, implementing 2PC is both time-consuming and resource consuming. As a design principle, it is better to avoid transactions in MSA. If at all transactions are mandatorily required, in contrast to the ACID transaction in conventional systems, *Basically Available, Soft state, Eventually consistent* (BASE) transactions are implemented with design patterns such as the *Saga pattern*. BASE transactions are suitable for applications with large web sites and a large number of replicated datasets. In the Saga pattern, each atomic task is considered as a local transaction, the task is committed locally, and the status is relayed to a central coordinator. If any of the local transactions fail, then the coordinator instructs every participating service to roll back the committed change. The rollback process is again executed as another local transaction. In this way, the BASE transactions provide eventual consistency of data. In addition, MSA adopts the Command Query Responsibility Segregation (CQRS) pattern which mandates the use two different database instances of which one instance is used for write operations and the other one is used for read operations. Having two database instances helps in reducing data contention issues and provides high availability and security. Thus, MSA provides data consistency with the Saga pattern, high security, availability, and performance with the CQRS pattern.

**Service Deployment**

Microservices can be deployed in bare metal servers, in a virtualized environment, or in containers. As mentioned in the previous chapter, a container is the best choice for deploying a microservice due to its small size.

**Security**

Since microservices are exposed to clients through their APIs, from a security perspective, it becomes important to ensure that the API of a microservice is well-defined, well-documented, standardized, and possesses core security characteristics, namely (i) confidentiality, (ii) integrity, (iii) availability, and (iv) reliability. An API can guarantee confidentiality and integrity by permitting only authenticated and authorized users to access their relevant services. In addition, an API must always be available to handle requests and process them reliably. APIs should be managed with the necessary security policies, such as Quality of Service, auditing, dynamic data filtering, and other security mechanisms.

In MSA, since the application is split up into services, other than the generic security mechanism, each service can implement its own security requirements. In practice, for simple applications, the required security mechanisms are typically implemented in the API gateway itself or as a separate service. Sensitive applications typically implement both API gateway level security and service level security.

The following sections handle three architectural aspects/elements. They are:

(i) Design principles of microservices
(ii) Prerequisites for service communication (elements of communication)
(iii) Communication models

## 3.2 Design Principles of Microservices

The first core element of MSA is microservices. Microservices are created by partitioning the application into a collection of services based on functionality, usually according to Martin Fowler's Single Responsibility Principle (SRP). The application should be designed to consist of *several single-purpose microservices.* The main design criterion of microservices is that they "*do only one thing and do the thing well.*" The services should be self-contained and independent. One service should not interfere with another service for its functionality so it is capable of independent deployment.

The general practice of decomposing an application into microservices is by applying the bounded context principle of Domain Driven Design (DDD). In simple words, while designing microservices follow the following steps:

(i) Start with the smallest possible microservice and create a boundary around it.
(ii) Check if there is any interaction that lies outside the boundary.
(iii) If so, extend the boundary to include the interaction or allow relaxed communications.
(iv) In this way, a microservice is refined based on a communication boundary until it comes out as a *separate bounded context.*

 The following key points may be considered while separating the bounded context.

 - If any two services need to interact a lot with one another, it means that they work for the same concept or function, and those two services should be combined into a single service.
 - While designing microservices, one should look for a separate *communication boundary.*
 - *The communication boundary also gets reflected in the autonomy of the microservices.* If one service interacts with other services for completing its purpose, obviously it is not autonomous, and the service should be redesigned to include the dependency.
 - *Here please note that the size of the service does not dictate the deployment; the autonomous nature of the service decides it.*

Thus the *design principles of microservices* include (i) the Single Responsibility Principle, (ii) design the microservices as per bounded context in Domain Driven Design. This indirectly emphasizes a separate communication boundary and autonomy of microservices. (iii) Check whether the service is capable of independent deployment.

Consider an example taken from [1]. This example explains the concepts of domain, subdomain, and services. The domain is a broad concept which has one or more subdomains. Subdomains are independent areas, and they are loosely coupled with one another. Each subdomain can have one or more microservices, which are identified based on a single business capability.

The domain involved in the above example is *retail banking*. Retail banking is also called consumer banking, which is individual-oriented, and offers a wide range of services such as (i) savings accounts, (ii) checking accounts, (iii) mortgages, (iv) personal loans, and (v) debit/credit cards to individuals. *Retail banking offers online banking to individuals. Usually, customers use online banking using web or mobile applications.* Another option through which the customers performs a purchase is through *Point of Sale* (POS). Here, a customer either swipes his card or enters his card with a chip into the merchant's terminal. These transactions can be made with a debit card or credit card.

According to Domain Driven Design, the domain, i.e., retail banking, is divided into subdomains. In addition, according to Conway's Law, subdomain boundaries are determined in part by the *communication structures* or *organizational structures* within an organization. Thus, the subdomains for retail banking are identified from the organizational structure as (i) self-service banking, (ii) customer and card management, (iii) deposit account, (iv) product lending and credit, and (v) mortgages.

Now each subdomain has distinct or independent bounded contexts. For each subdomain, independent functional areas are identified, as given in Table 3.1.

Consider that *retail banking* introduces *customer-centric payment services* in order to meet the goals of customer retention. *This service allows a customer to purchase their products based on their investments, accounts, assets, and interactions with the bank rather than simply based on their account balance.*

*Various subdomains and bounded contexts along with the new customer-centric payment services are placed in the retail domain, as shown in* Figure 3.2.

**Table 3.1 Bounded Contexts in Various Subdomains for a Retail Domain**

| *Subdomain* | *Bounded Context* |
|---|---|
| Self-service banking | (i) online banking and (ii) Point of Sale |
| Customer and card management | (i) customer information, (ii) customer authentication, and (iii) payment and transactions |
| Deposit account | (i) savings account and (ii) checking account |
| Product lending and credit | (i) product lending and (ii) credit card |
| Mortgage | (i) mortgages |

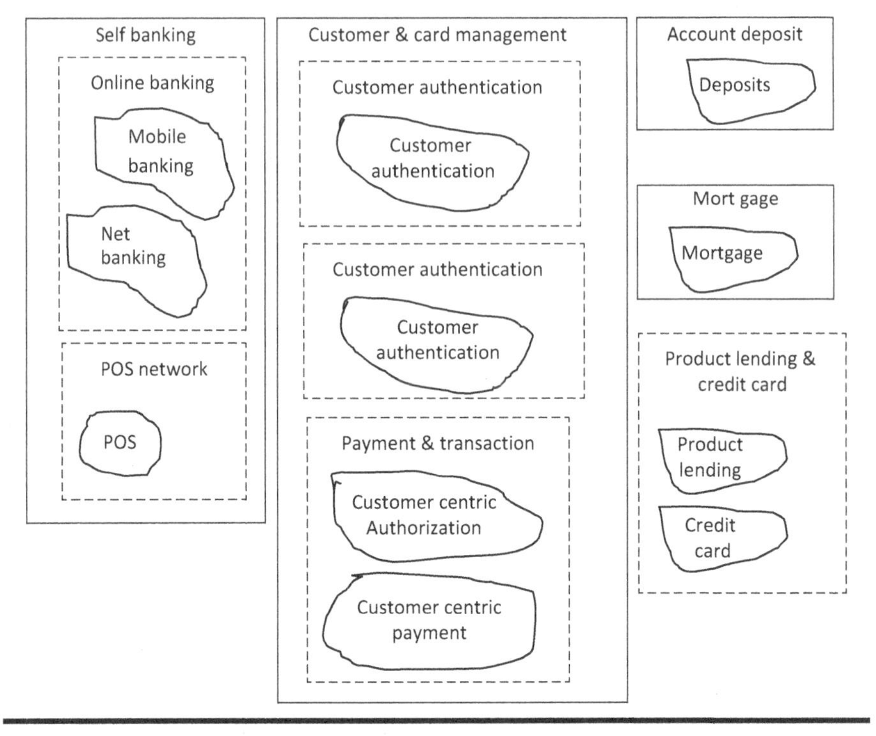


**Figure 3.2 Subdomains and bounded contexts in a retail banking domain.**

## 3.3 Prerequisites for Service Interaction/ Communication

*Note: Elements discussed in this section work in unison to bring about communication between services. Hence, the elements can be perceived as prerequisites for service communication/interaction.*

Microservices Architecture serves as an architecture for applications which require frequent deployment and continuous release. These applications are developed using an agile software process model. MSA gives freedom to developers in choosing technologies, programming languages, and operating systems, tools, etc. for developing microservices; i.e., MSA supports polyglot development. With this polyglot feature, each microservice can have its own programming language and platform, as shown in Figure 3.3. In Figure 3.3, there are three services: Microservice-1 is developed using Python and Linux, microservice-2 is developed using .NET and Windows, and microservice-3 is developed using Java and Linux. This illustrates the difficulty in communication. Naturally, a middleware platform has to be established to hide the heterogeneity in the environment of the microservices. In addition, there should be standardization (i) in the way APIs are designed and exposed and (ii) in data serialization formats.

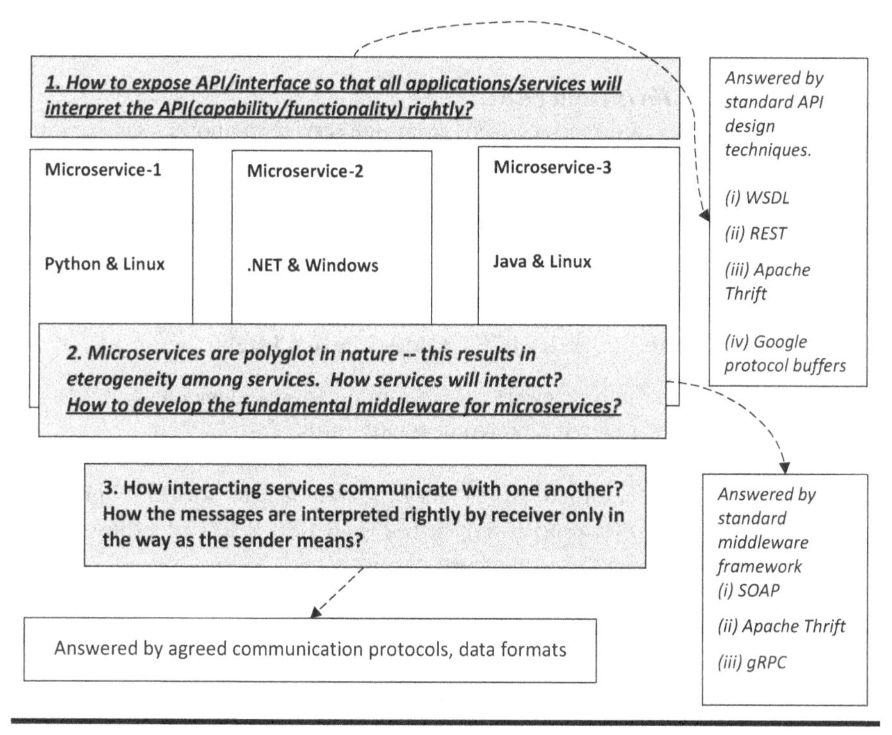


**Figure 3.3 Prerequisites for service interaction.**

When services need to communicate with one another, a number of questions will arise.

(i) How will one service come to know about the capabilities of other service? How does a service expose its functional capability to others?

*A service exposes its capabilities through an Application Programming Interface. An API describes the complete details of all method signatures and their calling semantics.*

(ii) How to standardize API design so that a service interprets the API correctly, as in how the provider meant/interpreted it?

There are some standard mechanisms or techniques to design API. They are:

***WSDL, REST, Apache Thrift,* and *Google Protocol Buffers***

(iii) Since in heterogeneous environment as the programming languages, technologies and platforms of services are disparate in nature, it becomes necessary to establish a middleware which should hide all the heterogeneity. Is there middleware providing frameworks already in place? So that developers can focus on the core application rather than developing middleware support for microservices communication?

There are some standard communication middleware platforms for MSA. They are:

***SOAP, Apache Thrift,* and *gRPC***

(iv) How are data and messages sent from one service to another service interpreted correctly?

*Services need to use agreed-upon protocols and data formats.*

**ESSENTIAL PREREQUISITES FOR MICROSERVICE COMMUNICATION:**

Two parties (sender and receiver) can communicate seamlessly and successfully only when the following prerequisites are fulfilled.

(i) At first, the sender should expose its functional capabilities through an Application Programming Interface (API). Unless a service exposes its interfaces, other services cannot communicate with it.
(ii) Sender and receiver should use the same communication model and protocol.
(iii) Sender and receiver should agree the data formats for communication.
(iv) MSA does not mandate any constraints on the programming languages, technologies, platforms, etc. used for implementing microservices. Hence, every service or even the same application can have its own programming language, operating system, database model, etc. The polyglot nature of MSA results in a heterogeneity environment. Hence, middleware is required to hide the heterogeneity and to provide the required platform on the top of heterogeneity so that the services can communicate easily. In this context, the middleware platform becomes an essential prerequisite for communication.
(v) Ultimately, a service should expose its URL in a registry so that others can retrieve its location and access it according to its API.

## 3.4 Communication Models for Microservices

The first obvious question that occurs is:

Why do the services need to communicate with one another if each service is independent?

*Key:* The services are independent as far as a particular business capability is concerned. This means that a microservice does not need to depend on another service to complete its functional capability. For example, consider a microservice: *customer authentication service.* The functionality of this service is given as follows:

*Take the user credentials entered by the customer and verify the input data against the customer table. If the credentials are fine, the service approves the user as an authenticated user; otherwise, the service rejects the user as an unauthenticated user.* Now, this service is functionally independent.

Consider another service: *customer-centric payment service*. Consider that a customer is interested in buying a product from a Point of Sale. He swipes his card, and the purchase request reaches the *customer-centric payment service* for payment. Here, the *customer-centric payment service* needs to communicate with other services, the *user authentication service*, and the *customer-centric payment authorization service*. In this example, the *customer-centric authorization service* allows the purchase by checking the account balance, his credit limits, and his interactions with the bank. Consider that the service performs the verification as follows.

*If product price <=account balance + credit card limit + credit gained by a user by his behavior then allow the purchase otherwise disallow the purchase.*

Once the *customer-centric payment service* gets the required information and approval from the *customer payment authorization service*, it proceeds to accept the payment from the customer. The interactions among different services are shown in Figure 3.4.

For the above example, after choosing the product, the user swipes the card and enters the PIN number. Now his request is taken to *customer-centric payment service* (assume that the user has already set his preferences with the bank and hence bank approved his customer-centric payment as he is a trusted user with good credit). This service performs the following:

(i) Checks for user authentication.
(ii) If it finds the user as an authenticated user, it invokes the *customer-centric authorization service*. This customer-centric authorization service in turn

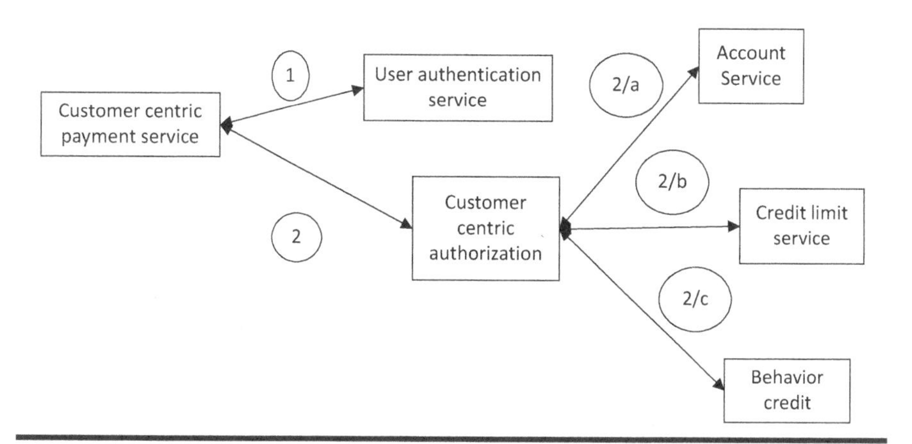


**Figure 3.4 Communications/interactions among microservices for producing a useful task.**

accesses three different services, namely, *account service, credit limit service,* and *behavior credit service.*
With account service, it gets the permissible balance that can be withdrawn
With credit card service, it gets the permissible credit limit for the user
With behavior credit service, it gets the earned credit

(iii) It checks whether payment can be allowed or not.

(iv) Ultimately, the payment service will either execute payment or reject the payment (Please note: For simplicity, the amount transfer and database transaction portion is not taken at this moment). From the above example, one should have understood that within an application, a service may produce a single functional capability, but that alone is not sufficient to realize useful business tasks. In order to produce or deliver useful business tasks, the services need to interact with one another by sending commands or queries or notifications or messages, etc. Thus, one service needs to interact with other services to produce useful business process.

Basically, there are two kinds of communication styles [2, 3], namely, synchronous communication and asynchronous communication as shown in Figure 3.5.

Different communication styles are explained in detail in the subsequent sections.

## 3.5 Synchronous Communication

In synchronous communication, the sender and receiver should be connected with each other during communication. The sender (or client) sends a request to the receiver and goes into a blocked state or waits until it receives a response from the receiver (or server). In MSA, one service may invoke another service for information,

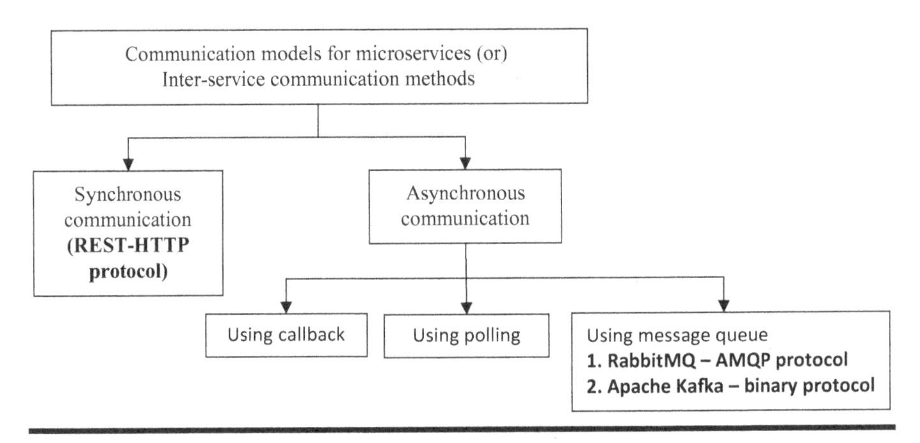


**Figure 3.5 Communication models for microservices.**

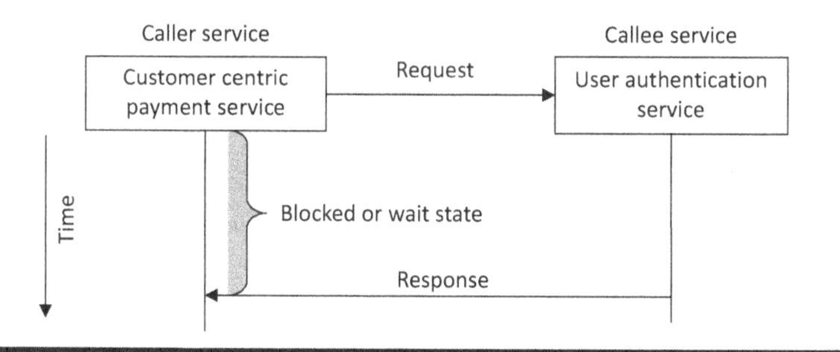


**Figure 3.6 Synchronous communication.**

and the caller service has to wait until it receives a response from the other or callee service. This is shown in Figure 3.6. Sender and receiver communicate with each other in a point-to-point manner.

Microservices use a REST architectural style, which implicitly uses a HTTP protocol to communicate with each other synchronously. HTTP is a synchronous protocol in which a client sends a request and waits for a response from the server. The client can continue its work only if it receives a response from the server.

(*Please note: The rest of this section first discusses the key points of REST architecture, and then presents how microservices use REST to implement synchronous communication.*)

### 3.5.1 Representational State Transfer (REST) Architecture

Microservices Architecture took genesis in 2014. Initially, microservices-based applications were developed using a Representational State Transfer (REST) architectural style, which was developed by Roy Fielding in 2000. REST is an architectural style for designing and developing loosely coupled services that use HTTP as a means of communication [4]. REST basically considers microservices as similar to web/internet resources. i.e., similar to how web resources are identified and located using a URL on the World Wide Web, REST considers microservices as web resources, and it identifies and locates microservices using a URL. Even the web itself is an example of the implementation of REST architecture. REST architecture consists of three components, as shown in Figure 3.7. They are:

- Resources
- Actions
- Representation

**Resources**

When one develops an application with REST architecture, the fundamental step is to identify resources and how they are linked with each other. In MSA, resources

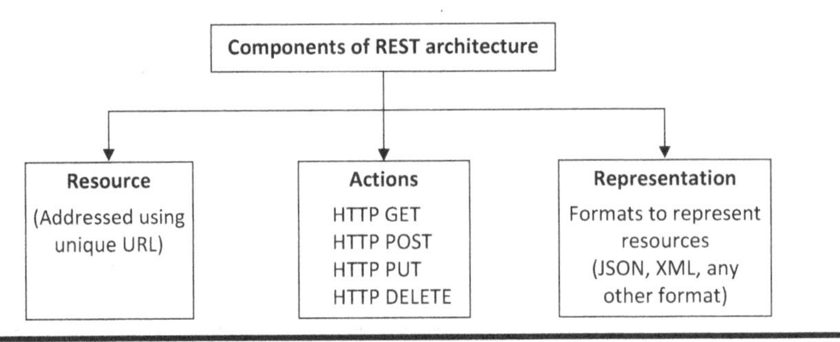


**Figure 3.7 Components of the REST architecture.**

refer to microservices. Each service can be addressed with a Uniform Resource Locator (URL). The URL of the resource is used to identify the resource. Hence, each resource must have a unique URL. The application developer has to carefully design URLs for the resources. Consider an example: *The author information of a book.* The developer has to decide whether the author information of a book has to be designed as a separate resource with its own URL or as part of a book resource itself. This would be based on the usage of the concerned part. In case author information of a book is frequently used by users, then it can be designed as a separate resource.

### Actions

REST uses HTTP methods to take different actions, as described in Table 3.2, on the resources.

It is clear that REST is very simple as it uses a URL to locate a resource and uses different HTTP methods to perform *Create*, *Read*, *Update*, and *Delete* (CRUD) operations on the resources.

### Representation

In REST, resources can be represented using any format because HTTP implicitly supports any type of content (binary, text, image, audio, video, etc.) in the body. Very frequently, the resources are represented using JSON and XML.

**Table 3.2 REST Actions Using HTTP Methods**

| *HTTP Method* | *Description of Action on the Resource* |
|---|---|
| HTTP GET | To get details of a resource |
| HTTP POST | To create a new resource |
| HTTP PUT | To modify an existing resource |
| HTTP DELETE | To delete an existing resource |

**Core Features of REST**

- REST provides a simple architectural style for developing a loosely coupled services based application. Services are considered as resources.
- Each service can be addressed using a URL address, and each service has its own data. According to MSA, each service is functionally independent, but needs to interact with other services for the exchange/update of data. REST architectural style provides the four basic database operations, namely CRUD using HTTP methods.
- With REST, services can interact directly with each other without requiring any additional infrastructure.
- REST is not linked to any platform or technology or any language.
- REST is implicitly coupled to HTTP. Since HTTP has a built-in caching framework, a caching layer can be added either by the server or client.
- One of the main criteria of microservices is that the services are subject to frequent deployment and hence there may be many versions of services. With REST architecture, the version number can be included in the URL itself and hence requesting a particular version of the resource is easy (example: http://www.xyz.com/service-B/v1/employees).

## 3.5.2 REST and HTTP Methods for Synchronous Communication

How REST uses different HTTP methods for performing CRUD operations is discussed below with an example.

### HTTP GET

Consider a GET request, *GET www.xyz.com/service-B/employees/5649 HTTP/1.1 format=json*, as shown in Figure 3.8. In this request, *GET denotes that the read action is to be performed on the resource identified by the path "/service-B/employees/5649" which is residing in the server "www.xyz.com"*.

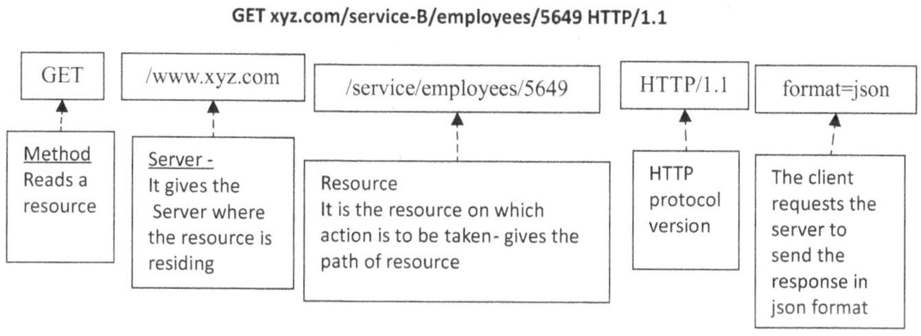

**Figure 3.8 How REST uses a HTTP GET request.**

The GET method does not change the state of the resource. It retrieves the state or information of the resource.

How the two microservices, service-A and service-B, are communicating using a REST-HTTP GET request is shown in Figure 3.9.

As in Figure 3.9, service-A places a read request to service-B in the *www.xyz.com* server. Now, in service-B, the operation whose URITemplate matches with the path in the client's request will get executed. That is, in the above example, the URITemplate of the method GetEmployee (ID) is *"/employees/empid"*. This URITemplate gets matched with the path portion of the HTTP request. i.e., *"/employees/5649"* of the HTTP request. Hence, the method GetEmployee (ID) will get executed. Also, in the above request, the client requests the server to send the response in a *JavaScript Object Notation* (JSON) format. Thus , Synchronous communication between microservices is typically implemented using REST.

- *REST architecture/style* is a simple URL-based architecture which implicitly uses *HTTP GET, POST, PUT and DELETE methods for performing CRUD operations.*
- Transports the request and response using a *HTTP transport protocol.*
- Provides any data in any format and *JSON/XML* is commonly used.

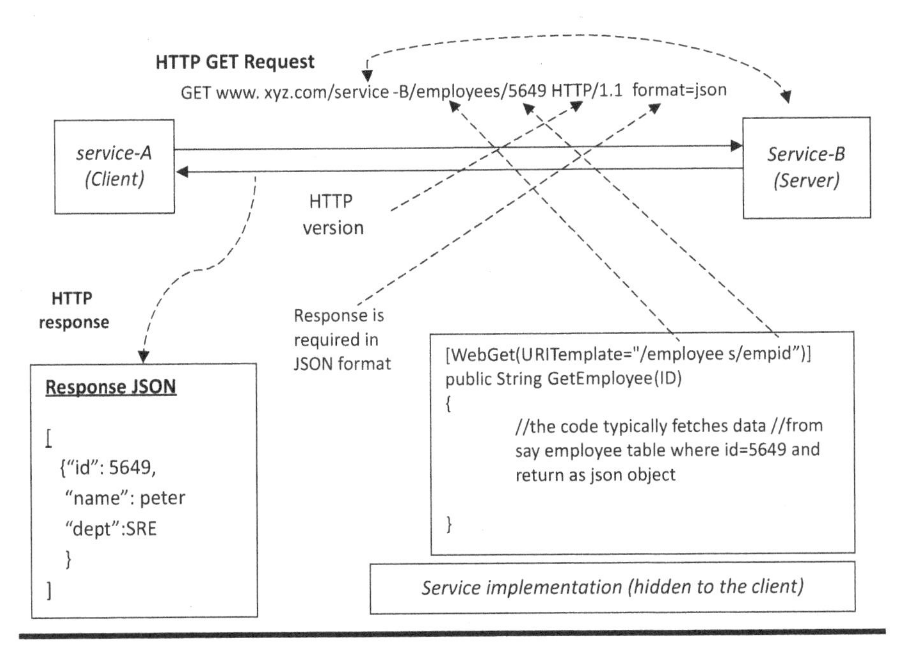


**Figure 3.9 Typical REST GET request and response.**

### HTTP POST

REST uses a HTTP POST request to create a new resource (i.e., typically *to create a new row in a database on the server*). The syntax of the POST method is shown in Figure 3.10.

### HTTP PUT

REST uses the PUT method to update any changes in the existing records of a database. Along with the request and request header, JSON content is attached in the request body. Typical syntax of the PUT method is shown in Figure 3.11.

### HTTP DELETE

REST uses the DELETE method to remove or delete a row in a database. Typical syntax of the DELETE method is shown in Figure 3.12.

```
POST www.xyz.com/service-B/employees/3708 HTTP/1.1
Content-Type: application/json

{
 "employee": {
  "id" :3708,
  "name": "ganesh",
  "siteRole": "Publisher"
 }
}
```

JSON data to create a resource

**Figure 3.10 The HTTP POST method to create a record.**

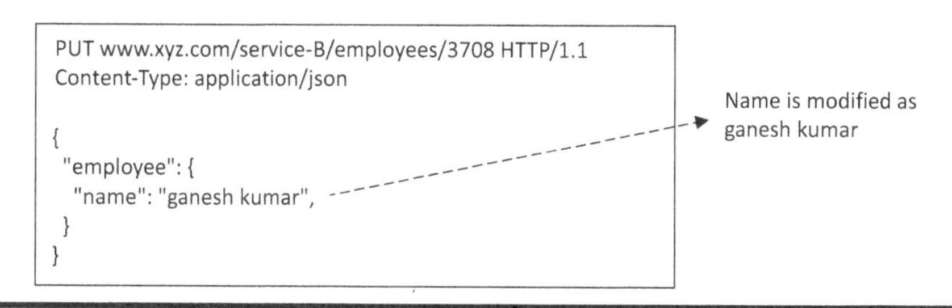
PUT www.xyz.com/service-B/employees/3708 HTTP/1.1
Content-Type: application/json
{
"employee": {
"name": "ganesh kumar",
}
}
Name is modified as ganesh kumar

**Figure 3.11 HTTP PUT request.**

```
PUT www.xyz.com/service-B/employees/3708 HTTP/1.1
```

3708 denotes the ID of record which is requested for delete

**Figure 3.12 HTTP DELETE request.**

### *3.5.3 Why Synchronous Communication Is Not Encouraged in Microservices?*

Consider a simple synchronous communication between four services, say service-A, service-B, service-C, and service-D as shown in Figure 3.13.

As in Figure 3.13, service-A makes a request to service-B and waits until it receives a response from service-B. Service-B sends a request to service-C which in turn makes a request to service-D. In each interaction, the caller has to wait until the callee sends a response. Due to the block or wait state of synchronous communication (as shown in Figure 3.13), the request–response cycles will become long. The performance of the application will become very poor. Hence, synchronous communication is not encouraged even for queries. The primary objective of MSA is to that each microservice is independent, autonomous, and available to the client irrespective of other services of the application. When synchronous communication is employed, the objective of MSA itself will get disturbed.

## 3.6 Asynchronous Communication

In asynchronous communication, the client (caller) sends a request to the server (callee) and does not wait for the response from the server. There are three ways to receive a response from the server: (i) using the callback function, (ii) using the polling method, and (iii) using a message broker.

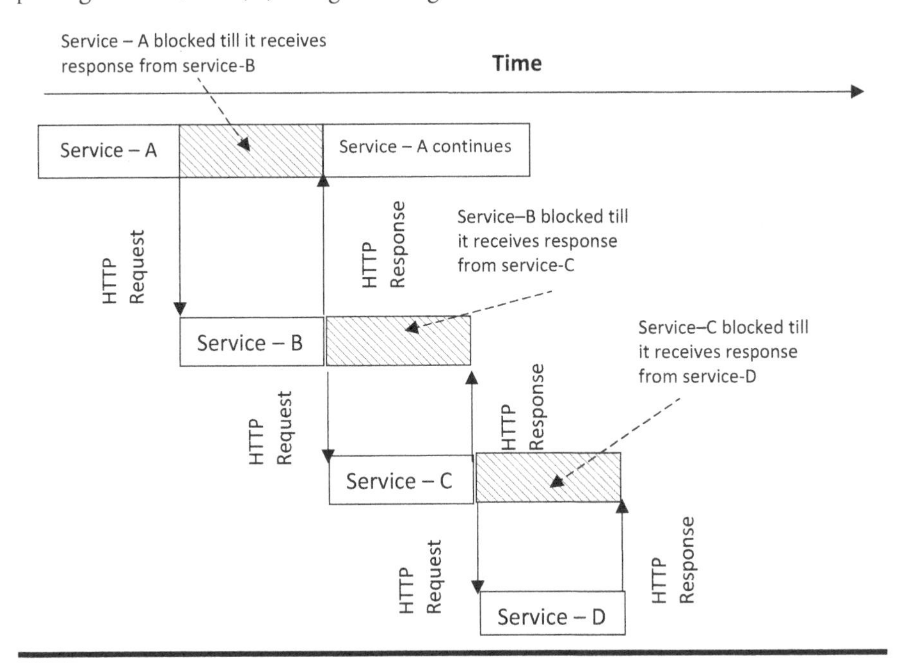


**Figure 3.13 Blocked state in synchronous communication.**

**(i) Using the Callback Method**

In this method, the client (caller) sends a request to the server. While sending a request to the server, the client also sends a reference to the callback function (the callback function is a function in the client) which will be invoked by the server after it processes the request. So, as soon as the request is processed, the server invokes the callback function in the client. With this invocation of the callback function, the client understands that the response is ready, and it will go for further processing. This is shown in Figure 3.14.

**(ii) Using the Polling Method**

Asynchronous communication using the polling method is shown in Figure 3.15.

In the polling method, the client will send a request to the server. The server acknowledges the client for the receipt of the request. The client will continue its work. In addition, the client polls the server for the status of the request at regular intervals of time until the server finishes the request.

**(iii) Using Message Queue**

In this method, the sender sends the messages to a queue, and the receiver takes the message from the queue as shown in Figure 3.16.

In the message queue method, the sender and receiver of the message are not directly connected to each other. Sender and receiver are connected through a message queue. They need not connect to the queue simultaneously. The sender sends the messages to the queue, and the queue stores the messages until the receiver retrieves the messages. The main advantage of the message queue is that it provides a high degree of decoupling between sender and receiver. This enables us to achieve high-performance, scalability, etc.

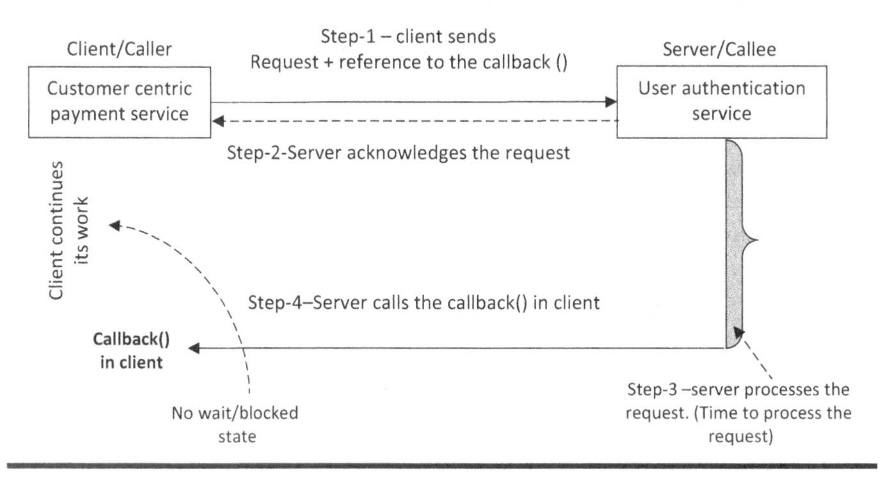


**Figure 3.14 Asynchronous communication using the callback() function.**

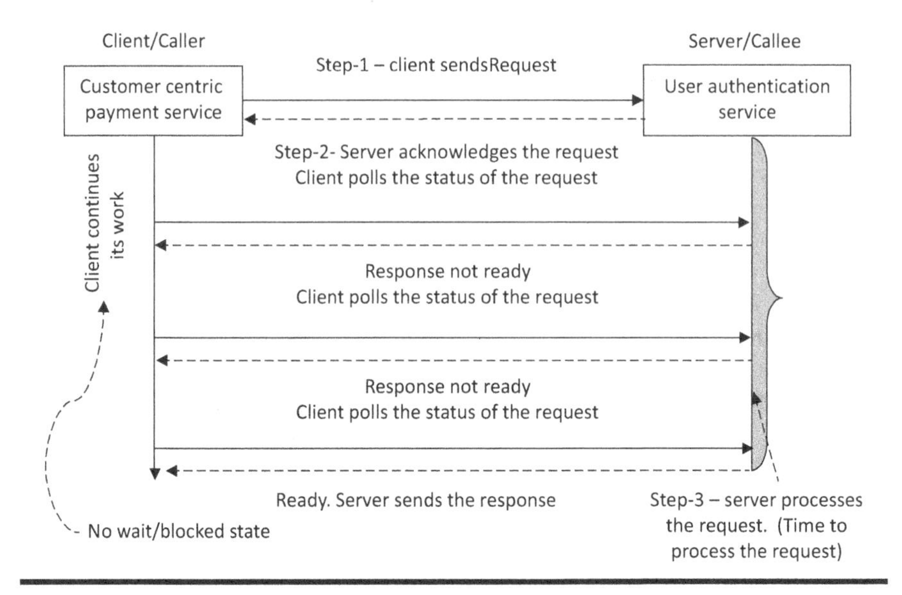


**Figure 3.15 Asynchronous communication using polling.**

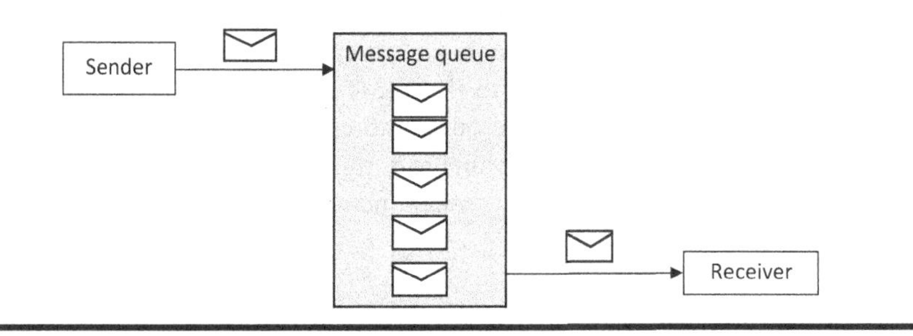


**Figure 3.16 Asynchronous communication using a message queue.**

Conventionally, message queues use their own proprietary protocols which do not provide cross-platform and cross-language support. Hence, nowadays, message queues are implemented using standard protocols.

Commonly used open protocols for message queuing include (i) AMQP, (ii) Simple/Streaming Text Oriented Messaging Protocol (STOMP), and (iii) Message Queuing Telemetry Transport (MQTT).

***Advanced Message Queuing Protocol (AMQP)***—Advanced Message Queuing Protocol is an open source message-oriented middleware that provides asynchronous messaging, including reliable queuing, topic-based publish-and-subscribe messaging, flexible routing, transactions, and security. AMQP provides reliability, scalability, and interoperability between different vendors.

***Simple/Streaming Text Oriented Messaging Protocol***—STOMP is a simple text-based protocol used for transmitting data across applications developed in different languages and platforms. It does not use the concept of queues and topics, but it sends semantics with a destination string. This protocol can be used when one needs a simple message queuing application without the demand for queues.

***Message Queuing Telemetry Transport***—MQTT provides publish-and-subscribe messaging (no queues). Its small footprint makes it suitable for embedded systems, Internet of Things (IoT) based applications, etc. For example, MQTT-based brokers can support many thousands of concurrent device connections. MQTT has a compact binary packet payload which makes it appropriate for applications such as sensor updates, stock price tickers updates, mobile notifications, etc.

There are many message queuing tools such as *IBM MQ*, *Java Message Service* (JMS), *Apache ActiveMQ*, *Apache Kafka*, *Apache RocketMQ*, *Sun Open Message Queue*, *Amazon Simple Queue Service*, *JBoss messaging*, etc. In MSA, asynchronous communication is commonly implemented using two popular open source message brokers, namely:

(i) Rabbit MQ
(ii) Apache Kafka

These two message brokers are described in detail in the following sections.

## 3.7 Asynchronous Communication with Rabbit MQ Message Broker

Message brokers are used as middleware between microservices where a microservice can send/deliver (publish) its messages to a broker, and other microservices that can connect to the broker and receive/subscribe to the messages. *The primary purpose of the message broker is to provide decoupling between a message producer and message consumer.* So, with a broker, the message producer is relieved from the communication-related aspects, and focuses on the core work. The broker is responsible for the reliable communication of the message to the receiver. Java Message Service is the most popular Java's asynchronous API. But the limitation of JMS is that it only supports Java language and thus it becomes insufficient for communicating with non-Java applications. Another popular and traditional message broker is RabbitMQ. RabbitMQ was developed by Rabbit Technologies Ltd which was acquired by SpringSource, a part of VMware. The RabbitMQ project became a part of Pivotal software and was released in 2013. *The initial goal of RabbitMQ was to provide an interoperable message broker. It provides support for cross-language and cross-operating systems. In contrast to earlier message queues, such as IBM queue or JMS or Microsoft Message Queue, RabbitMQ is a platform-neutral, language-neutral, open source message broker.* RabbitMQ is developed in Erlang. RabbitMQ runs on many operating systems and in cloud environments. It provides a wide range of developer tools for most popular languages.

RabbitMQ [5] was the first to implement *AMQP specification*. AMQP specification [6, 7] comprises two aspects as shown in Figure 3.17:

1. A set of messaging capabilities (application layer level, server-side services), called the AMQ model. The AMQ model consists of a set of components that route and store messages within a server and a set of rules which bind these components together. Precisely, this part of the specification gives a higher-level architecture for the message brokers.
2. A network level protocol called AMQP using a client application can interact with a message broker.

## 3.7.1 AMQ Model

The core components of the AMQ model is shown in Figure 3.18.

The core components of the AMQ model are (i) messages, (ii) message producers, (iii) message consumers, and (iv) message brokers/servers.

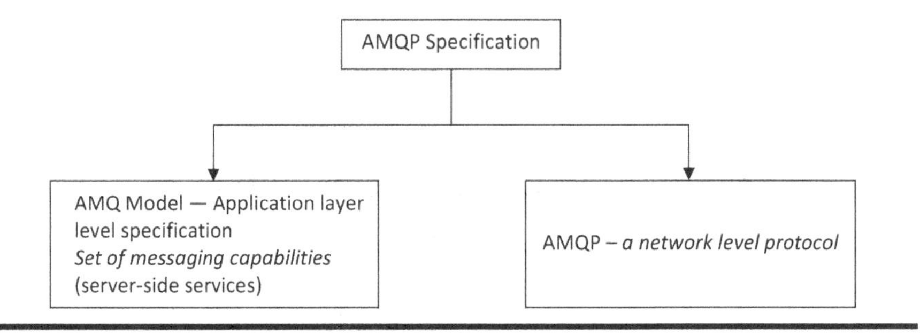


**Figure 3.17 Parts of AMQP Specification.**

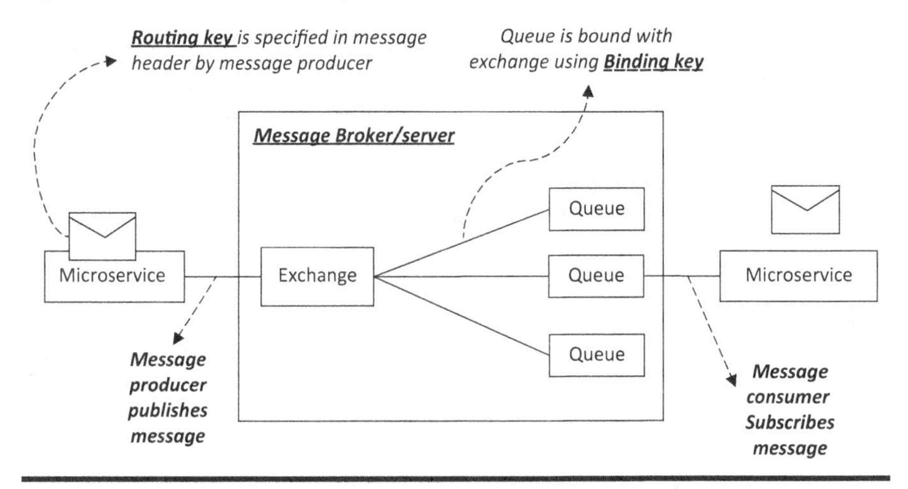


**Figure 3.18 The AMQ model.**

**Messages**—A message is an information packet consisting of two parts, namely, *a header and a body.*

**Message producers**—Message producers are applications that create messages and sends them to the broker. A message producer publishes its messages with what is called a *routing key*, which is used by the exchange component to route the message to the concerned consumer. The routing key is a message attribute. The routing key gives the virtual address to which the exchange routes the message.

**Message consumers**—Message consumers, are the applications that connect to the broker's queue and subscribe or receive their messages.

### Message Brokers/Servers

Message servers/brokers enable the messages published by a message producer to reach the intended consumers asynchronously. The broker has two key components:

1. Exchanges
2. Queues

Consider the RabbitMQ message broker. It is an open source message broker that implements AMQP specification. It ensures the messages from message producers reach the right consumers using their primary components, namely exchange and queue, as shown in Figure 3.19. It decouples producer and consumer. With a message broker, the producer and consumer need not be connected with one another. Producer and consumer are connected through a broker.

The message from a producer to a consumer moves through two intermediary components, exchange and queue.

### Exchange

*The exchange performs the function of routing messages.* The messages are published to an exchange inside the broker. The exchange then distributes copies of those messages to queues according to certain developer defined rules, and these rules are called bindings. Binding is a relation between an exchange and a queue. Each queue is bound with an exchange through a *binding key* (please refer to Figure 3.18).

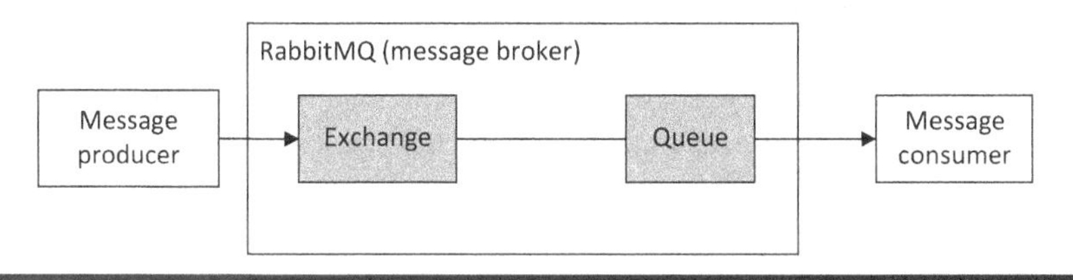


**Figure 3.19 Primary components of a message broker (example: RabbitMQ).**

**Queues**

The queue is a named entity that stores messages in the memory or on a disk (that were routed by the exchange) and delivers the messages to one or more consumers. Queues are two-sided components. The input side of a queue fetches messages from one or more exchanges while the output side of the queue is connected to one or more consumers. Each message will be stored in the queue until it is received by the message consumer. Each message queue is entirely independent and is a reasonably clever object. A queue has different properties such as *private/shared, durable/temporary, server-named/client-named*, etc. These properties are useful to implement a queue with different functional characteristics. For example, a private queue is meant to deliver the message to a particular or a single consumer, whereas a shared queue delivers the message to multiple consumers. Similarly, a subscription queue is a server-named queue and connected to a single consumer.

**Distribution of Messages in RabbitMQ/Types of Exchange**

A message producer publishes a message to a *named exchange*, and the consumer pulls the message from a queue which is bound with the exchange. *Here understand that the consumer has to create a queue and attach it to the required exchange. Also, understand that the consumer should know the name of the exchange. Only then can the consumer bind its queue with the named exchange. There may be multiple exchanges per queue, or multiple queues per exchange or one queue per exchange* (with one-to-one mapping). Now, a question arises? How does the message distribution occur? This is according to the type of exchange. *According to the type of exchange, the exchange routes the message to the concerned queue.*

There are different types of exchanges according to the way queues are bound with the exchange and how the exchange matches the binding of the queue against the message attributes, such as routing key or header values. They are:

1. Direct exchange
2. Fanout exchange
3. Topic exchange
4. Headers exchange

*1. Direct exchange*—Direct exchange routes the message by matching the routing key with the queue name. This is shown in Figure 3.20. As in Figure 3.20, the routing key holding the value "Queue-1" is matched with the name of the queue ("Queue-1"). This type of exchange routes the message for point-to-point communication. In this type of exchange, wildcard characters such as "*" or "#" are not supported.

*2. Fan out exchange*—In fan out exchange, the message is copied and sent to all queues connected to this exchange. The concept of fan out exchange is shown in Figure 3.21.

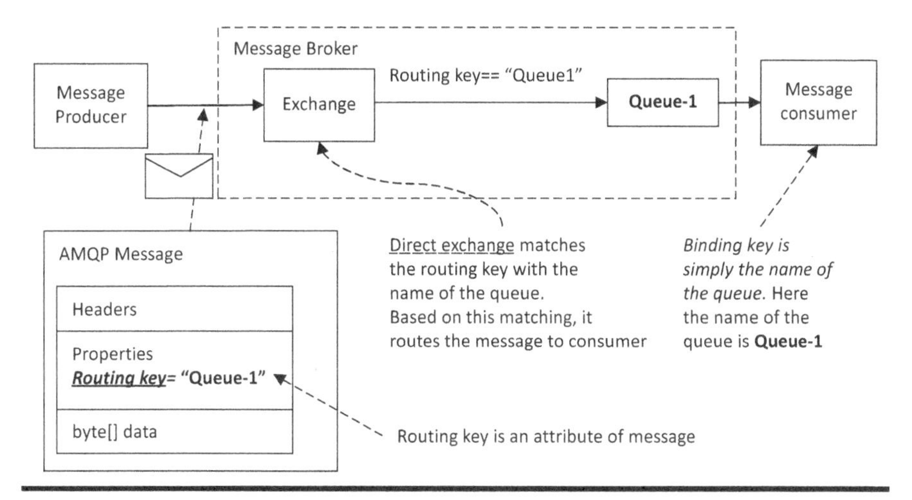


**Figure 3.20 Direct Exchange.**

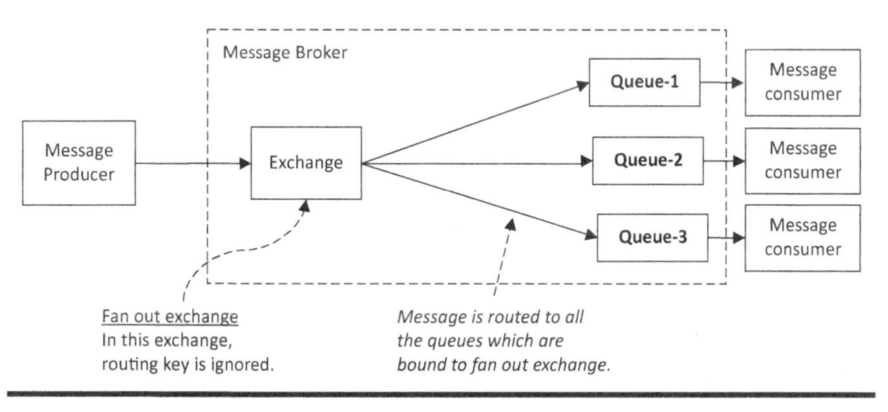


**Figure 3.21 Fan out exchange.**

In this exchange, the routing key is ignored. When a new message is published in a fan out exchange, then the message is sent to all the queues which are bound with the exchange. This exchange is more suitable for broadcasting a message to all concerned consumers.

*3. Topic exchange*—Message distribution in a topic exchange is shown in Figure 3.22. In topic exchange, the message is routed to some of the queues by matching the routing key against the patterns of the binding keys represented using wildcard characters.

This exchange basically provides a publish-subscribe message pattern in which publishers (message producers) categorize their messages into different classes (logical channels called topics) without knowledge of subscribers (message consumers). In topic exchange, a message is published with a routing key containing a series of words

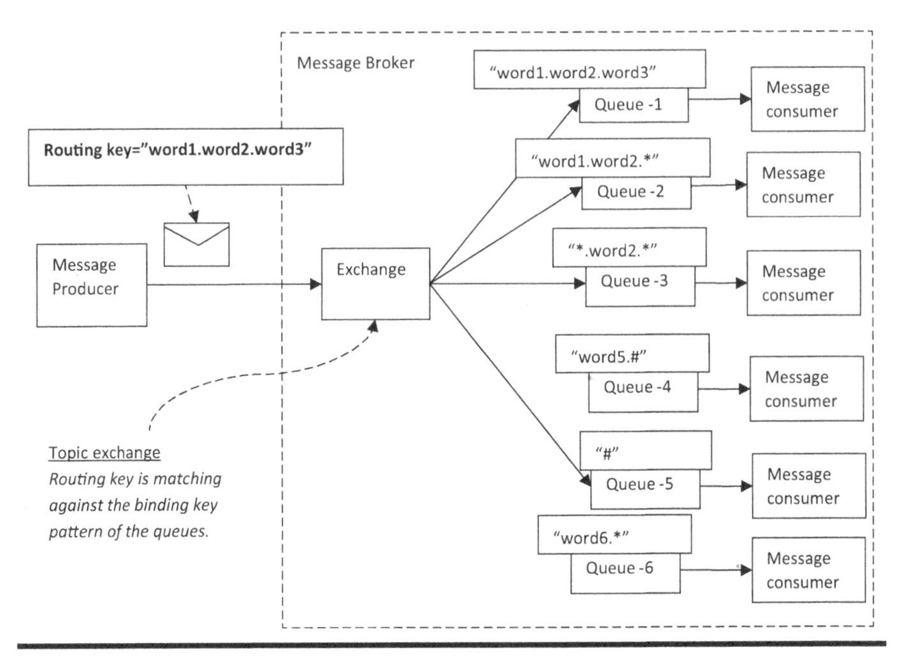


**Figure 3.22 Topic exchange.**

separated by a dot, say, for example, a routing key is "*word1.word2.word3.*" Queues binding to a topic exchange supply a matching pattern to the server to be used while routing the message. Patterns may contain an asterisk "*" to match a word in the specific position of the routing key, or a hash "#" to match zero or more words. As in Figure 3.22, since the binding keys of Queue-1, Queue-2, Queue-3, and Queue-5 found a match with a routing key, the message is forwarded to these queues, whereas there is no match between the routing key and binding key pattern of Queue4 and Queue6. So, the message is not forwarded to Queue-4 and Queue-6.

*4. Headers exchange*—Message distribution in a headers exchange is shown in Figure 3.23. In headers exchange, instead of matching a routing key with a binding key, one or more headers of the message are matched with the expected headers specified by the queue.

In topic exchange, there is only one criterion, namely the routing key is matched against the binding key. But in headers exchange, more than one criterion is specified as key-value pairs in the header of the message and is matched against the key-value pairs specified in the queue. In a header exchange, a bounded queue specifies whether all the key-value pairs are to be matched with headers (i.e., through the match option "all") or if any of the key-value pairs is to be matched (i.e., through match option "any"). Consider the headers exchange in Figure 3.23. Its message headers consist of three key-value pairs. They are {"key1"="value1," "key2"="value2," "key3"="value3"}. Also, there are three queues, Queue-1, Queue-2, and Queue-3.

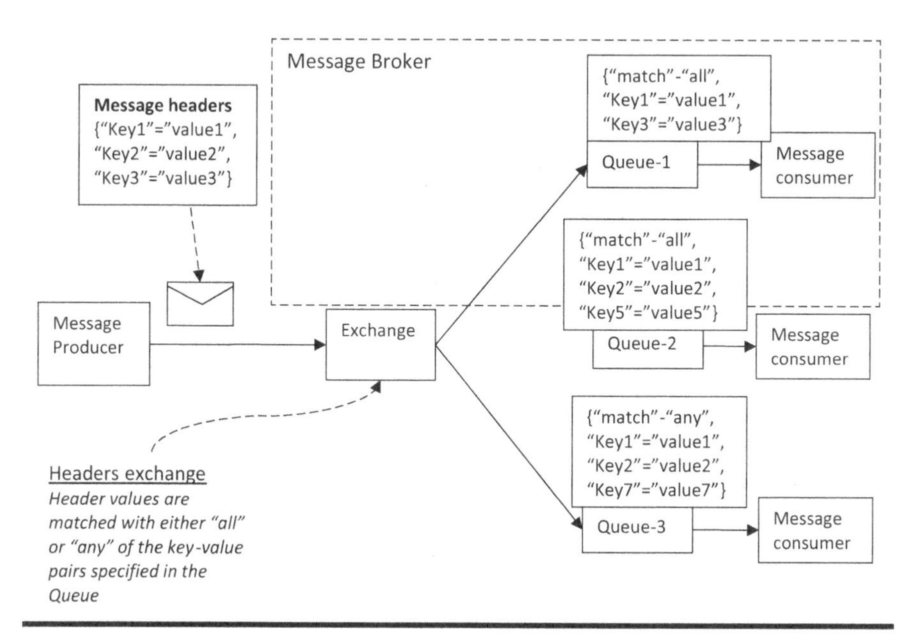


**Figure 3.23 Headers exchange.**

Queue-1 specifies that the exchange has to match all the key-values specified. There are two key-values. They are {"Keyl"="valuel," "Key3"="value3"}. Since these two are in message headers, the exchange forwards the message to Queue-1. For Queue-2 which specifies that all key-values have to be matched against headers, as the header does not contain "Key7"="value7," the message will not be forwarded to Queue-2. In the case of Queue-3, the queue specifies a match for any one of the key-value pairs against the headers. Since there are two matches for "Keyl" and "Key2," the message will be forwarded to Queue-3.

## 3.7.2 Advanced Message Queuing Protocol

AMQP specifies three architectures, namely (i) command architecture, (ii) transport architecture, and (iii) client architecture.

### 3.7.2.1 AMQP Command Architecture

A message producer connects to a message broker using a TCP/IP connection. AMQP is a connected protocol. The connection can carry multiple channels.

- The client (message producer) creates a TCP/IP connection with the server using the *Connection* class. The client sends the protocol header to the server/broker.
- The server responds with the protocol version and properties along with supported security mechanisms.

- The client chooses a security mechanism.
- The server starts the authentication process for the client.
- The client completes authentication.
- After authentication is completed, the server goes to negotiate parameters, such as frame size, etc., with the client.
- After fixing protocol parameters, the client establishes a connection with the server.
- It opens a channel over the connection. The server confirms the channel is ready for use.
- Then the client and server use the channel according to their needs.

The AMQP protocol divides its commands into five core classes of functionality. They are (i) basic, (ii) channel, (iii) exchange, (iv) queue, and (v) transaction.

To provide an insight into how messages are published and consumed using the above core classes and their methods, the essential steps are given in Listings 3.1 and 3.2, respectively.

### *3.7.2.2 AMQP Transport Architecture*

In AMQP, the messages are transported over a reliable stream-oriented TCP/IP connection (i.e., TCP/IP socket connection). Each connection can have many channels that carry messages in the form of frames. In order to distinguish them, each frame contains a channel number. AMQP is a binary protocol and information is organized as "frames" of various types. Frames carry protocol methods and other information. The typical structure of the frame is given in Figure 3.24.

Each frame consists of (i) a frame header, (ii) a payload, and (iii) a frame-end.

*(i) Frame header*—The frame header gives the type of frame, channel number, and size of the frame.

```
Steps to publish messsage
Step 1 – create connection
connection = Connection()
Step 2 – create channel
channel = connection.channel()
Step 3- create exchange using the property of Channel
channel.exchange.declare('exchange_name', 'direct')
Step 4 - publish the message using Basic class' publish method with routing key
channel.basic_publish(exchange='exchangeName', routing_key=severity,
body=message)
```

**Listing 3.1 Typical steps involved in publishing using AMQP**

***Steps to consume messsage***

Step 1 – create connection

*connection = Connection()*

Step 2 – create channel

*channel = connection.channel()*

Step 3- declare exchange

*channel.exchange_declare(exchange ='exchangeName', type='direct')*

Step 4 - declare queue

*channel.queue_declare(queue=queue_name, exclusive=True)*

Step 5 - bind the queue with exchange

*severity = 'routingKey'*

*channel.queue_bind(exchange='exchangeName', queue=queue_name, routing_key=severity)*

Step -6 consume message

*channel.basic_consume(callback, queue=queue_name, no_ack=True)*

*channel.start_consuming()*

**Listing 3.2 Typical steps involved in consuming messages using AMQP**

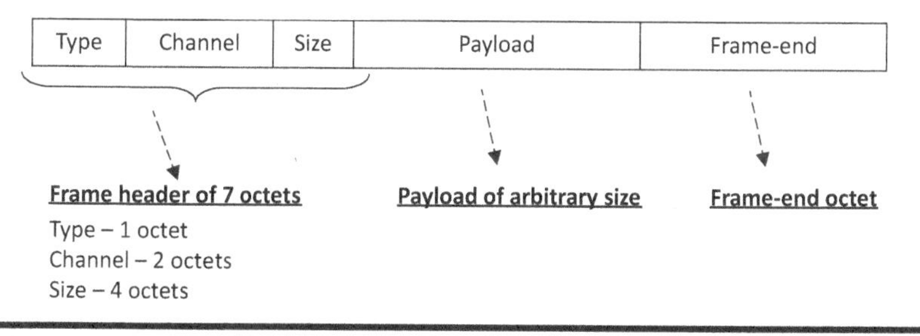


**Figure 3.24 Typical frame structure.**

Frames can be of different types such as a protocol frame, method frame, content header frame, body frame, and heartbeat frame. A protocol frame is used to establish a connection between the message producer and message broker. Method frames carry commands such as RPC request/response commands. Content header frames carry properties of content related methods. For example, a content header frame may give the type of content of a message that is going to be published using the publish method. Body frame contains the actual content of the message. Heartbeat frames are used to check whether the concerned peers over the connection are alive. If one peer does not respond to the heartbeat signal, then the other peer disconnects the connection.

*(ii) Payload*—The payload varies according to the frame type, so each type of frame will have a different payload format

*(iii) Frame-end*—Frame-end refers to a single byte which is used to indicate the end of the frame.

AMQP uses exceptions to handle errors. Any operational error (message queue not found, insufficient access rights, etc.) results in a channel exception. Any structural error (invalid argument, the bad sequence of methods, etc.) results in a connection exception. An exception closes the channel or connection, and returns a reply code and reply text to the client application.

#### *3.7.2.3 AMQP Client Architecture*

AMQP recommends the following architecture for AMQP clients. A message producer/consumer should establish a four-layered architecture, as shown in Figure 3.25, to interact with the message broker and consume the message from it.

This layer may be a socket for a synchronous I/O or a socket for an asynchronous I/O.

***Framing layer***—Framing layers converts the AMQP commands which are represented in higher-level languages to a lower-level wire format by serialization.

***Connection Manager Layer***—The connection manager layer is responsible for establishing the connection between the message consumer and broker. It manages the connection, session, channel, error handling, transfer of messages, etc.

***API layer***—The API layer exposes sets of APIs to applications and abstracts the internals of AMQP to developers. Developers can simply invoke the methods of the API to perform the message consumption easily.

***I/O layer***—This layer is the socket used to read and write the message at the lower/socket-level.

### *3.7.3 Where to Use RabbitMQ*

RabbitMQ is designed as a general purpose message broker. As mentioned earlier, prior to AMQP, there were many proprietary or commercial message queues or asynchronous message tools such as Microsoft Message Queue, IBM message queue. Since applications are developed using different languages and platforms, there are compatibility issues when these applications need to be integrated through

| Framing layer |
|---|
| API layer |
| Connection Manager Layer |
| I/O layer |

**Figure 3.25 AMQP client architecture.**

commercial message queues. In order to standardize the message queuing and brokering requirements, the AMQP specification was developed. RabbitMQ was the first message broker to implement AMQP. Thus RabbitMQ serves as an ideal choice for bringing interoperability and provides compatibility between applications and brokers. So, the purpose of RabbitMQ is to implement AMQP. RabbitMQ offers several patterns of communications, such as point-to-point, request/reply, and topic-subscribe, etc. Another key feature of RabbitMQ is that it uses a smart broker and dumb consumer model, focused on the consistent delivery of messages to consumers to consume without any difficulty. RabbitMQ has a wide range of features:

- Reliable delivery.
- Flexible routing.
- Federation.
- High Availability.
- Security.
- Multiple protocol support.
- Tracing support.
- Easy to use UI through which one can monitor and control the different functions and features of a message broker.
- Management tools and other features.
- It is mature.
- It provides cross-language support for various languages such as Java, .NET, node.js, Ruby, PHP, and many other languages.
- It has different plugins for different integration needs.

***Usage scenarios***

RabbitMQ fits as a suitable choice for:

- When an application is in need of *reliable asynchronous messaging* for high-performance applications.
- When an application needs to work with different messaging protocols, such as AQMP 0-9-1, STOMP, MQTT, and AMQP 1.0.
- When an application needs finer-grained consistency control/guarantees on a per-message basis and needs a variety of communication patterns, such as point-to-point, request/reply, and topic/subscribe messaging.
- When an application deals with *complex routing to consumers.*

***Advantages of RabbitMQ***

- Compatibility: RabbitMQ allows applications developed using different programming languages or operating systems to work together.
- Interoperability: RabbitMQ provides cross-platform and cross-language support.

- Decoupling: Separating the producers from the consumers has many advantages.
- Availability: If a consumer is unavailable, the messages sent from the producer will be held in the queue until the consumer is available again.
- Scalability: RabbitMQ provides reasonable scalability.
- Fast.
- Polyglot.
- Simple management.
- No Erlang knowledge needed.
- Great documentation and community.

***Limitations of RabbitMQ***

- Performance is limited as the broker itself has a very heavy weight.
- Once the consumer reads the message from the queue, the message is removed from the queue.
- Since RabbitMQ is developed in Erlang, reading, and understanding Erlang syntax is tough, and extending RabbitMQ is difficult for the same reason.
- RabbitMQ has poor scalability for handling too many events in a short time.
- *More importantly, if a particular message has to be sent to more than one consumer, then a separate queue will be maintained for each consumer, and the message has to be copied to each consumer.*

### 3.7.4 AMQP and JMS

When one reads about messaging, one obvious question will arise: What is the difference between the Java Message Service and AMQP? The *key* is given in Table 3.3.

## 3.8 Asynchronous Communication with an Apache Kafka Message Broker

### 3.8.1 Need for Apache Kafka (High Throughput Message Broker)

After going through RabbitMQ architecture, the question that may strike the reader is:

*Why another message broker? What is the need for Apache Kafka?*

In an application such as LinkedIn, there are different individual publish/subscribe queue systems, as shown in Figure 3.26.

**Table 3.3 Differences between JMS and AMQP**

| *Feature* | *JMS* | *AMQP(/RabbitMQ)* |
|---|---|---|
| Description | Java Message Service is an API that is part of Java EE for sending messages between two or more clients. There are many JMS providers such as OpenMQ HornetQ (JBoss), and ActiveMQ | AMQP gives an architecture for a message broker as well as provides application level and network level protocols for applications to interact with a message broker |
| Messaging model | JMS provides two types of communications:<br>(i) One-to-one communication<br>(ii) Publish-subscribe communication | AMQP provides four types of communications:<br>• Direct<br>• Fanout<br>• Topic<br>• Headers |
| Data types | JMS supports different data types | AMQP is a binary protocol |
| Technologies | JMS supports only Java | RabbitMQ, which implements AMQP, supports many technologies and provides cross-language support (please note: JMS is not helpful for non-Java applications). With the advent of AMQP, cross-language flexibility became real for open source message brokers |

In Figure 3.26, there are three individual queues, the metric queue, user tracking queue, and database log queue, etc. One or more message producers are likely to publish their messages with their topics. Also, one or more consumers may subscribe their interested topics. *In applications with large web sites, there are many such queues and data is continuously moving between applications. Each message queue has its own custom communication protocols and ultimately moving data between different applications itself is a challenging task for developers. So, Kafka has its origins in moving data between internal systems,* as shown in Figure 3.27.

As in Figure 3.27, Apache Kafka provides a fast, highly scalable, highly available, distributed publish/subscribe messaging model for internal systems of applications that allow multiple consumers to consume messages.

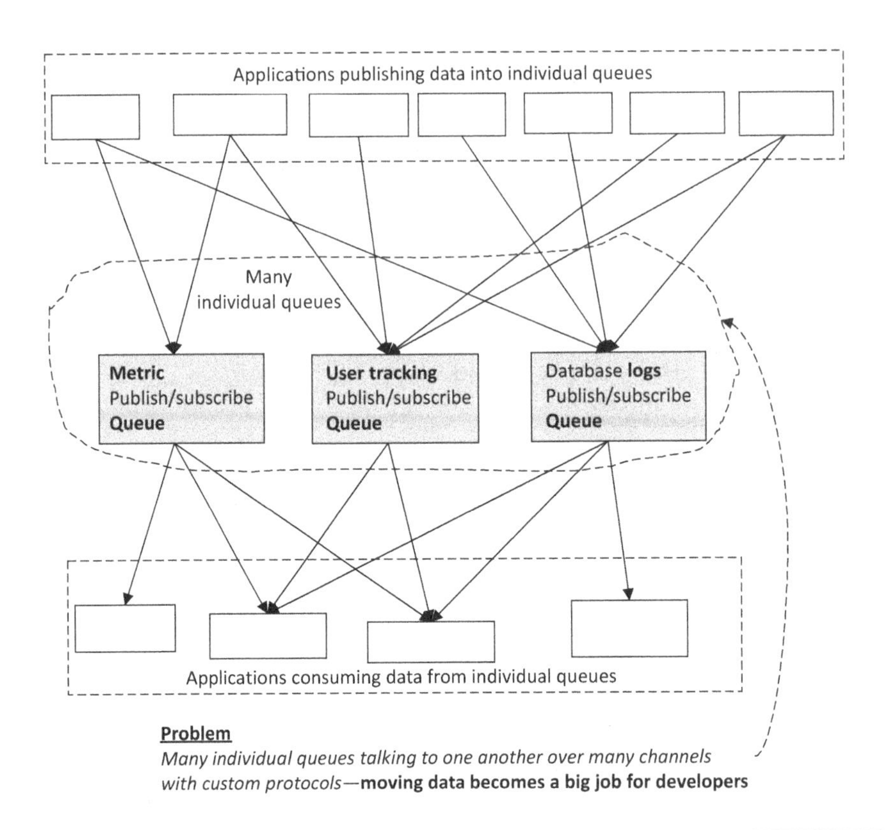


**Figure 3.26 Problems with individual message queues—The origin of Apache Kafka.**

### 3.8.2 Comparing the Origin of Kafka with RabbitMQ

Again, another question comes to mind. *Can RabbitMQ be used for moving data between internal applications?*

Obviously, RabbitMQ can be used for delivering data between internal applications as long as the throughput is around 20 K to 50 K messages per second. But there are situations where messages are arriving in high volumes and streams (typically, 2 million messages per sec) which are typically processed by many big data processing applications; in this case, Kafka fits as a better choice. (*Please note that Kafka is not meant to replace RabbitMQ. RabbitMQ is developed with interoperability between applications producers/consumers and a message broker with an AMQP protocol, whereas Kafka is developed with high throughput for message transfer and multiple consumers in mind.*)

The origin of Rabbit MQ is shown in Figure 3.28.

- Conventional queues use Dynamic Random Access Memory (DRAM) for their data store. Though RAM provides very low latency, the cost of RAM is very expensive. Systems will become very costly if they need to communicate

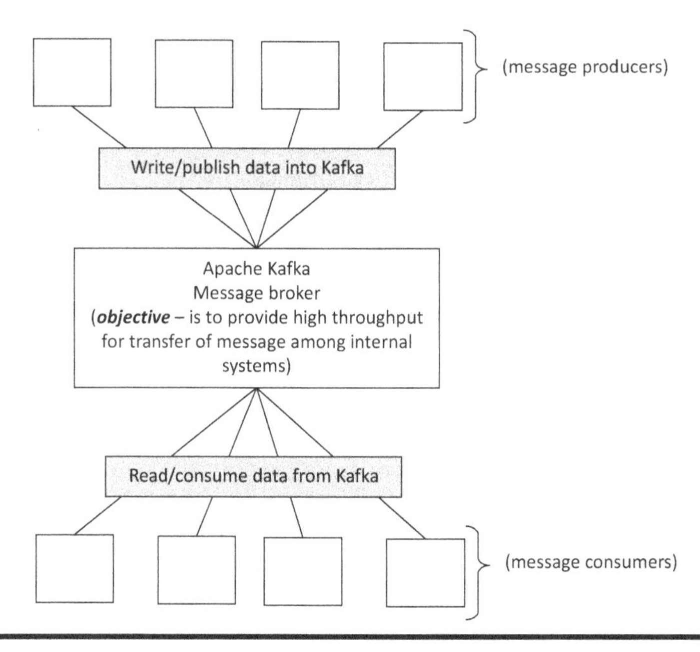


**Figure 3.27 Apache Kafka as a message broker with high throughput for internal systems.**

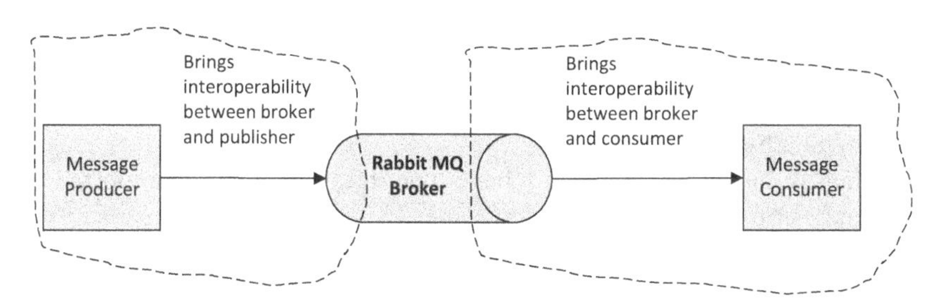


Objectives of Rabbit MQ are (i) to bring interoperability among message producer, broker and message consumer. Broker interoperates with producers and consumers that are implemented in disparate operating systems & programming languages
(ii) to implement AMQP
(iii) to decouple producer and consumer & to provide asynchronous messaging
(iv) to provide open standard for asynchronous messaging

**Figure 3.28 The origin of Rabbit MQ.**

hundreds of GBPS of data. In RabbitMQ, messages are stored in DRAM as long as possible. When the available DRAM is completely full, then RabbitMQ start storing the messages on the disk without having a copy in DRAM. This severely impacts performance. But, Kafka relies on the file system for storage and caching. The major problem with the file system is that they have high seek time. *But in Kafka, seek operations are never used.* In Kafka, the file system is accessed with sequential I/O. This leads to a very low latency.

- *Kafka gives emphasis to the replication of messages across clusters so as to provide distributed replicated and safe data storage.* (Please note: Rabbit MQ does not cope well with network partitions.)
- Apache Kafka uses a queue data structure, which provides a time complexity of O(1). This enables very good performance
- In addition, it provides a binary data format (i.e., with data modification for serialization or deserialization). This also enhances performance.

*Thus, where Kafka is applicable? Typically Kafka is useful for delivering messages to big data processing platforms. Apache Kafka is integrated with Apache Spark and Apache Flink.*

Kafka originated on LinkedIn in 2010 as a way to connect its different internal systems.

#### 3.8.2.1 Primary Objectives of Kafka—High Scalability, Availability, and Throughput (The Concept of Partitions in Kafka)

The primary objective of Kafka is to provide:

1. Efficient persistence. The Kafka architecture is designed to retain the message in the log for the specified message retention time, which is quite long.
2. Support for multiple consumers reading messages. Kafka provides a partition to support multiple consumers consuming a message, and hence Kafka provides high scalability.
3. High throughput (i.e., the number of messages that can be transported from producer to consumer in a unit of time).
4. Ability to write messages into log files with efficient I/O patterns.

To understand the aim of Apache Kafka, consider an online retail textile application. *The application provides an online purchase facility to its customer requests. Certainly, customers from different countries of the world are likely to access the application. Imagine that the textile shop is very popular and many orders are likely to be received on a daily basis. Also, the textile application has its branches in different locations. The application architecture team decided to process the orders received from customers as follows.*

(i) Orders received by customers in India will be processed by its application running in New Delhi.
(i) Orders received by customers in Sri Lanka will be processed by its application running in Colombo.
(ii) Orders received by customers in China will be processed by its application running in Beijing.

Now Kafka helps in transferring the orders to the concerned processing applications as described below.

Here, orders are messages. In Kafka, message producers publish messages into a named "topic." Assume that the topic is "order." While creating a topic, one has to specify the number of partitions required. If there is no need to partition the messages, then the number of partitions will be zero. That is, the messages published to the topic will not be split into partitions. All messages will be in the same and single partition. In addition, messages can be associated with keys. Keys serve like metadata to the messages. Also, Kafka uses key-values to assign a partition to the messages. That is, messages with the same key are published into the same partition.

Consider that the orders received from India are tagged with a key say "key-1." Similarly, orders received from Sri Lanka are tagged with a key say "key-2" and orders received from China are tagged with a key say "key-3."

Consider that in the above example, the topic is created with a number of partitions = 3 (partition-0, partition-1, partition-2). This means that the messages published into the topic are split into three partitions. The next question is: How do the messages split into partitions? Messages with the same key will go into the same partition. Messages with no key will randomly be placed into a partition by a Kafka broker. (While understanding Kafka, please keep in mind that message publishers and message consumers belong to same application and the developer knows very well in advance which messages are produced by publishers and how the messages are consumed.) Here Kafka plays the role of distributing the messages from publisher to consumer with a high throughput so that different consuming applications can simultaneously process the messages in different partitions. This is shown in Figure 3.29.

Another facility provided by Kafka architecture is that replication. When a topic is created, one can specify replication factor so that topic is replicated according to replication factor and the replications are distributed into different Kafka brokers as shown in Figure 3.30. Here replication gives high availability and fault-tolerance.

### 3.8.3 Kafka Architecture

Apache Kafka is developed in Scala and Java and started out at LinkedIn in 2010 as a way to connect different internal systems. A message producer publishes its message to a topic. This topic may be subscribed to by many or multiple applications. Apache Kafka is an open source, *distributed*, replicated commit log [8, 9]. Kafka does not contain the concept of a queue. In Kafka, messages are stored in partitioned, append-only log files called topics [10, 11]. The generic architecture of Kafka is shown in Figure 3.31.

As mentioned earlier, Kafka puts emphasis on partitions and replications. In general, a topic is created with:

1. Topic name
2. Number of partitions
3. Replication factor

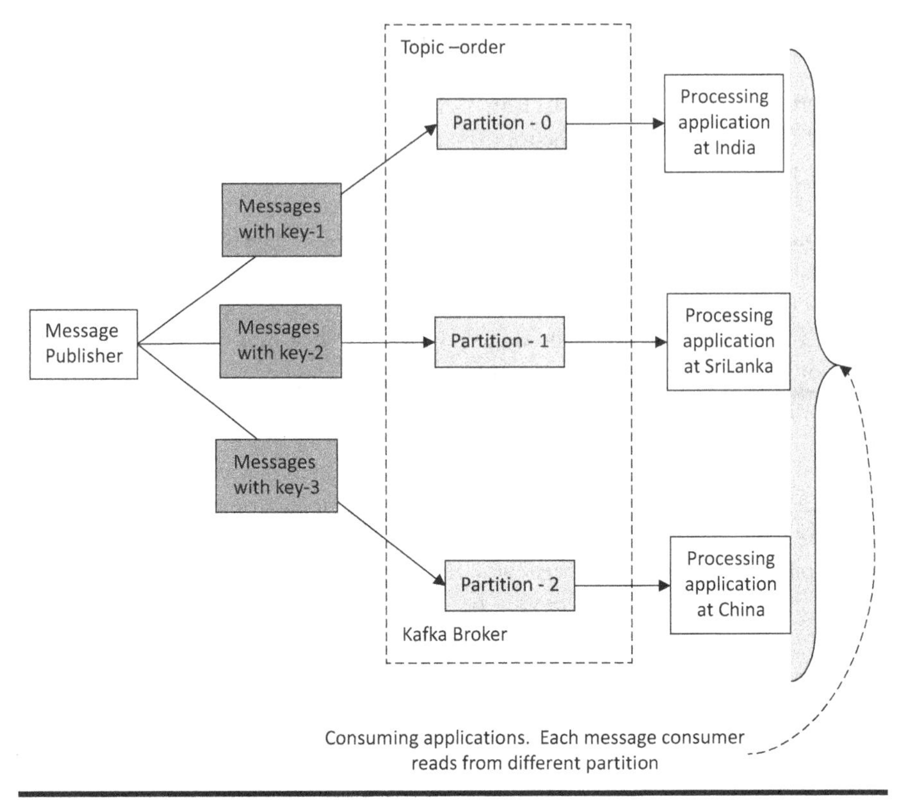


**Figure 3.29 Kafka handles multiple consumers with required scalability using partitions.**

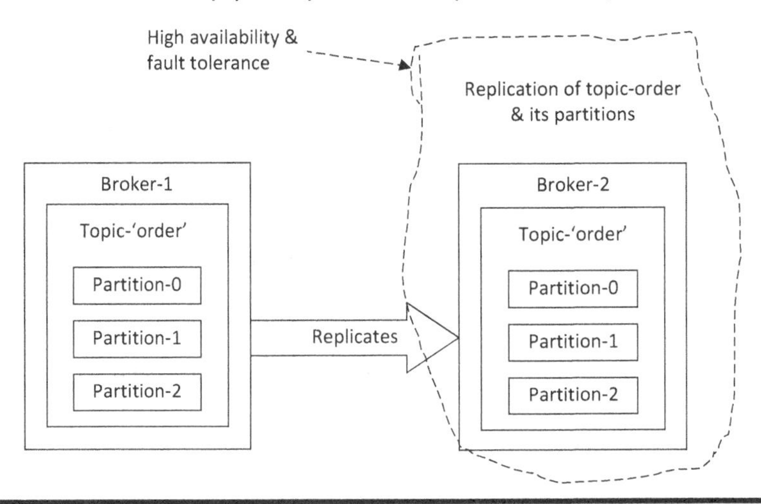


**Figure 3.30 Replication in Kafka architecture.**

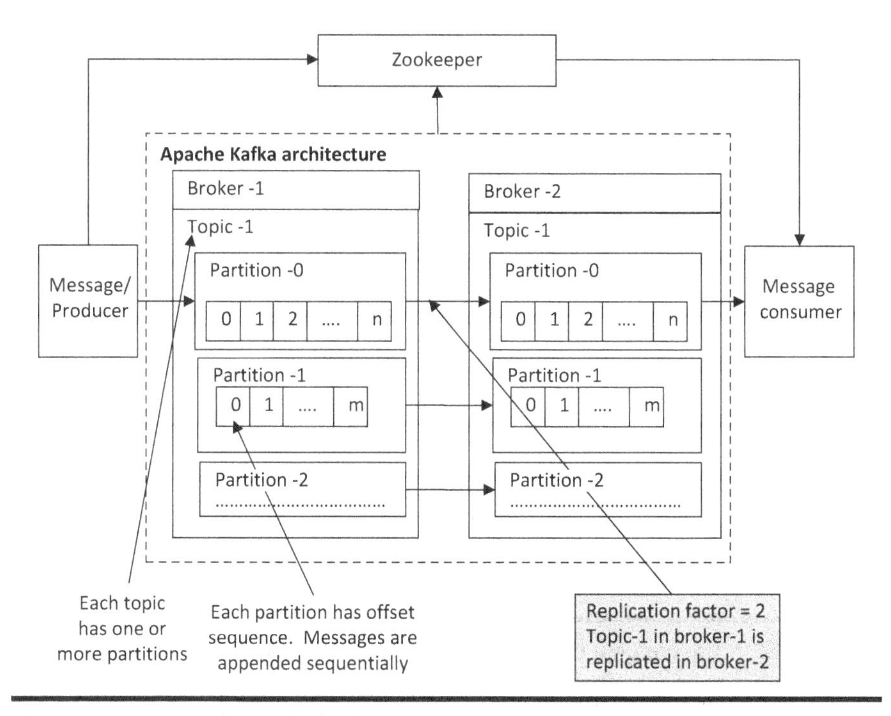


**Figure 3.31 Generic Kafka architecture.**

The Apache Kafka broker consists of multiple brokers. Each broker is stateless and can handle hundreds of thousands of message reads/writes per second. In Kafka, messages are stored as key-value pairs. Keys contain metadata about the messages and the values are the actual data, and it can be any type of data, such as byte arrays, strings, or any object that can be stored in any format or JSON, etc. These messages are stored in *topics*. Each topic is identified by a unique name. Message producers push their messages into topics. Topics are divided into *partitions* (please refer to Figure 3.32). Partitions are replicated across brokers. In a partition, each message is given an incremental ID called *offset* which has scope only within the partition. Messages can be pushed with or without an ID. If messages are pushed without an ID, then those messages may be pushed into any partitions as chosen by the broker. If messages are pushed with an ID, the messages having the same ID will get pushed into the same partition. Also, in a partition, the messages are pushed in a sequence. Once the data is published into topics, it cannot be updated.

A partition can be viewed as a log. Message producers write data into a log. Message consumers read from the log. One key aspect of the Kafka broker is that it is a lightweight broker; it does not have even queue. It is the responsibility of the consumer to keep track of message reader. Kafka's broker does not even know whether a consumer has read a message or not. Kafka is so designed as a *thin broker* to yield *higher throughput*, reliability, and replication in contrast to conventional

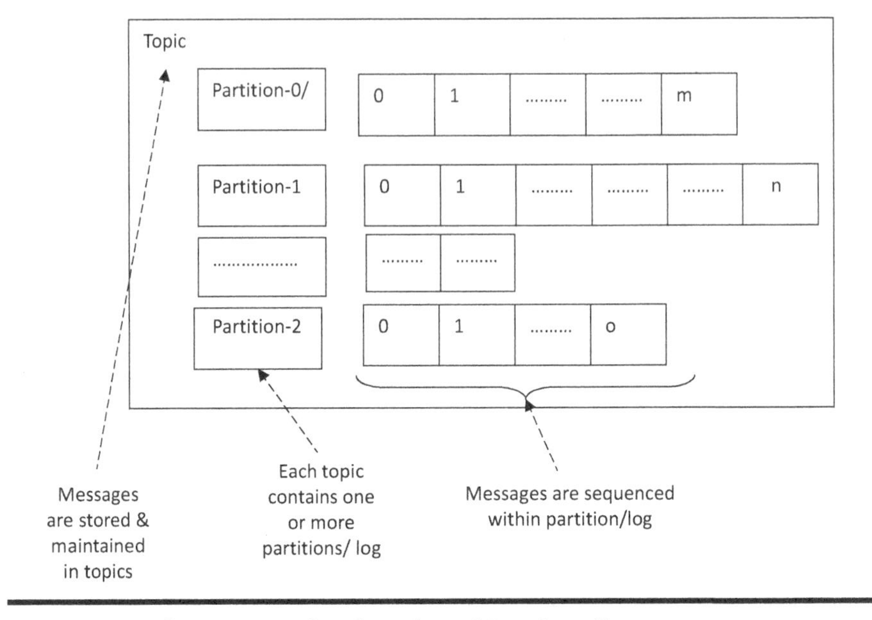


**Figure 3.32 The concept of topic and partitions in Kafka.**

brokers. Basically, the broker is huge log storage which keeps on appending the messages. Since the brokers are stateless, external programs such as ZooKeeper are used to maintain the state and serve as synchronizer and status coordinator. Zookeeper basically keeps track of topics, partitions, brokers, clusters, etc.

Kafka is built around different kinds of APIs, such as:

- Producer APIs
- Consumer APIs
- Stream APIs
- Connector APIs

Message Producers interact with the Kafka architecture using a set of APIs called producer APIs. Message consumers interact with the Kafka architecture using a set of APIs called consumer APIs. Stream APIs are used to push and pull streams. Connector APIs are used to connect message producers and message consumers to Kafka.

### *3.8.4 How Consumers Read Data from Kafka with Message Ordering?*

Consider that a message publisher publishes data into a topic. In real applications, data can be generated at a greater speed. Say, for example, in a sensor network-based application; different sensors generate data at a higher speed. But consuming applications may not be able to consume the message as quickly as the data is being generated. So, there is a critical need to scale the consumption of data from topics. That's why the topic is split into different partitions and within a partition the sequence of messages is kept in order. Now consumers can access data from different partitions without disturbing the ordering of the messages)

As in Figure 3.33, consider three consumergroups, namely, *consumergroup-1*, *consumergroup-2*, and *consumergroup-3*. Consumergroup-1 consists of one consumer (consumer-1), consumergroup-2 consists of two consumers (consumer-1, consumer-2) and consumergroup-3 consists of three consumers (consumer-1, consumer-2, consumer-3). As per the Kafka design, to facilitate slow consumers/long processing consumers, the topic is split into partitions. In each partition, messages can only be appended as per their occurrence. Within each partition, the sequence and ordering of messages are maintained. In order to facilitate the consumption of different parts of topic/messages by different consuming applications, partitions are created. In the first consumergroup-1, since there is only one consuming application, it alone has to process all the messages in the topic. But if we add more than one consumer to a group, then Kafka allows different consuming applications of the same group to access different partitions. Since there is only one consumer in consumergroup-1, all partitions are given to consumer-1 of group-1. In consumergroup-2, there are two consumers. Here the number of consumers matches the number of partitions. Now, partition-1 will be accessed by consumer-1 and partition-2 will be accessed

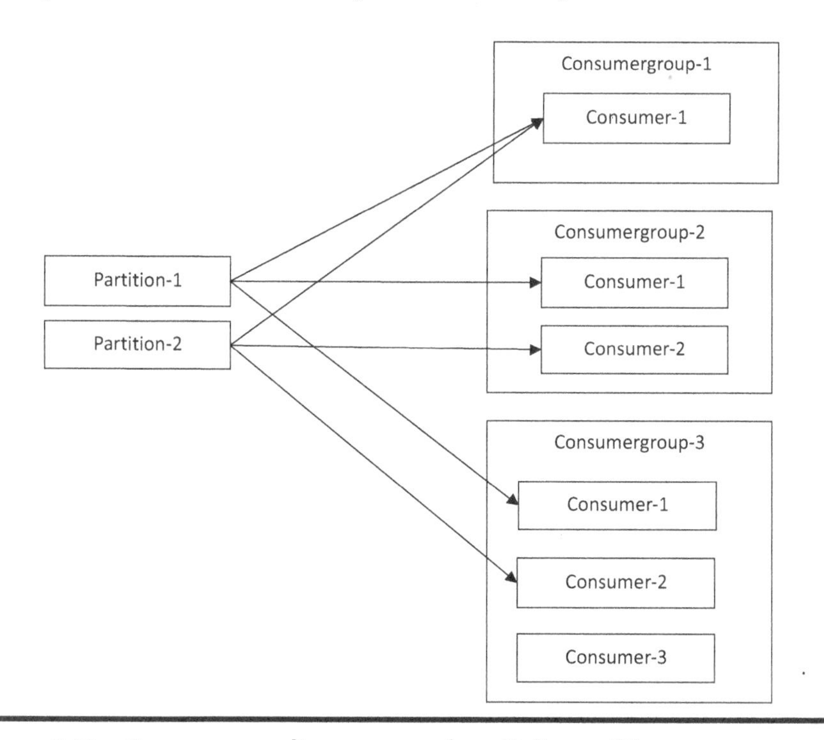


**Figure 3.33 Consumers reading messages from Kafka partitions.**

by consumer-2. The rule of thumb for achieving high scalability is: *The number of partitions should be the same as the number of consuming applications in a group.* If the number of consumers is more than the number of partitions as in consumergroup-3, then the excess number of consumers will be idle. For example, in consumergroup-3, there are three consumers, whereas there are only two partitions. Consumer-3 of consumergroup-3 will be idle. Thus, the key points are:

1. When multiple consuming applications are involved, consumers are grouped. Each consumergroup can have one or more consumers. The developer has to design the number of partitions with the number of consumers in mind.
2. Different consumers of the same consumergroup are allowed to access different partitions of the topic simultaneously. *But different consumers of the same consumergroup cannot access the same partition simultaneously.*
3. Consumers belonging to different consumergroups can access the same partition simultaneously.

(Note: if Kafka does not allow more than one consumer from the same group to access the same partition, the ordering of the messages may get altered. For example, consumer-1, a very fast consumer, consumes message-1, whereas at the same time consumer-2, a slow consumer, consumes message-2, and it would not have completed its task. Now, consumer-1 after finishing message-1 will go to message-3 as message-2 is tied up with a slow application, consumer-2.)

### 3.8.5 Kafka and Message Producers

Kafka is designed to handle multiple producers. Various combinations such as: (i) different producers may publish data in different topics, (ii) the same producer can publish messages in different topics, and (iii) multiple producers that can publish messages in the same topic are handled by the Kafka broker. Please see Figure 3.34, Figure 3.35, and Figure 3.36.

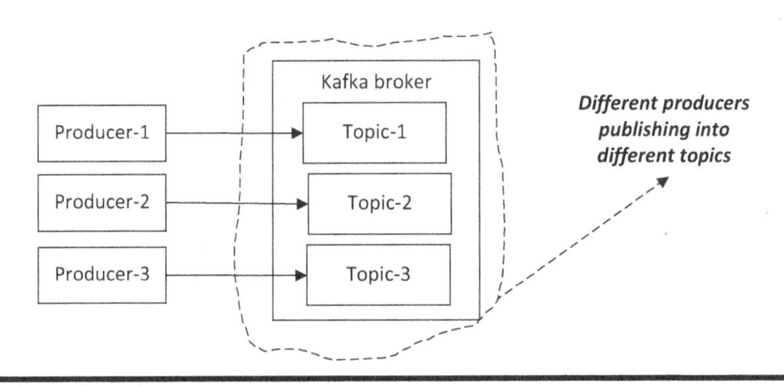


**Figure 3.34 Different producers publishing messages into different topics.**

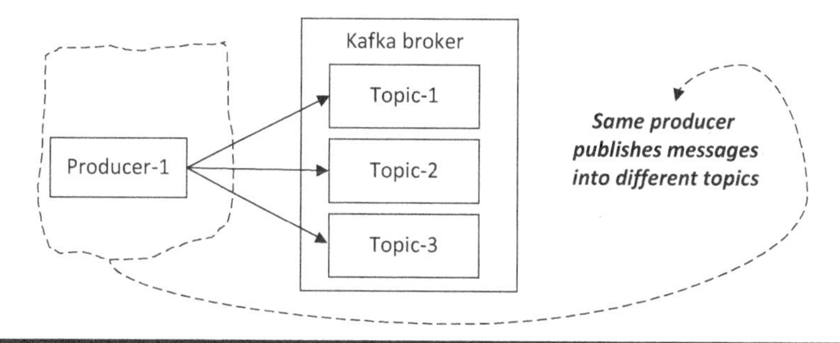


**Figure 3.35 The same producer publishing messages into different topics.**

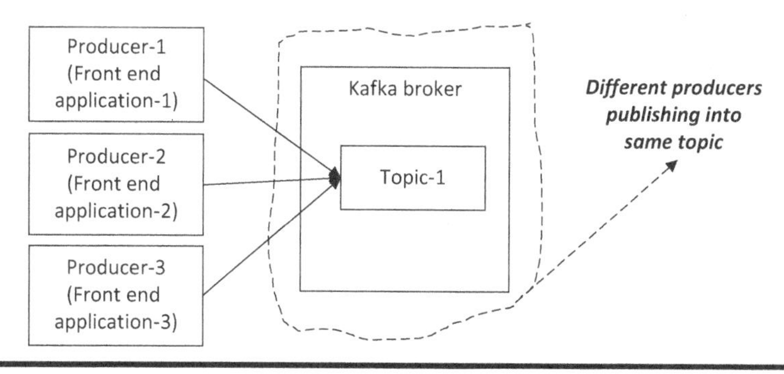


**Figure 3.36 Different producers publishing messages into the same topic.**

This capability of Kafka makes it ideal for aggregating data from many frontend applications (which are likely to monitor data for the same topic) and make it consistent. This helps consumer applications receive consolidated data from all applications without having to coordinate from multiple topics.

## 3.8.6 Important Features of the Kafka Broker

- *Scalability*

  Apache Kafka provides high scalability without any downtime. i.e., it gives high horizontal scalability. By adding many brokers, it can handle many message producers, consumers, events/messages, etc.
- *High throughput*

  Kafka can handle a high-volume of data even at a high-speed. It can handle hundreds of thousands of events/messages every second.
- *Fault-tolerant*

  The replication concept of Kafka makes it highly fault-tolerant and resilient. In the case of a node failure, Kafka automatically recovers with no downtime.

- *Highly durable*
  Apache Kafka replicates and archives the messages in Kafka servers. It does not delete or remove the message after the consumer has consumed the messages. Basically, the Kafka server can set a time for how long the messages have to be retained, say, for example, 24 hours. So, irrespective of whether the message is consumed or not, the server stores the data for 24 hours.
- *Low latency*
  Once the message producer pushes the data to the Kafka server, it is immediately available for the consumers without any delay.
- *High volume*
  Kafka can handle a huge number of messages with a high-volume storage.
- *Data transformation*
  Kafka offers methods for transforming data streams from one format to another format.

### 3.8.7 Typical Use Cases of the Kafka Broker

(i) Kafka is preferred when high message throughput is required.
(ii) Kafka is preferred when multiple consumers are involved.
(iii) Kafka is preferred when message retention is required.
(iv) Kafka is preferred when high scalability is required.
(v) Kafka uses real-time streaming applications that transform or react to the streams of data. Nowadays, Apache Kafka is replacing other stream processors such as Apache Storm and Apache Samza.
(vi) Event sourcing is a style of application design where state changes are logged as a time-ordered sequence of records. Kafka's support for storing very large amounts of log data makes it an appropriate choice for event sourcing.
(vii) The Kafka broker serves as an aggregation log server in a distributed environment. It collects log files from servers and stores them in a centralized server for processing by different consuming applications.
(viii) The Kafka broker is used for operational monitoring and archives the monitored status as messages.
(ix) The Kafka brokers are used for tracking user's activities such as web page views, searches, etc. Message producers publish user's web activities into the Kafka broker, which will be analyzed and processed by the consumers.
(x) Kafka is used very frequently for event sourcing.

Event Sourcing is an application architecture pattern which represents changes to an application as a time-ordered sequence of immutable events; i.e., in event sourcing, every change to the state of an application is considered as an event, and all the events are captured and stored in a sequence so that at any instant of time the state of an application can be modeled as a sequence of events.

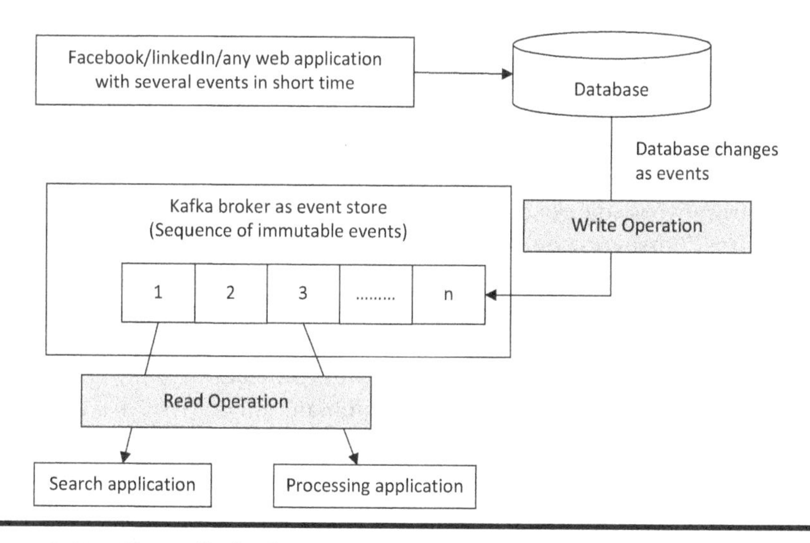


**Figure 3.37 The Kafka broker as an event store.**

There are many applications such as Facebook and LinkedIn, where changes made to databases should be notified to many processing applications, such as search applications, cache application, etc. Due to its high durability, high scalability, high-volume, fault-tolerance, and high-speed capabilities, the Kafka broker as a central event store from which processing applications can consume the events. This is shown in Figure 3.37.

### *Summary*

At first, the chapter presented an overview of the different architectural elements of MSA. Then it discussed the basic principles of designing microservices. After explaining basic design principles, it presented the need for interactions among different microservices to achieve useful business tasks. In this context, the chapter introduced two communication models, namely synchronous and asynchronous. It then described in detail how REST architecture is used to achieve synchronous communication. Next, it explained the need for standardizing asynchronous communication protocols and described AMQP as an open standard for asynchronous message-based communication. Then the chapter described how RabbitMQ implemented AMQP. Lastly, it elaborated on the design and work of high throughput message broker, Kafka. It clearly illustrated the distinguishing capabilities between RabbitMQ and Kafka with usage scenarios and typical use cases.

### *Exercises*

1. Consider online TV show websites such as Crackle or Tubi. Consider that the website should have well-defined categories such as TV Dramas, TV Comedies, Reality TV, and Crime TV. Now the website has to offer

personalized TV show recommendations to users according to their preferences. This will facilitate a user to find preferred content easily without too much of search time. Keeping this scenario in mind design a microservices-based architecture.

(Hint—Readers can refer the following web site:
https://www.edureka.co/blog/microservices-tutorial-with-example
https://fossbytes.com/best-sites-watch-free-tv-shows-online-legally/—compulsory assignment problem.)

2. Two services, A and B, are interacting with one another. A sends a command and initiates an action in B. The output of B only decides further actions in A. Now what kind of communication style is suitable?
3. Do we really require asynchronous communication? If so, list situations where asynchronous communication is useful?
4. Explain the architecture of RabbitMQ and list its limitations.
5. Consider stock exchange applications where the arrival of messages and their ordering are important. Explain how to design communication with other services? Which model do you prefer? (Hint: ordering is important in stock exchange apps).
6. Consider an example where message delivery is important, and the ordering of messages is not essential. Which communication model do you prefer?
7. What is the use of a ZooKeeper in Kafka?
8. Explain the message retention policy of Kafka and compare it with RabbitMQ? (Hint— Kafka retains messages for a long time compared to RabbitMQ. In RabbitMQ the message is deleted once it is delivered. But in Kafka messages are retained even after they are consumed by a client, so a client can read the message again).
9. Why do big IT players like LinkedIn, Microsoft, and Netflix use Kafka and not a JMS based queue)?

   (Hint—the scalability of Kafka)

## References


1. Matt McLarty. Designing a System of Microservices. 2017. Available at: https://www.apiacademy.co/articles/2017/05/designing-a-system-of-microservices.
2. Piotr Mińkowski. Communicating between Microservices. 2017. Available at: https://dzone.com/articles/communicating-between-microservices.
3. Hicham Layadi. Microservices: Why Asynchronous Communications? 2018. Available at: https://dzone.com/articles/microservices-why-asynchronous-communications.
4. Tom Nolle. How to Move Beyond REST for Microservices Communication. Available at: https://searchmicroservices.techtarget.com/tip/How-to-move-beyond-REST-for-microservices-communication.
5. Akash Bhingole. RabbitMQ in Microservices. 2018. Available at: https://dzone.com/articles/rabbitmq-in-microservices.

6. Erik Lupander. Go Microservices, Part 9: Messaging with RabbitMQ and AMQP. 2018. Available at: https://dzone.com/articles/go-microservices-blog-series-part-9-messaging-with.
7. Steve Vinoski. Advanced Message Queuing Protocol. 2006. Available at: https://www.researchgate.net/publication/3419866_Advanced_Message_Queuing_Protocol.
8. Jack Vanlightly. RabbitMQ vs Kafka Part 1 - Two Different Takes on Messaging. 2017. Available at: https://jack-vanlightly.com/blog/2017/12/4/rabbitmq-vs-kafka-part-1-messaging-topologies.
9. Stanislav Kozlovski. Thorough Introduction to Apache Kafka. 2017. Available at: https://hackernoon.com/thorough-introduction-to-apache-kafka-6fbf2989bbc1.
10. StackOverflow. Understanding Kafka Topics and Partitions. 2016. Available at: https://stackoverflow.com/questions/38024514/understanding-kafka-topics-and-partitions.

# Chapter 4

# Designing APIs and Developing Middleware Platforms for Microservices

***Objective***

This chapter's objective is to describe three major architectural elements related to communication, namely (i) designing API for microservices, (ii) developing middleware platforms, and (iii) data formats for communication. The reader will then understand why microservices require APIs, how to design APIs for microservices, and how to establish middleware platforms with existing standards and frameworks such as REST, SOAP, Apache Thrift, and gRPC. Further, the reader will understand different data formats for communication. By the end of this chapter, the reader will be able to visualize how different concepts, namely API, data formats, communication models, and middleware platforms, fit together to enable inter-service interaction and hence integration.

***Preface***

In the previous chapter, the reader would have understood that one microservice can interact with another microservice either synchronously or asynchronously with an existing architectural style such as REST, or an asynchronous message broker such as RabbitMQ and Apache Kafka. Having communication models alone is not sufficient to enable interaction between microservices. One service can invoke another service only if the second service exposes its capability through an Application Programming Interface (API). As microservices are developed using different technologies, programming languages, and operating systems, there is a need to have fundamental middleware platforms for services to communicate and interact with one another to produce useful applications or business processes. Also, the interacting services should agree with data formats so that the messages/data sent between services will get interpreted correctly (i.e., a receiver interprets a message exactly in the same way as the sender means it). Thus, API, middleware platforms, data format, communication protocols, and message brokers work together to enable interaction among services.

This chapter will discuss: How to design API for microservices, how to establish a middleware platform with existing frameworks, and different data formats for communication.

This chapter intends to answer the following motivating questions:

1. Why do microservices need an API?
2. What is the use of an API?
3. Why do we need middleware platforms? What is the use of middleware platforms?
4. What data formats do microservices use?
5. How do API, middleware platforms, data formats, and communication protocols work together?

## 4.1 API Design Mechanisms and Middleware Platforms

In order to expose the method signatures or interface of a microservice to other services, standard mechanisms are needed. An Application Programming Interface (API) defines how a microservice allows other services or applications to use its functionality. APIs provide a detailed description of the service's interface. It contains elements like available methods and data structures for parameters and results. Typically, a microservice exposes its methods, signatures, or method declarations (while hiding the implementation of methods) to consumers so that consumers can invoke the service. According to the calling semantics of the methods, the client will invoke the service. Thus, APIs are essentially interface definitions, and they are very much essential for a client to be able to consume a service. The next question that arises is: *How to design the API of a microservice?*

The design of an API is very important because, with the growth of the internet, a microservice needs to handle thousands of queries and requests from several users in a short time. So, it is essential to design the API such that it interacts with the right systems developed using the right languages and technologies to produce the right output and deliver it to the right people at the right time. Also, the design of an API should take a users' experience into account. Precisely speaking, the design

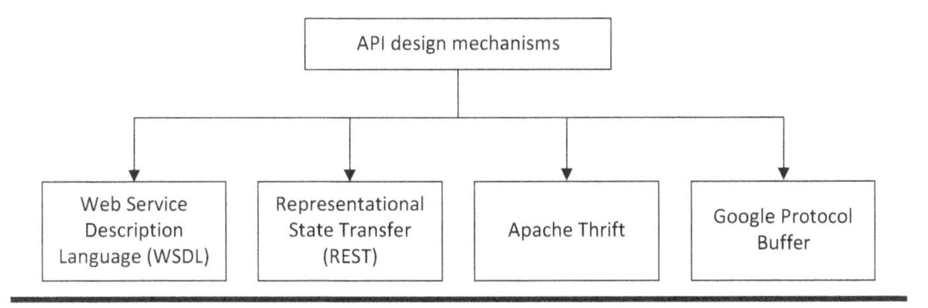


**Figure 4.1 API design mechanisms.**

of an API should be holistic so that the needs of a user's experience are fulfilled. There are four standard mechanisms, as shown in Figure 4.1, to design APIs.

Standard mechanisms for designing APIs include:

- Web Service Description Language (WSDL)
- Representational State Transfer (REST)
- Apache Thrift
- Google Protocol Buffer (Google Protobuf)

As discussed above, to hide heterogeneity in programming languages and operating systems, middleware platforms are essential. Middleware platforms work in collaboration with an API (also called an interface definition). Common middleware platforms, along with their respective APIs are shown below.

As shown in Figure 4.2, there are four different combinations of middleware platforms and API designs. They are:

1. Web Service Description Language and Simple Object Access Protocol (SOAP)
2. Representational State Transfer with no extra middleware
3. Apache Thrift IDL and Apache Thrift code generation middleware tools
4. Google Protocol Buffer interface definition with gRPC middleware

## 4.2 WSDL and SOAP (Traditional API and Middleware Platform for Web Services)

Traditionally in SOA, web services used Web Service Description Language for interface description and Simple Object Access Protocol for constructing messages. These technologies are not used in MSA. (*Note: These two technologies are discussed just to provide an insight on how web services have used APIs and middleware.*)

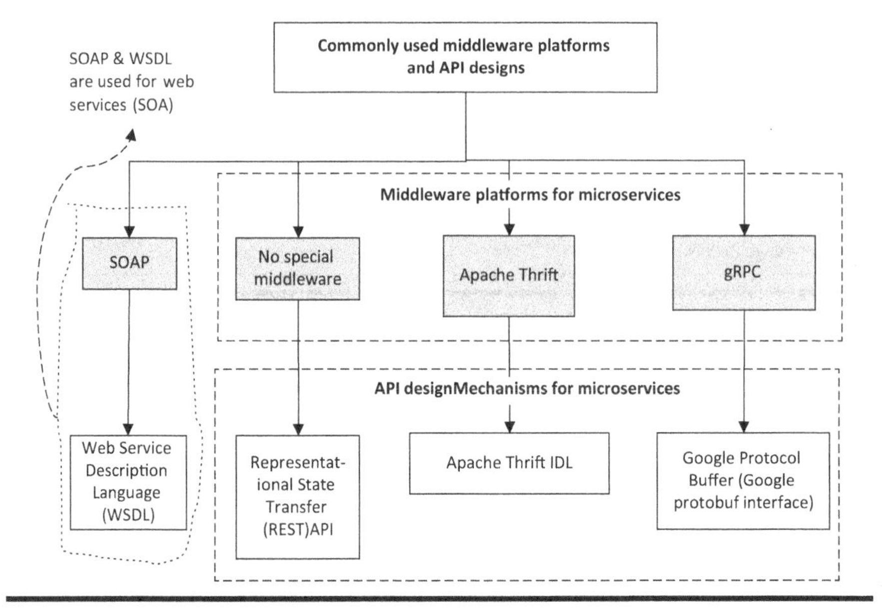


**Figure 4.2 Commonly used middleware platforms and API mechanisms for microservices.**

### *4.2.1 Web Service Description Language*

WSDL is an XML-based open standard used to expose the interface of a web service. WSDL consists of two parts, namely an abstract part and a concrete part. The abstract part describes the functional capabilities of the service. That is, it describes the operations of the web services. The concrete part of a service description describes the URL and port where the service is available. With a WSDL document, a service is described using six elements, namely <definitions>, <types>, <message>, <portType>, <service>, and <port>. <definitions> is the root element of the WSDL document which contains all the other elements. A typical structure of an WSDL document is shown in Figure 4.3.

WSDL includes information about:

- The data types it uses
- Parameters it requires and returns
- Groupings of functionality
- The protocol to be used to access the service
- The location or address of the service

As in Figure 4.3, the <port Type> element is a set of one or more operations. So, a <portType> element consists of one or more <operation> elements. Each operation is likely to have one or more input messages (arguments) and output messages (return values). Each <operation> typically contains zero or more input and output messages. The <message> element is typically a part of a complex data type which is defined under the <types> element. For understanding, WSDL elements are shown diagrammatically in Figure 4.4.

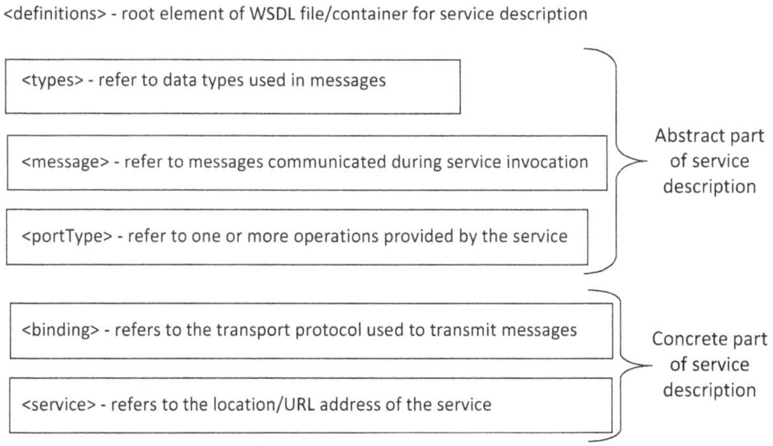

<definitions> - root element of WSDL file/container for service description

<types> - refer to data types used in messages

<message> - refer to messages communicated during service invocation

<portType> - refer to one or more operations provided by the service

Abstract part of service description

<binding> - refers to the transport protocol used to transmit messages

<service> - refers to the location/URL address of the service

Concrete part of service description

**Figure 4.3 Typical structure of a WSDL document.**

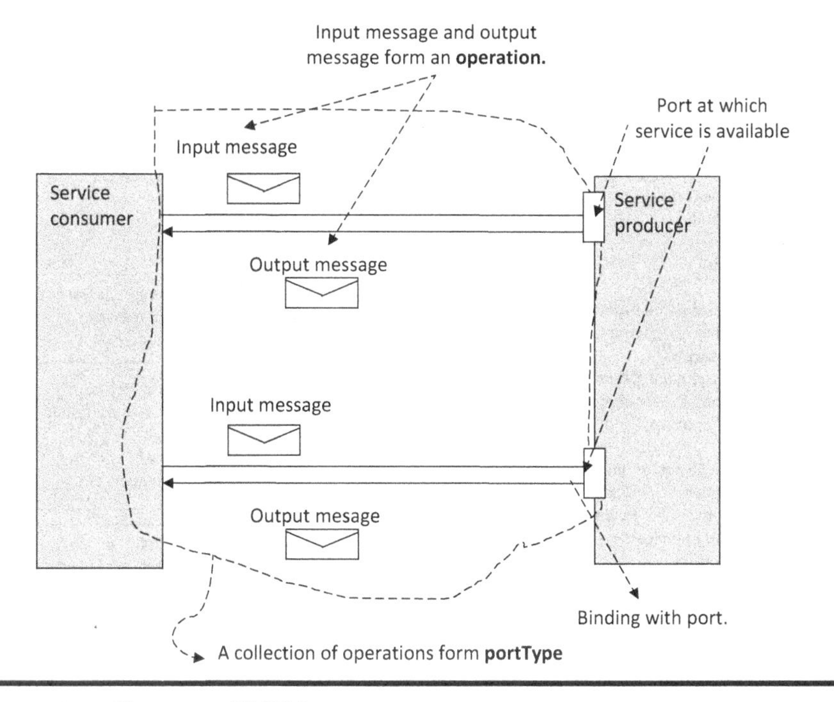


**Figure 4.4 Elements of WSDL.**

To provide an understanding of how a WSDL file will look, a sample WSDL for adding two integers is given in Listings 4.1 and 4.2. (Note: Inbuilt Java packages and .NET frameworks generate WSDL documents corresponding to the web services. Developers need not worry about how to develop an WSDL.)

### 4.2.2 Simple Object Access Protocol

As mentioned in the first chapter, the Simple Object Access Protocol is an open web services protocol that enables communication between heterogeneous applications. SOAP was developed by Dave Winer, Don Box, and Bob Atkinson, in

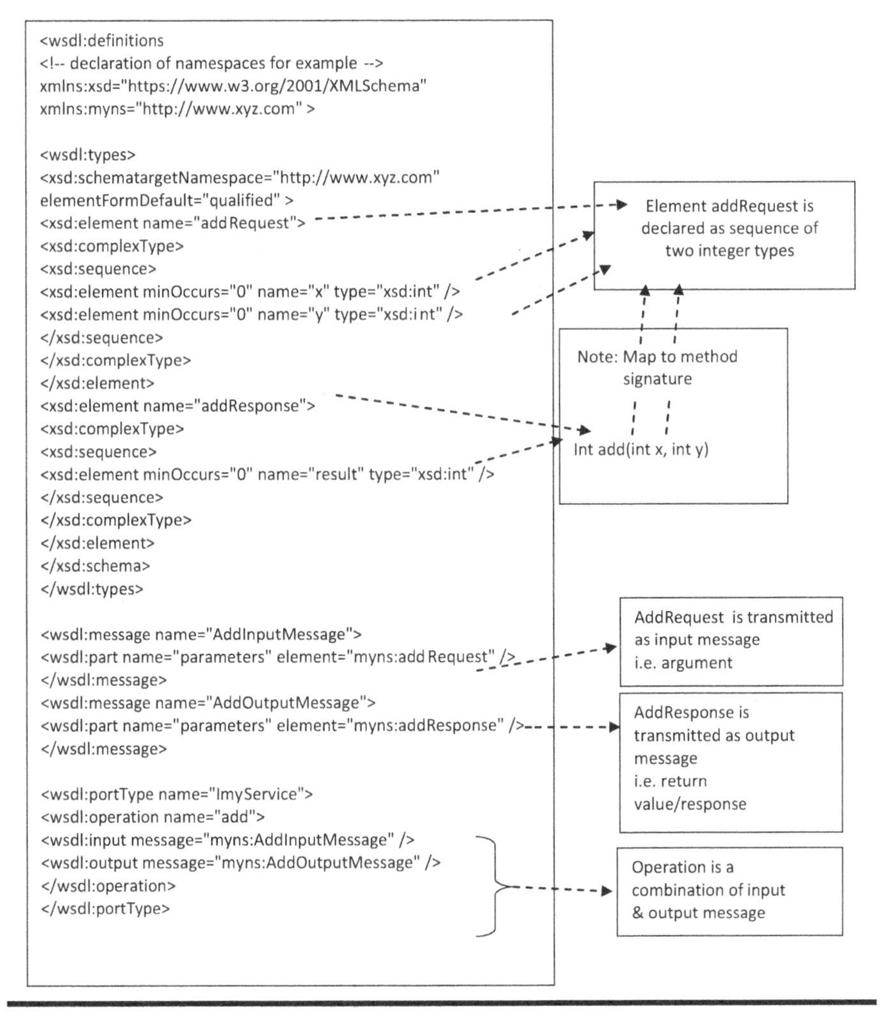


**Listing 4.1 The abstract part of a sample WSDL file.**

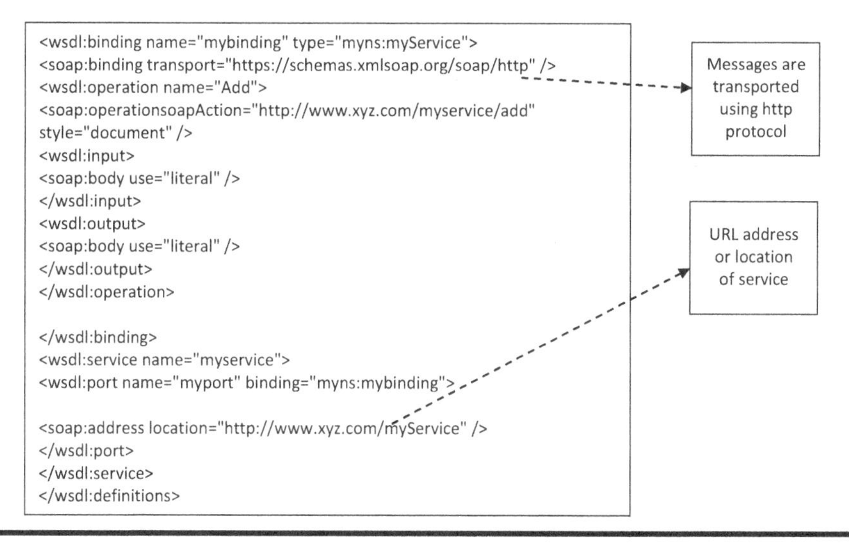
<wsdl:binding name="mybinding" type="myns:myService">
<soap:binding transport="https://schemas.xmlsoap.org/soap/http" />
<wsdl:operation name="Add">
<soap:operationsoapAction="http://www.xyz.com/myservice/add"
style="document" />
<wsdl:input>
<soap:body use="literal" />
</wsdl:input>
<wsdl:output>
<soap:body use="literal" />
</wsdl:output>
</wsdl:operation>
</wsdl:binding>
<wsdl:service name="myservice">
<wsdl:port name="myport" binding="myns:mybinding">
<soap:address location="http://www.xyz.com/myService" />
</wsdl:port>
</wsdl:service>
</wsdl:definitions>
Messages are transported using http protocol
URL address or location of service

**Listing 4.2 The concrete part of WSDL.**

collaboration with Microsoft in 1998. *SOAP is an XML-based messaging protocol which defines the format of XML messages. The sender and receiver should adhere to the standard so that the message will be interpreted correctly by the receiver* (i.e., the interpretation of the messages will be correct). How WSDL and SOAP work in unison to achieve service invocation is shown in Figure 4.5.

As shown in Figure 4.5, in service invocation, there are two entities. They are (i) a service provider who provides the service over the network for service consumers/clients to use and (ii) a service consumer who consumes the service. Service providers and service consumers interact according to a Service Level Agreement (SLA).

Following are key points describe the SOAP protocol and how it works in unison with WSDL.

1. At first service provider exposes the interface of service using WSDL while hiding the implementation details.
2. The service provider publishes/exposes the interface through (i) public service portals, (ii) service registry, (iii) Point of Sale sites, and (iv) email or other communication media.
3. Service providers generate a server-side skeleton by giving a WSDL document (*.wsdl*) as an input to a *WSDL-target language compiler*. Here the server has to ensure whether the compiler generates mapping from the WSDL to the targeted language (i.e., language in which service is implemented). Please refer to Figure 4.5.
4. The client has to obtain the WSDL in order to access the service as a WSDL only contains the calling semantics of a service as well as the URL of the

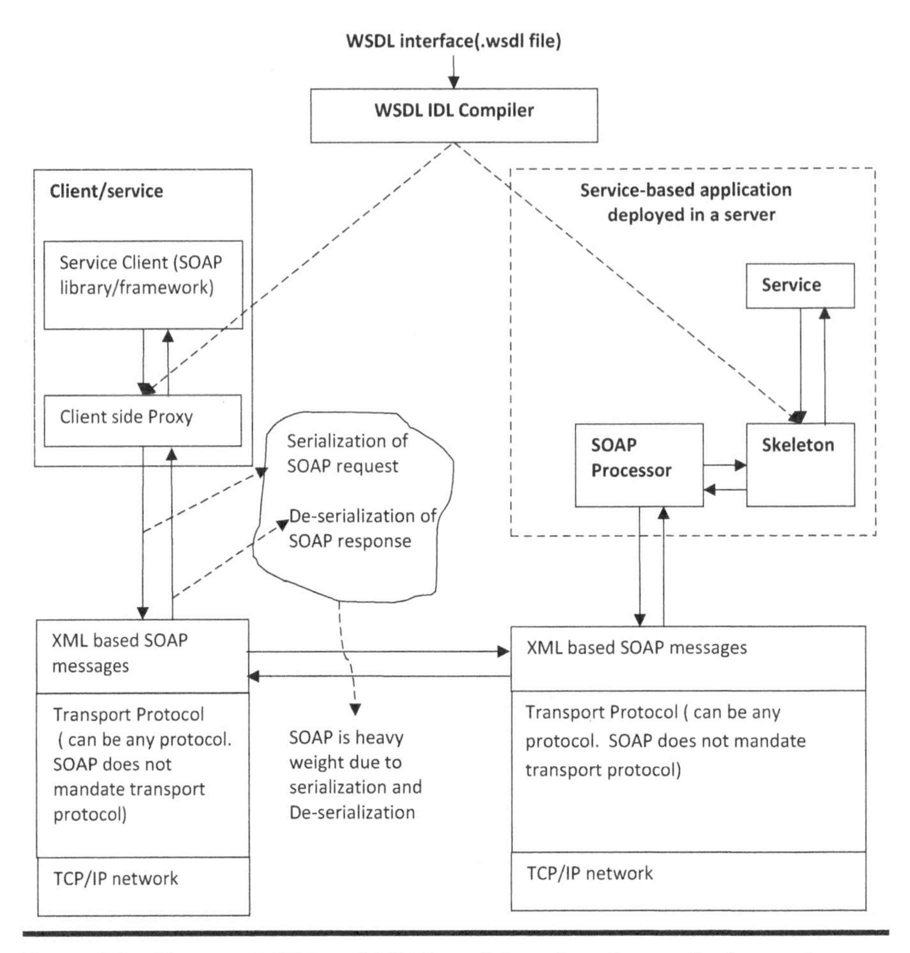


**Figure 4.5 The way WSDL and SOAP work in unison for service invocation.**

service. The service consumer can obtain the WSDL via different means, as mentioned above.

5. After obtaining a WSDL, the consumer generates the client-side proxy using a *WSDL-target language compiler.* Here also, the client has to use the correct WSDL compiler, which supports the mapping of the WSDL-targeted language of the client. *Please refer to* Figure 4.5.
6. According to the calling semantics defined in WSDL, the client constructs a SOAP message using SOAP libraries/frameworks in a higher-level language such as Java, .NET, etc. The higher-level request is given to the client-side proxy (which serves as a local service instance for the client).
7. The request in a high-level language is serialized as an XML message and sent over transport protocols such as HTTP. SOAP frameworks assist in

serialization and deserialization so that the developer can focus on the actual application development without worrying about how to generate SOAP messages and how to perform the serialization/deserialization of SOAP messages.
8. On the server-side, the request is de-serialized and given to the skeleton.
9. The skeleton invokes the service.
10. The response is again serialized and sent to the client.
11. In client-side, the response is de-serialized and given to the client application.

Unique characteristics of SOAP includes:

1. A messaging protocol that enables applications to interact irrespective of languages and platforms, as it uses XML, which is text-based protocol.

   It does not mandate any transport protocol as in Figure 4.5 (though developers use HTTP). But SOAP is a heavyweight protocol as it requires the serialization and deserialization of method arguments and objects.

   In addition, According to the service contract/interface, SOAP requests and response should be updated.
2. SOAP provides extensibility and it provides neutrality over a transport protocol.
3. SOAP has a large data handling capability.

The following are the soap requests (see Listing 4.3) and soap responses (see Listing 4.4) corresponding to the invocation of the service which implements the addition of two integers in the WSDL, as given in Listing 4.1.

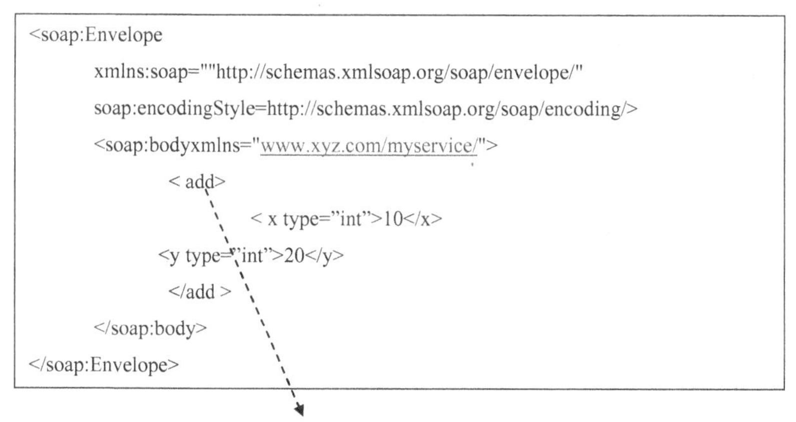

```
<soap:Envelope
        xmlns:soap=""http://schemas.xmlsoap.org/soap/envelope/"
        soap:encodingStyle=http://schemas.xmlsoap.org/soap/encoding/>
        <soap:bodyxmlns="www.xyz.com/myservice/">
                < add>
                        < x type=”int”>10</x>
                <y type=”int”>20</y>
                </add >
        </soap:body>
</soap:Envelope>
```

**SOAP is tied up with service interface/contract. (add is operation defined in interface) So, when there is change in service interface, accordingly SOAP message has to be modified**

**Listing 4.3 Sample SOAP RPC request.**

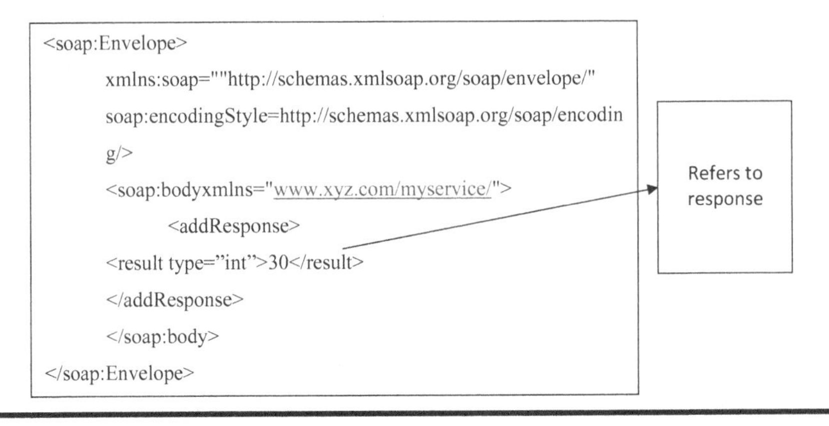

```
<soap:Envelope>
        xmlns:soap=""http://schemas.xmlsoap.org/soap/envelope/"
        soap:encodingStyle=http://schemas.xmlsoap.org/soap/encodin
        g/>
        <soap:bodyxmlns="www.xyz.com/myservice/">
                <addResponse>
        <result type="int">30</result>
        </addResponse>
        </soap:body>
</soap:Envelope>
```



**Listing. 4.4 Sample SOAP RPC response.**

As seen in Listing 4.3, a SOAP RPC request is constructed with an operation name as an element under the SOAP body. Within this element, sub-elements are declared for each argument along with its type. In the above *add operation* example, there are two integer arguments, namely "x" and "y."

As seen in Listing 4.4, according to SOAP convention, an RPC response is constructed by specifying the name of the *operation with the response appended at the end*. Then the response is constructed with the element <result> along with the data type of the return value.

## 4.3 API Design and Middleware Platforms for Microservices

There are three commonly used combinations of technologies for designing APIs and constructing middleware platforms, which include:

- *REST* API design with no special middleware platform
- *Apache Thrift* API design with Apache Thrift generated middleware
- *Google Protocol Buffer* API design with gRPC middleware

### *4.3.1 REST API*

#### *4.3.1.1 REST API Design Using a URL Template*

As mentioned earlier (please refer to Chapter 3), REST architecture [1, 2] considers services as resources which are located using URLs themselves. So, the URL of the REST request contains the location of a service. The path of the URL is mapped to the concerned method of the service. In addition, the action to be taken on the resource or method to be invoked is also passed through the same URL. In this way, REST gives a very simple way of accessing services.

Consider a service, say "myservice," having a method signature, int add (int, int).

Now for this service, the API or interface is constructed as a URL template. *The URL template is a way to specify, (i) the location of the resource/microservice, (ii)the path of the resource, (iii) the action to be taken, i.e., method to invoked on the resource/ microservice, and (iv) the parameters to be passed to the method (keep in mind that the parameters must be substituted before the URL is invoked).* For the above method, the *URL template* can be constructed as shown in Figure 4.6.

Following are the key points while writing REST APIs:

*Basically, the API/interface is a set of method signatures. Each method signature has a method name, zero or more arguments, and zero or more return values.*

*Service name and method name are given in the URL path.*

*The big question is: How to convey the arguments?*

*The key is: Arguments can be passed as path variables. In the above example, there are two path variables, {a} and {b}.*

It implies that the *method "add" has two arguments "a" and "b."*

REST architecture supports four types of parameters. They are:

- *Header parameters*—Parameters included in the request header. Typically these parameters are related to authorization.
- *Path parameters*—These parameters are declared within the path of the end-point, i.e., before the query string (?). Path parameters are usually specified with curly braces. Example: {a}.
- *Query string parameters*—These parameters are specified after the query string (?). These parameters take the form of a key-value pair. Example: ?username=."raj".
- *Request body parameters*—These parameters are included in the request body. The JSON format is extensively used.

Now, it is clear that a developer can expose a service using a URL template. On the other side, a service consumer can use this URL template and can consume the

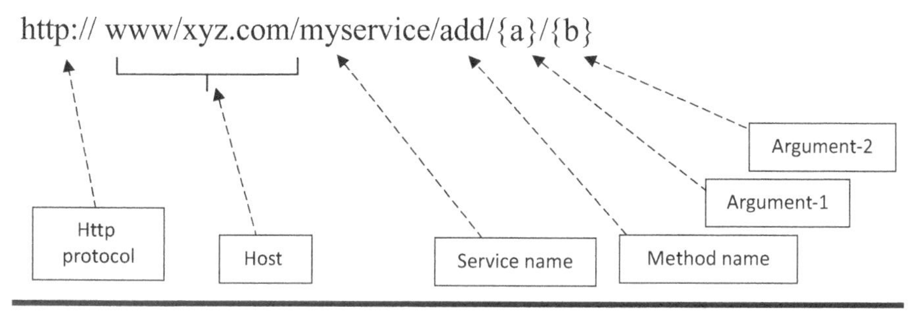


**Figure 4.6 REST API design using a URLTemplate.**

service. Now according to the REST architecture, a service consumer can access the service using a HTTP GET request as:

```
GET www.xyz.com/myservice/add/{10}/{20} HTTP/1.1
```

Now consider the service implementation side. The service and its method should be mapped with an @path annotation, as shown in Figure 4.7.

#### 4.3.1.2 The Need for REST API Standardization/ Limitations with URL Template Design

With the above discussion, a reader would have understood that a REST API can be constructed using a URL template. *However, there is a limitation when trying to express all the required aspects with a URL template. There is no provision to include the data type of arguments. But, data types of arguments are very important.* The reason for this limitation is that REST APIs follow an architectural style, not a specific standard. REST simply exploits the already existing technologies such as URL and HTTP technologies to locate a resource as well as specify the action to be taken on the resource. When a service is developed by a few internal teams of an enterprise, exposing the REST API via a URL template may be useful. *But when the number of services grow and when there are many consuming applications, it is essential to develop a REST API according to standard specifications.* However, several REST specifications have been developed to provide standards in the way that REST APIs are described.

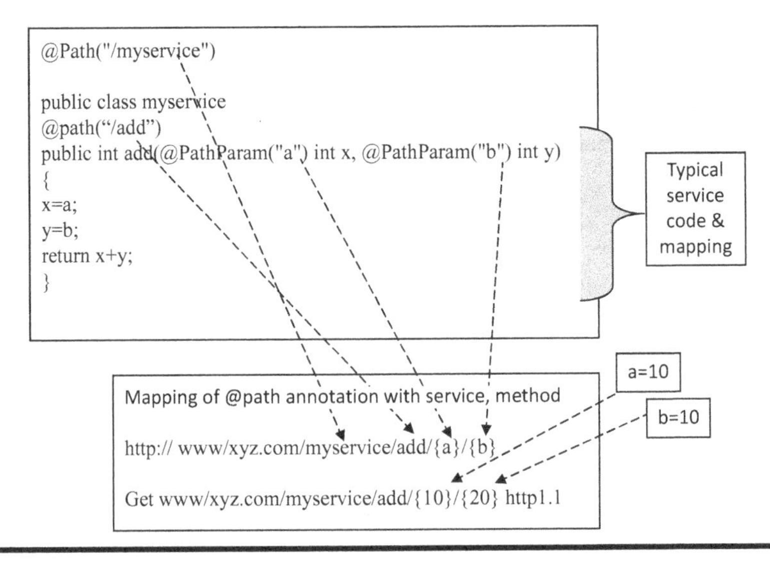
@Path("/myservice")
public class myservice
@path("/add")
public int add(@PathParam("a") int x, @PathParam("b") int y)
{
x=a;
y=b;
return x+y;
}
Typical service code & mapping
Mapping of @path annotation with service, method
http:// www/xyz.com/myservice/add/{a}/{b}
Get www/xyz.com/myservice/add/{10}/{20} http1.1
a=10
b=10

**Figure 4.7 Mapping elements of a URL template to different parts of service implementation.**

### 4.3.2 Standard REST API Specifications

The three most popular REST API specifications are:

- *OpenAPI (formally called Swagger)*
- *RESTful API Modeling Language (RAML)*
- *API BluePrint*

#### 4.3.2.1 Open API Specification (Swagger)

Swagger [3] is a set of rules or a specification for describing, producing, consuming, and visualizing REST APIs. The format is both machine-readable and human-readable. Swagger began its development in 2010 by Reverb Technologies. In 2015, SmartBear software acquired the Swagger API specification from Reverb Technologies and maintains it under the sponsorship of the Open API Initiation Foundation of Linux. In 2016, the Swagger specification was renamed the OpenAPI specification

An API is a contract that service providers and service consumers need to follow in an exact manner. Since making changes to an API is difficult, the design of an API should involve multiple stakeholders. OpenAPI definitions are formalized plain-text documents that can reside in a repository, e.g., on GitHub, similar to code artifacts. So, the design and development of an API can collaborate with multiple stakeholders.

OpenAPI specification provides support for developing server-side as well as client-side code generation. Swagger generates a description of a REST API using standard data serialization formats, namely Yet Ain't Markup Language (YAML) and JSON, which is language-neutral.

For public APIs, all of the benefits mentioned above make an API better, and that alone is a big part of attracting developers to integrate it and build applications with it. But OpenAPI offers a provision for publishing OpenAPI definition. It also allows client developers to use their preferred tools in combination with an open API. Developers who work with a large number of APIs will be happy to use just one toolchain for all integrations instead of multiple proprietary APIs/interfaces.

One can visualize how microservices, REST API, and Swagger fit together, as shown in Figure 4.8.

Before looking into what a Swagger specification will look like, one should note that there are two different approaches for designing an API [4], namely (i) the API-First approach (also known as the Design-First approach) and (ii) the Code-First approach, as shown in Figure 4.9.

***API-First or Design-First Approach***

API-First or Design-First approach is a top-down approach in which the first APIs are designed and then following API design, the services corresponding to the respective APIs are developed. This is shown in Figure 4.10.

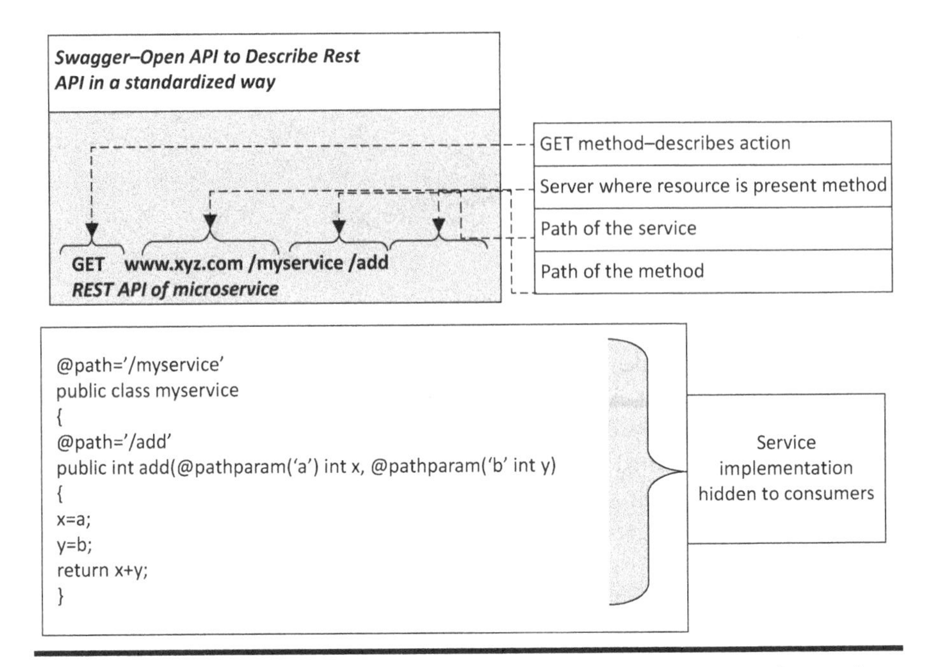


**Figure 4.8 How microservice, REST API, and Swagger descriptions fit together.**

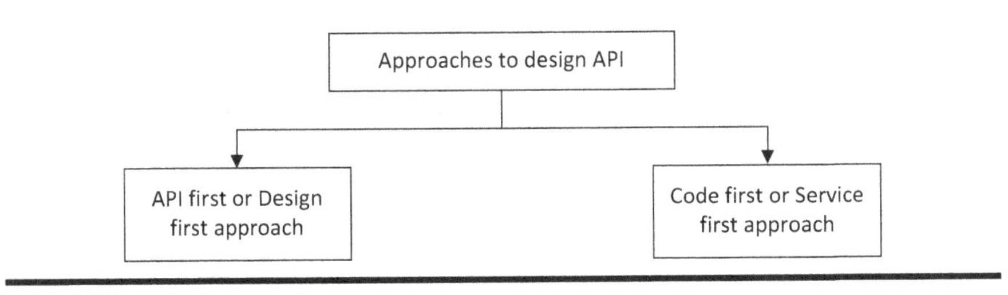


**Figure 4.9 Approaches to API design.**

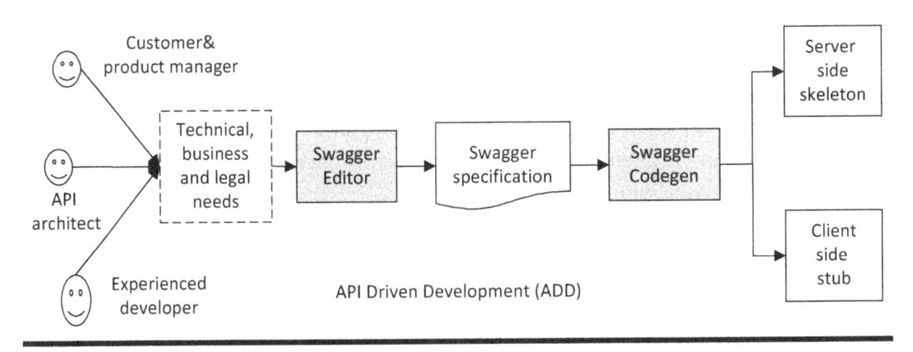


**Figure 4.10 API-First approach.**

As shown in Figure 4.10, at first, API experts develop API specifications by taking into account the needs and ideas of the various stakeholders of an application, such as developers, product managers, and external consumers. The design of an API should attend to technical, business, and legal needs.

With Swagger, API specification is developed using the Swagger Editor. After designing an API, a *server-side skeleton* and *client-side stub* are generated using *SwaggerCodeGen tools*

*Why a Design-First Approach*

API specifications should meet the needs of various stakeholders as APIs are important resources that are going to reside in repositories and be used by many teams. APIs are the central resource which enables all the team members to work together

One should note that the APIs cannot undergo any changes simply as APIs are important resources that are used by different internal and external stakeholders. Implementation of applications may undergo changes frequently without disturbing the APIs. Hence, most large and modern applications prefer to use an API-First approach. This approach is also called a *API Driven Development* (ADD) or contract the first approach. This approach enables the integration of services as well as communication among services.

*Benefits of the Design-First Approach*

In general, for any application, the Design-First approach is preferred to the Code-First approach due to the benefits given below.

- A well-designed and well-developed API is preferred for *high adoption* and *high consumption of services.*
- Well-designed APIs help customers to understand quickly.
- Well-designed APIs facilitate the integration of services easier.
- Well-designed APIs improve reusability of services significantly.
- Well-designed APIs yield high customer satisfaction.
- A Design-First approach identifies any bugs in an API in the design stage itself.

*When an application has a well-developed API architecture and experienced developers and is to be involved with external customers, the Design-First approach is a good choice.*

*Code-First or Service-First Approach*

The *Code-First or Service-First Approach* is a bottom-up approach in which services are developed first, and then following the service classes and code, APIs are generated using different tools, as shown in Figure 4.11. As shown in Figure 4.11, from the services classes and REST APIs, Swagger specification is developed using the Swagger Editor. Swagger is typically configured to work in an integrated

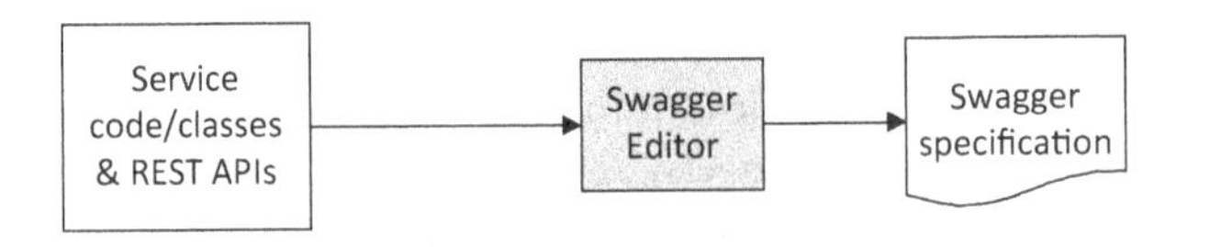


**Figure 4.11 A Service-First or Code-First approach.**

environment such as *Java Spring Boot* which generates an OpenAPI specification by taking in service classes, code, and REST APIs.

When APIs are developed for internal use (i.e., no external customers are not involved), then the Code-First approach fits as a suitable choice [5], and it offers (i) *speed*, (ii) *automation*, and (iii) *reduced process complexity*. In addition, this model can be adopted even by programmers with less experience.

A typical REST API specification using Swagger/OAS for a GET request and the response of http://www.xyz.com/myservice/add/{a}/{b} are given in Listing 4.5a and b, respectively.

*Features of Swagger*

As mentioned earlier Swagger (developed by SmartBear) provides formal documentation for a REST API. Swagger provides three important facilities, (i) Swagger Specification, (ii) an interactive User Interface/Editor, and (iii) code generation tools.

Swagger as an OpenAPI specification defines a standard, a formal interface to RESTful APIs which can be interpreted by both humans and computers. The Swagger specification describes a standard structure with typical components such as:

(i) *OpenAPI specification version*—Version of the Open API specification

(ii) *Info object*—Given metadata about an API

It contains sub-parts namely, (i) title, (ii) description, (iii) terms of service, (iv) contact, (v) license, and (vi) version.

(iii) *Server*—Represents the server in which the resources are available

It contains sub-parts namely, (i) URL (URL of the target host), (ii) description, and (iii) variables.

(iv) *Paths*—Paths give the relative paths to the individual endpoints of resource operations.

(v) *Operation*—An operation object represents a single API operation along a path.

(vi) *Extern docs*—Extern docs help refer to an external resource.

*Features*

- Swagger facilitates effective communication among services.
- Swagger provides an easy and flexible orchestration of services to achieve the usefulness of the entire application.

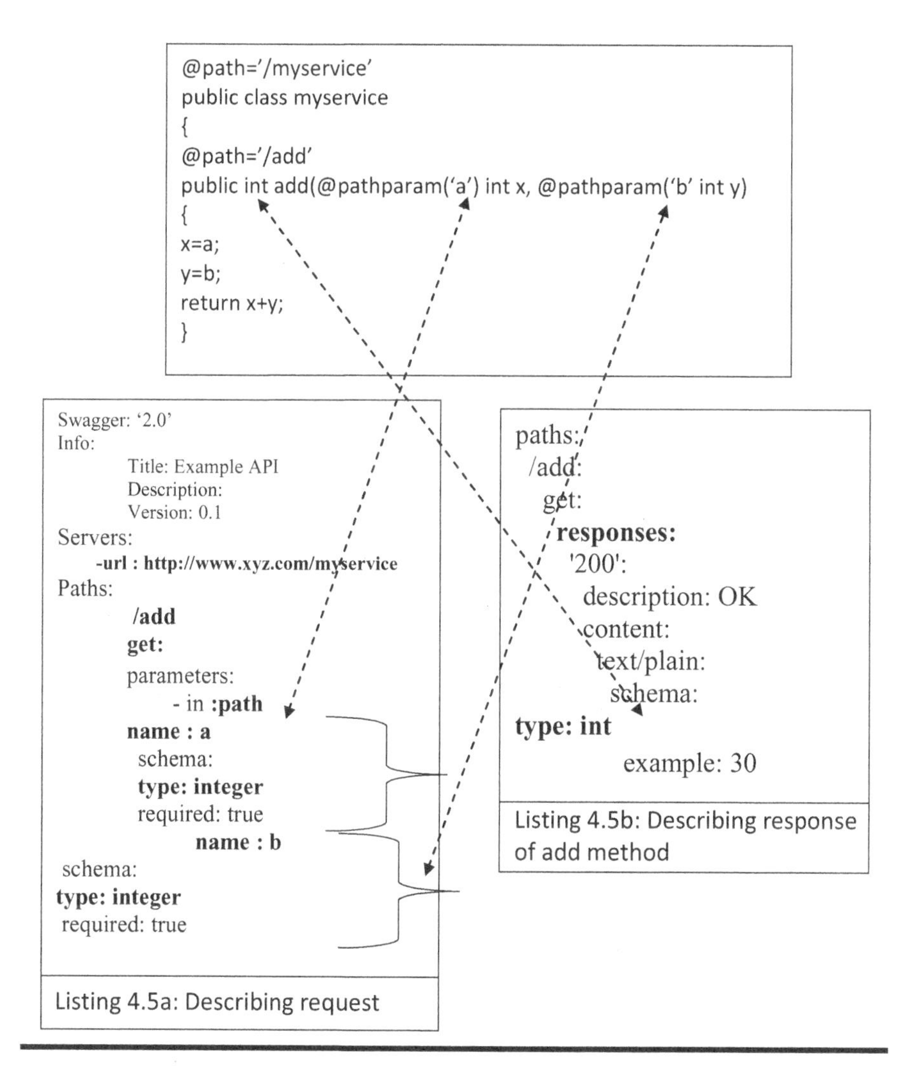

@path='/myservice'
public class myservice
{
@path='/add'
public int add(@pathparam('a') int x, @pathparam('b' int y)
{
x=a;
y=b;
return x+y;
}
Swagger: '2.0'
Info:
Title: Example API
Description:
Version: 0.1
Servers:
-url : http://www.xyz.com/myservice
Paths:
/add
get:
parameters:
- in :path
name : a
schema:
type: integer
required: true
name : b
schema:
type: integer
required: true
Listing 4.5a: Describing request
paths:
/add:
get:
responses:
'200':
description: OK
content:
text/plain:
schema:
type: int
example: 30
Listing 4.5b: Describing response of add method


**Listing 4.5 (a) Describing a request. (b) Describing the response of add method.**

- The Swagger interface defines the common SLA between clients and services.
- It generates server and client templates.
- It creates test cases for development and testing.
- Swagger provides an API editor called *SwaggerHub* for intelligent design, and domains to quicken API design delivery and ultimately achieves a *quicker time-to-market*.
- Swagger is a framework that describes an API in a common language that everyone can understand. Swagger is used to describe REST APIs.
- It describes as well as debugs and tests any issues related to APIs.

- The key feature of Swagger is that it is both human- and machine-readable. Swagger is extensively used for *describing*, *publishing*, and *discovering* microservices.
- Swagger is language independent.
- Swagger provides easy-to-understand, concise, interactive documentation, client SDK, and discoverability.

*Pros*

- OAS/Swagger generates server code, client code, and documentation.
- It allows for quick changes to the API.
- It is open source.
- It has large community support.
- It has a high adoption rate, *and hence it has lots of documentation.*
- It has strong framework support.
- It has the largest language support of any open source framework.

*Cons*

- It increases project complexity by using additional tools and libraries.
- It generates a lot of code that the user might not understand.
- It does not allow for code reuse.

#### 4.3.2.2 REST API Modeling Language

RAML is an acronym standing for RESTful API Modeling Language [6]. RAML, a vendor-neutral, open-specification language, built on YAML 1.2 and JSON for describing RESTful APIs. RAML, was created in 2013 by Uri Sarid from MuleSoft as an alternative to Swagger, focusing on both human and machine readability (YAML format). RAML is backed by MuleSoft, VMware, Akana Software, Cisco, and others, with a focus on API design, as its name indicates (RESTful API Modeling Language).

- RAML provides source code generators for client and server. Hence, source code and comprehensive user documentation can be created.
- RAML is used to manage REST API lifecycle completely. There is a lot of useful tooling built around RAML. This means that one can design an API visually, test it, and get user feedback without writing a single line of code. In contrast to Swagger, RAML is a pure Design-First approach.
- RAML's focus lies on designing clean and readable descriptions, which is why YAML has been chosen as their design markup language.
- Due to the human-centered approach, RAML has strong support for reusable patterns. RAML allows code reuse and design patterns. Also, RAML checks whether an API remains consistent throughout API development.

- The RAML community claims that the biggest strength of RAML is that descriptions can be understood by non-technical stakeholders. (It is the vision behind the API definition.)
- With RAML, an API can be sent to potential API users for mock-up test. Also, RAML allows for integration with popular API tools such as Postman.
- As RAML makes it easy to design, prototype, and get feedback on API designs, bugs are detected before the production stage.

To provide a basic idea on how a RAML uses syntax to express an API design, RAML requests and responses are given in Listings 4.6 and Listing 4.7, respectively.

*Pros*

- RAML has a strong visual-based IDE and online tooling with collaboration focus.
- It provides a single specification to maintain.
- It allows for the use of design patterns.

*Cons*

- It lacks strong documentation.
- It supports only limited code reuse.

```
#%RAML 1.0
title: myservice has an operation with name 'add' which takes two integer arguments and
returns the sum of arguments
version: v1
protocols:  HTTP
baseUri: http://www.xyz.com/myservice

/add
get:
queryParameters:
    x:
displayName: x
      type: int
      description: one of the two operands
      example: 10
      required: true
    y:
displayName: y
      type: int
      description: one of the two operands
      example: 20
      required: true
```

**Listing 4.6 A simple REST API GET request in RAML.**

```
/add:
  get:
    responses:
     '200':
       description: OK
       content:  plain/text
type: int
           example: 30
```

**Listing 4.7 A simple REST API GET response in RAML.**

#### *4.3.2.3 API BluePrint*

API BluePrint [7] is an open source, documentation-oriented web API specification used to specify, describe and document web RESTful API description language (*Note: Web APIs are APIs offering one or more publicly exposed endpoints as interface/contract for clients so that they can interact and consume the application.*) API BluePrint was created by Jakub Nesetril as a more human-readable alternative (*Markdownformat*) to Web Application Description Language (WADL) and Swagger, and was launched by Apiary in 2013 with a focus on *consumer-centric API documentation*. The specification evolved to cover full API lifecycle needs and tooling for mocking or testing.

- API BluePrint is essentially a set of semantic assumptions laid on top of the Markdown syntax used to describe a web API.
- API BluePrint provides an API Design-First approach.
- It is more consumer-oriented.
- API BluePrint is widely-used due to its vast number of features and tools. It uses *Markdown Syntax for Object Notation* (MSON) which is the plain-text syntax for the description and validation of data structures.

*Markdown syntax* was developed by John Gruber and released in 2004. Core elements of Markdown data format/syntax include Headings, Emphasis, List, Images, Links, and Blockquotes.

1. Headings

    Example:

    # this is a level 1 tag

    ## this is a level 2 tag

    (please note there are two ## tags in a level 2 heading which distinguishes it from a level 1 heading tag which has only one #)

2. Emphasis

    Example:

*This text will be italic* (* is used to indicate the text in italic)
_This will also be italic_ (_ is also used to indicate the text in italic)
**This text will be bold** (** is used for making bold)

3. List

   Markdown syntax supports a list of items.

   Example:

   item 1
   item 2
   item 2(i)
   item 2(ii)

4. Images

   Markdown provides support for including a reference to images.

5. Links

   Markdown provides support for including a reference to links

6. Blockquotes

   Block quotes are simply prefixed by the > symbol.

APIs in API BluePrint can be developed using the Apiary Editor on Apiary.io, because of its built-in helpers and instant preview. To provide some basic level idea, API for www.xyz.com/myservice/add will be something like as seen in Listing 4.8 (Note: This listing is given only to show how API BluePrint uses Markdown syntax to develop API specification).

*Pros*

- API BluePrint provides good online tools.
- It has good community involvement.

```
FORMAT: 1A
HOST: https://www.xyz.com
# /myservice
## [/add]
### [GET]
+ parameters
  + a(integer, required) – one of the integer argument
  + b(integer, required) – one of the integer argument
Response 200
  + Body(integer)
  Example
        30
```

**Listing 4.8 Example of an API which uses API BluePrint specification.**

*Cons*

- Since API BluePrint is recently developed and new to the API market, it has a low adoption.
- It lacks advanced constructs.
- REST does not require additional technical knowledge as with SOAP. It has a unique feature in that it uses the HTTP protocol and code leveling tools.

### 4.3.3 Apache Thrift API Design and Middleware Platform

Apache Thrift [8] was developed by Facebook, and is at present maintained by Apache.

#### 4.3.3.1 Apache Thrift IDL and Code Generation

Apache Thrift is a software framework for implementing Remote Procedure Call (RPC) in services, with cross-language support. It is a framework for scalable cross-language services development, with a *code generation engine to build services* using different languages such as C++, Java, Python, PHP, Ruby, Erlang, Perl, Haskell, C#, Cocoa, JavaScript, Node.js, Smalltalk, OCaml, and Delphi, etc.

*Thrift defines a special Interface Description Language* (IDL) to define data types and service interfaces which are stored as *.thrift* files. A service developer who adopts a Thrift API should expose his service interface using Thrift IDL (the reader can recall that a conventional SOAP service uses WSDL for interface description). The Thrift IDL is used to develop a client-side stub and server-side skeleton. Server and client-side languages may be different. One can specify the languages for stub and skeleton. This is shown in Figure 4.12.

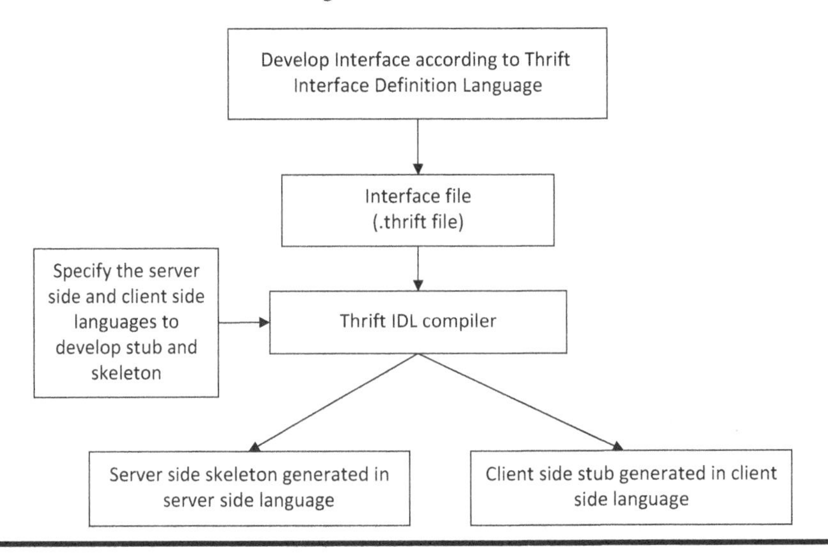


**Figure 4.12 Apache Thrift Code generation steps.**

An important strength of a Thrift compiler is that it not only generates stubs and skeletons in the required/opted language but also generates the client and server-side source code for RPC communication. So, one can just view Thrift as a set of code generation tools that allow developers to build RPC clients and servers just by defining data types and service interfaces in IDL. Thus, the primary main strength of a Thrift API is the ability to generate client and server code across a wide range of programming languages. Developers only need to write the handlers on the client and server.

### *4.3.3.2 Thrift Layers of Communication*

- A Thrift framework provides a rich set of options for data formats and transport protocols which work on the top of TCP/IP network. This is shown in Figure 4.13.

The data, method arguments or method signatures in language-specific format, are converted into an appropriate form, say, for example, binary or JSON

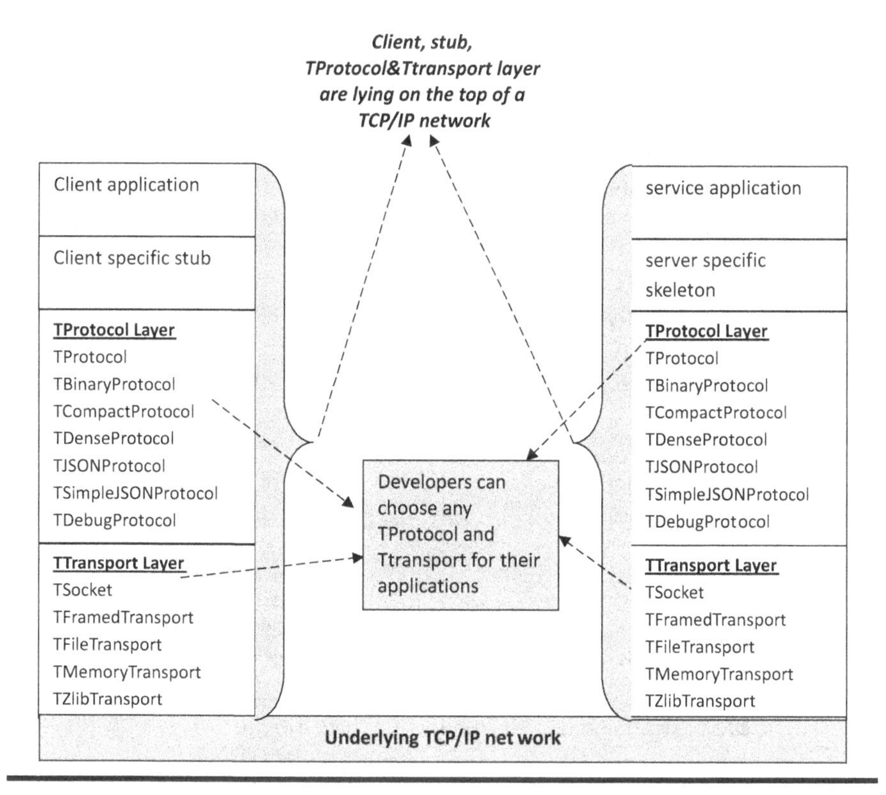


**Figure 4.13 Thrift layers of communication on the top of the TCP/IP network.**

using TProtocol support. As shown in Figure 4.13, Thrift provides different *TProtocols*, such as *TProtocol, TBinaryProtocol, TCompactProtocol, TDesneProtocol, TJSONProtocol, TSimpleJSONProtocol, TDebugProtocol*, etc. Out of these various protocols, a developer can choose his/her required one. Similarly, Thrift is not tied to any specific transport protocol. Thrift provides different transport protocols such as *TSocket, TFramedTransport, TFileTransport, TMemoryTransport, TZlibTransport.*

### 4.3.3.3 How to Use Thrift API and Tools

This section highlights the usage of *Thrift* with a simple example. In this example, a service called *AddService* is exposed using a Thrift API. This example covers how to write the API, how to generate stubs and skeletons, implementation of an interface, and developing server.

*Step 1—How to develop the interface.*
The interface is defined using the keyword *service* of the IDL. Service can include one or more methods or signatures. Listing 4.9 shows the interface of *AddService* which adds two integer values.

*Step 2—How to generate stub and skeleton.*
The interface file *Add.thrift* is given to an IDL compiler to generate stub and skeleton in the required server and client language. For example, consider that the server-side language is Java. Then the command "*$thrift–gen java AddService.thrift*"

will generate the server-side skeleton file, *AddService.Iface*. The implementation code (also called the handler code) for interface (*AddService.java*) will be as in Listing 4.10.

*Step 3—How to develop server (in this example a synchronous blocking server is considered).*
Let us consider a file *AddServer.java* as given in Listing 4.11.

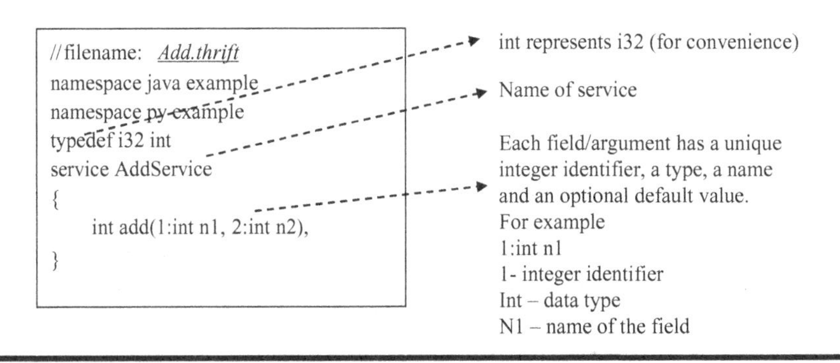


**Listing 4.9 A Thrift interface (syntax according to Thrift IDL).**

```
//AddService.java  (handler class)
package example;
import org.apache.thrift.TException;
public class AddServiceImpl implements AddService.Iface
{
   public int add(int num1, int num2) throws TException
  {
     Return num1 + num2;
   }
 }
```

**Listing 4.10 *AddService.java*—implementation file for *AddService.thrift*.**

```
public class AddServer
{
        public static AddService handler;
        public static AddService.Processor processor;
        public static void main(String [] args)
        {
                try
                {
                handler = new AddService();
                processor = new AddService.Processor(handler);
                Runnable simple = new Runnable()
                {
                        public void run()
                        {
                                simple(processor);
                        }
                };
                new Thread(simple).start();
                } catch (Exception e) {  }
        }

        public static void simple(AddService.Processor processor)
        {
        try
         {
                TServerTransport serverTransport = new TServerSocket(9090);
                TServer.Args args = new TServer.Args(serverTransport);
                args.processor(processor);
                args.protocolFactory(new TBinaryProtocol.Factory());
                TServer server = new TSimpleServer(args);
                System.out.println("Starting the simple server...");
                server.serve();
        } catch (Exception e) { }
        }
}
```



**Listing 4.11 *AddServer.java*.**

The Thrift framework automatically generates a processor class (*AddService.processor*). This processor class contains methods to (i) write something to the output stream and (ii) read something from the input stream. The *AddServer.java* is developed using the processor and handler classes. The purpose of the above listing is to highlight how the Thrift framework offers different protocols and how the developer can choose their desired protocol for serialization and transport. One should note that Thrift achieves higher performance due to the availability of binary and compact protocols for serialization.

#### 4.3.3.4 When to Use Thrift

Though REST is good for the web, the stack composed of REST, HTTP, and JSON are not optimal for the high performance required for internal data transfer. Indeed, the serialization and deserialization of these protocols and formats will be a bottleneck for the internal data transfer when Thrift fits as a natural choice.

*Disadvantages*

Thrift is poorly documented.

### 4.3.4 Google Protocol Buffers (Protobuf, GPB) and Google RPC

#### 4.3.4.1 Google Protobuf

Google's Protocol Buffers (referred to as Protobuf) [9] is *a language-neutral, platform-neutral extensible mechanism for serializing structured data.* Protobuf supports representing data in a way that can be used by multiple programming languages. Protocol Buffers is Google's IDL, which is used to describe an interface for the microservices. The Protobuf provides a simpler, faster, smaller, flexible, automated mechanism for serializing structured data. Whatever data is to be serialized should be constructed as *.proto* files. An example of a *.proto* file is given in Listing 4.12.

The *.proto* file in Listing 4.12 defines a message type called Person. The Person message type consists of three fields, namely *id*, *name*, and *email*. A message is an aggregate containing a set of typed fields. Many standard simple data types are

```
message Person {
  required int32 id = 1;
  required string name = 2;
  optional string email = 3;
}
repeated Person employee=10;
}
```

Each field has a unique identifier which is used to identify the field in binary format.

**Listing 4.12 Message in a *.proto* file.**

available as field types, including bool, int32, float, double, and string. One can also add further structure to messages by using other message types as field types. If a field is mandatory, it should be declared with the "required" keyword. Similarly optional fields are declared with the keyword "optional." Each field is given a unique identifier which is used to identify a field in the serialized binary data format. Basically *.proto* files are used to declare the messages which will be communicated between a service consumer and service producer. The service consumer and service producer may be working on disparate machines having different operating systems and programming languages. Hence, it becomes essential to have a higher-level stub and skeleton developed with the required target languages for the server and client.

At present, Google Protobuf compiler includes *Protobuf IDL which concerns the target language mapping* of the languages, namely (i) C++, (ii) Java, (iii) and Python. Currently, there are some new ongoing projects which develop *ProtoBuf IDL which concern the target language mapping* for other languages such as C, C#, Haskell, Perl, and Ruby.

An important key aspect of Google Protocol Buffer is that it defines the messages in a platform and language independent manner (i.e., it supports the languages for which ProtoBuf IDL to the concerned language mapping exists).

#### *4.3.4.2 Google RPC with Google Protobuf*

Now, an important question arises. Having described messages using Google Protobuf, how does one perform the communication between service consumer and service provider?

The key is with Google RPC (GRPC). Google RPC is commonly used in combination with Protobuf, i.e., Protobuf is used for API design and GRPC is used for the development of required middleware (which hides the heterogeneity in operating systems and programming languages) for communication. Please keep in mind that both are developed by Google

Thus:

- *Google Protocol Buffers play two roles, (i) they describe the interface definition of a service and (ii) they serialize data from a language-specific format to a binary format and vice versa.*
- *Google RPC is an RPC framework which is used to define a service and its methods in a way that can be called remotely by specifying their parameters and return type. The key point to note is that GRPC uses Google Protobuf for interface description and data serialization.*

The role of GRPC and Google Protocol Buffer are shown in Figure 4.14.

On the service-side, after developing an interface using Google Protobuf as an a *.proto* file, the *.proto* file will be given as an input to a Protocol Buffers Compiler for the generation of a stub and skeleton in the desired language in which client

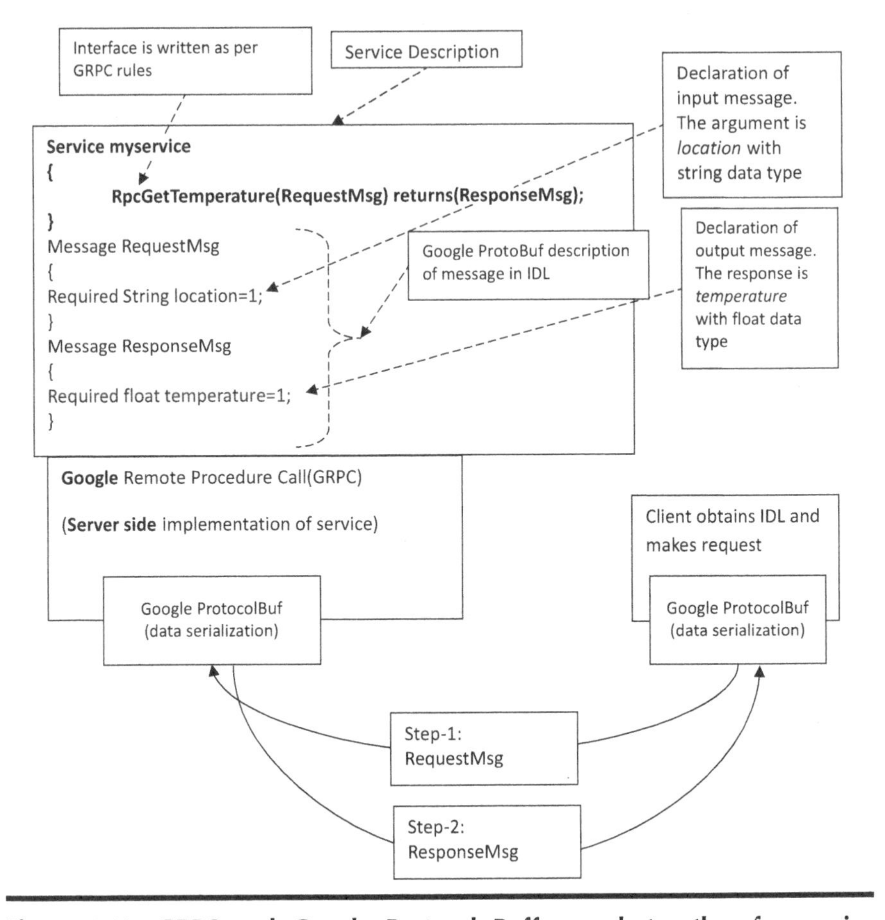


**Figure 4.14 GRPC and Google Protocol Buffer work together for service communication.**

and server are being developed. (*Please note that during compilation, one can specify the target languages such as C, Java, Python, etc. in which stub and skeleton have to be generated.*) This is shown in Figure 4.15.

The binary format generated by the Google Protobuf is much smaller than a normal JSON and conversion/parsing is very fast. The generated code also provides methods to create the protocol object instance and read–write it to any byte stream like a file, network, etc.

## 4.4 Data Serialization Formats for Inter-Service Communication

Data serialization refers to the process of converting data structures and objects from a language-specific format into some universal text or binary format so

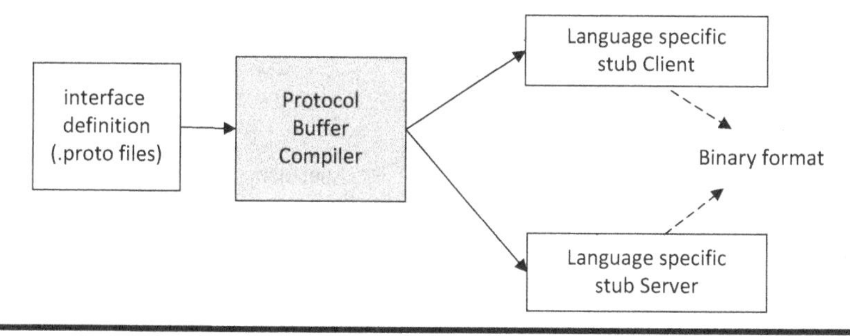


**Figure 4.15 Generation of skeleton and stub using a protocol buffer compiler.**

that the data can be stored in memory or sent over the network or shared with other applications which are running on different platforms. The process of converting language-specific data into XML is an example for serialization. Similarly, deserialization refers to the process of converting back the data format from XML into the language-specific format. There are some universal formats which support the sharing of data among different applications and different platforms.

They are:

- eXtensible Markup Language (XML)
- JavaScript Object Notation (JSON)
- Yet Another Markup Language/Yet Ain't Markup Language
- AVRO

## *4.4.1 XML*

Extensible Markup Language is a markup language that defines a set of rules for describing structure and data types of data in a format that is both human and machine-readable. XML is in a text-based format. It is both language independent and platform independent. It is a World Wide Web Consortium (W3C) specification.

Elements and attributes are the basic building blocks of XML. An XML element begins with a start tag and ends with a matching end tag.

For example, an element will look like:

<name>Kamal</name>

Attributes are key-value pairs that describe the properties of elements.

Example:

<employee id="5649"> Kamal</employee>

XML documents have a root node under which the data is described. A simple XML file is shown in Listing 4.13.

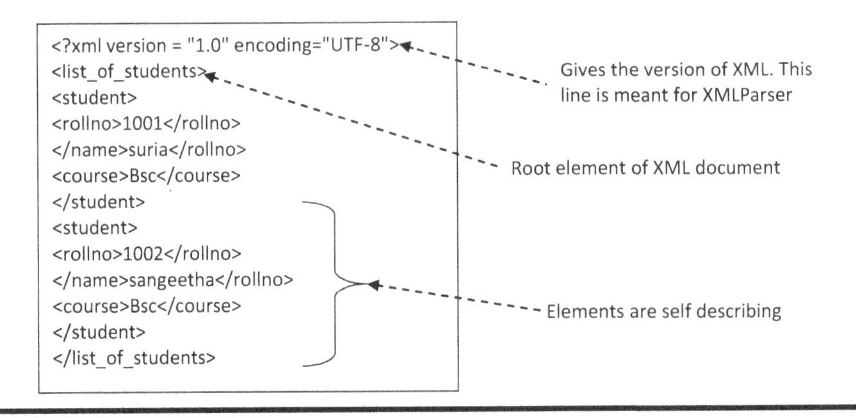
<?xml version = "1.0" encoding="UTF-8">
<list_of_students>
<student>
<rollno>1001</rollno>
</name>suria</rollno>
<course>Bsc</course>
</student>
<student>
<rollno>1002</rollno>
</name>sangeetha</rollno>
<course>Bsc</course>
</student>
</list_of_students>
Gives the version of XML. This line is meant for XMLParser
Root element of XML document
Elements are self describing

**Listing 4.13 A simple XML document.**

XML provides a few important technologies such as namespace and a robust schema language called XML schema Definition (XSD). An XML namespace is similar to the concept of the package in Java. An XML namespace is a mechanism to avoid the ambiguity in naming XML elements and attributes. The purpose of an XSD schema is to define and describe a class of XML documents by using schema components which constrain a document, its structure, its constituent parts, their data types, and their relationships.

It supports a wide range of data types:

- XML is extensively used over the internet and in web applications.
- XML is extensible.

In practice, XML is used as a data storage format in:

1. Many SQL databases such as IBM DB2, Microsoft SQL Server, Oracle, PostgreSQL
2. Many NoSQL databases such as BaseX, eXistDB, MarkLogic
3. Many web application APIs such as Amazon Elastic Cloud Compute (EC2) web service, eBay, LinkedIn, etc.

### 4.4.2 JavaScript Object Notation (JSON)

JSON stands for JavaScript Object Notation. It is a lightweight, self-describing, open standard for data interchange. JSON data format is both human- and machine-readable. All languages, IDEs, and microservices use JSON as a means of data interchange. JSON is a subset of JavaScript. It supports the fundamental primitive data types such as string, number, object, array, boolean, and null. The other two important data structures of JSON are:

- A collection of name/value pairs.
- An ordered list of values.

Some important features of JSON include (i) Simplicity, (ii) Openness, (iii) Self-describing, (iv) Internationalization, (v) Extensibility, and (vi) Interoperability.

Listing 4.14 shows how a simple JSON file is generated using Java.

After execution of the above program, the contents of *student.json* will be as given in Listing 4.15.

Similarly, the contents of a JSON file can be read using a JSONParser, as shown in Listing 4.16.

The output of the above program is:

```
{"rollno": 1001, "name": "Peter"}
```

In practice, JSON is widely-used in:

(i) many NoSQL databases such as MongoDB, CouchDB, and Riak
(ii) many web application APIs such as Twitter, Google Maps, YouTube, and Facebook

```
#simple java program that generates a simple JSON file
import org.json.simple.JSONObject;
import org.json.simple.JSONString;
import java.io.*;
public class JSONWriteExample
{
        public static void main(String[] args)
        {
        JSONObject obj = new JSONObject();
        obj.put("rollno", "1001");
        obj.put("name", "Peter");
        FileWriter file = new FileWriter("student.json")
        file.write(obj.toJSONString());
        file.flush();
          }
}
```

**Listing 4.14 Simple Example in Java that writes data in a JSON format.**

```
{
"rollno": 1001,
"name": "Peter"
}
```

**Listing 4.15 Contents of *student.json*.**

```
import org.json.simple.*
import org.json.simple.parser.*;
import java.io.*;
import java.util.Iterator;
public class JSONRead
{
  public static void main(String[] args) throws Exception
  {
JSONParser parser = new JSONParser();
     Object obj = parser.parse(new FileReader("student.json"));
JSONObjectjsonObject = (JSONObject) obj;
System.out.println(jsonObject.toString());
  }
}
```

**Listing 4.16 Reading JSON using JSONParser.**

While reading JSON, an obvious thought will come to the reader's mind. What are the similarities and differences between JSON and XML. The key is given in Table 4.1.

### 4.4.3 YAML Ain't Markup Language

YAML Ain't Markup Language (YAML, pronounced *yaamel*) is a data serialization standard for programming languages. It was developed by Clark Evans in 2001. Initially, YAML was treated as Yet Another Markup Language. But later, in order to emphasize that YAML is mainly *data-oriented* and not document-oriented, the expansion of YAML was interpreted as YAML Ain't Markup Language.

- YAML describes data objects with its own syntax in YAML documents.
- YAML defines data using three basic structures, scalar, sequence, and map.
- Almost all languages are provided with YAML parsers which are used to read *.yaml* files and YAML emitters which are used to write data as YAML documents.

To show how data is structured in YAML, a few examples are given below.

*Scalars* denote simple variables such as string, integer, boolean variable, etc. Listing 4.17 shows an example of defining scalar using YAML:

- All items of a *sequence* (or list) should begin with the same intent, and each item should begin with "-".
- List/sequence structured data is denoted by the symbol "%."

A sequence/list of birds is represented in Listing 4.18.

**Table 4.1 Comparison between XML and JSON**

| | *XML* | *JSON* |
|---|---|---|
| ***Differences*** | | |
| Nature of data language | XML is a markup language | JSON is not a markup language |
| Schema | XML has schema | JSON has no schema |
| namespace | XML has namespace | JSON has no namespace |
| Verbose | Verbose in nature | Not verbose |
| extensibility | Extensible | Not extensible |
| Secure | XML is more secure | JSON is less secure |
| Data types | XML provides rich data types<br>XML does not support an array | JSON supports only limited data types<br>JSON supports array |
| Verbose | XML is more verbose<br>Each element has a start tag and end tag<br>The addition of tags adds extra weight data payload and hence in data transmission | |
| Object model | XML does not align with object models of programming languages | JSON aligns with object models of programming languages<br>The direct mapping to common programming language objects makes JSON significantly easier to work with as a developer |
| ***Similarities*** | • Both are open standards<br>• Both support Unicode, i.e., both support internationalization<br>• Both self-describe data<br>• Both are platform and language-neutral<br>• Both are interoperable | |

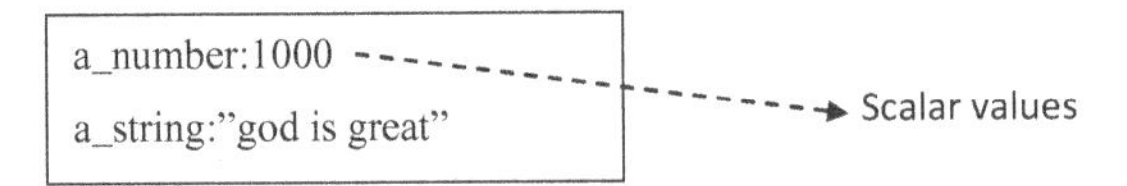


**Listing 4.17 Scalar values in YAML.**

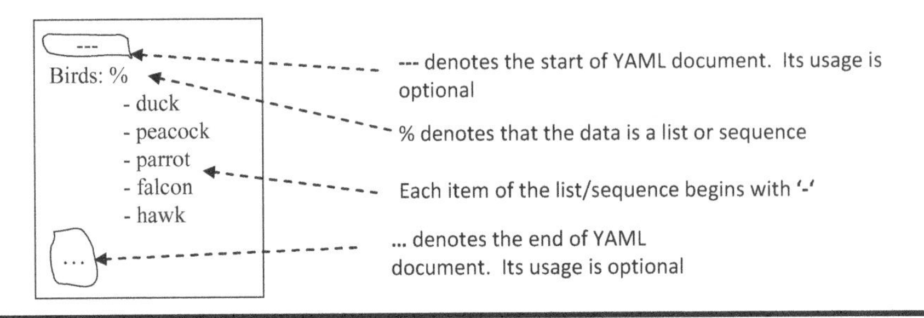


**Listing 4.18 Example of a list data structure in a YAML document.**

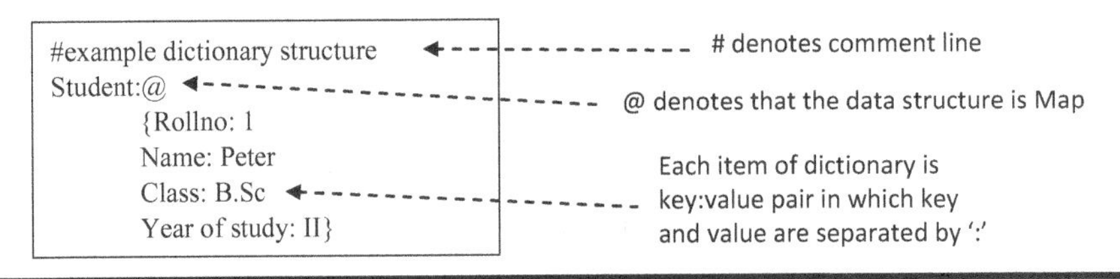


**Listing 4.19 Example of mapping in YAML.**

- The *map* contains a set of key:value pairs in which key and value are separated by ":" as shown in Listing 4.19.
- Map data structure is denoted by the "@" symbol.

To provide an insight into how easy it is to covert a language-specific format to a YAML format consider the following listings. Listing 4.20 shows how a *yaml* file can be read in a Java application, and Listing 4.21 Shows how data is written into a *yaml* file from Java.

### 4.4.4 Apache Avro

Apache Avro was developed by Doug Cutting. It is a remote Procedure Call and serialization framework developed with Apache's Hadoop project. It uses JSON for defining data types and protocols and serializes data in a compact binary format. It offers rich data types and it converts the data in higher-level language into a more compact, binary format. It also provides support for describing service interfaces. (Please note: Though Apache Avro has facilities for interface description and RPC framework, *its ability of data serialization is heavily used in Hadoop projects*. Hence, Apache Avro is discussed in this section.).

```
#writing reading yaml file using Java Application.
Consider a YAML file say for example birds.yml file

#birds.yml
Birds: %
        -parrot
        -peacock
        -eagle

#java application reads birds.yml
import java.io. *;
import org.ho.yaml.Yaml;
public class test
{
        public static void main(String args[]) throws Exception
        {
        System.out.println(Yaml.load("birds.yml");
        }
}
```

```
The output will be:
Birds={parrot, peacock,
eagle}
```

**Listing 4.20 Example to show how a *.yml* file can be read using Java.**

```
import org.ho.yaml.Yaml;
public class Example {
  public static void main(String [] args) throws Exception {
    List <Object> object = new ArrayList<Object>();
object.add("One");
object.add(2);
object.add(455);
Yaml.dump(object, new File("mydata.yml"));
  }
}
```

**Listing 4.21 Example to show a Java program write data into *.yml* file.**

The core facilities of Apache Avro are shown in Figure 4.16.
Features of Apache Avro include:

- It provides rich data structures.
- It serializes the data into a more compact binary data format.
- It is fast to serialize the data.
- It provides a container file to store persistent data.
- It provides a RPC framework.
- It can be easily integrated with dynamic languages.

**Schema Definition with JSON**

Schema is represented using JSON by using *JSON primitive data types* (null, boolean, int, long, float, double, bytes, and string), *JSON objects, and complex types* (record, enum, array, map, union, and fixed). Avro schema files have the file extension *.avsc*.

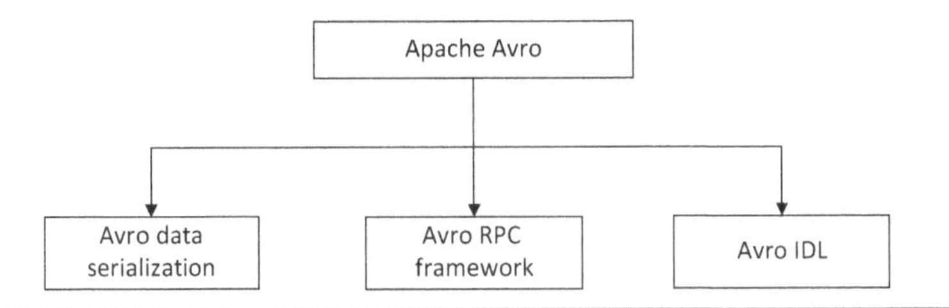


**Figure 4.16 The core facilities of Apache Avro.**

```
{"namespace": "www.xyz.com",
"type": "record",
"name": "Student",
"fields": [
{"name": "student_name", "type": "string"},
{"name": "student_rollno", "type": "int"},
{"name": "student_marks", "type": "int"]}
]
}
```

**Listing 4.22 Schema example in Apache Avro (*student.avsc*).**

Consider a simple schema file *student.avsc* given in Listing 4.22. The *student.avsc* file describes the schema for a complex type with a "record" data structure in Avro. Here, the name given to the type is *student*. The student record consists of three primitive fields, namely name, rollno, and marks. Also, the data types of the fields should be mentioned in the schema.

### Serialization and Deserialization of Data

With Apache Avro tools, classes can be automatically created by compiling the schema file. For example, the following command, given in Figure 4.17, will create a class. (In this example, *student.class* will get generated.)

Now objects can be created from classes and serialized into files. Listing 4.23 is given to show how Apache Avro provides the facility to:

1. Create objects from automatically created classes.
2. Serialize objects into files.
3. Deserialize data from the file as objects.

### Avro IDL

Avro includes support for describing IDL. The Avro IDL( previously called GenAvro) describes the interface of services in a file with the extension *.avdl*, and the interface file is converted into a protocol file with the extension *.avpr*. IDL tools are used for creating interface files and generating protocol files.

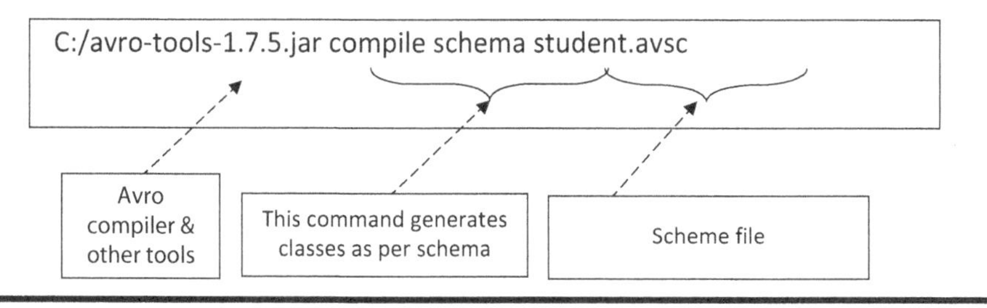


**Figure 4.17 The automatic creation of classes from a schema.**

```
//creation of object
Student mystudent = new Student("Rajkamal", 1001, 450);

//writing object into file - serialization
DatumWriter<Student>mywriter = new DataWriter<Student>(Student.class)
DataFileWriter mydatawriter = new DataFileWriter(mywriter);
Mydatawriter.create(mystudent.getSchema(), new File("students.avro");
Mydatawriter.append(mystudent);
Mydatawrite.close()

//reading objects from file – deserialization
DataFileReaderdata FileReader = new DataFileReader(students.avro, datumReader);
while dataFileReader.hasNext()
{student = dataFileReader.next();
dataFileReader.close();
}
```

Student class

**Listing 4.23 Avro data serialization and deserialization.**

***Summary***

This chapter has introduced WSDL, REST APIs, Apache Thrift APIs, and the Google Protocol Buffer in detail, with examples such as the techniques for designing APIs for microservices. Special emphasis has been given to differentiating API designs and the need for middleware, such as SOAP, Apache Thrift middleware, and gRPC, to establish the communication among different applications or services that are developed in different programming languages and run on different operating systems. The chapter has presented the most popular combinations for API design and middleware development frameworks, which include WSDL with SOAP, REST APIs, and its standard specifications, namely Swagger, RAML, and API BluePrint. The chapter discussed that as REST follows a simple URI(text)-based architecture for accessing services and taking actions within it, it does not require any special middleware. After presenting REST and its specifications, this chapter elaborately discussed the concept of Thrift APIs, the supporting tools of Thrift, the Google Protocol Buffer, and gRPC. Ultimately the chapter described various data formats, XML, JSON, YAML, and Apache Avro.

***Exercises***

1. Briefly explain the role of middleware platforms and APIs in microservices-based application development.
2. Explain how WSDL and SOAP meet the needs of communication among web services.
3. Consider an operation called GetTemperature. This operation takes location as its argument and returns the temperature of the location as a response. Create a service Weather and declare the above operation in it. Design IDL in REST. Add documentation to the IDL using Swagger.
4. Consider a situation where the data needs to be presented in a binary format. In addition, the data needs to be packed as compressed as well as encrypted data. What kind of API would you design? Why?
5. List the advantages of Thrift over REST.
6. Explain how GRPC and Google Protocolbuf meet the needs of the interactions among microservices.
7. What is the special characteristic of JSON that makes it so popular?
8. Compare different data formats for microservices. As a developer, which format do you prefer for your microservices-based application? Justify your ideas.

# References

1. Viktor Farcic. REST API with JSON. 2014. Available at: https://technologyconversations.com/2014/08/12/rest-api-with-json/.
2. What is a REST API? Documenting APIs. Available at: https://idratherbewriting.com/learnapidoc/docapis_what_is_a_rest_api.html.
3. OpenAPI Specification. Swagger. Available at: https://swagger.io/specification/.
4. Keshav Vasudevan. Design First or Code First: What's the Best Approach to API Development? 2018. Available at: https://swagger.io/blog/api-design/design-first-or-code-first-api-development/.
5. https://dzone.com/articles/design-first-or-code-first-whats-the-best-approachwhen to use API-first code-first
6. About RAML. RAML. Available at: https://raml.org/about-raml.
7. API Blueprint tutorial. APIARY. Available at: https://help.apiary.io/api_101/api_blueprint_tutorial/.
8. Thrift protocol stack. ThriftTutorial. Available at: https://thrift-tutorial.readthedocs.io/en/latest/thrift-stack.html
9. https://developers.google.com/protocol-buffers/docs/proto3

# Chapter 5

# Service Discovery and API Gateways

***Objective***

The objective of this chapter is to introduce two related concepts, namely, service discovery and the API gateway. By the end of this chapter, the reader will understand how clients access MSA-based applications, which are comprised of several microservices, through a single-entry point, an API gateway, and supported service discovery mechanisms.

***Preface***

From the previous chapters, the reader will know that microservices can expose their interfaces through APIs and they can interact with each other synchronously or asynchronously using a REST protocol or asynchronous message brokers such as Rabbit MQ or Apache Kafka. Now, the obvious question is:

*How does one service come to know about the other services?*

The key lies in service discovery.

Further, in simple architectures, services are likely to be deployed statically in a single location. But in MSA, since services are allowed to scale independently, service locations become highly dynamic.

*If so, how is service discovery done in MSA?*

Another question that arises is:

We know services are limited in their functionality. Very frequently an MSA application is likely to contain 10 to 100 or more microservices. How do external clients who are likely to work from public networks, such as the internet, access the application? If a client's request is realized by ten services, will it be good for the external client to access all ten services via a public network? Or *can we make the entry point an architectural element?*

The key lies with an API gateway.

Thus, this chapter discusses two essential topics, namely service discovery and API gateways in detail.

## 5.1 The Need for Dynamic Configuration for Microservices Discovery

In order to consume a service, a client should know the IP address/URL address and port of that service instance. The process of finding or discovering the location of the desired service is called service discovery. In traditional applications, running on physical hardware, the network locations of service instances were relatively static. But in MSA, each microservice is allowed to scale independently. Typically, microservices are deployed in a cloud environment. As more and more services and their instances are added to the system, service locations start to change, i.e., services may get created and may get deleted in just a couple of minutes. Service locations start to change, and they become highly dynamic. Hence, the dynamic configuration of the location of microservices becomes essential. As the changes in services take place in a short time span, a matter of minutes, the dynamic configuration of service locations should facilitate an automated service. To meet the automatic and dynamic configuration of service locations, a separate service (called a *discovery service*) should need to be specifically designed to hold the addresses of all other services of the application [1]. Now, it becomes the responsibility of the discovery service to keep all updated locations of available service instances. It becomes sufficient for a consuming service to know only about the *discovery service. In practice, the discovery service is implemented as a service registry where services register themselves and the details of their locations. The services can only be discovered by clients if they are registered in the registry. Thus, service registration is a prerequisite for discovery.*

## 5.2 Service Registry

A key component of service discovery is a service registry, which is a database that contains the locations of all available service instances. It contains the currently-available instances of each service and their connection details. Microservice instances register their details using a *publish API*, using, for example, the POST method of a REST/HTTP API from the registry. This is shown in Figure 5.1.

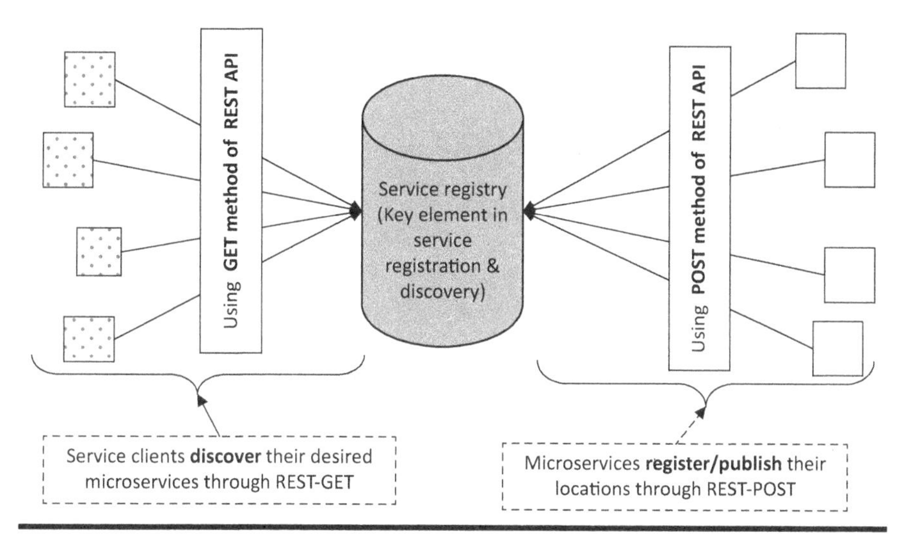


**Figure 5.1 Service registry as a key element in registration and discovery.**

Similarly, service consumers search and find the location of their desired services using a *discovery API*, for example, the GET method of a REST/HTTP API from the registry. The service registry should be readily available and up to date. In order to provide high availability, a registry may be implemented using a cluster of servers with the help of replication protocol to maintain the consistency of data among servers in the cluster.

## 5.3 Service Registration

The service registry is the key element for registration and discovery. The process of registering the location (host and port address) of a service instance along with other metadata such as (i) authentication credentials, (ii) protocols, (iii) versions numbers, and/or (iv) environment details in a central registry is called *service registration*.

Service registration can take place in two ways: (i) self-registration and (ii) third-party registration.

**Self-Registration**

In self-registration, service instances themselves register their name, network location, and port, as shown in Figure 5.2.

After registration, the metadata is refreshed repetitively. Once the service is completed, it deregisters by sending a delete request or by not sending a refresh request. The service registry discards the service if it does not receive a refresh within the specified time.

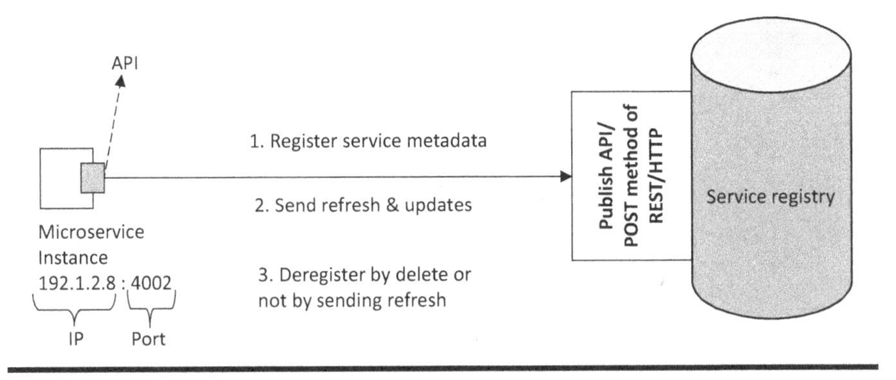


**Figure 5.2 Self-registration.**

## Third-Party Registration

In third-party registration, another component called *service registrar* registers and deregisters the available services with the service registry, as shown in Figure 5.3. Examples of third-party service registrar tools include:

1. ZooKeeper
2. Etcd
3. Consul
4. Eureka

As shown in Figure 5.3, the service registrar component obtains the service metadata of all services and registers them with the registry. It also checks the healthiness of the services and sends a heartbeat to the registry. In addition, it tracks the changes in service metadata by subscribing to the services events. It updates the changes with the registry.

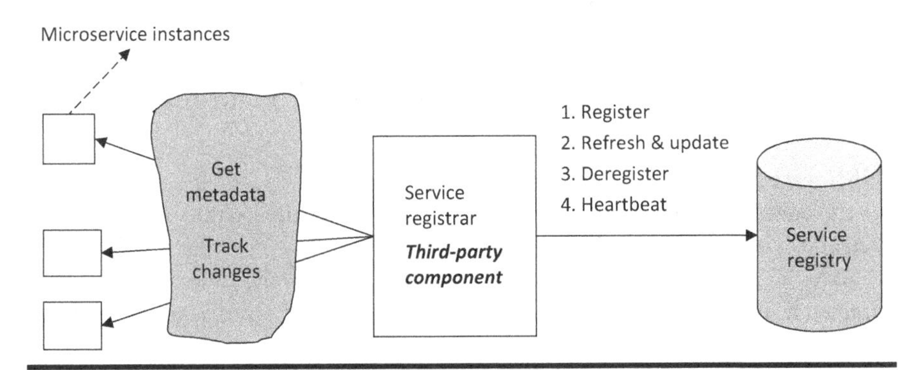


**Figure 5.3 Third-party registration.**

Consuming services first query the service registry to retrieve the details of their required microservice instance and then they connect to it. The registry maintains a heartbeat mechanism to see if services are still active and if not removes them from the registry.

## 5.4 Service Discovery

The process of searching and finding the desired service from the registry is called service discovery. There are two types of service discovery mechanisms, namely (i) client-side discovery and (ii) server-side discovery.

### *5.4.1 Client-Side Discovery*

In client-side discovery, the client is responsible for discovering the service locations of available services, and itself has to submit the request to the appropriate service instance by using a load-balancing algorithm. So, the client contains both a service discovery mechanism and a load-balancing algorithm. As shown in Figure 5.4, consider that there are four service instances that have registered their metadata in the registry. The client discovers the required service using a service discovery mechanism (Step-1—Service discovery). In the above example, four instances will be discovered. Now, the client executes the load-balancing algorithm (Step-2—Load balancing) to find the service with fewer requests, for example, instance-3

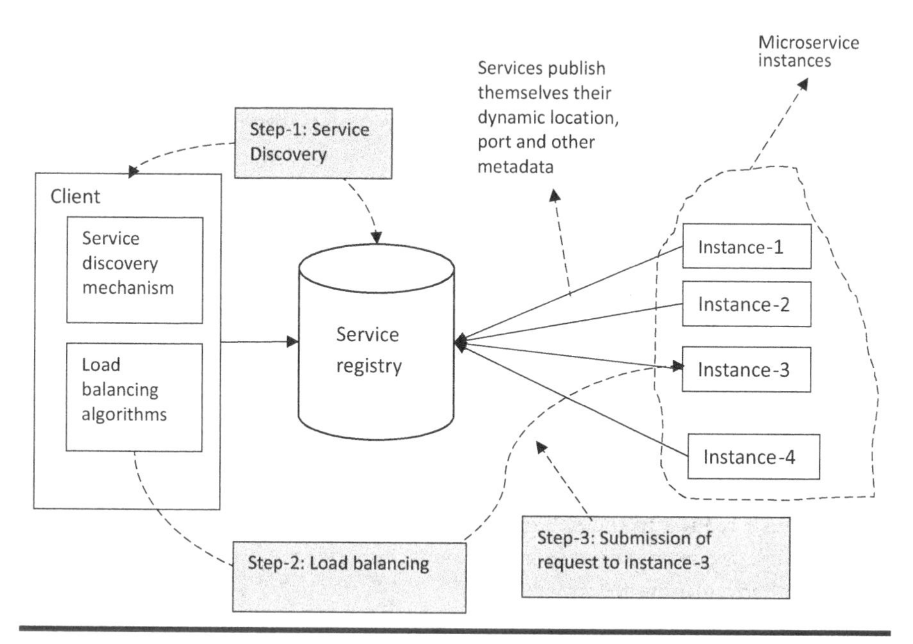


**Figure 5.4 Client-side service discovery.**

is relative with the lesser load. Now the client submits its request to instance-3 (Step-3—Submission of request to instance-3).

In addition, the client also has to track the changes in service metadata. This is done either by polling or by subscribing to service events related to the metadata.

**Advantages**

There is no need to implement service discovery related code in the API gateway.

**Limitations**

- In client-side discovery, a client is forced to query the service registry (Step—1 in Figure 5.4) before performing the actual requests. This requires clients to deal with additional concerns such as load balancing, authentication, etc. [2].
- The client needs to know the fixed endpoint (or endpoints in the case of a clustered registry) to contact the registry.

### *5.4.2 Server-Side Service Discovery*

In server-side service discovery, the client will make a request to a load balancer/API gateway. The load balancer is responsible for discovering the appropriate service instance for the given request and directs the request to the appropriate service instance.

As shown in Figure 5.5, the load balancer should contain the service discovery mechanism and load-balancing algorithm.

- It queries the service registry and finds the service instances which fulfill the client' request (Step 1—Discovery).
- It performs load balancing (Step 2—Load balancing).
- Then submits the client's request to it (Step 3—Request submission).

In addition, the load balancer has to keep track of the service metadata. It tracks the changes by either polling the registry or by subscribing to the events related to metadata changes.

**Advantages**

- The client code is simpler as it does not have to deal with discovery. It simply makes a request to the API gateway/load balancer/router.
- The client does not need to know about the service registry or about multiple instances running for service.
- It simply interacts with the API gateway/router which is has a static IP address.

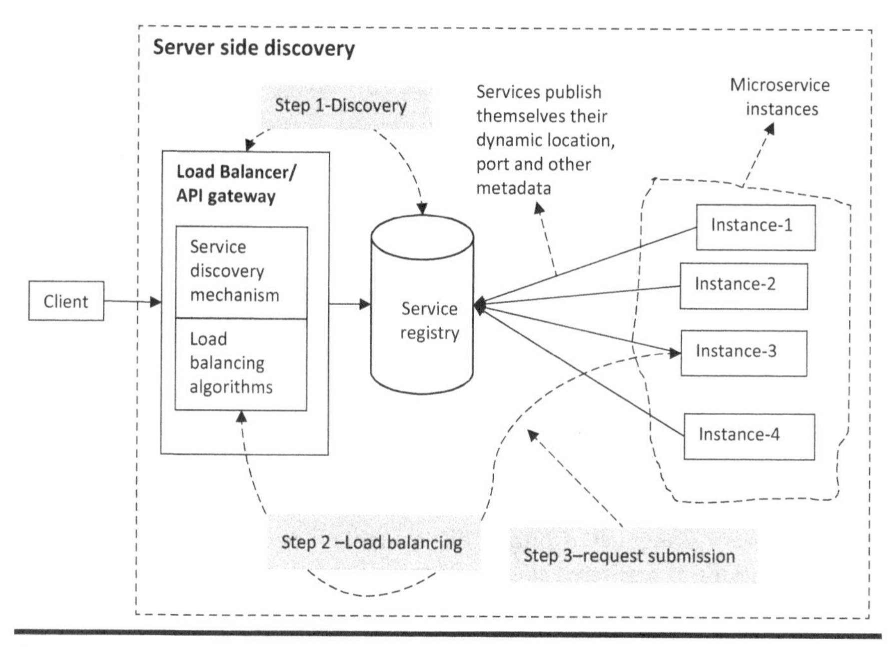


**Figure 5.5 Service side discovery.**

**Disadvantages**

- Discovery, load balancing, and other required code related to service discovery have to be maintained in a separate component API gateway/router/load balancer on the server-side. In addition, this component has to be deployed and maintained separately.
- The API gateway/router/load balancer should be made highly available.

## 5.5 Service Discovery Tools

Existing open source tools for service discovery are of two types [3], as shown in Figure 5.6.

### *5.5.1 General Purpose Discovery Tools*

General purpose tools are actually general purpose data stores. They are typically used for coordination. These tools can be used as service registries as discussed below.

**ZooKeeper**
ZooKeeper is an Apache project that originated from Hadoop. It is a distributed, hierarchical, eventually consistent configuration store that was used to maintain

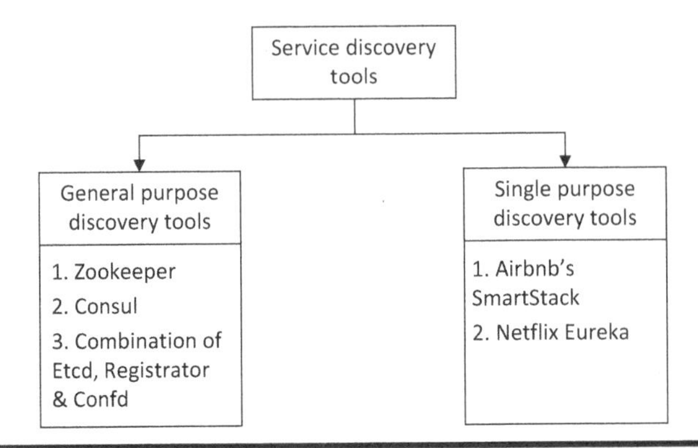


**Figure 5.6 Types of service discovery tools.**

the various components of the Hadoop cluster. By design, ZooKeeper is not a service discovery system. It is only a distributed configuration store that provides notifications to registered clients. With this, it is possible to build a service discovery infrastructure, as shown in Figure 5.7. However, every service must explicitly register with ZooKeeper, and the clients must then check in the configuration [4].

In ZooKeeper key-value entries can be viewed using an ACC Console. There exists an ACC command zk dump which dumps the ZooKeeper configuration entries as key-value pairs [5].

**Advantages**

- Mature
- Robust
- Feature rich

**Disadvantages**

- ZooKeeper's usage of Java gives it many dependencies and makes it more resource intensive.
- The rich features of ZooKeeper make it more complex.

**Consul**

Consul is a decentralized fault-tolerant service from the HashiCorp Company [6]. This means that the Consul architecture consists of a cluster of replicated Consul servers which maintain the data of all service instances.

As shown in Figure 5.8, A Consul agent is installed in each host. Services register their metadata with the Consul server through a Consul agent. Any change in metadata also gets updated in the server. Consul agents interact with the Consul

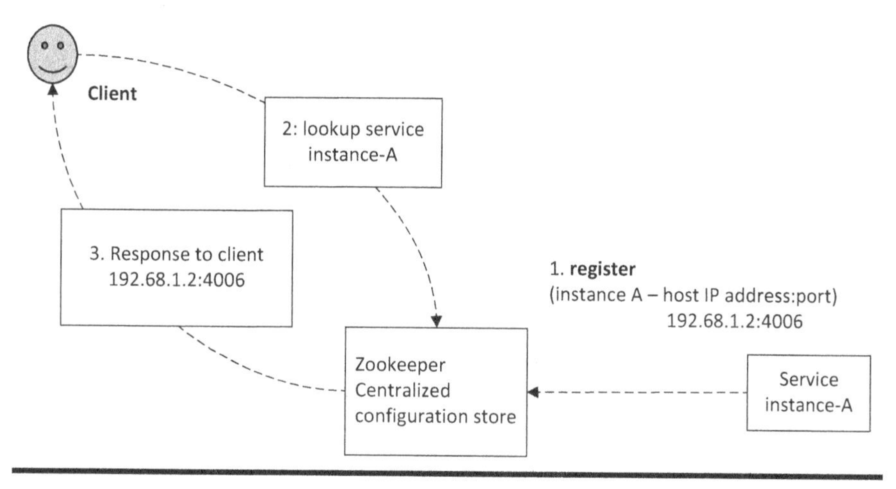


**Figure 5.7 ZooKeeper for service discovery.**

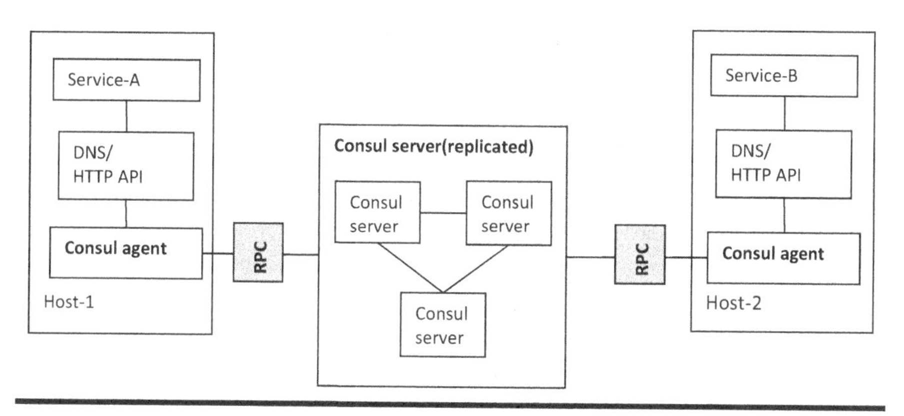


**Figure 5.8 Service discovery with Consul.**

server using a RPC. All Consul agents register the metadata of the service instances deployed in their respective hosts with a Consul cluster. Similarly, when a service wants to search and find its desired service, it makes a request to the Consul agent through a DNS API or HTTP API. The agent will interact with the Consul cluster and find the desired service. Thus, the Consul agent performs two tasks, (i) registering the metadata of microservices with the server and (ii) finding the desired services for clients.

**Combination of Etcd, Registrator, and Confd**

One of the generic registry tools, etcd, is an open source, distributed key-value store developed by CoreOS. It provides a reliable way to store data across a cluster of machines and is accessible through HTTP. It features a hierarchical configuration system that can be used to build service discovery; it is very easy

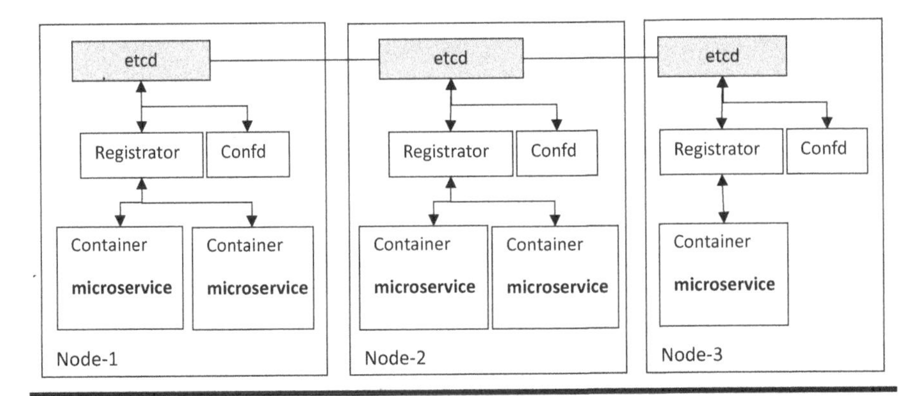


**Figure 5.9 Service discovery using etcd, registrator, and confd in a container environment.**

to deploy, setup, and use; it provides reliable data persistence; it is secure; and it provides very good documentation. Typically etcd is combined with other tools like a registrator and confined to service discovery objectives [7]. This is shown in Figure 5.9.

As discussed in Chapter 2, microservices are commonly deployed in containers. There may be one or more containers in a node. Etcd is a distributed key-value store (see Figure 5.9). The tool *registrator* is used to inspect the containers and automatically registers and deregisters the services deployed in the containers. In addition, another tool called *confd* is a configuration management tool used to keep the data in etcd up to date. Thus, etcd serves as a key-value store, registrator registers/deregister service metadata, and confd keeps the files in etcd up to date.

## 5.5.2 Single-Purpose Service Registry Tools

**Airbnb's SmartStack**

Airbnb's SmartStack is a combination of two custom tools, namely *Nerve* and *Synapse*, that leverage *haproxy* and *ZooKeeper* to handle service registration and discovery. This is shown in Figure 5.10. Both Nerve and Synapse are written in Ruby.

- The nerve runs as a separate process along with the application service. It is responsible for registering services in ZooKeeper. Applications that expose an endpoint to HTTP services are continuously monitored by Nerve and registered in ZooKeeper according to availability.
- Synapse also runs as a separate process in the client and is responsible for service discovery. It queries ZooKeeper for currently registered services and reconfigures a locally running *haproxy* instance. Any client always accesses the local haproxy instance, which will route the request to an available service.

**Netflix Eureka**

Netflix Eureka is a REST (Representational State Transfer)-based service registry that is primarily used in the AWS cloud for locating services. Service discovery using a Eureka server is shown in Figure 5.11.

Service instances register their host address, port, and other metadata with the Eureka server. The Eureka server is a cluster of replicated servers. The server serves as the registry where the locations of service instances exist. Services instances (called

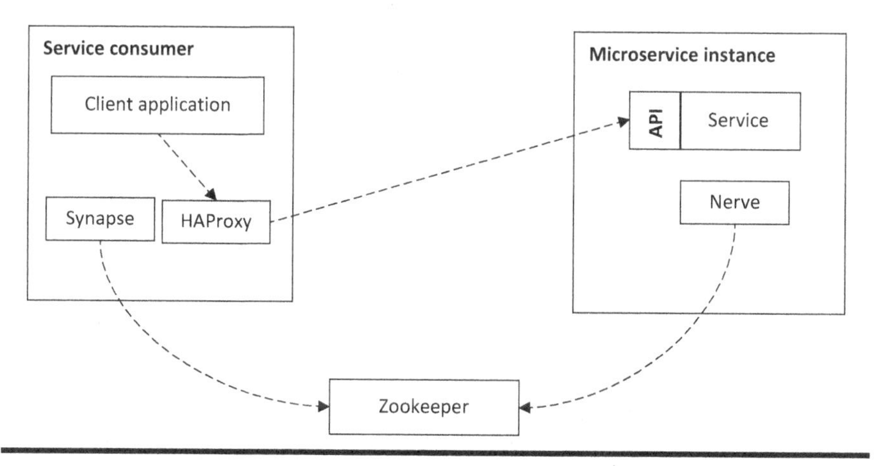


**Figure 5.10 Airbnb's SmartStack for service discovery.**

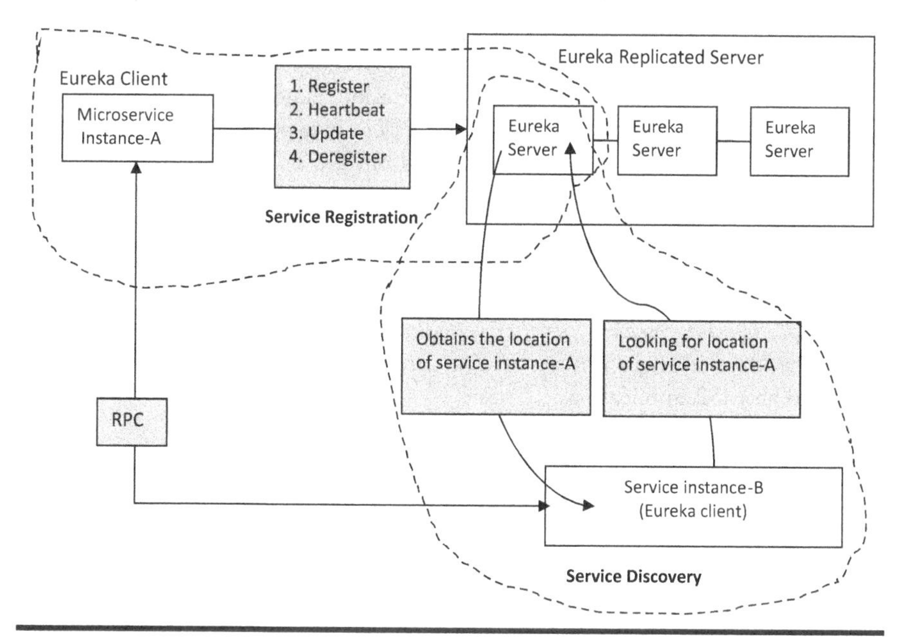


**Figure 5.11 Service discovery using Eureka.**

Eureka clients) interact with the Eureka server using a REST API and register their details with the server using the POST method.

Similarly, the service consumers (these are also called Eureka clients) can discover their desired service instances from the Eureka server by interacting with it using REST GET.

Features of Eureka include the following:

- It provides high availability.
- It provides a graphical web interface to interact with.
- It is a dedicated service discovery solution.
- It is simple, as well as robust.
- It is an open source solution, so no licensing is required.
- Deploying Eureka in multiple AWS regions is a fairly straightforward task as the clusters between regions do not communicate with one another.
- Eureka servers are resilient.

## 5.6 API Gateway

### *5.6.1 The Need for an API Gateway (Single-Entry Point to MSA Applications)*

When an application is developed using MSA, it will be developed as a collection of small microservices designed according to the single responsibility principle. An important aspect of an MSA application is *how to design the client access or invocation for the application*. In a conventional application, exposing the endpoint of the server URL is not difficult; the number of services involved will only be very few. But in MSA, for example, an Amazon application, there are hundreds of microservices involved, even in the launch of a single web page. Typically modern applications, such as LinkedIn, eBay, Amazon, or any other commercial application, tend to have larger websites, and obviously they have to deal with a huge number of microservices. *So, designing how clients are going to access (i.e., whether directly or through some intermediary) an MSA application becomes important.* The following are the key challenges while providing direct access/communication between a client and an MSA application.

1. The microservices of the application are distributed in nature. Each and every service has a specified number of instances according to the required scalability. Similarly, each service instance has its own endpoint. To realize a useful business process, it is necessary to invoke multiple participating services. When a client makes a call to every service over the internet, invoking different services become very inefficient. It involves heavy network traffic, and network latency increases. Implementing client code becomes very complex.

2. One big practical difficulty is that, when service APIs are developed, very frequently the API architects and developers only keep the internal teams in mind, and they tend to develop an API with poor documentation. So, clients find it very difficult to match their requirements with exposed APIs.
3. Each and every service has its own data formats. The services may use different techniques for API designs.
4. The services may use different transport protocols.
5. The services may use different communication protocols.
6. In order to access different services, the client code has to deal with the above heterogeneity.

In order to alleviate the above difficulties, the concept of an API gateway was developed. Thus, an *API gateway serves as single-entry point and enables invocation of services over high-speed LAN.*

Clients make requests from the external internet. Without an API gateway, if a client is making direct communication, many service requests have to go through the internet, which gives poor performance. When the client makes its request to a gateway, the gateway invokes the services within a high-speed Local Area Network (Figure 5.12).

### 5.6.2 Key Functions of the API Gateway

The main purpose of the API gateway is to serve as a frontend entry point to an MSA application. In addition, the API gateway is typically designed to provide the following key functions, as given in Figure 5.13.

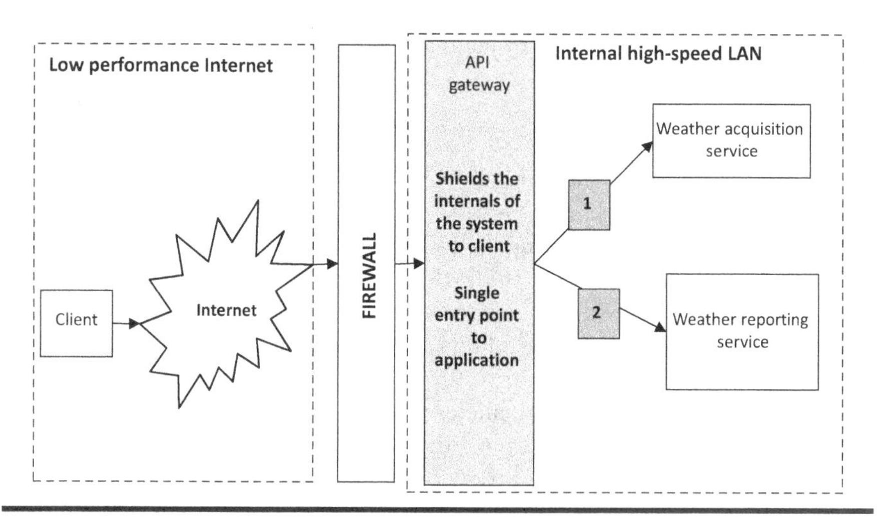


**Figure 5.12 An API gateway invoking services over a high-speed LAN.**

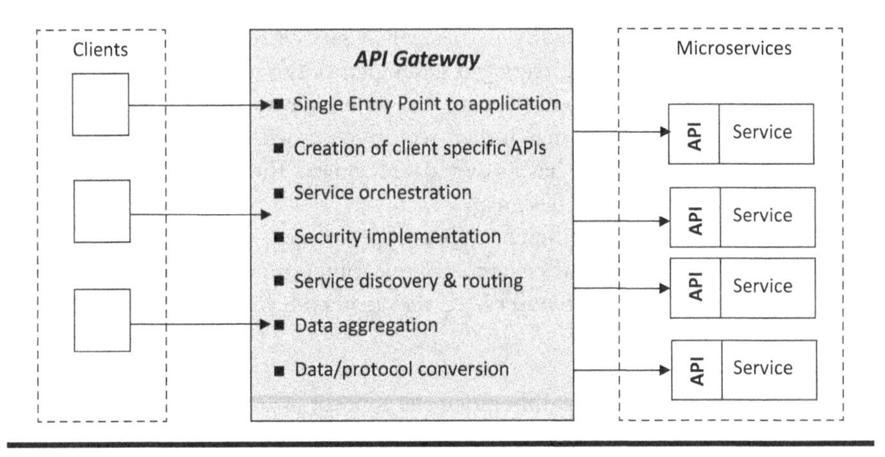


**Figure 5.13 Key functions realized at the API gateway.**

Key functions that are implemented with an API gateway include:

- A single-entry point to the application
- Creation of custom client-specific APIs for applications
- Service orchestration
- Implementation of security
- Service discovery and routing
- Data aggregation

### 5.6.2.1 Creation of Client-Specific APIs at API Gateway

An API gateway abstracts the internal system and provides a client-specific API, as shown in Figure 5.14. Here the key point is a client can access the application using a variety of devices such as:

1. Smartphones with iOS.
2. Smartphones with Android.
3. Laptops or desktops.
4. Any connected device/Bring Your Own Device (BYOD).
5. Pervasive device/Internet of Things (IoT) devices, etc. Thus, different types of clients such as mobile clients, browsers or a traditional server applications or other services, as shown in Figure 5.14, may be interacting with the API gateway.

Internally, in an MSA application, microservices typically use a REST API, Apache Thrift, or Google Protobuf to express their APIs. Now the question is how this generic API will interact with a variety of clients. Here, the API gateway plays a crucial role. It generates client-specific APIs with the required adapter code from the generic API and facilitates the interaction with different kinds of clients.

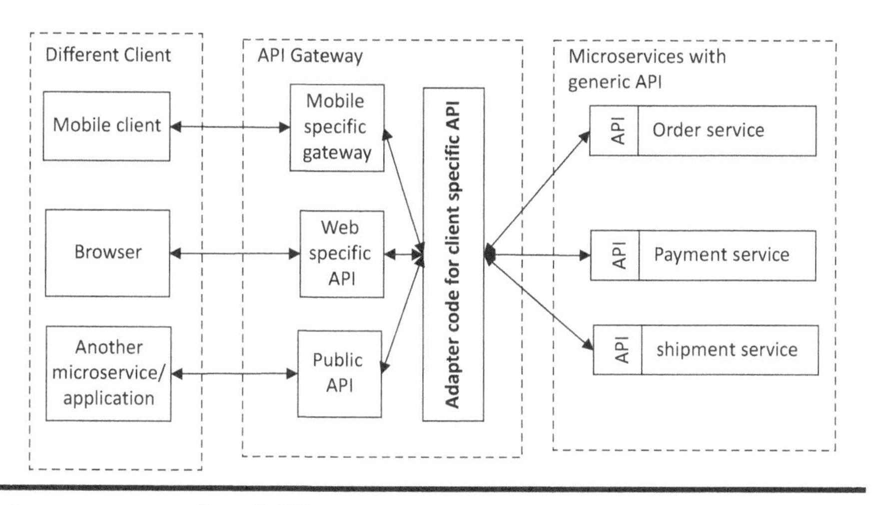


**Figure 5.14 Creation of different client-specific APIs in an API gateway.**

### 5.6.2.2 Service Composition at the API Gateway

There may be situations where more than one service needs to be invoked in order to fulfill a client's requirement. A client may request, for example, the "*travel plan service*," as shown in Figure 5.15. Consider that this service can be realized using three atomic services from different domains. They are the *trained booking service*, *hotel booking service*, and *cab booking service*. The train booking service books tickets from the source to the destination with the date of journey specified. Consider that the destination is the place of stay. Also, consider that the consumer wishes to stay in a hotel at the destination until the date of return. Now, the hotel booking service is used to book a hotel for the desired number of days at the destination location up until the date of return. Similarly, during a stay at the destination, the client wishes to visit different tourist locations. Now the cab booking service is used to book a cab for different locations. Here the key point is that only with the confirmation of

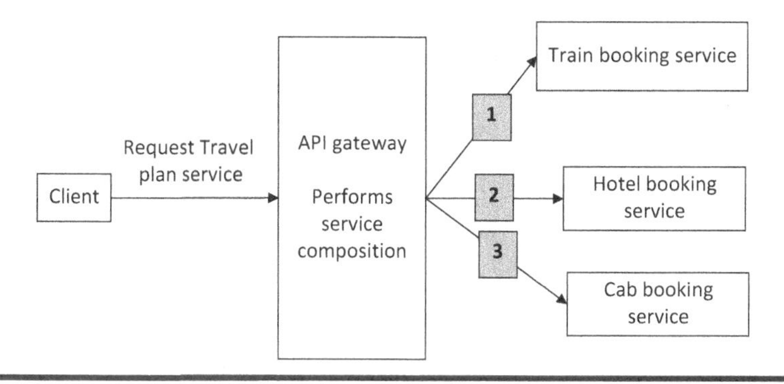


**Figure 5.15 Service composition at the API gateway.**

train tickets, can the hotel be booked. Similarly, only after booking the hotel, can the cab be booked to reach different sightseeing locations from the booked hotel.

Now, when a client makes a request to the "travel plan service," the API gateway performs the service composition by combining the above three services, as shown in Figure 5.15.

The API gateway reduces the number of round trips between the client and the MSA application by composing the three services. There are two important aspects of composition which have to be considered: (i) What are all the services to be invoked in order to fulfill the request and (ii) what is the order and the execution pattern in which the services need to be invoked? These two aspects should be known prior to service composition. Again, there are two techniques to implement service composition. They are (i) service orchestration, where a centralized coordinator will handle the execution of the workflow of the concerned business process, and (ii) service choreography, where the logic of the business process is distributed among different services themselves. (Please note: service orchestration and service choreography are discussed in Chapter 6.)

#### 5.6.2.3 Security Implementation

With MSA, an application is split into multiple microservices, and an access request to each service needs to be authenticated and authorized. This means that the same security logic needs to be implemented in each service. It is inefficient to have every microservice take on the overhead of authenticating the user and then loading the user details from the user information microservice. In practice, every request is authenticated in the API gateway layer. How token-based authentication is implemented in the API gateway is shown in Figures 5.16 and 5.17.

Step 1—Client submits his credentials to the identity server to get an access token.

Step 2—The identity server validates the credentials. If the user is an authenticated user, the server sends an *opaque reference access token* to the client. That is, the identity server will store the contents of the token in a data store and will only issue a unique identifier for this token back to the client. This reference access token is a random and encrypted token which is used outside the network. Step 3—Once the client obtains the reference access token for further requests, it sends both the request and the access token.

Step 4—The API gateway sends the access token received from the user to the identity server.

Step 5—The identity server validates the access token and returns a JSON Web Token (JWT) to the API gateway. *JWT is a token by value, and it contains both user information and access/permission information.*

Step 6—The API gateway uses the JWT token inside the network. It sends the client request to the concerned microservice along with the JWT. Now, the microservice checks for authorization by using the contents of the JWT.

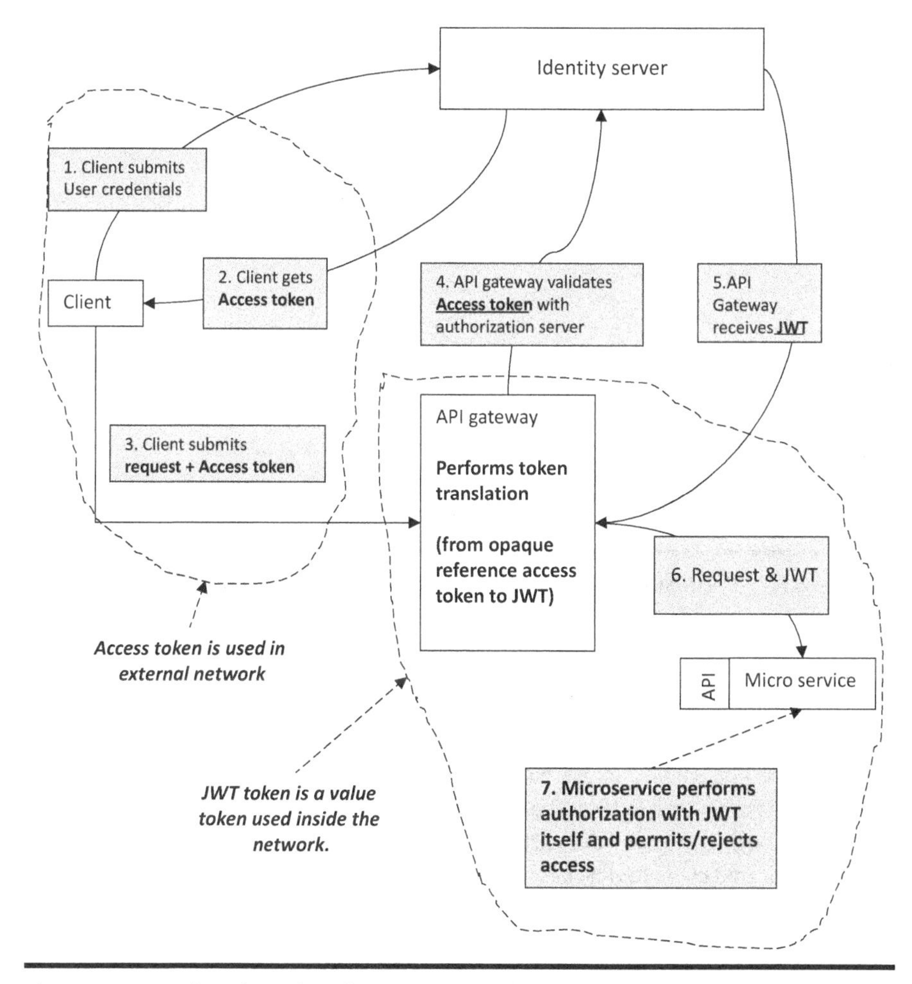


**Figure 5.16 Token-based authentication at the API gateway.**

Step 7—A JWT token is self-contained, carrying in its payload all the identity information (including authorizations), which avoids the need to perform additional calls (for example, a database query) to obtain user information (please see Figure 5.17).

JWT tokens consists of three parts:

1. Header—The header contains a hashing algorithm and type of token.
2. Payload—The payload contains all authorization information and expiry of the token.
3. Signature—The signature refers to the header and payload, which is digitally signed with the server's private key.

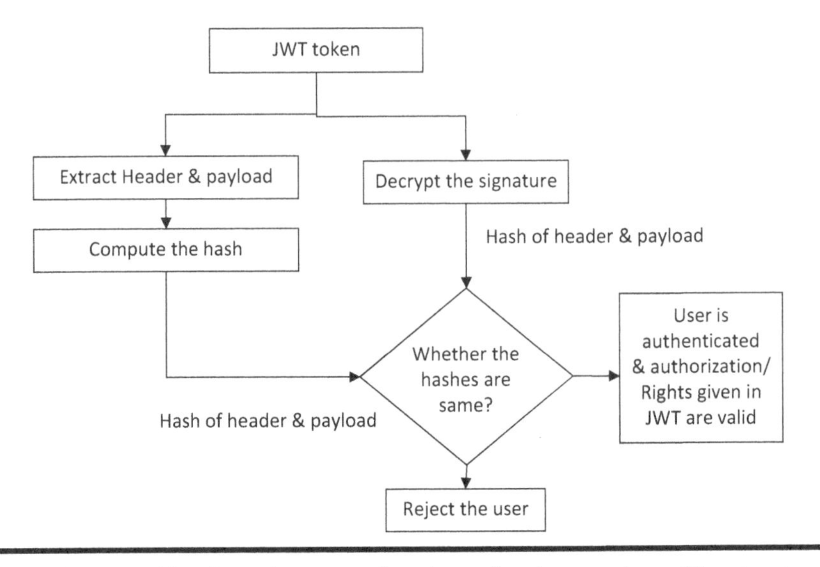


**Figure 5.17 Verification of a JWT token in each microservice without external calls.**

When a JWT is received by a microservice, what happens is:

The microservice extracts the header and payload. It uses the same hash algorithm to compute the hash of the header and payload. Consider this hash as *hash value-1*. Now, it decrypts the signature with the public key of the server. This signature is actually a hash of the header and payload. Consider this decrypted hash value as *hash value-2*. If both the hash values are same, the service will conclude that the client is an authenticated client and he has the permissions and roles as defined in the payload. In this way, it performs an authorization check at the service level and also prevents many calls to the database server for querying authorization details.

In addition, the API gateway has to refresh the JWT before its expiration. It has to send a refresh request to another endpoint, and it gets the same JWT with a new expiration set. Alternately, if JWT expires, the gateway can request new JWT.

### 5.6.2.4 Service Discovery and Routing with an API Gateway

As mentioned earlier, service discovery can be performed in two ways: (i) client-side discovery and (ii) server-side discovery. Server-side discovery can be implemented with an API gateway as shown in Figure 5.18.

When a client makes a request, the API gateway searches in the service registry to find where the desired service is available to match the client's request. If it finds a match, then it routes the request to the concerned service. Another point to note here is that each and every microservice has its own version. *Versioning* can also be handled by an API gateway. The API gateway can be designed to archive the updated endpoints of different versions of the microservices within it. When a client

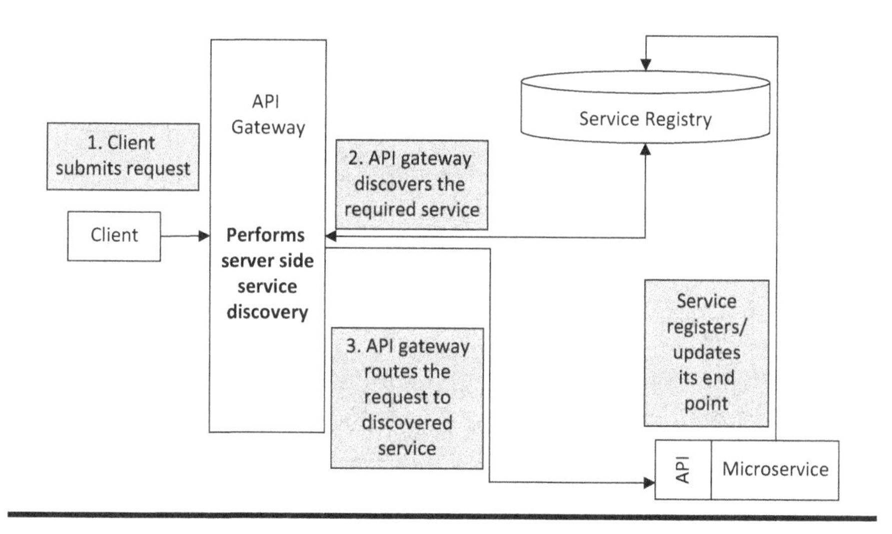


**Figure 5.18 Service discovery and routing with an API gateway.**

makes a request, it handles the request with an updated version of the microservice and routes the request appropriately.

### *5.6.2.5 Data Aggregation with an API Gateway*

As mentioned earlier, in MSA architecture, the microservices are designed with two major design criteria, namely (i) each service should perform single responsibility and (ii) each service should own its private data without sharing. This results in many simple services with their respective data. There are situations where a client may look for data which is actually tied up with different microservices. Now, an API gateway can be designed to aggregate the data from concerned microservices by invoking the services and returning the aggregated data to the user.

As shown in Figure 5.19, the client looks for the orders placed and the amount paid by customer id "5649". The relevant data is tied up with three services, namely the customer service, order service, and payment service. Now the API gateway invokes the three services, obtains the data, combines it as aggregated data, and returns it to the client.

### *5.6.2.6 Data Format/Protocol Conversion at the API Gateway*

As MSA does not mandate any constraints on the technologies used for the development of microservices, they tend to use different data formats for serialization or different protocols for transport. When a request is made with API gateway with a request having different data formats or protocol formats, then the API gateway has to perform the required data and protocol conversion and routes the request to concerned microservice. This is shown in Figure 5.20.

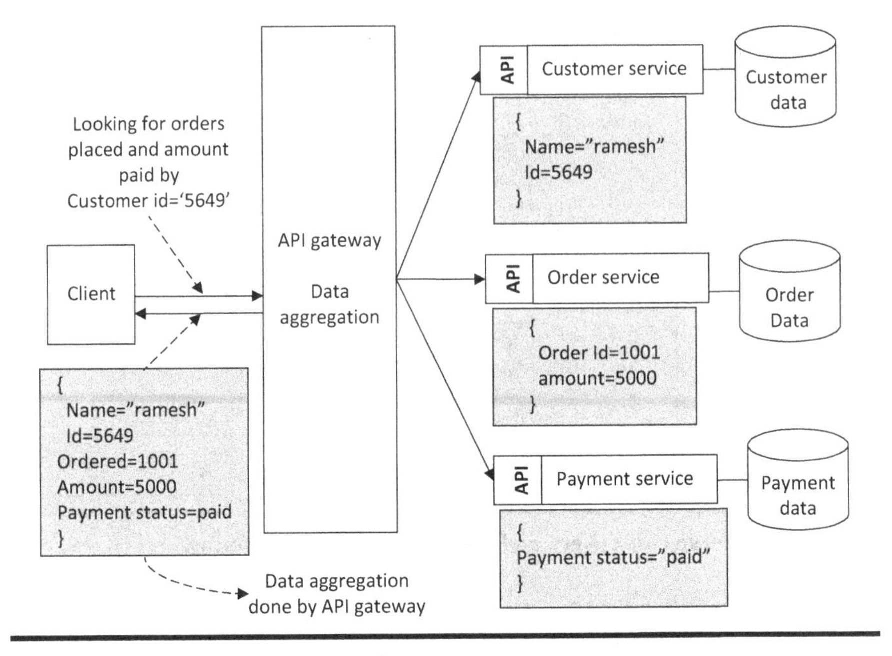


**Figure 5.19 Data aggregation with an API gateway.**

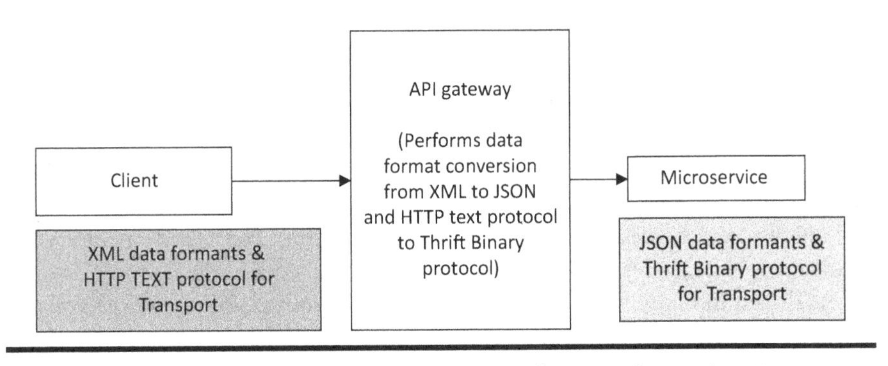


**Figure 5.20 Data format conversion and protocol conversion at the API gateway.**

### *5.6.2.7 Edge Functions at the API Gateway*

The API gateway can also be designed to include the following edge functions:

1. Request rate limiting—The API gateway determines how many requests there are for a service within one second, and it can limit the requests to a particular service.
2. Caching—The API gateway can be designed to cache the results of frequently accessed services and hence the API gateway itself can return the results from the cache to clients without making a request to the services.

3. Metric collection—The API gateway can be designed to collect different metrics such as service or API usage or data accesses to calculate billing.
4. Logging and Auditing—The API gateway can also be designed to include the logging of different operations and further audit those logged events.

**Key Benefits of the API Gateway**

The key benefits of the API gateway include:

1. Provides a single-entry point to the application.
2. Makes the service calls within a high-speed LAN network.
3. Prevents the direct exposure of application to clients.
4. Makes the client code simple. For example, it handles data format conversion or protocol conversion.
5. Performs service discovery and required routing.
6. Reduces the number of client requests by performing service composition and data aggregation.
7. Performs common core services such as authentication and authorization; otherwise, every service has to perform such services.

**Drawbacks of an API Gateway**

As the API gateway is the primary component with which all clients interact, it turns out to be a highly available and scalable component. So it has to be appropriately developed, deployed, and managed. It should be designed in such a way that it should not become a bottleneck for the development and deployment of applications. API gateway functions should be kept as minimal as possible. Only essential functions should be moved to the API gateway.

#### *5.6.2.8 API Gateway—Monitoring and Other Design Considerations*

As the API gateway serves as a single-entry point to an application and it performs various key functions, such as discovery, composition, security, data aggregation, protocol/data transformation, etc., monitoring the API gateway and designing the API gateway with required scalability, availability, and governance guidelines become very important [8]. An API gateway can be monitored by collecting:

- Data related to system status and health
- Network-related data
- Security alerts
- Logs
- Backup and recovery related logs

- Performance related data
- Runtime exceptions
- The number of requests per API

General status related data helps to verify whether the API gateway is up and running. Performance related data is used to understand the load on the system. From the performance related data, one can design how the API gateway has to be scaled. An API gateway can be scaled horizontally (by increasing the number of API gateway instances) or vertically (a single API gateway is equipped with the necessary hardware and software to handle the required scalability).

In addition, the API gateway should be carefully designed to provide the necessary availability to the application. API Gateway instances are usually deployed behind standard load balancers, which periodically query the state of the API Gateway. If a problem occurs, the load balancer redirects traffic to the hot standby instance. The desired level of availability is achieved using three different models, namely:

1. Active/standby
2. Active/passive
3. Active/active

In an *active/standby* model, the standby system is in the turned off state. This system will take over when the active system fails. When failure occurs, the standby system will be made operational, the necessary state is brought, and then it continues its active operation.

In an *active/passive* model, the standby system is turned on, and it is in an operational state, but it does not contain the current state of the active system. During failure, the current state is brought into a passive system, and it will continue the active operation

In an *active/active* system, the standby system also maintains the same state as that of the active system, and it provides zero downtime. When high availability is required, an API gateway should be designed with this model.

Ultimately as the number of APIs increases, it becomes crucial to introduce design guidelines for API designs such as:

1. Defining standards for API definitions
2. Keyword-based API categorization
3. Verification for conformance with API definitions

Along with design guidelines, the monitoring of various activities of the life cycle of the API have to be carried out, such as:

1. Routing to APIs
2. Monitoring API utilization

3. API versioning
4. Rate limiting per API usage
5. Load balancing, etc.

### *5.6.2.9 Open Source Tools for an API Gateway*

An API gateway is a vital piece of infrastructure, as requests will pass through this platform component. Some of the open source API gateway tools include Ambassador and Kong.

**Ambassador**

Ambassador is an open source Kubernetes-native API gateway built on Envoy, designed for microservices. It was developed by Datawire. Ambassador essentially serves as an ingress controller. An ingress controller sits in front of many services with a cluster and routes the traffic to different services in the cluster. The ingress controller is integrated with a service proxy such as Envoy. This is shown in Figure 5.21.

Kubernetes is an open source container orchestration platform which was originally designed by Google and maintained by the Cloud-Native Computing Foundation. The main function of Kubernetes is to orchestrate and manage containers. Kubernetes is a container-centric management platform which provides a different quality of factors such as reliability, availability, and scalability to cloud-native applications. Similarly, the Envoy proxy is the other open source tool developed at Lyft, which is primarily used to provide load balancing. In addition, it can

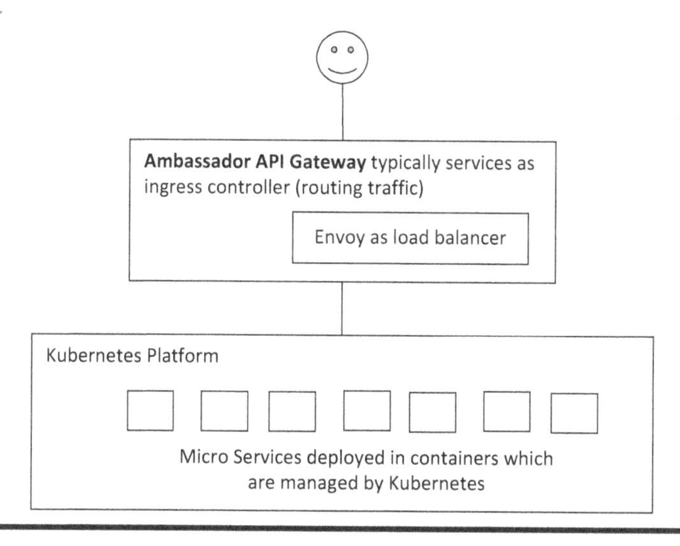


**Figure 5.21 Ambassador as an API gateway routes the traffic to services deployed in Kubernetes.**

also provide observability and the monitoring of data, rate limiting, circuit breaking, service discovery, active/passive health checking, shadowing, outlier detection, statistics, logging, and tracing. Thus, Ambassador serves as ingress controller which works in unison with Envoy and which performs load balancing in Kubernetes platform.

**Kong**

Kong is an open source API gateway which was developed at Mashape. It is written in Lua. Typically, Kong is built on the top of reliable technologies, namely, NGINX, OpenResty, Cassandra, and other plugins, as shown in Figure 5.22.

NGINX is an open source, high-performance HTTP web server. OpenResty is a full-fledged web application platform which extends NGINX by bundling a NGINX core, many modules written in Lua libraries, third-party NGINX modules, and their external dependencies. It is designed for developers to easily build scalable web applications, web services, and dynamic web gateways. Apache Cassandra is a highly scalable, high-performance distributed NoSQL database designed to handle large amounts of data across many commodity servers, providing high availability. On top of these technologies, Kong serves as an open source API gateway for microservices having REST APIs. Kong sits in front of any configured API, and it is the main entry point of any HTTP request. It can be integrated with open source, distributed databases such as Cassandra.

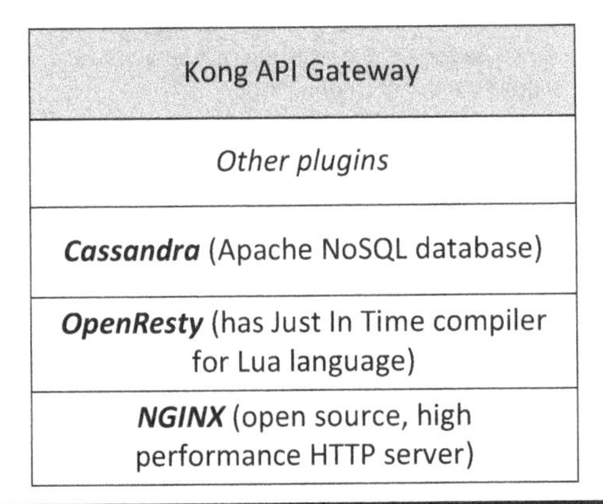


**Figure 5.22 A Kong API gateway on the top of other technologies.**

***Summary***

In this chapter, two major architectural concepts, namely service discovery and the API gateway, were discussed. The need for automatic discovery was emphasized as in modern cloud-based applications the endpoints of services keep on changing. Three key aspects of discovery, namely service registration, service registry, and service discovery, were also discussed. Overviews of existing service discovery tools were described. After describing service discovery, and their related concepts, how an API gateway becomes an essential entry element for MS- based applications was also described. Different key functions, namely the creation of client-specific APIs, service discovery, service composition, protocol/data format transformations, security implementation, were described. An overview of popular API platforms and tools was presented.

***Exercises***

1. Why do we need service discovery?
2. Explain dynamic service discovery?
3. List the key concepts of service discovery? Explain each in detail.
4. Write some notes on the different service discovery tools.
5. Consider that you are developing a small MSA application with four services. Also, consider that your clients are internal to the enterprise. In such a situation, how do you design an entry point to the application? Do you need an API gateway in this case? Justify your answer.
6. Explain the role of an API gateway in MSA.
7. Write some notes on popular open source API gateways.

# References

1. Alejandro Duarte. Microservices: Service Registration and Discovery. 2018. Available at: https://dzone.com/articles/getting-started-with-microservices-2.
2. Sebastian Peyrott. An Introduction to Microservices, Part 3: The Service Registry. 2015. Available at: https://auth0.com/blog/an-introduction-to-microservices-part-3-the-service-registry/.
3. Jason Wilder. Open-Source Service Discovery. Jason Wilder's Blog. 2014. Available at: http://jasonwilder.com/blog/2014/02/04/service-discovery-in-the-cloud/.
4. Simplicity Itself Team. Service Discovery Overview. Available at: http://www.simplicityitself.io/learning/getting-started-microservices/service-discovery-overview.html.
5. Nagarajan Sivaraman. Role of ZooKeeper in webMethods API Portal. 2019. Available at: http://techcommunity.softwareag.com/web/guest/pwiki/-/wiki/Main/Role+of+ZooKeeper+in+webMethods+API+Portal;jsessionid=B704F7EEDE2F7D0CB81A96C4DE62D58F.
6. Vladislav Chernov. Consul Service Discovery Part 1. 2016. Available at: https://dzone.com/articles/consul-service-discovery-part-1.

7. Viktor Farcic. Service Discovery: Zookeeper vs etcd vs Consul. 2015. Available at: https://technologyconversations.com/2015/09/08/service-discovery-zookeeper-vs-etcd-vs-consul/.
8. Sanjay Gadge and Vijaya Kotwani. Microservice Architecture:API Gateway Considerations. 2017. Available at: https://www.globallogic.com/wp-content/uploads/2017/08/Microservice-Architecture-API-Gateway-Considerations.pdf.

# Chapter 6

# Service Orchestration and Choreography

***Objective***

This chapter introduces two service integration/composition techniques, namely service orchestration and choreography for composing individual services so as to achieve a useful business process. It introduces the above concepts using traditional orchestration and choreography languages. Then it discusses how microservices are integrated flexibly and easily with the help of readily available orchestration platforms and workflow engines.

***Preface***

From the previous chapters, the reader will have understood that microservices are based on the Single Responsibility Principle, and they are independent in implementing simple and limited functions. In order to realize a useful business process, the individual microservices need to be composed in a specific pattern. The process of combining individual services is called service composition, which can be performed using two techniques, service orchestration and choreography. In orchestration, a central coordinator contains the processing logic and invokes the individual services according to the desired pattern, whereas in choreography the processing logic is distributed between the individual services so that after the execution of a service it invokes its subsequent service according to the essential preconditions.

This chapter describes the basics of these two techniques, along with orchestration and choreography languages/standards. The chapter presents a simplified description of commonly used orchestration languages, namely Web Services Business Process Execution Language (WS-BPEL), XML LANGuage (XLANG), Business Process Modeling Notation (BPMN), and commonly used choreographic languages such as Web Service Choreography Interface (WSCI) and Web Service Choreography Description Language (WS-CDL).

After describing the basic concepts of orchestration and choreography, the chapter discusses the need for well-developed platforms and tools to monitor and handle the execution of business processes by composing microservices without any failures or operational issues. It discusses various workflow engines and orchestration platforms for microservices such as *Camunda*, *Zeebe*, *Conductor*, *RockScript*, *JOLIE*, and *Jexia*. Ultimately it discusses that simpler business processes can be implemented with event architectures such as Apache Kafka, and complex business processes involving a huge number of microservices are implemented with the help of well-established workflow engines such as Zeebe in combination with Apache Kafka as an event store.

This chapter answers questions such as:

1. What is service composition? What is the necessity for service composition?
2. Why do we require orchestration and choreography?
3. How do microservices employ choreography?
4. Won't it be a burden to manage the workflow for developers?
5. Is there any tool or platform to manage the workflow?

## 6.1 Service Composition

Microservices are typically designed with the Single Responsibility Principle. So, each service has a limited function. Very frequently, it becomes essential to combine the functions of more than one microservice in order to realize a business process/goal. The process of combining more than one service in order to realize a bigger business process according to a specific execution pattern is called service composition. As mentioned earlier, service composition can be performed primarily with two approaches, namely service orchestration and service choreography, and also by using a combination of the two (Figure 6.1).

In service orchestration, a central coordinator coordinates the execution of participating services according to execution pattern or workflow (i.e., the order and pattern in which different services will be invoked), which is expressed using traditional workflow languages such as Business Process Execution Language or using

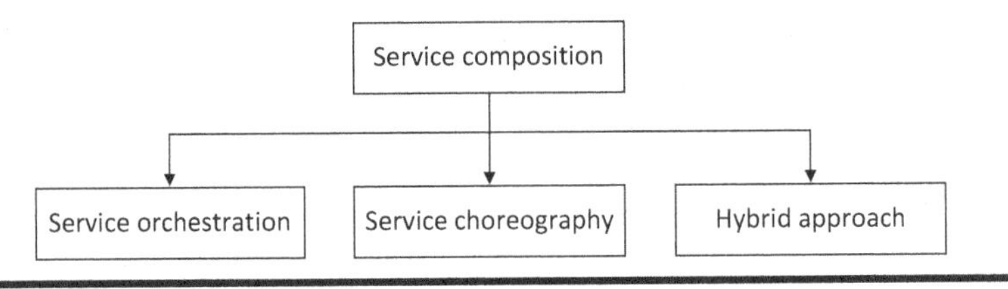


**Figure 6.1 Different approaches to service composition.**

Business Process Modeling Notation that defines the steps of a business process using graphical notation.

In service choreography, there is no centralized coordinator and the logic for realizing a business process is spread between the participating services themselves using choreography specification language such as Web Service Choreography Interface or Web Services Choreography Description Language (WS-CDL). Choreography serves as a programming model for composite application development by defining a system view of service interactions. Choreography understands who works with whom and it can cover any complex operation. Choreography describes (i) what each service does, (ii) how each service interacts with other services, and (iii) how the local interactions contribute to big business processes.

In addition, choreography can include the orchestration of sub-processes also. This means that composition can take place by using a combination of both orchestration and choreography.

## 6.2 Service Orchestration

The primary objective of MSA is to break the given application logic into many independent and loosely coupled microservices according to the Single Responsibility Principle. Since the services are independent and self-contained with their own private data, they can scale independently without affecting the rest of the application. With MSA architecture, the application consists of many microservices with each service capable of delivering a simple, single, and limited functionality. In order to realize a business process, the individual services need to be composed according to a specific execution pattern. Service orchestration is an approach to service composition where a centralized coordinator performs the composition of services according to a particular execution pattern expressed using languages such as BPEL and BPMN. This is shown in Figure 6.2.

In service orchestration, there is a centralized coordinator which contains the processing logic, and which invokes the other participating microservices. Participating microservices behave like normal services, and they do not even know that they are participating in an orchestration. Whenever the coordinator invokes the participating services, they will execute in a usual manner.

### *6.2.1 Orchestration Languages*

Orchestration and choreography languages concentrate on how to specify or express a business process, which is realized by more than one service. It is essential to understand that existing orchestration and choreography languages and standards are developed primarily for SOA. Most of them are XML-based standards and notations (as SOA aims to bring interoperability). But the purpose of MSA is different; it aims to facilitate the frequent deployment and continuous delivery of an application by breaking the application into independent microservices with polyglot support. So, as far as MSA is concerned, it is not necessary to use only XML-based orchestration or choreography languages.

(*Please note: For MSA, the orchestration/choreography languages and standards are not directly used by developers. To facilitate developers, workflow engines and orchestration platforms and tools (which are internally based on BPMN/BPEL) are built, and they are available as readymade solutions with cross-language and cross-platform support.*)

So, any developer can easily and flexibly interact with existing workflow engines such as Zeebe, RockScript, Conductor, JOLIE, etc.

(*Please note: In order to provide a deeper understanding, the basic concepts of orchestration and choreography are discussed using traditional SOA languages. Then an overview of workflow engines and orchestration platforms for microservices is presented.*)

Basically, a business process consists of more than one task which is executed according to a specific execution pattern so that the desired business process is achieved. For example, consider the processing of an order placed by a customer. This process consists of different tasks such as:

(i) Creation of an order once the customer places an order.
(ii) Receive payment from the customer for the goods ordered.
(iii) Ship the goods to the customer.
(iv) Send notifications.

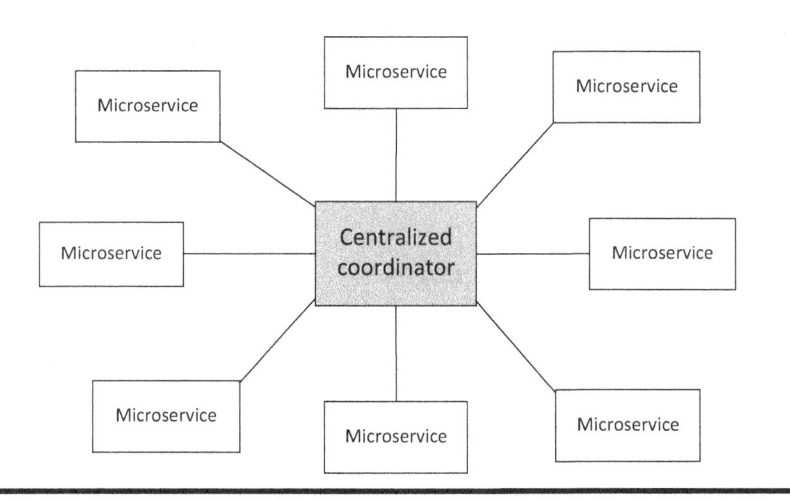


**Figure 6.2 Service orchestration.**

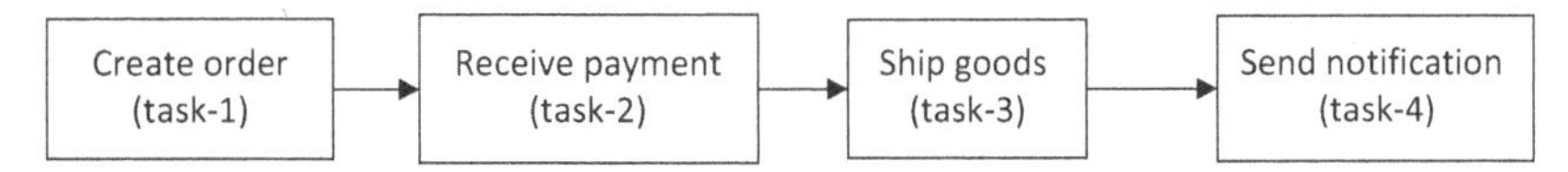


The above tasks are executed in the given ordering. task-1→task-2→task-3→task-4
i.e. sequential workflow

**Figure 6.3 Example workflow.**

Now these four tasks should be executed in the execution pattern given as a workflow, as shown in Figure 6.3.

There are standard languages and notations to represent the workflow of business processes. The workflow may be a simple sequential workflow, as in Figure 6.3, or it may be complex and include the parallel execution of more than one task, executing tasks chosen from different choices, or the execution of tasks based on conditions or iterations, etc.

Some of the commonly used orchestration languages include:

- Business Process Modeling Notation
- Web Services Business Process Execution Language (WS-BPEL/BPEL)
- XML LANGuage (XLANG)

**Business Process Modeling Notation**

BPMN [1] was developed by the Business Process Management Initiative team of the Object Management Group in 2011. BPMN was developed to define the steps of a business process using graphical structures similar to the activity diagram of Unified Modeling Language (UML). BPMN is a standard that is used to describe individual processes as well as interactions among different processes using diagrammatic notations called a Business Process Diagram (BPD), so that various processes and their interactions can be understood by different stakeholders/users of the process, namely business analysts, technical developers, and business managers.

- BPMN is simple and easy to use but has the ability to model complex business processes. It enables developers, analysts, and business managers to communicate business processes in a standardized manner.
- Workflows are modeled by designing the starting event of the business process: business decisions such as branching, iterations, and outputs/results.
- BPMN maps directly to BPEL which was developed using a Pi-Calculus branch of Process Calculi. Pi-Calculus is a formal method of computation for dynamic and mobile processes which ensures that business processes can be directly mapped to any business modeling executable languages for immediate execution.
- Workflows can be exported and imported as BPMN or BPEL files providing an activation layer which enables users to generate applications based on BPMN and BPEL modeling.

### Business Process Execution Language

- Business Process Execution Language for Web Services (BPEL4WS) or Web Services Business Process Execution Language [2] specification was developed and published by Microsoft, IBM, and BEA.
- BPEL is an XML-based language used to define enterprise business processes within Web services.
- The objective of BPEL is to standardize the format of business process flow definition so that different companies can work together seamlessly to achieve a common goal.
- BPEL describes interactions among services and thus supports business transactions.
- Processes written in BPEL can orchestrate interactions among services, and the processes can be executed on any platform.
- BPEL supports two different types of business processes.
  - Executable processes: Models the actual behavior of a participant in a business interaction. It follows the orchestration paradigm and can be executed by an orchestration engine.
  - Abstract processes: Uses process descriptions that specify the mutually visible message exchange behavior of each of the parties involved in the protocol, without revealing their internal behavior. BPEL is used to model the behavior of both executable and abstract processes.
- Important core constructs of BPEL are described in Table 6.1.

**Table 6.1 Basic Constructs of BPEL**

| *Construct* | *Description* |
|---|---|
| <invoke> | Invokes a service |
| <receive> | Waits for client input |
| <wait> | Simple wait for some time |
| <assign> | Used to manipulate variables |
| <throw> | To throw exceptions |
| <reply> | To generate response |
| <terminate> | To terminate the process |
| <sequence> | To have a sequential execution of services |
| <flow> | To have a parallel execution of services |
| <switch case> | To branch into a different logic |
| <while> | To define a loop |

**XLANG**

- Xml LANGuage (XLANG) is an XML-based language for defining business processes from Microsoft. XLANG is used in Microsoft's BizTalk Server and was based on the WSDL language with extensions that describes the behavior of services [3].
- XLANG is a notation for the automation of business processes based on web services for the specification of message exchange behavior among participating web services.
- XLANG has both low-level data types, such as integer and string, as well as high-level constructs such as messages, ports, correlations, and service links to define business processes. In addition, XLANG has process control statements such as *while* or *scope.*
- XLANG statements generally fall into one of two categories, namely (i) simple statements and (ii) complex statements.
- Simple statements act on their own, such as to *receive* or *send.*
- Complex statements contain a group of simple statements or complex statements, such as scope, parallel, and listen.
- In practice, the BizTalk Orchestration Engine executes XLANG files that are produced by a BizTalk Orchestration Designer. Orchestration Designer is a rich graphical tool for visually designing business processes. It generates XLANG files that have an *.odx* extension and contain additional visualization information in their headers and custom attribute information in their bodies.

### 6.2.2 Service Orchestration in Detail (with BPEL)

In this section, orchestration is discussed in detail with process logic defined in BPEL. Consider the example of the purchase order process. This process performs the following tasks:

- Task-1—Receives the purchase order from a customer
- Task-2—Computes the amount to be paid for the items in the purchase order
- Task-3—Receives Payment
- Task-4—Ships goods
- Task-5—Notifies the customer

Service-1, service-2, service-3, service-4, and service-5 are the services that perform task-1, task-2, task-3, task-4, and task-5, respectively. Now the logic for processing a purchasing order is created using Business Process Execution Language. BPEL is a markup language for composing a set of services according to a specific execution pattern in order to realize a composite process. In this example using BPEL,

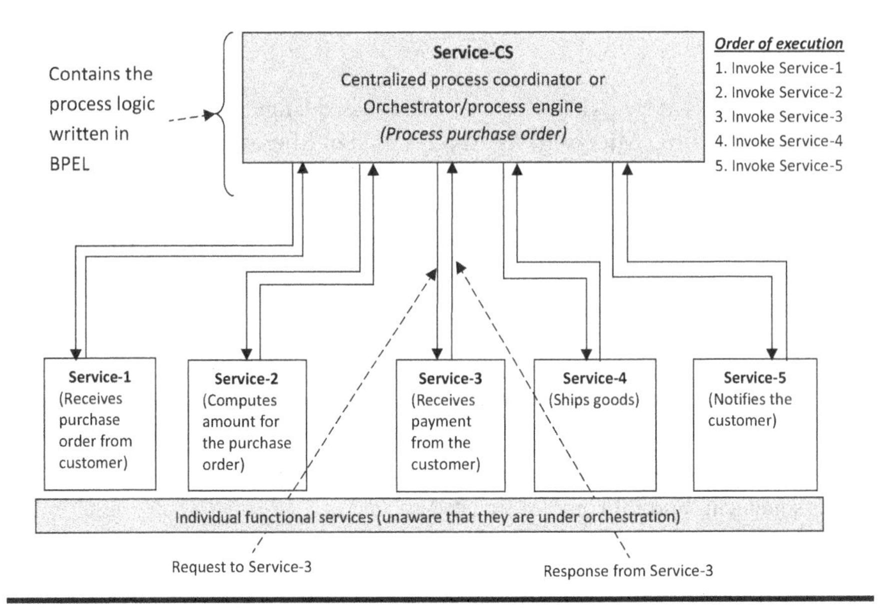


**Figure 6.4 Service orchestration.**

a composite service "service-CS" is created. This service invokes the other services according to the logic written in BPEL. Now, service-CS becomes the central controller for implementing the business process as shown in Figure 6.4, where the processing logic is with service-CS. The individual services are not aware that they are involved in a process.

To provide more of an idea of orchestration, the logic for processing a purchasing order is illustrated through a higher-level schematic, as shown in Figure 6.5, and a sample pseudo-code, in Listing 6.1.

As shown in Figure 6.5, there are two logical entities, (i) processing logic and (ii) individual services. Processing logic has a composite service, which is the coordinator. Individual services get executed in the usual manner when they are invoked even without knowing that they are taking part in the composition.

The above illustrations emphasize that the processing logic is centralized. It invokes the required individual services according to the process logic.

As shown in Figure 6.6, the top layer represents the presentation layer through which clients interact with an MSA-based application. The client's request is supported by a centralized orchestration which contains the processing logic. The orchestration layer invokes different services in the appropriate pattern so as to fulfill the client's request. It takes inputs from the presentation layer and interfaces with the underlying services to produce a business goal. The service layer consists of different kinds of services such as business services, application services, common or utility services, etc.

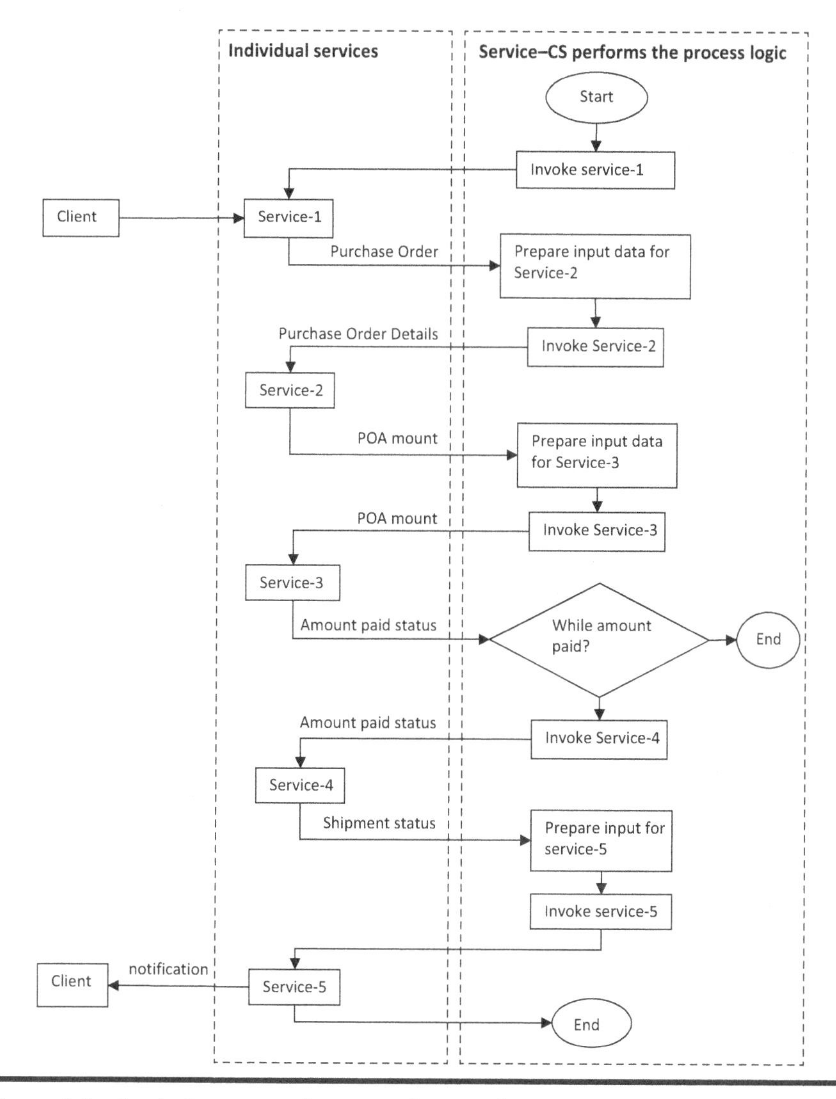


**Figure 6.5 Logic for processing a purchase order.**

### *6.2.3 Service Orchestration in Microservices*

Service orchestration in microservices can be implemented using two methods, as shown in Figure 6.7.

Service orchestration in MSA can be performed:

(i) Using an API gateway as the orchestration layer. This means that the API gateway itself will contain the processing logic of a business process.
(ii) Using a separate composite microservice which invokes the participating microservices.

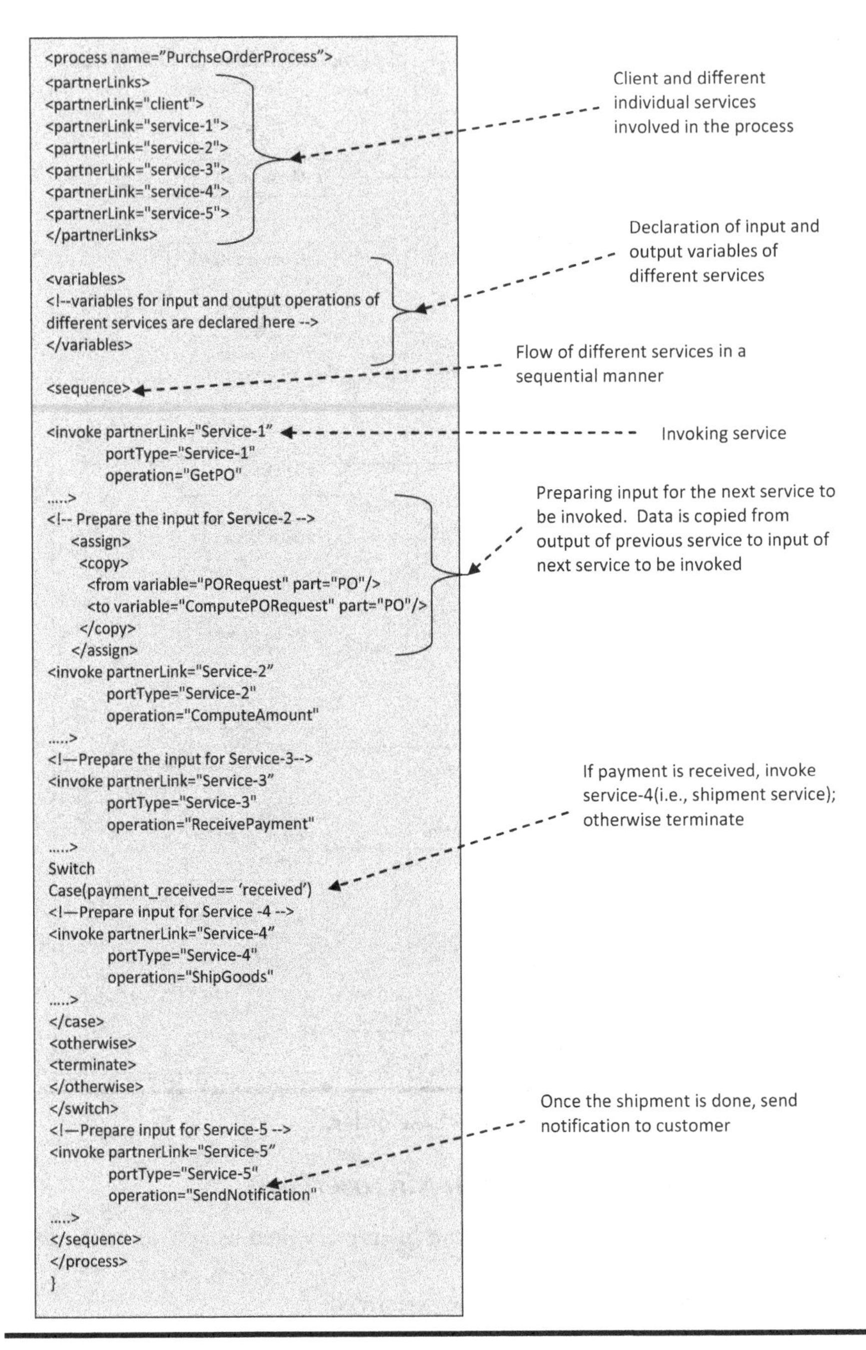

```
<process name="PurchseOrderProcess">
<partnerLinks>
<partnerLink="client">
<partnerLink="service-1">
<partnerLink="service-2">
<partnerLink="service-3">
<partnerLink="service-4">
<partnerLink="service-5">
</partnerLinks>

<variables>
<!--variables for input and output operations of
different services are declared here -->
</variables>

<sequence>

<invoke partnerLink="Service-1"
        portType="Service-1"
        operation="GetPO"
.....>
<!-- Prepare the input for Service-2 -->
   <assign>
    <copy>
     <from variable="PORequest" part="PO"/>
     <to variable="ComputePORequest" part="PO"/>
    </copy>
   </assign>
<invoke partnerLink="Service-2"
        portType="Service-2"
        operation="ComputeAmount"
.....>
<!—Prepare the input for Service-3-->
<invoke partnerLink="Service-3"
        portType="Service-3"
        operation="ReceivePayment"
.....>
Switch
Case(payment_received== 'received')
<!—Prepare input for Service -4 -->
<invoke partnerLink="Service-4"
        portType="Service-4"
        operation="ShipGoods"
.....>
</case>
<otherwise>
<terminate>
</otherwise>
</switch>
<!—Prepare input for Service-5 -->
<invoke partnerLink="Service-5"
        portType="Service-5"
        operation="SendNotification"
.....>
</sequence>
</process>
}
```

Client and different individual services involved in the process
Declaration of input and output variables of different services
Flow of different services in a sequential manner
Invoking service
Preparing input for the next service to be invoked. Data is copied from output of previous service to input of next service to be invoked
If payment is received, invoke service-4(i.e., shipment service); otherwise terminate
Once the shipment is done, send notification to customer

**Listing 6.1 Sample process logic code in BPEL.**

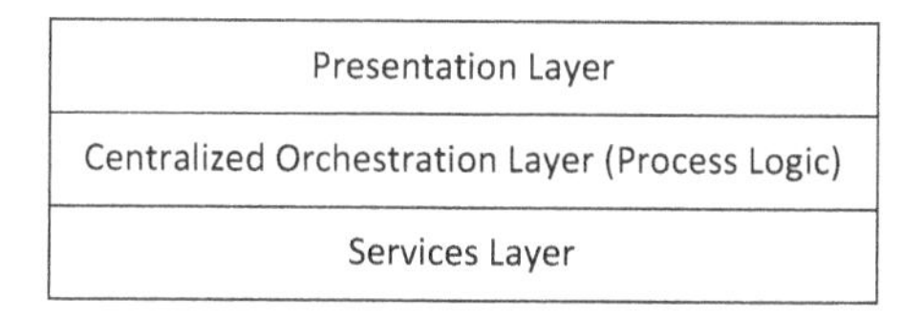


**Figure 6.6 Layers of service orchestration.**

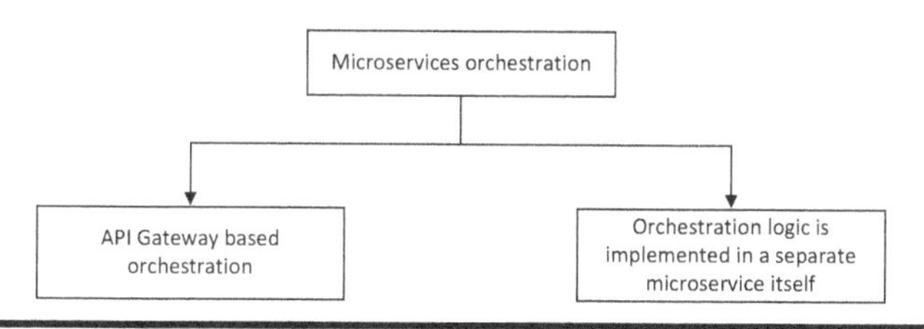


**Figure 6.7 Methods of orchestration in MSA.**

Orchestration using an API gateway is shown in Figure 6.8.

The processing logic is kept in the API gateway. When a client requests a business process, the API gateway serves as the centralized coordinator and executes the business logic with it. It then returns the results to the client.

Alternately, the orchestration logic can be implemented as a composite service which invokes the participating services according to the desired pattern.

## 6.3 Service Choreography

In the service choreography technique, the processing logic of the business process is not at a centralized place, but distributed among the individual services. Choreography describes the collaboration between a collection of services, the interactions in which the participating services engage to achieve this goal, and the dependencies between these interactions, including control-flow dependencies, data-flow dependencies, message correlations, time constraints, transactional dependencies, etc. [4]. Choreography does not describe any internal action that occurs within a participating service. In choreography, all participating services are treated equally, and the required processing logic is distributed among all participating services, as shown in Figure 6.9.

Service choreography can be implemented by incorporating the business process logic among participating services using languages such as a Web Service Choreography Interface and Web Service Choreography Description Language.

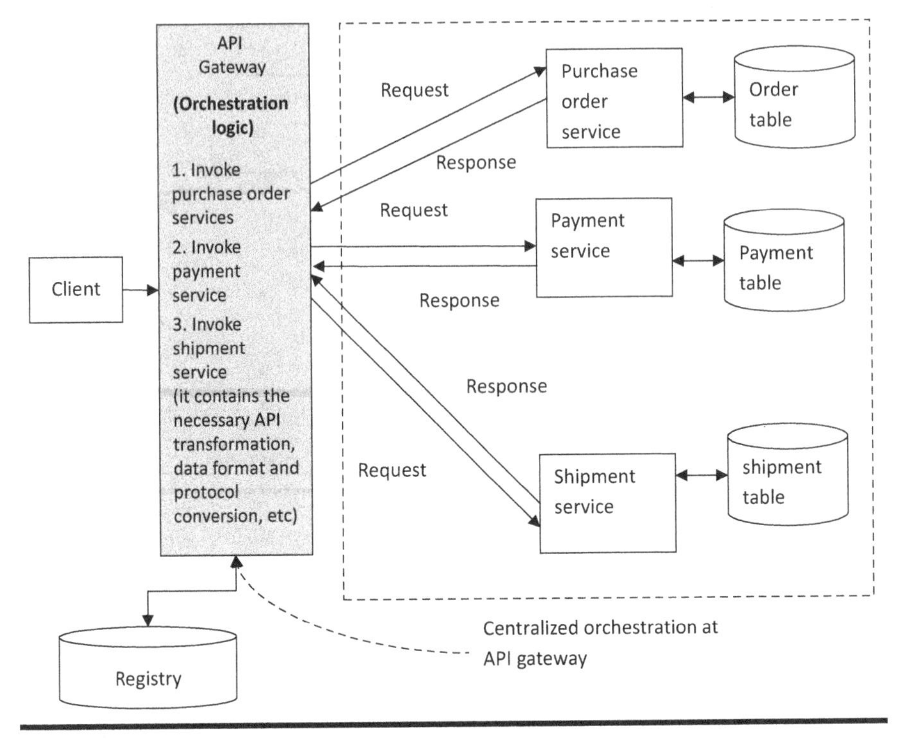


**Figure 6.8 An API Gateway-based orchestration.**

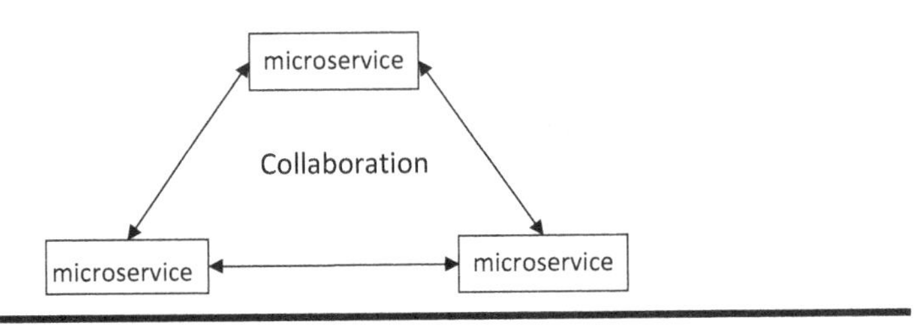


**Figure 6.9 Service choreography.**

## *6.3.1 Choreography Languages*

### Web Service Choreography Interface

- A Web Service Choreography Interface is an XML-based language that describes the flow of messages exchanged by a service participating in a choreographed interaction with other services.
- WSCI was developed by Sun, SAP, BEA, and Intalio.
- A WSCI interface describes the observable behavior, including both temporal and logical dependencies for each web service *as a flow of messages*. So, a WSCI consists of a set of interfaces, one for each service taking part in the choreography.

WSCI describes the behavior of a service in terms of two activities, atomic activity and complex activity. Atomic activities are mapped to operations defined in WSDL. A complex activity consists of more than one atomic activity. Atomic activities contained in a complex activity can take place in Sequence or Parallel or as a Choice. WSCI provides control-flow structures such as while, loop, switch, and other conditional structures [5].

**Choreography with WSCI**

In choreography, the processing logic of the business process is included in the participating services themselves. This has been referred to as *smart endpoints and dumb pipes* by James Lewis and Martin Fowler, which means that the participating services are smart. They contain the intelligence of processing logic. Each participating service knows what to do after executing its part, and accordingly it invokes the subsequent service. The processing logic is choreographed with the help of choreography languages such as Web Service Choreography Interface and Web Service Choreography Description Language. WSCI works in conjunction with WSDL. This is shown in Figure 6.10.

Typically, there are two interfaces for each service.

Static interface—The functional capabilities are described using WSDL. This is a static interface. This interface does not show how a service interacts with other services. WSDL is a static interface and describes the functional features of a service. The root element of WSDL is <definitions>.

Dynamic interface—How one service interacts with other services is captured in the dynamic interface. Within the <definitions> element of WSDL of a service itself, the choreographic stuff of that service is included.

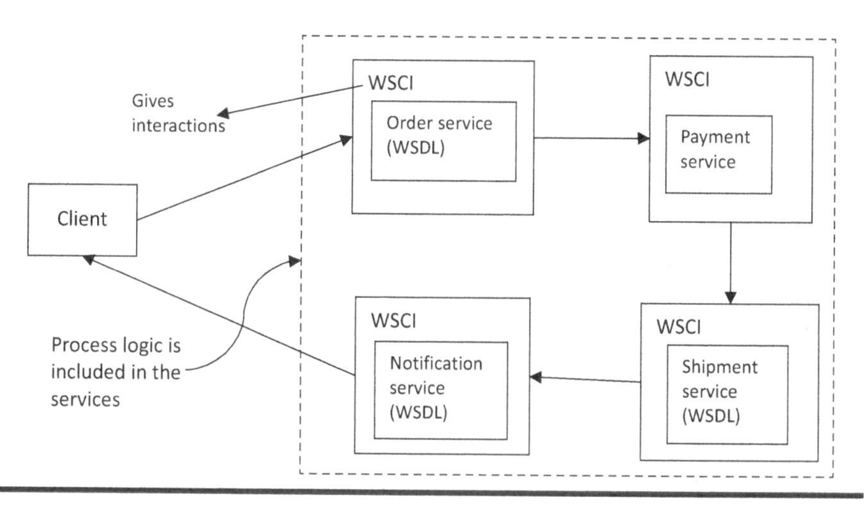


**Figure 6.10 WSCI works in conjunction with WSDL.**

WSCI gives a collaborative extension to WSDL with different specification structures such as message correlation, sequencing rules, exception handling, transactions, and dynamic collaboration.

## Web Service Choreography Description Language

- Web Service Choreography Description Language is an XML-based language that describes peer-to-peer collaborations of web service participants by defining their common and complementary observable behavior; where ordered message exchanges result in accomplishing a common business goal.
- WS-CDL is not explicitly bound to WSDL.
- WS-CDL choreography description is contained in a package and is essentially a container for a collection of activities that may be performed by one or more of the participants. There are three types of activities:
  - *Control-Flow Activities*—control-flow activities are of three types, namely Sequence, Parallel, and Choice. Sequence activities describe that execution of a sequential flow of activities where activities are ordered in a sequence. Parallel activities run simultaneously. Choice activity describe the execution of one activity chosen among a set of alternative activities.
  - *WorkUnit Activities*—A *WorkUnit* activity describes the conditional and, possibly, repeated execution of an activity with a set of guard and repetition conditions.
  - *Basic Activities*—Basic activities include:
    - Interaction
    - NoAction
    - SilentAction
    - Assign
    - Perform

The activities *NoAction* and *SilentAction* describe that no action is performed by a named role which does not affect the rest of the choreography. The Assign activity is used to transfer the value of one variable to another variable. The *Perform activity* is used to call another choreography.

The most important element of WS-CDL is the interaction activity. An interaction describes an exchange of information between participating services with a focus on the receiver of the information. Interactions have one of three purposes: to make a request, to make a response (respond), or to make a request that requires a response (request–respond). An interaction activity description has three main parts corresponding to (i) the participants involved, (ii) the information being exchanged, and (iii) the channel for exchanging the information.

## 6.4 The Need for Orchestration and Choreography Platforms for Microservices

Basically, microservices are designed with limited functionality to realize a useful business goal; it becomes essential to combine different services. Orchestration and choreography are used as the common models of integrating services where the processing logic is distributed among different services.

- When applications grow in size, the number of services involved grows and the overall flow of the process will become difficult to monitor and troubleshoot; i.e., when the number of services grows, the success of the end-to-end process is no longer guaranteed due to expected deadlocks and other issues.
- The choreography approach does not provide the functionality to handle errors in operational issues, failures, or timeouts. The errors are simply reported to the client without any handling mechanisms.

To help the developers, various choreography platforms such as Camunda and Zeebe have been developed. With these platforms, developers can simply incorporate the required workflow or choreography patterns, monitor the business process with visual diagrams, and control the process with efficient error handling mechanisms.

### *6.4.1 Camunda*

Camunda Business Process Management is a lightweight, open source, orchestration platform for Business Process Management. Camunda BPM was released by Camunda, a BPM software company. Camunda BPM can be used as a standalone process engine. It can also be embedded directly with applications developed using Java, .NET, and more. Camunda BPM is a highly available and scalable engine. Camunda defines the workflows using ISO standard BPMN and thus provides a common language for both technical and non-technical users of the applications. Camunda facilitates developers to define the workflows/business processes visually as well as collaborate with other developers. The two major aspects of Camunda include (i) a BPMN for defining workflows/business processes and (ii) a command pattern to execute different tasks

At a higher-level, the architecture of Camunda [6] is as shown in Figure 6.11.

The public API layer allows client applications to interact with the process engine. BPMN is the core of Camunda. It executes the workflows represented in BPMN XML files. The job executor is responsible for processing asynchronous background work. The process engine features a persistence layer responsible for persisting process instance states to a relational database. It is clear that Camunda represents the workflow of a process using BPMN. Consider an example workflow as given in Figure 6.12.

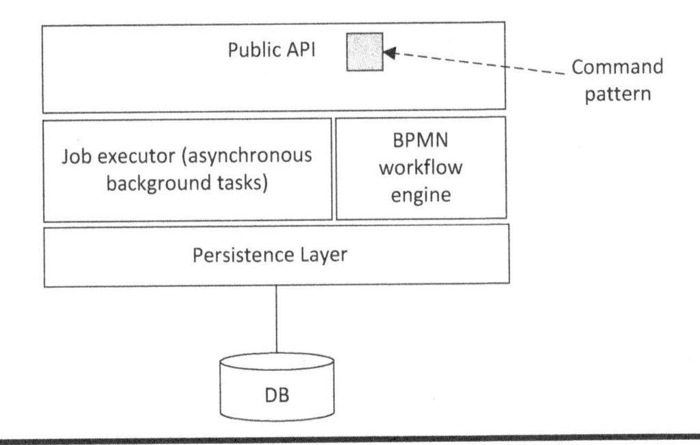


**Figure 6.11 Higher-level architecture of Camunda.**

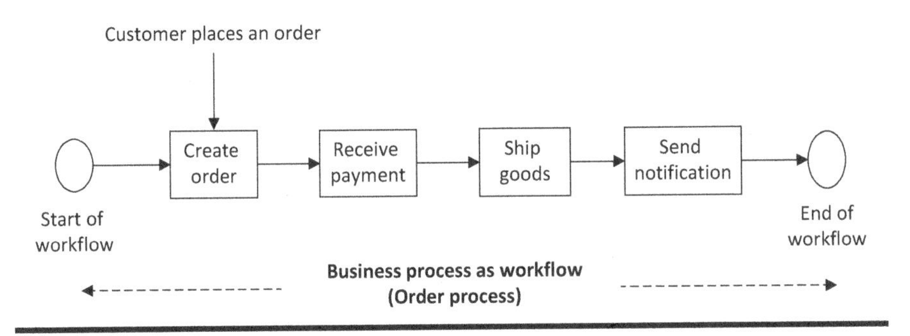


**Figure 6.12 Workflow for order processing.**

In orchestration, the execution of the workflow is initiated by the client through a public API. The execution engine performs the execution of various services by using asynchronous commands and events. Consider, for example, *processing of an order* placed by the customer. As shown in Figure 6.12, the processing of the order consists of a sequence of tasks, namely *create order, receive payment, ship goods*, and *send a notification*. Consider that these services are implemented by an *order service, payment service, shipment service*, and *notification service*. The BPMN engine of Camunda invokes and executes the above workflow as per the order given. Once a customer places an order, the *order service* performs the task of order creation. After creating the order, the engine invokes the *payment service* which receives payment from the customer. Once the payment is received, the engine invokes *ship goods*. After the goods are shipped, the engine invokes the *notification service* which sends a notification to the customer.

## 6.4.2 Zeebe

Zeebe, a new open source project for microservice orchestration, was released by Camunda, the Business Process Management software company in 2018. Zeebe is used to define orchestration flows visually using BPMN and ensures that once started flows are always carried out fully along with retrying steps in case of failures. Zeebe maintains a complete audit log so that the progress of flows can be monitored and tracked. Zeebe is a big data system and scales seamlessly with growing transaction volumes.

Features of *Zeebe* include:

- Visual workflows
- Audit logs and history
- Horizontal scalability
- Durability and fault tolerance
- Fully message-driven
- Easy to operate
- Language agnostic

The architecture of Zeebe [7] is shown in Figure 6.13.

The Zeebe workflow engine consists of four main components, namely client, gateway, broker, and exporter.

***Client***—Client is an application which connects to via a gRPC Zeebe workflow engine to execute a business workflow along with handlers for operational issues.

***Gateway***—Gateway is the single-entry point to a Zeebe cluster. All client requests are submitted to a gateway, which in turn submits to a Zeebe cluster. Gateways can be added in number to achieve high availability and load balancing.

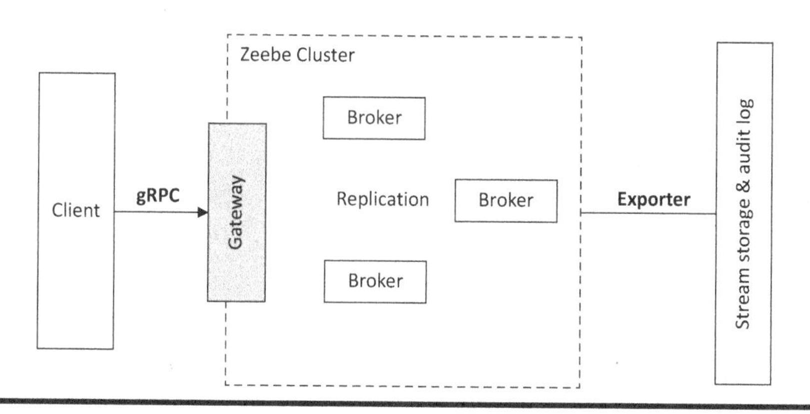


**Figure 6.13 Architecture of Zeebe.**

***Broker***—A broker is the distributed workflow engine which can be replicated for fault tolerance and scalability.

***Exporter***—An exporter consists of API to log all events and state changes that occur in Zeebe in storage.

### *6.4.3 Event-Based Choreography Using Apache Kafka and Zeebe Workflow Engine Zeebe*

In MSA, choreography is commonly implemented using asynchronous messages (or events). Consider an example of asynchronous message/event-based choreography. In decentralized event-based architecture, changes in the state of application are captured as events. The participating services of a business process will become totally loosely coupled from one another; still, they carry out the business process by publishing their events, subscribing their events, and taking actions according to the requirements. Apache Kafka can be used as an event store. Kafka archives all events that occur in the application; i.e., at any instant, the state of the application is obtained by Kafka. Also, each and every service subscribes to its required events and initiates its relevant tasks. (*Please note: as mentioned earlier, each service contains the processing logic (decentralized process logic).*)

When the number of services involved in a business process is small, a simple Kafka architecture is sufficient as each service subscribes to its required messages/events which initiate necessary commands/actions in the services, which subscribe to the events. But when the number of services involved increases, i.e., when the business process involves several services with a complex workflow and distributed services, a workflow engine is required to handle the flow of the business process.

To manage the flow of the business process, Zeebe workflow engine is used in combination with Apache Kafka, as shown in Figure 6.14. Zeebe monitors the orchestration to check whether the workflow is taking place without any operational issues. This means that Zeebe monitors, controls, and manages the workflow by providing different functional features such as:

- Handling operational issues
- Monitoring of working
- Optimizing the workflow
- Creating audit logs
- Providing fault tolerance
- Scalability

Consider the example of order processing using a publish-subscription-based event architecture. Consider four services, *order service*, *payment service*, *shipment service*, and *notification service*. When a customer places an order with the order service, the order service publishes an "order created" event. Consider that the payment service subscribes to the "order created" event. Now the payment service requests payment from the customer. Once the amount is received, it publishes a "payment received" event which in turn is subscribed to by the "shipment service."

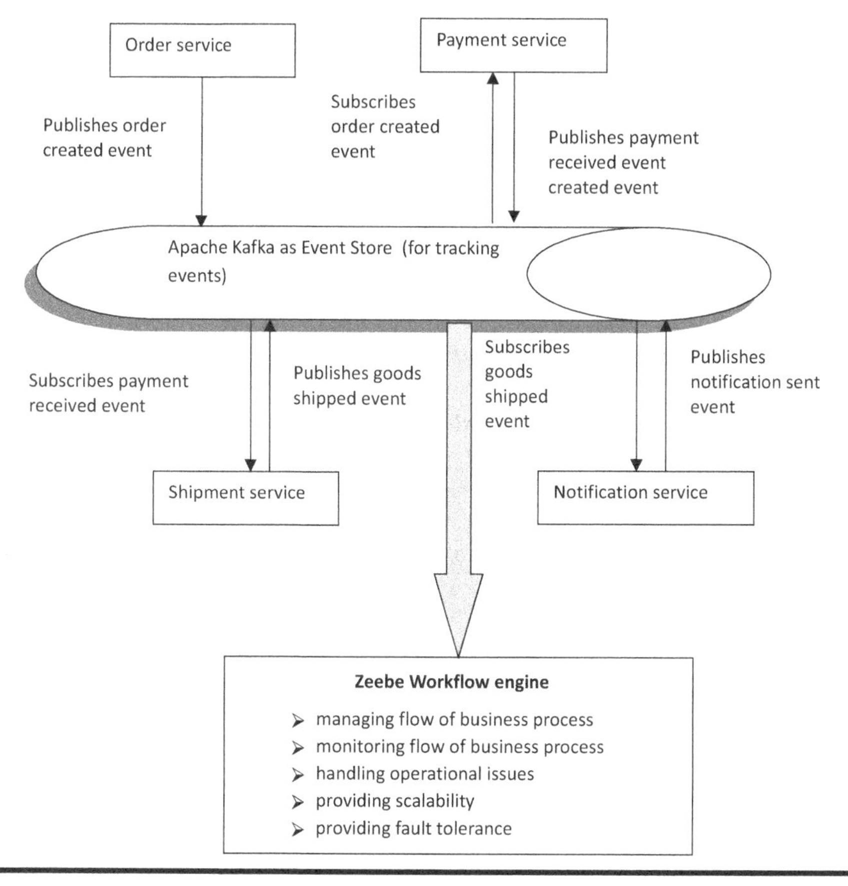


**Figure 6.14 Event-based choreography in MSA using an Apache Kafka and Zeebe engine.**

Now the shipment service ships the goods and publishes an "items shipped" event. On this event, the notification service notifies the customer.

Here, the publishing and subscribing services are totally decoupled. A publishing service does not anything about subscribing services. That is a publishing service that does not even know which services are subscribing it. So, it is the responsibility of the subscribing service to take appropriate action. Thus, asynchronous message-based communication facilitates choreography in a very loosely coupled manner. An important aspect is that the events in the event store are consumed by the Zeebe workflow engine which manages the flow of business process reliably by:

- Handling operational issues
- Monitoring and controlling the execution according to workflow
- Providing scalability
- Providing high availability
- Providing fault tolerance

### 6.4.4 RockScript

RockScript is an open source scripting language and engine for integrating and orchestrating microservices in the style of Event-Driven Architecture (EDA). It was developed by Tom Baeyens. The RockScript engine is an orchestration framework that allows the coordination of transactional activities within distributed microservice systems. Since microservices commonly use JSON over HTTP for their interactions, implementing transactions is difficult. During a transaction, the participating service may fail or crash. *In order to keep consistency when combining multiple microservice interactions for a business process, a record of the call graph and completions and failures must be kept and managed.*

- RockScript engines capture what must happen in response to an event, i.e., events are used as triggers which initiate commands in other services. RockScript ensures the flow of event-command patterns and ensures the successful execution of the workflow.
- With RockScript, it is easy to write small scripts that are connected to events being fired in enterprise systems and to establish trigger connections to scripts.
- RockScript executions are resilient, and the runtime engine ensures that script executions can recover from application and infrastructure crashes.
- The runtime state of each script execution is stored across a cluster using an event sourcing approach, and therefore script executions do not consume resources like threads and memory when they are waiting for asynchronous activities to complete.
- The use of event sourcing also allows the inspection of what happened when something went wrong, such as a server crash, and it is possible to attempt recovery from the last saved execution position.

### 6.4.5 Conductor

The conductor is a workflow orchestration engine that runs in the cloud.

**Features**

- The conductor is a distributed server ecosystem which defines and manages business process workflows in the cloud environment.
- It defines the execution flow using JSON Domain Specific Language (DSL).
- It provides visibility and traceability to process flows.
- It controls the execution of tasks in a workflow with the help of workers.
- It has the ability to pause, resume, restart, retry, and terminate the tasks.
- It allows the reuse of existing microservices.
- It provides a user interface to visualize, replay, and search the process flows.

- It provides high scalability.
- It provides event handlers to control workflows via external actions.
- Applications developed using Java and Python are supported by conductor.

### 6.4.6 *JOLIE*

- Java Orchestration Language Interpreter Engine (JOLIE) is an open source project which was started by Fabrizio Montesi in 2006, at the University of Bolognaan. JOLIE is an interpreter and engine for orchestration programs [8]. It is implemented in Java, and hence it can run on multiple operating systems including Linux-based operating systems, OS X, and Windows.
- The execution of JOLIE programs is mathematically supported by SOCK process calculus. JOLIE extends SOCK with support for various data structures, message types, typed session programming, integration with Java and JavaScript, code mobility, application containment, and web programming.
- JOLIE inherits all the formal semantics of SOCK and provides a C-like syntax which allows the programmer to design the service behavior and the service deployment information separately.
- The service behavior is exploited to design the interaction workflow and the computational functionalities of the service, whereas the service deployment information deals with service interface definition, statefulness, and service session management.
- The primary advantage of JOLIE is that it offers both a simple syntax for dealing with service composition and it is also based on formal semantics which avoids ambiguity.
- By means of JOLIE, it is possible to implement both simple services and complex orchestrators, scaling from handling a few clients to a very high number of connections with invokers and composing services.
- JOLIE offers a programmer-friendly syntax like C and Java that allows for the fast prototyping of services and their subsequent incremental refinement.
- JOLIE offers powerful primitives such as aggregation, embedding, and redirection for service composition. Using these primitives, the services are composed to yield another service which enables the creation of service hierarchies (services containing other services) and building seamless bridges between services that use different interaction protocols or data encodings.
- JOLIE provides a clear separation between the service behavior and its deployment information. This helps in easy implementation of same service behavior but with different communication media and protocols. Bindings and communication protocols for interaction with other services can be dynamically changed. Event new communication protocols can be dynamically added by developing simple Java libraries, called JOLIE extensions. The ability to extend its communication capabilities has proven to be a key factor in integrating JOLIE with a wide range of existing technologies.

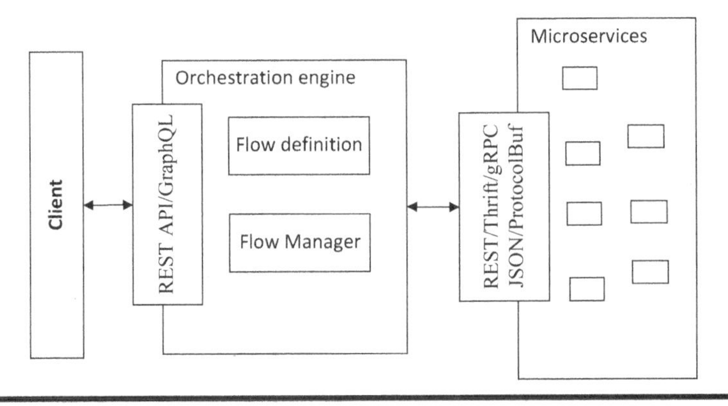


**Figure 6.15 Architecture of Jexia.**

### 6.4.7 *Jexia*

Jexia is an orchestration service, and when it receives a single request from the client, it invokes one or more backend microservices in order to fulfill the request. Jexia orchestration service is fast, simple, dynamic, small, configurable, and easy to use. One of the unique features of Jexia is the flexibility it provides to add new services dynamically to the workflow engine. A higher-level architecture of Jexia workflow engine [9] is shown in Figure 6.15.

As shown in Figure 6.15, in a Jexia orchestration engine, a client application can interact with an orchestration engine using a REST API or GraphQL. The orchestration logic or workflow for business processes are defined in DSL. This represents the flow definition. At any time, new services can be added dynamically into the flow definition. The execution of the workflow is managed by the flow manager. The flow manager interacts with backend microservices by providing support for different middleware such as REST/Thrift/gRPC as well as for different data formats such as JSON or Protobuf.

***Summary***

This chapter described two major techniques, namely, service orchestration and service choreography for composing individual services so as to realize higher-level and useful business processes. It outlined different orchestration languages and choreography languages. It emphasized that there is no need for MSA developers to deal with conventional choreography or orchestration languages; rather, they can simply make use of existing workflow engines and orchestration platforms and tools. The chapter described various facilities provided by the workflow engines such as the visual monitoring and execution of workflow and routines to handle operational failures, errors, and timeouts. The chapter provided an overview of various orchestration platforms such as Camunda, Zeebe, Conductor, RockScript, JOLIE, and

Jexia. Ultimately the chapter highlighted that MSA uses orchestration for distributed, large business processes, and choreography for local business processes.

***Exercises***

1. Why do we need service composition? Consider yourself as an application architect. Assume that you need to integrate a few services to achieve a business process? Explain in detail the issues with service integration.
2. Explain the difference between service orchestration and service choreography.
3. Explain in detail when you should follow service orchestration and when should you prefer service choreography.
4. Explain the need for orchestration platforms for microservices.
5. How does orchestration and choreography in MSA differ from that of SOA?
6. Explain in detail how the orchestration of a large complex business process can be achieved using Apache Kafka and Zeebe. Explain with a real-time e-commerce example.

# References


1. Object Management Group. Business Process Modeling Notation, V1.1. 2008. Available at: https://www.omg.org/bpmn/Documents/BPMN_1-1_Specification.pdf.
2. Matjaz B. Juric. A Hands-on Introduction to BPEL. Available at: https://www.oracle.com/technetwork/articles/matjaz-bpel1-090575.html.
3. Definition of XLANG. PC Mag. Available at: https://www.pcmag.com/encyclopedia/term/55039/xlang.
4. https://www.bptrends.com/publicationfiles/03-05%20WP%20WS-CDL%20Barros%20et%20al.pdf
5. María-Emilia Cambronero, Gregorio Díaz, Enrique Martínez, and Valentín Valero. A comparative study between WSCI, WS-CDL, and OWL-S. 2009. Available at: https://www.researchgate.net/publication/221648366_A_comparative_study_between_WSCI_WS-CDL_and_OWL-S.
6. Architecture Overview. Camunda Docs. Available at: https://docs.camunda.org/manual/7.9/introduction/architecture/.
7. Architecture. Zeebe Documentation. Available at: https://docs.zeebe.io/basics/client-server.html.
8. Fabrizio Montesi, Claudio Guidi, and Gianluigi Zavattaro. Composing Services with JOLIE. 2007. Available at: http://www.cs.unibo.it/cguidi/Publications/ecows07.pdf.
9. Maarten Bezemer. Microservice Orchestration. 2017. Available at: https://medium.com/jexia/microservice-orchestration-9ee71160882f.

*Chapter 7*

# Database Transactions in MSA

***Objective***

The objective of this chapter is to introduce the concept of database transactions in MSA. By the end of this chapter, the reader will know how data is decentralized among different microservices, and how transactions can be carried out in such a decentralized environment with high availability and eventual consistency.

***Preface***

In the previous chapters, the reader has been gradually taught the fundamental concepts of MSA, communication models, API design techniques, middleware support for MSA, service discovery, API gateways, and techniques such as service orchestration and choreography for service integration or composition. It is now the right place to introduce another important concept, database transactions. MSA differs drastically from conventional approaches due to its unique design principle that every microservice should have an independent data store, and can access the data tied up with another service only through its API. Another aspect with MSA is that the microservices are in general distributed. These features make implementing transactions in MSA tough. In addition to transaction concepts, there is another important requirement that MSA applications are likely to have for large websites, for example, Amazon, Facebook, Twitter, eBay, etc. These applications should be highly available to users, as per the CAP theorem which states that either consistency or availability and not both can be achieved in a distributed data store. As availability is of prime importance in e-commerce and modern applications, MSA applications tend to use Basically Available Soft state Eventually consistent (BASE) transaction.

In this context, this chapter describes in detail how conventional transactions with Atomicity, Consistency, Isolation, Durability (ACID) properties could be implemented using a Two-Phase-Commit Protocol, how MSA databases are decentralized among several services, how modern applications have availability as their primary need, how high availability and eventual consistency are obtained using design patterns such as a Command Query Responsibility Segregation (CQRS) pattern and Saga pattern. This chapter answers questions such as:

1. What is the CAP theorem?
2. What are BASE transactions?
3. When should one go for ACID transactions and BASE transactions?
4. Why MSA chooses BASE transactions?
5. How are eventual consistency and high availability achieved?

## 7.1 Database Transactions and ACID Properties

A transaction is a single logical unit of work which is executed as a collection of database operations against a database. Consider an example, say, a *credit card bill payment* for a transaction. A *credit card bill payment* is a transaction, i.e., a logical unit of work consists of two database operations, namely (i) a debit savings bank account and (ii) a credit card account. Only when these two operations are completed, the transaction will be complete.

As shown in Figure 7.1, a transaction contains more than one database operation. In order to maintain the accuracy of the database, the transaction should fulfill a criterion that states that either all the operations contained within a transaction should be executed or none of the operations should be executed. If this is

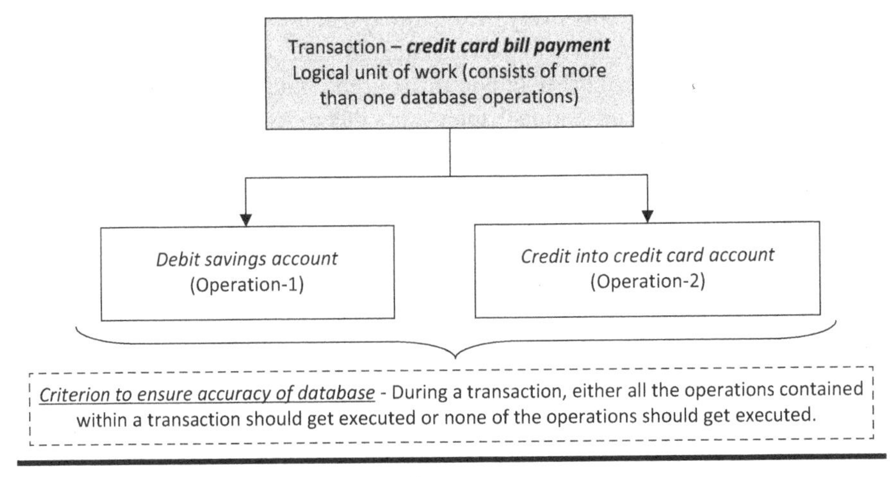


**Figure 7.1 Transactions—an example.**

not fulfilled, then the accuracy of the database cannot be maintained. In order to ensure accuracy, consistency, and integrity, each transaction should contain Atomicity, Consistency, Integrity, and Durability properties [1].

***Atomicity***—The Atomicity property emphasizes that a transaction should occur in its entirety. This means that all the operations contained in a transaction should occur or none of the operations should occur. Atomicity ensures the accuracy of the database. In the example shown in Figure 7.1, an amount of $100 has to be paid through the a credit card bill payment transaction. Now to fulfill this transaction, two operations have to be carried out. *An amount of $100 has to be debited from the savings account, and the same $100 has to be credited into the credit card account.* Only then can the accuracy of the database can be maintained. This is why the Atomicity property specifies that either all the operations should happen or none of the operations should happen.

***Consistency***—The Consistency property emphasizes that a transaction should occur according to serialization in order to preserve the consistency of the database. Basically, there are two operations involved with databases, read operations and write operations. These two operations can access the data with different combinations such as read–write, write–read, write–write, and read–read. Keep in mind that a read–read operation does not have any conflicts. A database can be read by multiple read operations simultaneously without any issues. But when two operations, one read and one write or two write operations are taking place simultaneously, a conflict will occur.

For example, consider two database write–write operations. An amount of $100 has to transferred from account-A to account-B and account-C both. Now this work/requirement has to take place as two database transactions (say transaction-1 and transaction-2) with serialization (i.e., transactions should take place serially). In transaction-1, an amount of $100 has to be debited from account-A and credited in account-B. In transaction-2, an amount of $100 has to be debited from account-A and credited into account-C. If they happen simultaneously, an error may occur as follows. Say, for example, the balance in account-A is say $1000. If the transactions are allowed to occur simultaneously, then both the transactions will consider the balance in account-A as $1000 and after the execution of both the transactions, the balance in A will be wrongly saved as $900, whereas the actual balance is only $800. Hence, in order to maintain the accuracy and logical correctness and consistency of the database, transactions should occur serially. Database management systems typically use a *concurrency control mechanism* to implement serialization. *Each transaction is assigned a unique timestamp value when it starts. So, the database operations can be ordered according to the timestamp.*

***Isolation***—This property emphasizes that each transaction should occur in isolation. This means that when a transaction is in progress, the other transactions cannot see the intermediate results of the ongoing transaction. The locking mechanism is used to implement isolation. When a resource is accessed by a transaction, it is locked. If any other transaction needs to access the resource which is already

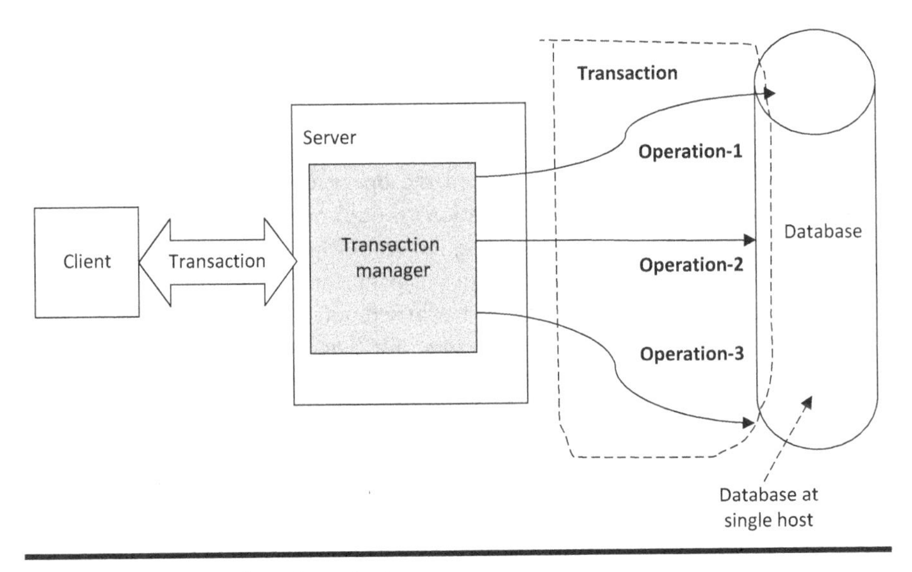


**Figure 7.2 Transactions in a single server.**

locked, the transaction manager has to check the type of lock (read lock and write lock) and type of access (read or write) and accordingly it will take the decision to release the resource.

***Durability***—Once a transaction completes successfully, the changes it has made into the database should be made permanent even if there is a system failure. The recovery-management component of database systems ensure the durability of the transaction. Transaction logs (which are flat files) can be used to rectify errors due to hardware failures. That is, a database management system reviews the transaction logs for any uncommitted transactions, and it rolls back uncommitted transactions.

**Database Transactions in a Single Server**

When the database is deployed in a single machine, i.e., with centralized databases, implementing a transaction is simple. Transactions are managed by a transaction manager as shown in Figure 7.2.

As shown in Figure 7.2, when the database is in a single server, a transaction manager manages the execution of a transaction in a single host without any difficulty.

## 7.2 Distributed Transactions and Two-Phase-Commit Protocol (in Conventional Systems)

When the database is distributed over different servers or hosts at different sites, as shown in Figure 7.3, a Two-Phase-Commit (2PC) Protocol [2] is used to manage the execution of the transaction.

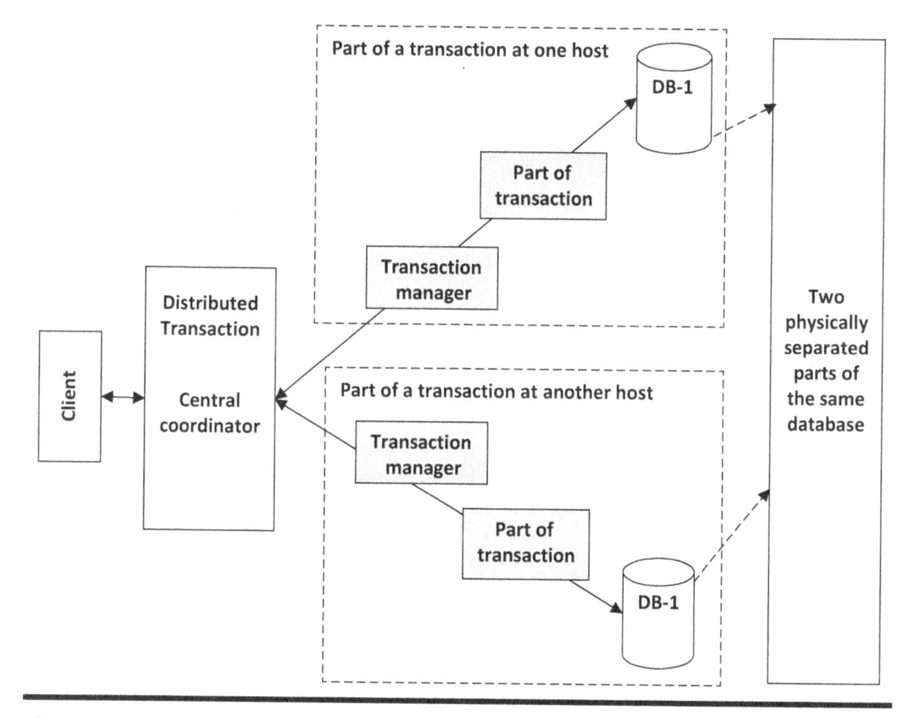


**Figure 7.3 A database distributed in more than one server.**

A distributed transaction is a database transaction in which two or more network hosts are involved. That is, a distributed transaction is a transaction which invokes database operations from several different servers. In Figure 7.3, a single database *DB-1* is distributed over two hosts. In each host, the transaction is managed by its local transaction manager. Also, in distributed transactions, one host is designated as a central coordinator (see Figure 7.3) which is the master, and other servers are participants (or slaves). The master node manages the distributed transaction using a Two-Phase-Commit Protocol. When a client initiates or sends a transaction to the transaction coordinator, the coordinator manages the execution of the transaction using the 2PC Protocol.

In a 2PC Protocol, there are two phases, the *prepare phase* and the *commit phase*. In the *prepare phase*, the coordinator sends a query to the transaction managers and different hosts to commit. Then the coordinator waits for an agreement message from all hosts.

After receiving the *ready/not ready signals* from all the participating transaction managers, the coordinator will make a decision whether to commit or abort (i.e., if the coordinator receives "ready" from all hosts, it will send commit to all hosts. If it receives "not ready" or fail from even one host, then it will abort the transaction). In the *commit phase*, it will send commit/abort to all participating hosts.

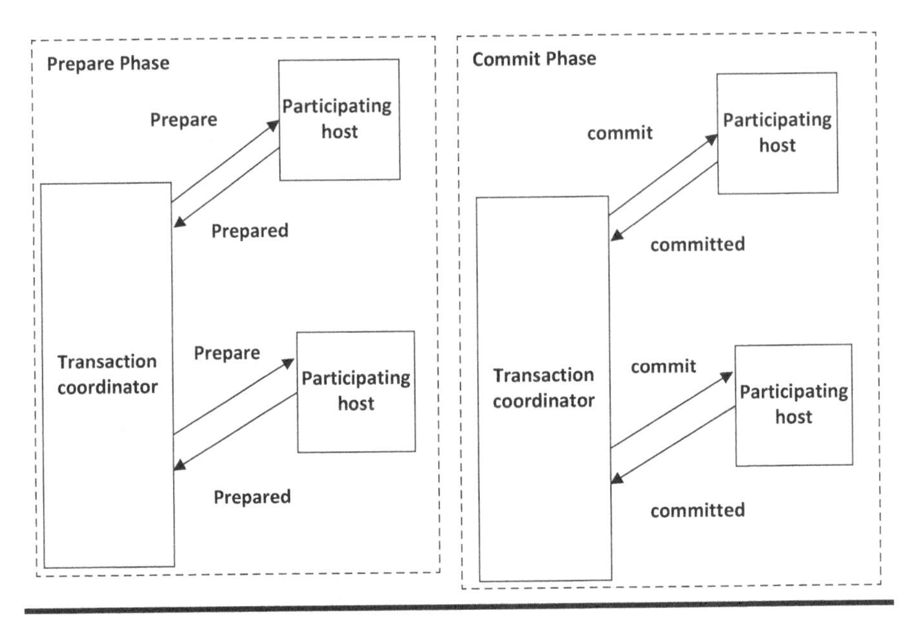


**Figure 7.4 The Two-Phase-Commit Protocol.**

After performing commit/rollback, the participating hosts send a committed signal to the coordinator. This is shown in Figure 7.4.

**Disadvantages of a Two-Phase-Commit Protocol**

- The Two-Phase-Commit Protocol is a blocking protocol, i.e., a node will block activity while it is waiting for a message from the coordinator node.
- A node will lock the resources when it is in a wait state. So, other processes will have to wait until the resources are released.
- Similarly, if the coordinator fails permanently, all participating nodes will have to wait forever.

## 7.3 Nature of Databases and Database Access in MSA

According to Microservices Architecture, an application is broken into many independent microservices based on the single responsibility principle. In order to provide full independence to services, each service needs to contain its own data. In practice, microservices may work with different tables of the same databases. So, they are likely to have different instances of the same databases, as shown in Figure 7.5, or the database itself may be split into different databases, tables, flat files, or NoSQL databases, which can be implemented using different technologies (i.e., polyglot persistence), as shown in Figure 7.6.

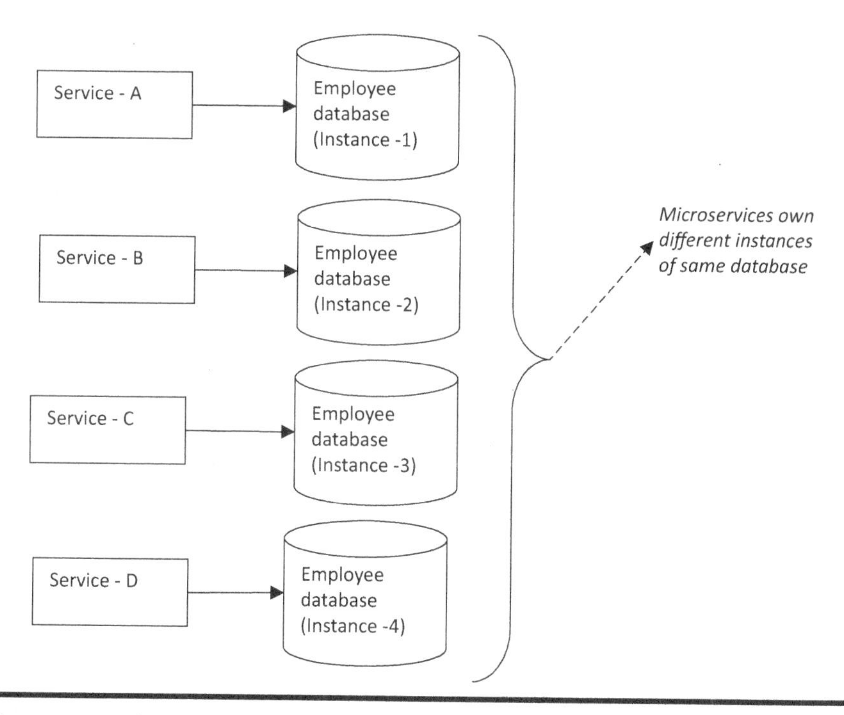


**Figure 7.5 Microservices having different instances of the same database.**

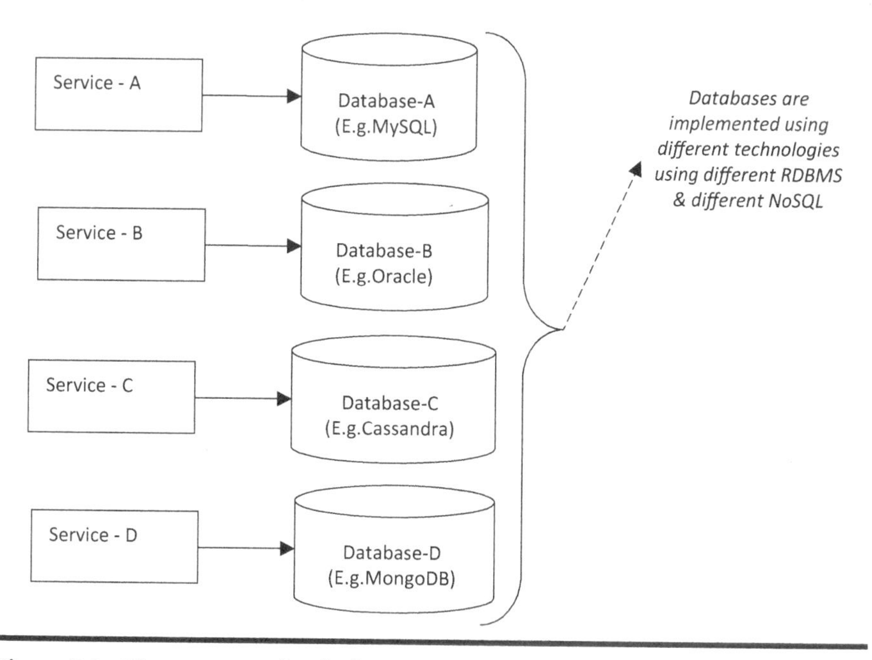


**Figure 7.6 The concept of polyglot persistence.**

In either case, each microservice is designed to work with its data independently. Each microservice has its own relevant dataset. When a microservice has its own database, it does not need to depend on other services. It can attain full independence and loose coupling with other services. Microservices are typically deployed in different servers or containers distributed over different locations. In addition, in MSA if a microservice needs to access the data associated with another service, it can do so only through the API of that microservice. The same database cannot be shared directly by more than one service. This is shown in Figure 7.7

Thus, in MSA:

- Each service should contain its own data.
- A service cannot share the same data tied up with another service. It can access data of another service only through its API.
- Databases may be SQL databases or NoSQL databases, flat files.
- Databases are distributed over different services and locations.
- Data is decentralized among different services.

## 7.3.1 Why Avoid ACID Transactions with 2PC in MSA?

The decentralized nature of data across different microservices has implications while data is updated. Since the data is tied up with different microservices, when a particular data is updated, all the services which need to handle that data need to

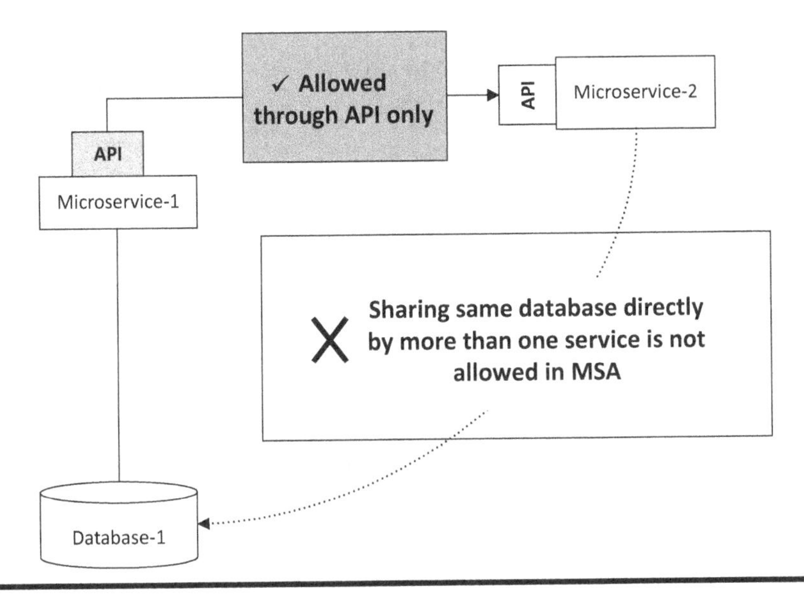


**Figure 7.7 Data access is only through an API.**

carry out the update and guarantee the consistency of the data. Also, data attached with one service can be accessed only through its API. Please remember, conventional applications having centralized databases use ACID transactions to achieve database consistency. But in MSA the data is tied up with several services. In addition, services are more likely to have NoSQL databases.

Implementing 2PC in a MSA environment has the following issues:

- Since there will be many services with their own relevant data, 2PC becomes very slow in MSA; i.e., implementing 2PC in MSA is time-consuming.
- It involves expensive disk operations.
- It is very much expensive as microservices deal with multiple databases which are of a *polyglot* nature. With the polyglot feature, microservices usually deal with a mix of both relational and non-relational sources, which still increases the complexity of implementing the transaction.
- In a centralized database, it is easier to perform join queries. But in microservices, since the data gets tied up with different microservices, and also with a polyglot persistence environment, performing join queries is still time-consuming and complex.
- NoSQL databases do not support 2PC.

### *7.3.2 BASE Transactions in MSA*

*MSA is extensively used in developing modern applications with large websites and a huge number of customers.*

Most of the modern applications such as eBay, Amazon, Netflix, etc. have to make their websites highly available to a large number of customers. That is, the availability of business websites becomes more important as it decides customer experience and customer satisfaction [3]. In order to provide availability, e-commerce web sites provide access to many proxy servers, and they extensively use replications of data. In addition, mild inconsistencies among the replications of data may not affect all the customers. These kinds of applications prefer to have availability in the first place, and they tend to adjust with the eventual consistency of the data. As an alternative to expensive and time-consuming 2PC, Dan Pritchett (with eBay) introduced the concept of Basically Available, Soft state, Eventually consistent (BASE) which is more suitable than ACID transactions in the case of large web sites having a huge number of replicated datasets or a distributed data store.

According to Eric Allen Brewer's CAP theorem, it is impossible for a distributed data store to simultaneously provide availability and consistency in the presence of a network partition.

Consistency—Every read receives the most recent write.

Availability—Every request receives a response with no guarantee that it contains the most recent write.

Partition tolerance—The system continues to operate despite an arbitrary number of messages being dropped (or delayed) by the network between nodes.

Thus, according to the CAP theorem, one has to choose either consistency or availability in applications with a distributed data store.

The nature of NoSQL databases in MSA and designing applications with large web sites and distributed data with MSA compels transactions to acquire BASE properties.

BASE Properties

- *Basically available*—states that the system should be always available.
- *Soft state*—indicates that the state of the system may change over time, even without input due to the eventual consistency model.
- *Eventual consistency*—indicates that the system will become consistent over time. It means that data updates will eventually ripple through to all servers, given enough time.

The success of high-volume web sites such as Google, Amazon, Twitter, and Facebook is that these applications trade-off consistency against availability; i.e., applications with large web sites and distributed data are now designed using MSA. They choose unlimited scalability, availability by trading off on consistency. Trading off on consistency enables higher levels of scalability and availability, and the new generation of websites are willing to do so.

In order to achieve high availability, applications tend to use several replicated servers. Any number of replication server instances can be added in order to provide the high availability of web sites to customers. *Also, note that the microservices are working with replicated servers through temporary data buffers and local data stores. Hence application tends to be in a soft state where the state of the system changes over time to bring consistency. The core idea of the soft state is that updating the memory and local data buffers are faster than updating disk operations, and hence responses can be delivered to customers very quickly.* Large commercial web sites have to mandatorily provide a sufficient level of user satisfaction and experience. The data updates will eventually ripple through to all servers, given enough time, and the database will become eventually consistent.

#### 7.3.2.1 How to Achieve the Basically Available Property in MSA

In general, there are two kinds of operations with data, namely:

(i) Reading data
(ii) Writing data

Reading data will not alter the state of data. For example, any number of customers can query their balance amount in their respective accounts. The key point is that any number of users can read a given database, table or record simultaneously without any conflict.

Consider, for example, Facebook, eBay, Amazon, etc. use several *replicated databases* at different locations in order to provide high availability of websites to customers. When users perform a *query or read operation*, they get the data from replicated servers. When a customer, for example, places an order or updates an existing order, it involves write operations and such write operations are carried out in *production databases*. The transaction will be logically completed, and the state of the transaction is saved or committed in the *production databases*. The *replicated databases* are continuously synchronized with the *production database* by using high-speed fiber optical networks. Ultimately, the data will become eventually consistent.

Thus, typically, read operations do not alter the state of databases whereas write operations bring changes in data (please see Figure 7.8). Also, note that changes made by write operations triggers actions in other services.

- ***Write operations bring in changes in databases.***

In microservices, since each service has its own private data instance, when a write command brings in changes in the data there may be some local inconsistencies among the microservices as long as the data is written to the disk. Here the reader may ask: When two users try to update the same record in the same table simultaneously, how do such updates take place?

Such write operations will take place in *isolation*. That is, update operations on the same record take place sequentially one at a time. If more than one user tries to update the same record, then the update operations are handled sequentially according to the time stamp on a "*first come first serve*" basis.

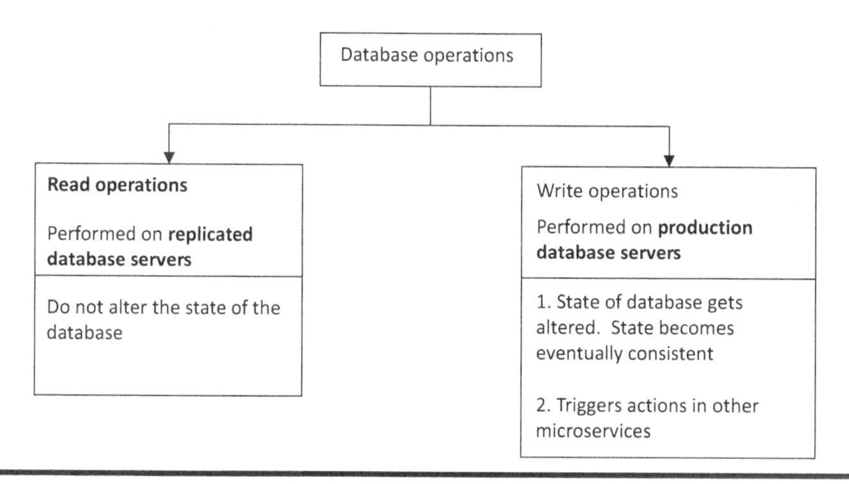


**Figure 7.8 Read and write operations on databases.**

■ ***Write operations trigger actions in other microservices.***

For example, consider two services, *inventory service* and *reorder service*. When a customer purchases some goods, after payment, the goods will be shipped to the customer. Now, the *inventory service will deduct the respective number of goods from the stock* database. The *reorder service* will also work with the stock database both at regular intervals and upon delivery of goods to find whether there is any need to place new orders for any goods by comparing the existing number of items against the preset threshold for goods. Whenever the *inventory service* updates the stock database, the same information needs to be sent to the *reorder service* so that it can take the appropriate action. Remember that the microservices are loosely coupled with one another and changes or data updates or business processes are taking place with the help of *event-driven architecture*. In MSA, availability is achieved by segregating read and write operations on different database instances. This is shown in Figure 7.9.

A specific example is presented below to show the significance of the segregation of read and write operations and to highlight the significance of how event-driven

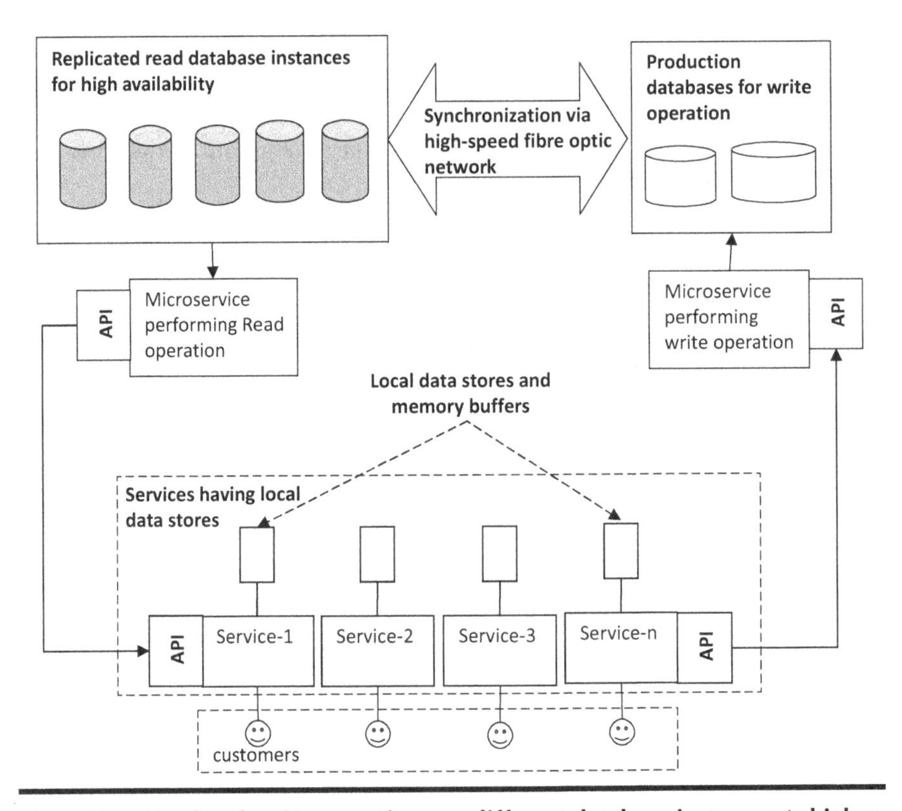


**Figure 7.9 Read and write operations on different database instances (a higher-level picture).**

architecture helps in publishing database write operations which in turn triggers actions in other interested services which subscribe to their events. For example, consider four services as follows:

*Order service*—This service takes orders from customers. It maintains the "order table" and "order detail table." It subscribes to the shipment event. Once a shipment is done, it updates the order status to "closed."

*Payment Service*—This service subscribes to order created events. Once the order is created, the payment service receives payment from customers when they pay. It maintains a "payment table." When a new order is created, it creates an entry into the payment table. When it receives payment, it updates the payment status and publishes a payment received event.

*Shipment Service*—The shipment service subscribes to the order created events and payment received events. Once the payment is received, shipment services ships the goods to the customer. It maintains a shipping table and publishes a "shipment done event."

*Inventory Service*—Once the shipment is done, the inventory service updates the stock table.

These services interact with one another with the help of event-driven architecture.

As shown in Figure 7.10, a customer places a new order with the order service. The order service creates a new entry in the order table. The entry contains an *order id, customer id, status, and amount.* It maintains the *order detail table* also. The *order detail table* contains details such as order id, item id, and quantity. Once an order is placed by a customer, the service publishes an order created event with an event bus. Services such as payment service and shipment service subscribe to the *order created event.* The payment service maintains the payment table. Once a new order is created, the payment service creates an entry in the *payment table.* As soon as the payment service receives the amount from the customer, it publishes a *payment received event* with an event bus. The shipment service subscribes to the *payment received event.* Once payment is received, it completes the shipment of goods to the customer, updates the shipment status in the *shipment table,* and publishes a *shipment done event* with the event bus. The ordered service subscribes to the shipment event, and once the shipment is done, it closes the order.

Thus, with the help of event-driven architecture, MSA can implement data-based related access operations, updates or triggers in other services

As mentioned earlier, there are two major kinds of operations, read operations, and write operations. In MSA applications, the read and write operations are segregated into two different operations; read operations will be performed by a separate microservice with its data instance and write operations will be performed by a separate microservice with its own data instance. Please keep in mind that the updates are eventually made consistent with the production servers of the applications. With this kind of design, the read services can scale to cater to the needs of a huge number of users. Also, note that the read operations do not alter the databases,

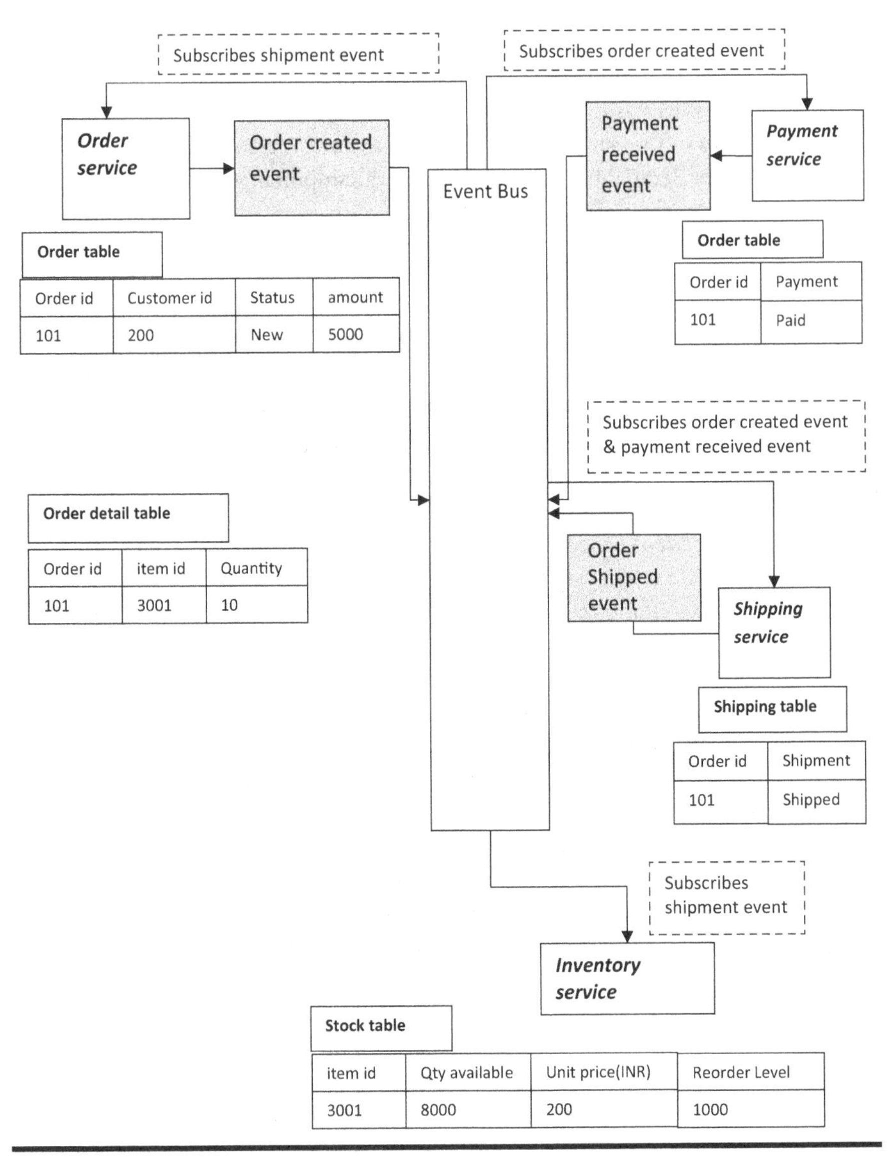


**Figure 7.10 Event-driven architecture for keeping informed about database changes (or events).**

and they are faster than write operations. This is commonly implemented with the help of a Command Query Responsibility Segregation (CQRS) design pattern [4], as shown in Figure 7.11.

How read operations are separated in an event-driven architecture is shown in Figure 7.12. Consider the same example of four microservices, namely an order service, payment service, shipment service, and inventory service. Consider the order detail table. The details of the order are accessed or read by the payment service to

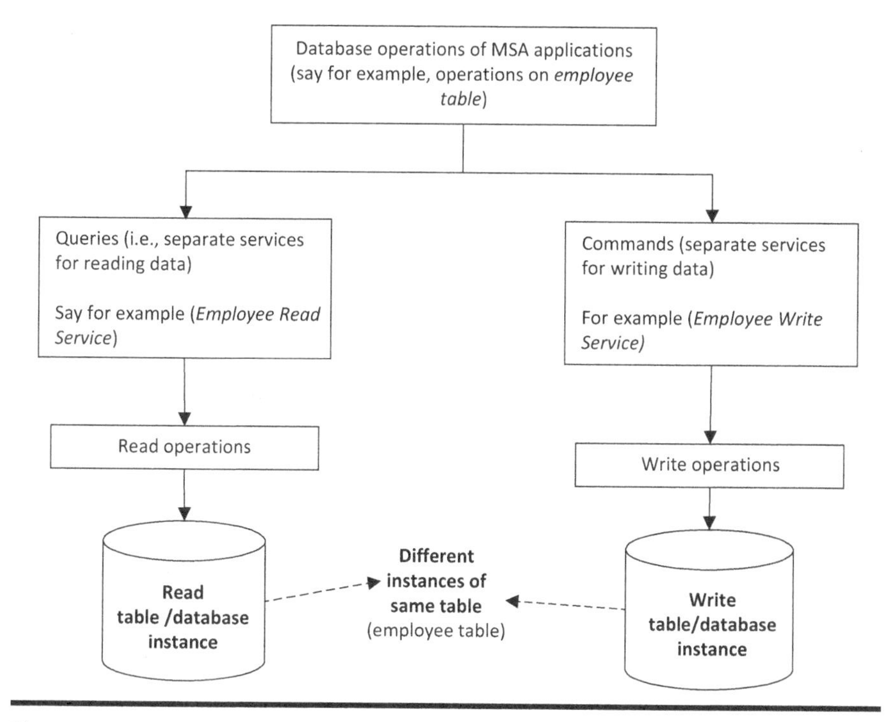


**Figure 7.11 Segregating read and write operations in data.**

compute the amount of order, shipment service to find out what are all the items to be shipped and by stock service to deduct those items from stock after shipment. Now consider a service called *orderdetailviewupdateservice.* This service subscribes to changes in the *orderdetailupdatedevent.* Basically, this view updater is a service which executes the select query in order to obtain the results of up to date records. It executes the select query and holds the results of the query typically as a materialized view object, as shown in Figure 7.12.

The other services which require order detail data will fetch the data from *order detail view,* which serves as the read instance for order details.

As shown in Figure 7.12, there is a sequence of database related operations that are implemented as:

(i) The command service (in this example, the order service) performs write operations in the database and publishes a data updated event (in this example, the order detail updated event).
(ii) The view update service (in this example, *orderdetailviewupdaterservice*) subscribes to the data update event. The data update (*orderdetailupdatedevent*) triggers *orderdetailviewupdaterservice* to execute the select command which in turn returns an updated materialized view ready for read accesses.
(iii) Now, other services such as the payment service, shipment service, and inventory service read the updated view.

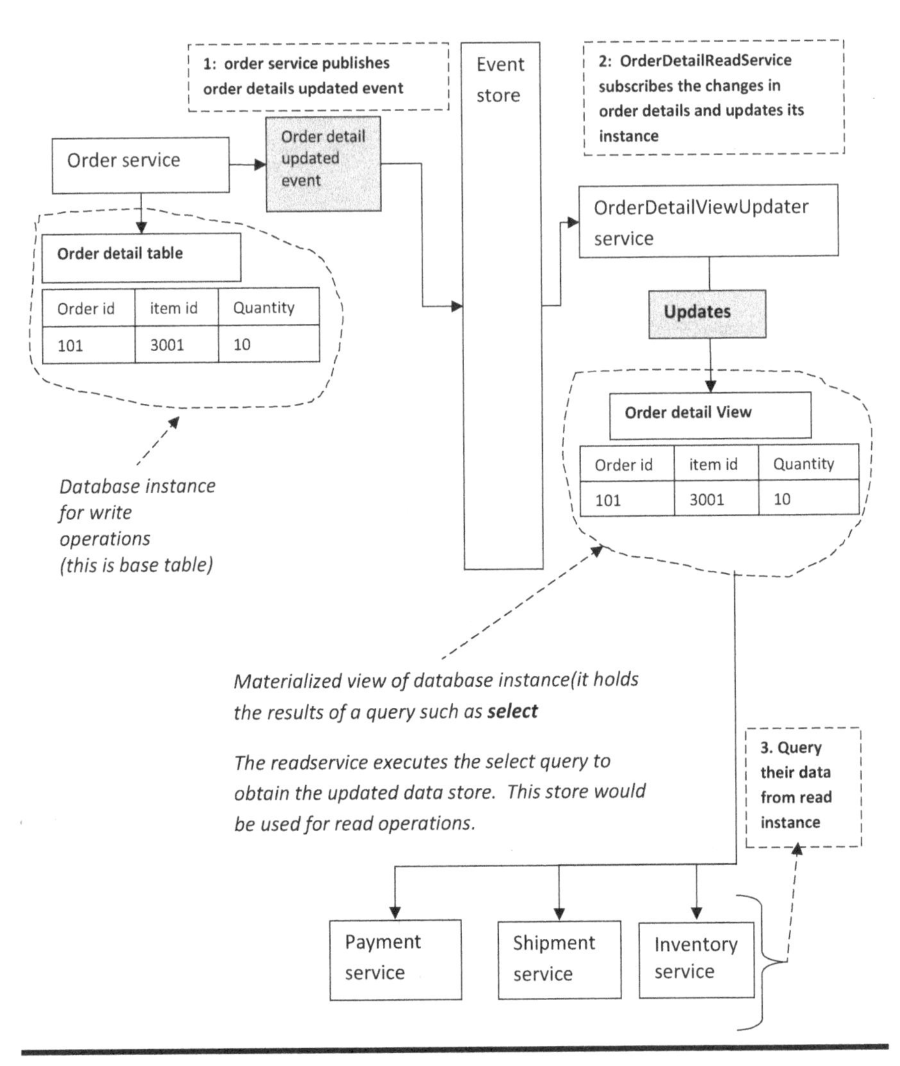


**Figure 7.12 Separating a write and read database instance (for better performance and availability).**

Overall, (i) database related operations and BASE transactions are implemented with the help of event-driven architecture.

(ii) Database operations are separated in read and write operations with separate database instances as well as separate services to handle them. The overall decentralized database operations are highlighted as shown in Figure 7.13.

From Figure 7.13, it is clear that the read and write responsibilities are allotted to different services. Similarly, separate tables/databases and views are maintained for read and write operations. A more important aspect is that the database operations, commands, and changes are published into the event store such as Apache Kafka.

The event store (i) stores the events and retains the storage of events until the pre-set retention time for them; (ii) the services which need to capture their events will subscribe to the events. The event store will notify those services which subscribe to their events. Now, the events (i) can trigger other services to take actions such as commands on the database (i.e., write operations, which in turn can publish its events, and it goes on), and they (ii) can trigger view update services to update their materialized views.

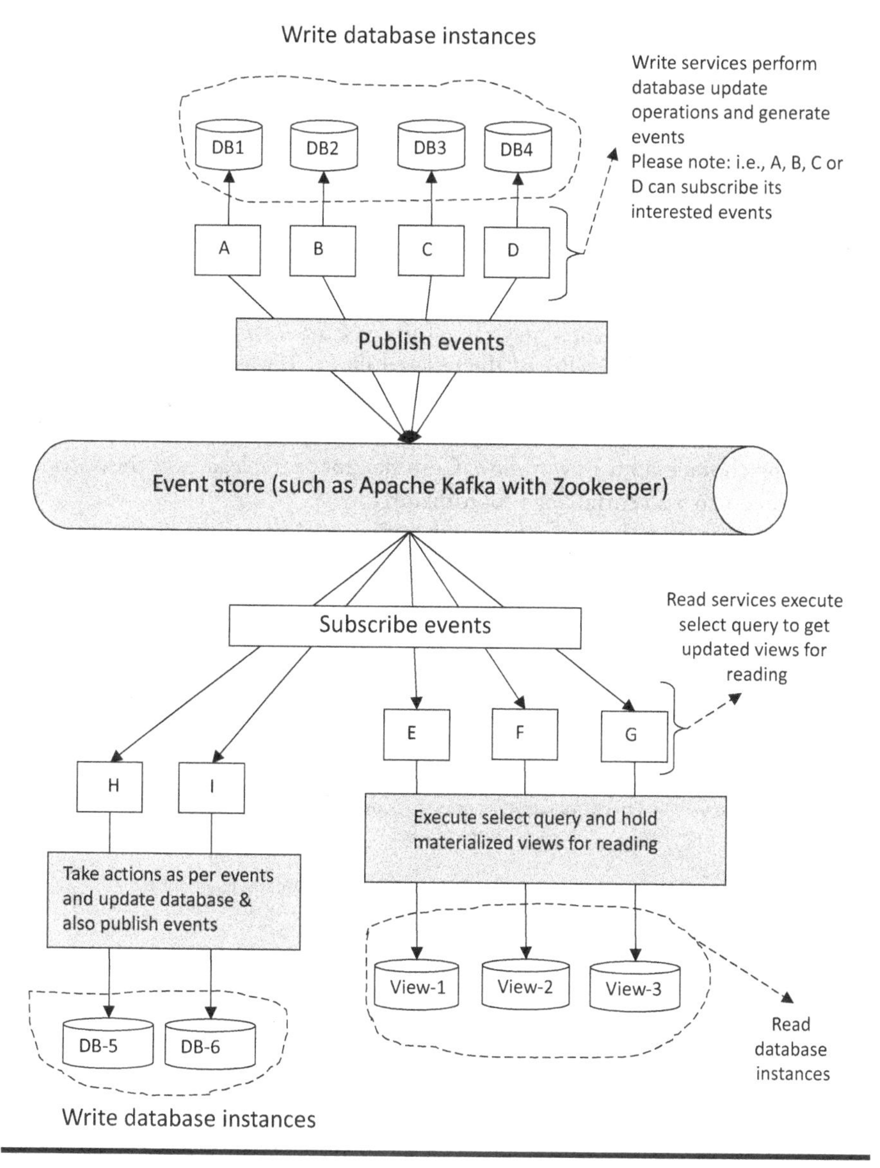


**Figure 7.13 Overall database operations with event architecture.**

### 7.3.2.2 How the Consistency is Brought in MSA (Saga Pattern)

Database consistency is implemented using a Saga pattern [5]. The Saga pattern describes how to solve distributed (business) transactions without a Two-Phase-Commit as this does not scale in distributed systems. The basic idea is to break the overall transaction into multiple steps or local transactions. Saga is a sequence of local transactions. After completing Saga, the overall consistency is taken care of by the Saga coordinator. The Saga has the responsibility of either getting the overall business transaction completed or of leaving the system in a known termination state in the case of an error by rolling back the process by executing compensation transactions in reverse order.

Saga transactions are illustrations with an example as following. Consider four services, an *order service*, *check availability service*, *payment service*, and *ship good service*.

*Example-1—successful Saga transaction*

In Example-1, a customer places an order for say ten *XZY branded cameras* with the *order service*, which creates an order. The *check availability service* checks with a stock table for the availability of the ordered items. The *payment service* receives payment and creates an appropriate entry in the payment table. The *shipment service* ships the ordered goods after payment. A Saga pattern can be implemented either using choreography or workflow. Consider, for example, a Saga transaction is implemented using a central Saga coordinator.

Example-1 is formulated as a Saga transaction as given in Listing 7.1

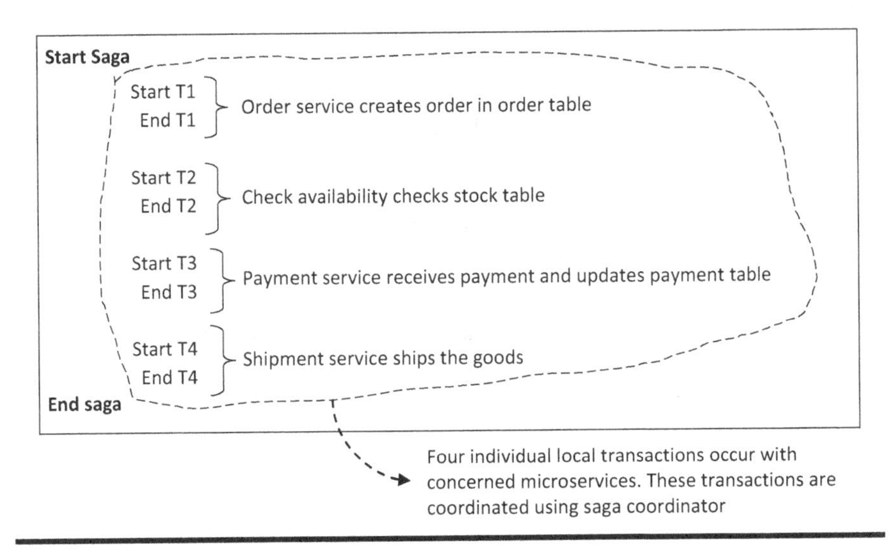


**Listing 7.1 A successful Saga transaction.**

How the Saga transaction is carried out in terms of local transactions in individual services against their local data stores is shown in Figure 7.14. The key point is that local transactions are taking place in a sequence. As in Figure 7.14, the Saga coordinator receives an end of transactions as a flag to indicate successful completion.

As every microservice performs its local transaction in sequence, there may be frequent chances that a service will not complete its local transaction successfully. If any service meets with failure while performing a local transaction, it sends an "*Abort Saga*" message to the Saga coordinator. With *Abort Saga*, the Saga coordinator executes compensating transactions to roll back the already committed local transactions in reverse order. The key point here is that every local transaction should have a corresponding compensating transaction which will be invoked in the case of failure.

Consider Example-2, an unsuccessful Saga transaction given in Listing 7.2.

As given in Listing 7.2, the Saga coordinator initiates *T1* with the order service, i.e., the order service creates an order entry once a customer places an order, for example, an order for the purchase of ten cameras. It sends an *End T1* message to the Saga coordinator. The coordinator initiates *T2* with the *check availability service*. Now the check availability service checks with the stock table. *It finds that the production for the ordered item has stopped*. Hence it gives a message "Abort Saga." Now the Saga coordinator executes *C1* which is a compensating transaction for *T1* to roll back the changes committed by *T1*. This is shown in Figure 7.15.

Thus, the Saga transaction consists of more than one local transactions which are executed in sequence according to a specific logic sequence by individual microservices against their local data stores. The Saga transaction proceeds as long as there is no failure and ultimately all local transactions get committed. If ,while

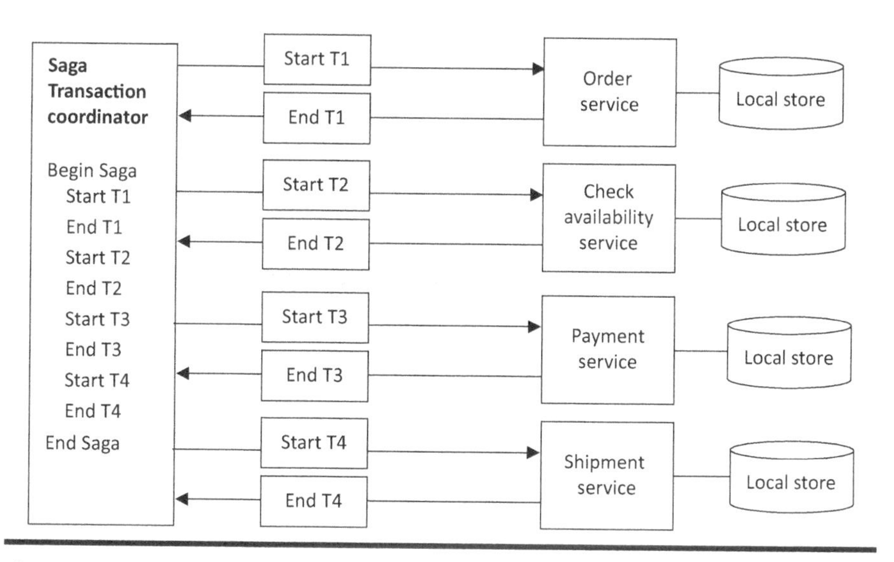


**Figure 7.14 A successful Saga transaction.**

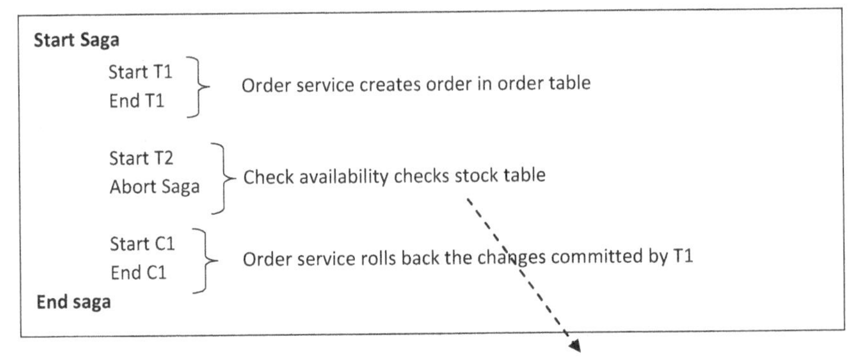


**Listing 7.2 Execution of a compensating transaction to roll back previous changes made.**

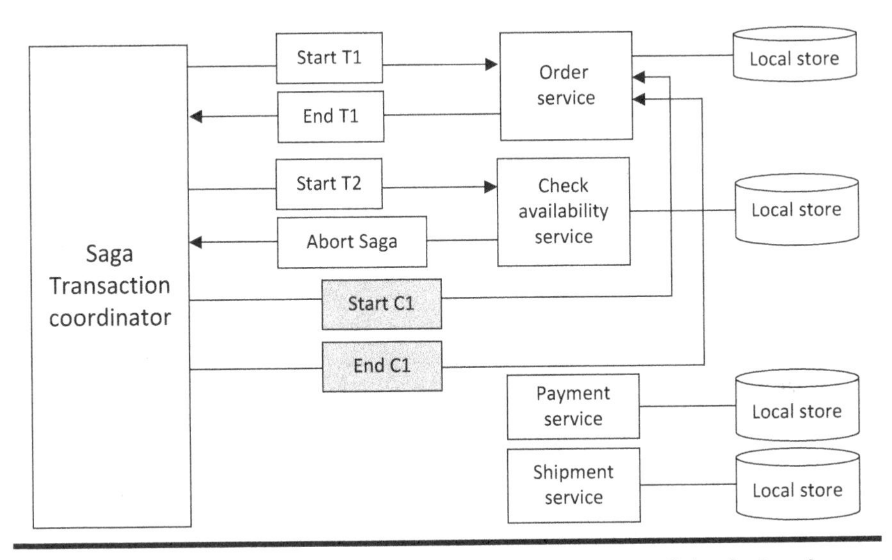


**Figure 7.15 The compensating local transaction (C1) to roll back the changes committed by T1.**

executing the Saga transaction, any of the local transactions with Saga fails, then compensating transactions will take place in reverse order for the previously committed changes in order to roll back the changes.

***Summary***

This chapter discussed an important concept in MSA: database transactions. First, it discussed how conventional applications use a Two-Phase-Commit Protocol to implement transactions in distributed databases but with limited distributions. Then the chapter discussed that in MSA, since each service has its own data store with NoSQL databases, implementing 2PC becomes inefficient. In addition, the chapter discussed that modern applications need to maintain the availability and scalability of applications to provide good customer service and customer satisfaction, and hence these applications trade-off consistency against availability. Thus, the chapter discussed how Basically Available Soft state Eventually consistent (BASE) transactions are implemented using a CQRS design pattern and Saga pattern with examples and rich schematics.

***Exercises***

1. What are the transactions?
2. Explain ACID properties?
3. How do transactions in MSA differ from that of conventional applications?
4. List out the requirements of modern applications.
5. Describe the CAP theorem.
6. What are the BASE properties?
7. How can high availability be implemented using CQRS?
8. How can consistency be implemented using Saga?

# References


1. ACID Properties in DBMS. Geeks for Geeks. Available at: https://www.geeksforgeeks.org/acid-properties-in-dbms/.
2. Shekhar Gulati. Two-Phase Commit Protocol. 2018. Available at: https://shekhargulati.com/2018/09/05/two-phase-commit-protocol/.
3. Y. Venkat. How to Implement Business Transactions in Microservices. Medium. 2017. Available at: https://medium.com/@venkat.y/how-to-implement-business-transactions-in-microservices-65e7223b04a5.
4. Shiju Varghese. Building Microservices with Event Sourcing/CQRS in Go using gRPC, NATS Streaming and CockroachDB. Medium. 2018. Available at: https://medium.com/@shijuvar/building-microservices-with-event-sourcing-cqrs-in-go-using-grpc-nats-streaming-and-cockroachdb-983f650452aa.
5. Ayush Prashar. Distributed Transactions and Saga Patterns. DZone. Available at: https://dzone.com/articles/distributed-transactions-and-saga-patterns.

# Chapter 8

# Patterns for Microservices-Centric Applications

***Objective***

The objective of this chapter is to present popular design patterns that are useful for the design, development, and deployment of microservices. By the end of the chapter, the reader will understand how different categories of patterns, such as decomposition patterns, composition patterns, observability patterns, database architecture patterns, cross-cutting concern patterns, and deployment patterns, are useful for MSA

***Preface***

Microservices Architecture is considered as the most efficient architectural pattern and style for producing and sustaining enterprise-grade applications which require frequent deployment and continuous delivery. Business applications and IT services are built using the unique capabilities of MSA. Not only fresh applications but also existing and legacy applications are being meticulously redesigned and remedied as microservices-centric applications. Thus, MSA is being proclaimed as the path-breaking and breakthrough approach for next-generation software engineering, which is propped up along with hardware engineering. The longstanding goals of software agility, reliability, scalability, availability, accessibility, sustainability, and security can be easily accomplished through the smart leverage of the Microservices Architecture. This chapter is prepared and presented in order to detail all kinds of useful and usable patterns toward microservices-centric application design, development, composition, and deployment. This chapter answers questions such as:

1. Why do we need design patterns? What are the benefits of design patterns?
2. How do we decompose microservices using design patterns?
3. Is there any pattern to model how services interact with one another without compromising their independent nature?
4. How do we model the database connections to microservices? Why can't microservices share the databases?
5. How do we design the API gateway?
6. How can we deploy microservices?
7. How can design patterns help in monitoring microservices?

## 8.1 A Macro-Level View of Microservices Architecture

For the sake of simplicity and for encouraging the risk-free utilization of Microservices Architecture, the time-tested layered approach is recommended. Experts have come out with different types of services that can be accommodated into a few different layers. With a macro-level view, layers of different types of microservices [1] can be realized, as given in Figure 8.1.

*Atomic/core microservices layer*—All the fine-grained self-contained atomic services form the bottom layer. These services typically perform the business logic of applications. Most of the existing technologies, such as SpringBoot, Dropwizard, etc. are focusing on building these services.

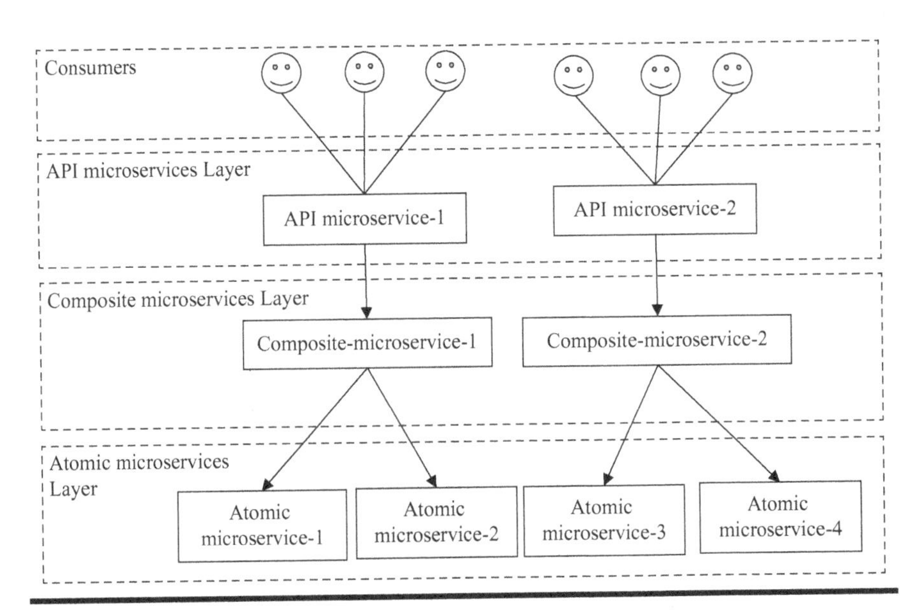


**Figure 8.1 Macro-level view of Microservices Architecture.**

*Composite microservices layer*—As atomic services offer limited functionality; they are combined to deliver useful business processes. Hence, composite services lie on the top of atomic services. These composite services are formed either by orchestration or by choreography. These services are coarse-grained. Along with composite services for business logic, there are also composite services which perform a number of services such as security, reliability, scalability, transaction support, resiliency, and stability, etc. Various technologies such as *Ballerina* which is a programming language designed for service compositions and network interactions and service mesh frameworks which can offload network communications are being used to develop composite services

*API/edge microservices layer*—The API/edge services layer lies on the top of the composite services layer. These services expose the APIs of both composite and atomic services to consumers. These are special composite services that perform basic routing functions, versioning of APIs, API security patterns, throttling, apply monetization, create API compositions, etc.

## 8.2 The Need for Patterns for Microservices Architecture

Design patterns are used to represent some of the best practices adapted by experienced object-oriented software developers. *A design pattern systematically names, motivates and explains a general design that addresses a recurring design problem in object-oriented systems.* It describes the problem, the solution, when to apply the solution, and its consequences. It also gives implementation hints and examples [2]. Design patterns have two major benefits. First, they provide a way to solve issues related to software development using a proven solution. The solution facilitates the development of highly cohesive modules with minimal coupling. They isolate the variability that may exist in the system requirements, making the overall system easier to understand and maintain. Second, design patterns make communication between designers more efficient. Software professionals can immediately picture the high-level design in their heads when they refer to the name of the pattern used to solve a particular issue when discussing system design [3]. As the patterns have evolved from best practices, they can be successfully applied to similar recurring problems. In the context of microservices, as microservices aim to provide fast and continuous deployment, employing a pattern will enable the a faster and more efficient continuous delivery. The goal of microservices is to increase the velocity of application releases; patterns can help mitigate the challenges associated with the design, development, and deployment of microservices-based applications [4]. Though MSA solves certain problems, it has several drawbacks, and hence the role of patterns gets elevated to beneficially leverage Microservices Architecture for building mission-critical applications. The typical MSA principles can be understood using Figure 8.2. MSA principles include (i) frequent deployment and continuous delivery, (ii) scalability, (iii) availability, (iv) resiliency, (v) independent and autonomous, (vi) decentralized governance, (vii) failure isolation, and (viii) auto-provisioning.

Applying all these principles brings in several challenges and issues. Here one can understand different issues and how the issues are tackled using different design patterns [5]. Different patterns are identified for implementing the above principles, and they are classified as shown in Figure 8.3.

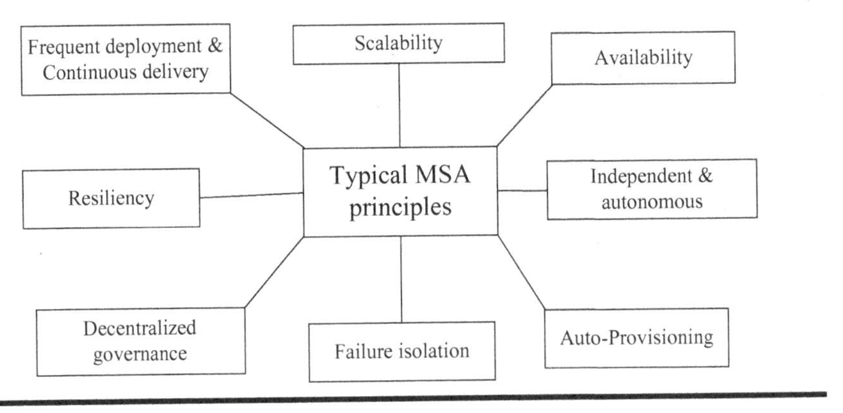


**Figure 8.2 MSA principles.**

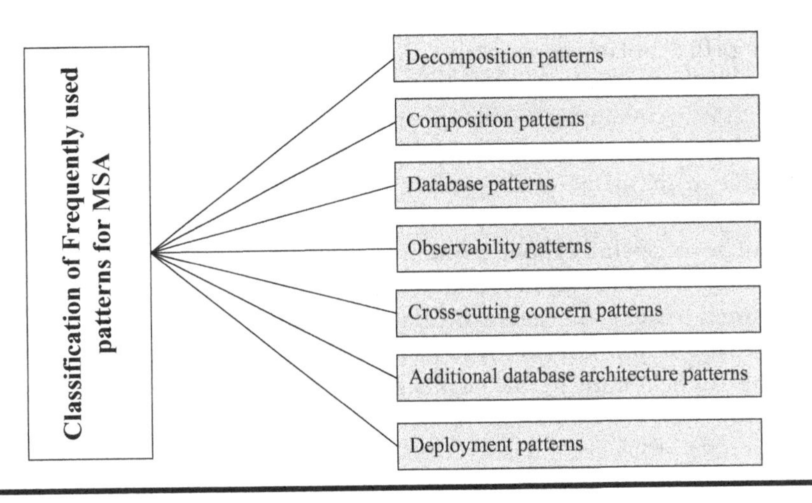


**Figure 8.3 Classification of frequently used patterns for microservices.**

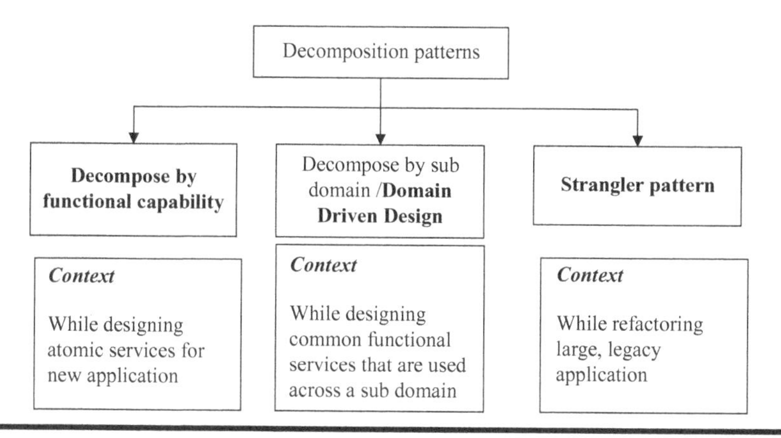


**Figure 8.4 Decomposition patterns.**

### 8.2.1 Decomposition Patterns

In MSA, an application is broken into independent microservices. Massive applications are partitioned into multiple interactive and intelligent microservices. Three patterns, as given in Figure 8.4, are discussed in this section.

**(i) Decompose by business capability pattern**

**Problem**—How to break large applications into smaller pieces? Decomposing large applications presents a significant challenge.

**Context**—While designing new applications which require frequent deployment and continuous delivery this pattern is used

**Solution—Decompose by business capability**—One viable approach is to decompose the application by business capability. A business capability is a business functionality that guarantees to deliver business value. For example, the capabilities of an insurance organization typically include sales, marketing, underwriting, claims processing, billing, compliance, etc. Each of these business capabilities is considered as a microservice to be expressed and exposed to the outside world to find and use.

**(ii) Decompose by subdomain/domain driven design pattern**

**Problem**—How do we decompose certain special business capabilities which need to be used across multiple functions/services?

**Context**—This pattern is used while designing new applications which require frequent deployment and continuous delivery. In addition, while segregating certain services as special functional services which will be used by multiple services across a subdomain, this pattern is used. There are certain other situations with certain classes of services, and they are being used across multiple services. Therefore, decomposing an application using business capabilities is not sufficient. For example, the order class will be used in order management, order taking, order delivery, etc. The challenge is: How do we decompose these special business capabilities?

**Solution—Decompose by subdomain**—The widely-known Domain Driven Design (DDD) is a viable answer. It interestingly uses subdomains and bounded context concepts to solve this unique problem. DDD breaks down the whole domain model into a number of subdomains. Now each subdomain will have its own model, and the scope of that model is called the bounded context. Microservices are developed around the bounded context. However, identifying subdomains is also beset with challenges. A thorough understanding of the business and its organizational structure comes in handy in overcoming these challenges.

**(iii) Strangler pattern**

**Problem**—How to refactor or rewrite legacy systems into modern applications?

As a part of legacy modernization, massive and monolithic applications are being analyzed and modernized. However, there are two options for doing this: rewrite or refactor. Rewriting or refactoring a large-scale application from scratch is definitely time-consuming and risky as there are no good documents for legacy applications.

So, Refactoring or rewriting legacy systems into modern applications is a difficult problem.

**Context**—While modernizing large, legacy applications by refactoring, a strangler pattern is used.

**Solution—The Strangler pattern**—The Strangler pattern reduces the above risk. Instead of rewriting/refactoring the entire application, replacing the functionality of the application step-by-step is suggested by this pattern. The business value of new functionality is realized and provided faster. The Strangler pattern emphasizes incrementally transforming monolithic applications into microservices by replacing a particular functionality with a new service as an individually deployable service, as shown in Figure 8.5. Once the new functionality is ready, the old component is strangled, the new service is put into use, and the old component is decommissioned altogether.

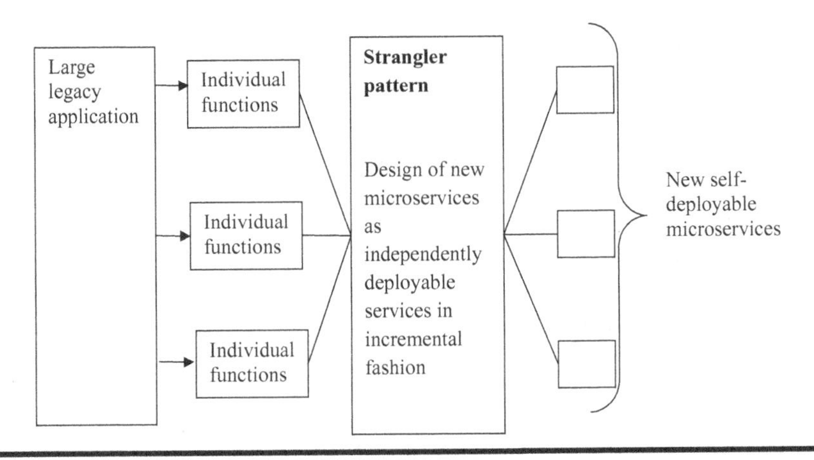


**Figure 8.5 The Strangler pattern for refactoring a large legacy application.**

### *8.2.2 Composition Patterns*

Frequently used composition patterns for MSA include:

(i) Aggregator patterns
(ii) Proxy patterns
(iii) Chained Patterns
(iv) Branch Microservice Patterns
(v) Shared resource patterns
(vi) API gateway patterns
(vii) The client-side UI composition patterns

**(i) Aggregator pattern**

**Problem**—Need to combine functions provided by more than one service.

**Context**—While developing composite services, as well as while realizing common functions such as load balancing, routing, discovery, and data/protocol conversion, there is a need to combine functions provided by more than one service. In such situations, the Aggregator pattern is used.

When breaking any business functionality into several smaller logical pieces of code (microservices), it is essential to think about the ways and means of empowering them to interact with one another. Also, the data sent by one service has to be unambiguously understood by the other service. If one service sends a message, it has to be completely understood and processed in order to accomplish what is commanded. As clients do not know how the provider's application is implemented, this data translation and protocol transformation have to be handled by a horizontal service such as an Aggregator service.

**Solution—Aggregator pattern**—How an Aggregator pattern is used to combine many functions is explained with a typical example, say, designing a web page which is comprised of many interface elements and each one corresponds to a function. In its simplest form, an Aggregator is a simple web page that invokes multiple services that implement a business function. This is commonly used in a microservices-based web application (see Figure 8.6).

The "Aggregator" is responsible for calling different services one by one.

Another option for Aggregator is when it is a higher-level composite microservice which can be consumed by other services. In this case, the Aggregator would just collect the data from each of the individual microservice, apply business logic to it, and further publish it as a REST endpoint. This can then be consumed by other services that need it. Consider that there are four different services, such as:

(i) Temperature service—gives the temperature of a location.
(ii) Wind speed service—gives the wind speed of a location.
(iii) Wind direction service—gives the direction in which the wind blows from.
(iv) Humidity service—gives the relative humidity of a location.

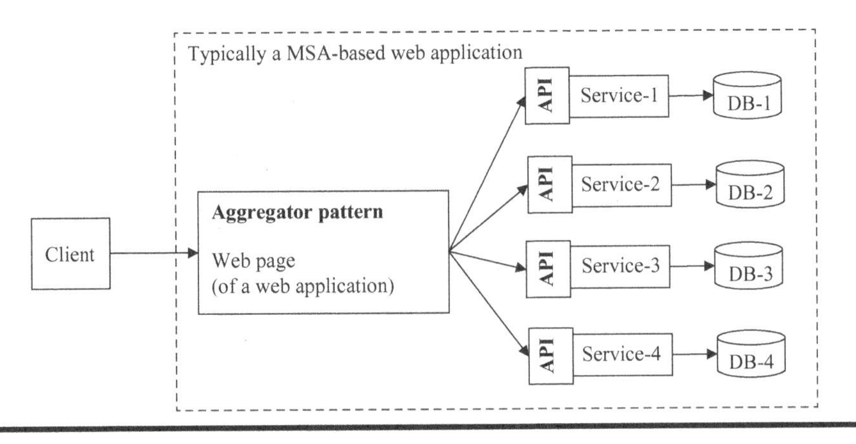


**Figure 8.6 A simple Aggregator pattern.**

Now, Assume that a client makes a single request, *find the weather*. Internally, the Aggregator service is designed to invoke the above individual services and to combine the results of the individual services. This is shown in Figure 8.7.

**(ii) Proxy pattern**

**Problem**—How to introduce controlled access to a microservice? Or how to hide the direct exposure of a microservice to clients?

**Context**—There may be situations where a developer wants to hide the direct exposure of the APIs of certain microservices to clients. That is, the access to a microservice needs to be controlled. In some other cases, additional functionality may be required while accessing an object. In these situations, the Proxy pattern is used.

**Solution—Proxy pattern**—A Proxy is a microservice which functions as an interface to another microservice for which direct access should be prevented. This is shown in Figure 8.8.

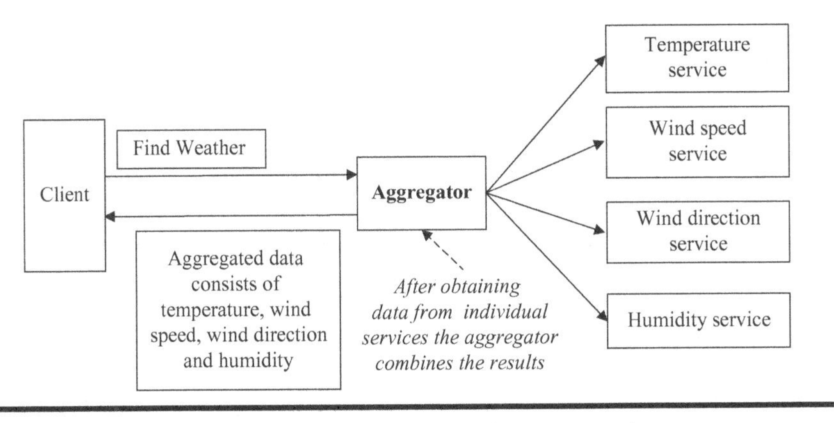


**Figure 8.7 An Aggregator pattern performing data aggregation.**

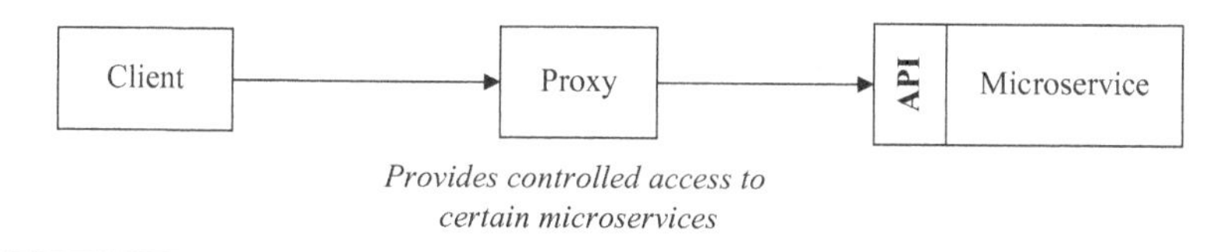


**Figure 8.8 A Proxy pattern.**

A proxy is a wrapper or agent object that is being called by the client to access the real serving microservice. It can provide additional logic. For example, a proxy can check preconditions before operations on the real microservices are invoked. It can check whether clients have the required access rights.

**(iii) Chained pattern**—This type of composition pattern will follow a chain-like structure. Here, the client communicates directly with the services, and all the services will be chained up in such a manner that the output of one service will be the input of the next service. The Chained pattern is shown in Figure 8.9. Please note that the business logic is tied up with individual services (choreography).

As shown in Figure 8.9, a Chained pattern is used to implement a travel plan service, which invokes a flight booking service, hotel booking service, and cab booking service as a chain.

**(iv) Branch microservice pattern**—This is the extended version of the Aggregator pattern and Chain pattern. The client can directly communicate with the service. Also, one service can communicate with more than one service at a time. The Branch microservice pattern is shown in Figure 8.10. Here a client invokes a service by inserting a smart card with an *insert card service.* Internally the insert card service invokes the *validate service* which validates the type of smart card.

**(v) Shared resource pattern**—This is actually a conglomerate of all the types of patterns mentioned earlier. In this pattern, the client or the load balancer will directly communicate with each service whenever necessary.

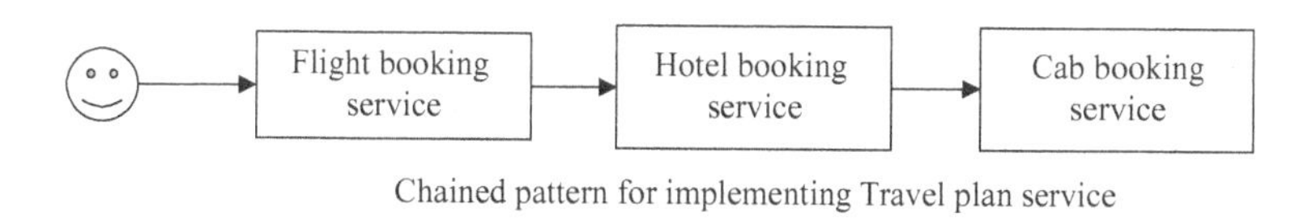


**Figure 8.9 A Chained pattern.**

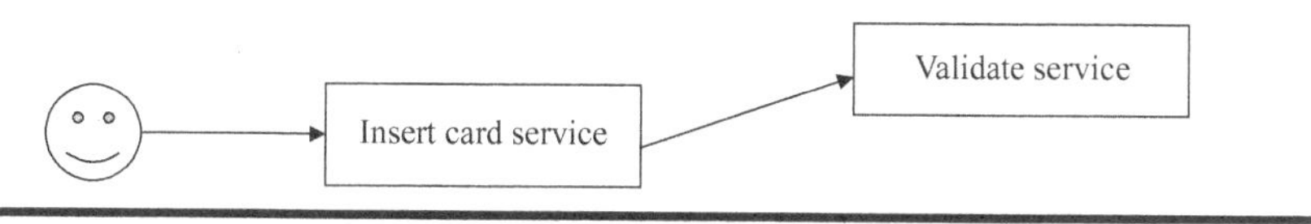


**Figure 8.10 A Branch microservice pattern.**

**(vi) API gateway pattern**

**Problem**—When an application is broken into atomic services, how does a client invoke and realize a useful business process?

**Context**—When an application gets broken down to a number of microservices, there are a few concerns that have to be addressed.

- Calling multiple microservices and abstracting producer information.
- There are multiple categories of input/output devices and channels. Application services have to receive and respond differently.
- Data and protocol translations are required to enable disparate and distributed microservices to collaborate with one another. There are multiple client types interacting with backend services and databases.

**Solution**—**API gateway pattern** helps to address the above-mentioned concerns. This is shown in Figure 8.11.

- An API gateway is the single point of entry for any microservice call.
- It also can work as a proxy service to route requests to microservices and their instances.
- It can fan out a request to multiple services and aggregate the results to send back to the client.
- One-size-fits-all APIs cannot fulfill different consumer's requirements. API gateways can create a fine-grained API for each specific type of client.
- It can also convert the protocol request (e.g., AMQP) to another protocol (e.g., HTTP) and vice versa.
- It can also offload the authentication/authorization responsibility of the microservice.

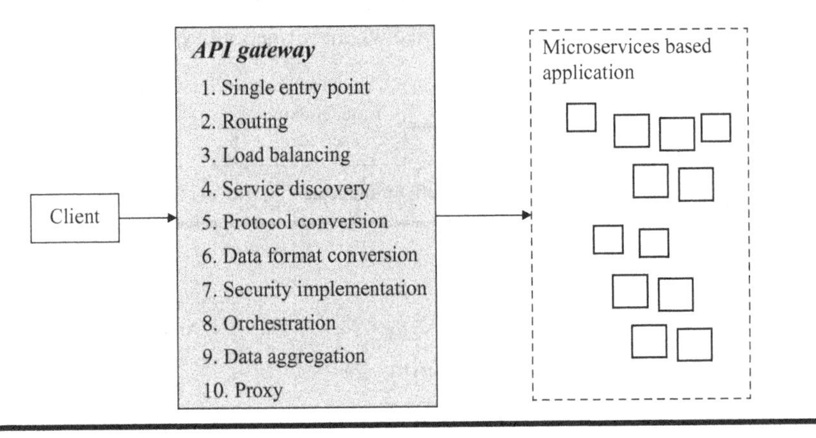


**Figure 8.11 An API gateway pattern.**

**(vii) Client-side UI composition pattern**

**Problem**—When the functional capability of an application is tied up among several services, how do you provide integrated and insightful information back to clients, when data/information has to be collected and composed of multiple services?

**Context**—While providing information to users, there is a need to combine output to provide an integrated view to users.

**Solution—Client-side UI composition patter**—As indicated above, microservices are developed by decomposing business capabilities/subdomains. That is, there are several services working together to fulfill business systems. Now, for giving integrated and insightful information back to the consumers, data/information has to be collected and composed of multiple services.

In the microservices era, the user interface (UI) has to be designed as a skeleton with multiple sections/regions of the screen/page. Each section has to make a call to an individual backend microservice to pull the data. There are a few enabling frameworks such as *AngularJS* and *ReactJS* that help to do this UI composition easily. These screens are known as Single Page Applications (SPA). This kind of setup enables the application to refresh a particular region of the screen/page instead of the whole page. *AngularJS is a JavaScript web application framework created by Google. It uses well-known components, designs, patterns, and development practices in a single framework to address the challenges encountered in developing a single page application. ReactJS is basically an open source JavaScript library which is used for handling the view layer for web and mobile apps. ReactJS allows for creating reusable UI components. React was first deployed on Facebook in 2011 and on Instagram.com in 2012.*

*React helps to create large web applications which can change data, without reloading the page. The main purpose of React is to be fast, scalable, and simple.*

### 8.2.3 Database Patterns

Frequently used database patterns include:

(i) Database per service pattern
(ii) Shared database per service pattern
(iii) Command Query Responsibility Segregator (CQRS) pattern
(iv) Saga pattern

**(i) Database per service pattern**

**Problem**—How to achieve independence in regard to databases?

In MSA, each service has to be independently designed, developed, debugged, delivered, deployed, and scaled. Further, they should also be loosely coupled. One service should not depend on other services. How can a service keep its own data? How to achieve independence in regard to databases?

**Context**—There may be many requirements, such as the following in regard to database operations and functions.

- Business transactions may enforce invariants that involve multiple services.
- Some business transactions may insist on querying data that is owned by multiple services.
- Databases have to be replicated in order to support high and horizontal scalability.
- Different services have different data model/storage requirements.

In the above situations, different database patterns are used.

**Solution—Database per service pattern**—Having understood the varying requirements, it is recommended to have a database instance for each microservice. Database access is only through the corresponding service's APIs. That is, a database cannot be accessed by other services directly.

For example, for relational databases, the options are:

- Private-tables-per-service
- Schema-per-service
- Database-server-per-service

Each microservice should have a separate database id, and one service cannot access other service's tables. Thus, data security is implemented through such separations.

**(ii) Shared database per service pattern**

**Problem**—How to share databases among more than one service?

**Context**—The predominant aspect is to empower every microservice with its own database. However, there are certain challenges, especially when we go for greenfield applications based on the proven DDD technique. Also, legacy applications are blessed with centralized and shared databases. Modernizing legacy applications using MSA brings forth other challenges as far as database architecture is concerned.

**Solution—Shared database per service**—The overwhelming success of microservices is due to a separate database for each service. For brownfield applications (referring to the applications which are modified or upgraded), having a separate database is ideal and sustainable. However, for greenfield applications (referring to the applications that are developed from scratch), one database can be associated and aligned with multiple microservices. The number has to be within two or three. Otherwise, the salient features (scaling, autonomy, etc.) of MSA are lost.

**(iii) Command Query Responsibility Segregation pattern**

**Problem**—How to achieve high availability for modern applications with large websites? Allocating one database for every microservice raises the question of how multiple services can be connected and questioned for certain database queries.

**Context**—When an e-commerce application has large websites, there is always a need to provide a sufficient availability of the web sites to a huge number of customers. In such situations, the CQRS pattern is used.

**Solution—Command Query Responsibility Segregation pattern**—This approach suggests splitting the application into two parts: the command side and the query side. The command side handles the Create, Update, and Delete requests, whereas the query side handles the query part by using the materialized views. In other words, CQRS is a way to dissociate writes (command) and reads (query). That is, we can have one database to manage the write part. The read part (materialized view or projection) is derived from the write part and can be managed by one or multiple databases. This is shown in Figure 8.12.

Generally, the read part is asynchronously computed, and hence both parts are not strictly consistent. The *Event sourcing pattern* is generally used to create events for any data change. The read part (materialized views) is kept updated by subscribing to the stream of events. The Event sourcing pattern ensures that all changes to the application state are stored as a sequence of events. This means that the state of an object is not stored. But all the events that impact the state of an object are stored. Then, to retrieve an object state, one has to read the different events related to this object and apply them one by one according to the time stamp.

**CQRS + Event sourcing**—Both patterns are frequently grouped together. Applying Event sourcing on top of CQRS means that each event is persisted on the write part of an application. Then the read part is derived from the sequence of events from an event architecture (please see Figure 8.12).

**(iv) Saga pattern**

**Problem**—How to implement a database transaction when it involves database operations in more than one microservice?

**Context**—In MSA, each service offers limited functionality with its own database. This tendency of microservices means a business transaction generally

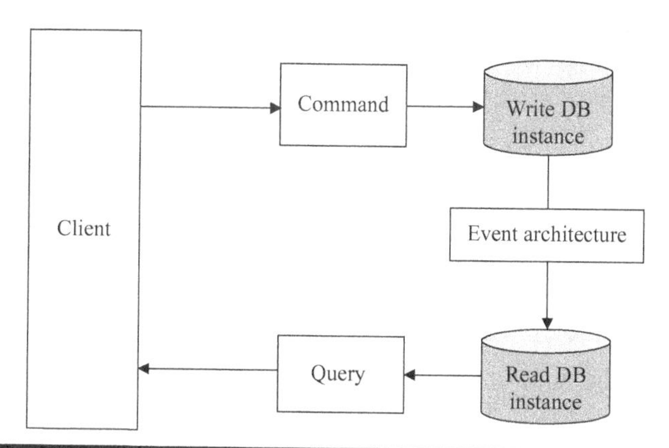


**Figure 8.12 Segregating read and write operations using a CQRS pattern.**

spans over multiple services (as data is tied up with different services). This kind of distributed transaction, bringing database consistency across the participating databases, is a real challenge. For example, for an e-commerce application where customers have a credit limit, the application must ensure that a new order will not exceed the customer's credit limit. Since *orders* and *customers* are in different databases, the application cannot simply use a local ACID transaction. The need for a *distributed transaction grows.* To exemplify this perpetual problem, consider the following high-level Microservices Architecture of an e-commerce system.

In the example above, one cannot just place an order, charge the customer, update the stock, and send it out for delivery. All these aspects cannot be accommodated in a single transaction. To execute this entire flow consistently, it is essential to create a distributed transaction. Dealing with transient states, eventual consistency between services, isolations, and rollbacks are scenarios that should be considered during the design phase.

**Solution—Saga pattern**—*A Saga is a sequence of local transactions* where each transaction updates data within a single service. The first transaction is initiated by an external request corresponding to the system operation, and then each subsequent step is triggered by the completion of the previous one. Each local transaction has a compensating transaction that is executed when the request fails. Let T1, T2, T3, ... Tn denote a set of local transactions that take place in a sequence. Each local transaction should have its own compensating transaction. Let C1, C2, C3, ... Cn denote the compensating transactions. The Saga pattern is used to handle failures in a distributed transaction.

In a Saga transaction, each database operation within the concerned microservice takes place as a local transaction. If all services complete their local transactions successfully, then the Saga transaction is completed successfully. If any of the local transactions meet with failure, then all the local transactions that have happened previously are rolled back by executing the compensating transactions in reverse order. For example, consider four services, *order service*, *payment service*, *check availability service*, and *shipment service*. The local transactions that occur in individual services along with compensating transactions are given in Table 8.1.

A successful Saga pattern will behave as shown in Figure 8.13.

If any local transaction fails, then the compensating transactions for the committed local transaction which have already occurred will take place in reverse order. For example, assume that a customer places an order for ten *XYZ laptops*. Also, assume that the customer paid the amount with a payment service. After payment is made, the check availability services check for the item in the stock table in order to notify the shipment service. Here, consider that the *ordered item is not in production*. Now, T3 fails. There are two transactions that have occurred already. In order to roll back T1 and T2, the compensating transactions, i.e., C2 and C1, will take place as shown in Figure 8.14.

**Table 8.1 Local Transactions and Their Compensating Transactions in Individual Services of a Saga Transaction**

| *Service Name* | *Description* | *Details of Local Transaction* | *Description of Compensating Transaction* |
|---|---|---|---|
| Order service | Customer places an order with order service | T1—creates an entry in the order table | C1—deletes the order entry |
| Payment service | Payment service receives payment from the customer | T2—receives payment and creates an entry in the payment table | C2—return the payment and deletes the entry in the payment table |
| Check availability service | The check availability service checks the availability of ordered goods in stock | T3—finds whether ordered items are available in the stock table. The item may be: (i) available (ii) out of stock (iii) not in production | C3—if the item is not in production, delete the item from catalog table |
| Shipment service | Ships the goods to the customer | T4—ships the items and makes an entry in shipment table | C4—deletes the record in shipment table |

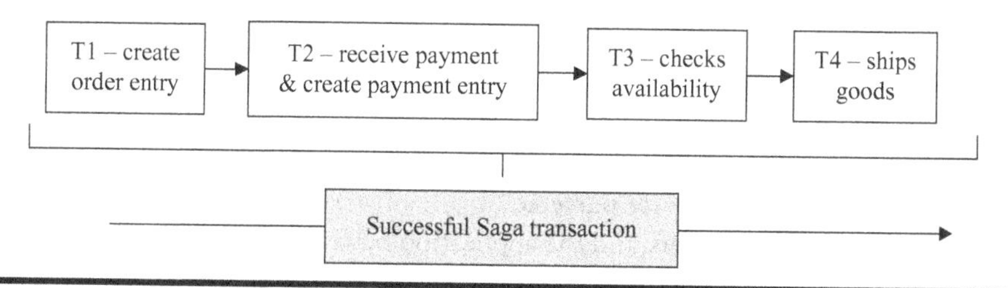


**Figure 8.13 A successful Saga transaction.**

There are a couple of ways to implement a Saga transaction.

- ***Events/Choreography***—When there is no central coordination, each service produces and listens to the other service's events and decides if an action should be taken or not.
- ***Command/Orchestration***—When a coordinator service is responsible for centralizing the Saga's decision making and sequencing business logic.

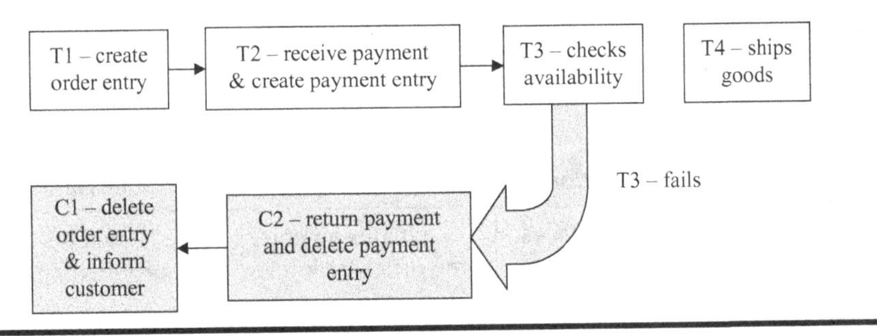


**Figure 8.14 Saga roll backs failed local transaction using compensating transactions.**

## *8.2.4 Observability Patterns*

Microservices are nothing more than regular distributed systems. The key differentiator is that the number of participating and contributing microservices for any distributed application is quite huge. Therefore, they exacerbate the well-known problems that any distributed system faces, like lack of visibility to a business transaction across process boundaries.

A system is said to be observable when one can understand its state based on the metrics, logs, and traces it emits. As there are many services and their instances, it is essential to aggregate the metrics for all instances of a given service, perhaps grouped by version. Metrics solutions play a crucial role in solving the observability problem. There are some observability patterns that are frequently used for microservices. They are:

(i) Centralized logging service pattern
(ii) Application performance metrics pattern
(iii) Distributed tracing pattern
(iv) Health check pattern

**(i) Centralized logging service pattern**

**Problem**—How to understand the application behavior through logs for a particular request?

**Context**—In the microservices world, an application consists of multiple service instances running on multiple machines. That is, service requests often span multiple service instances. Each service instance generates a log file in a standardized format. The challenge here is how to understand the application behavior through logs for a particular request?

**Centralized logging service pattern**—The *centralized logging service* aggregates logs from each service instance. Users can search and analyze the logs. They can configure alerts that are triggered when certain messages appear in the logs.

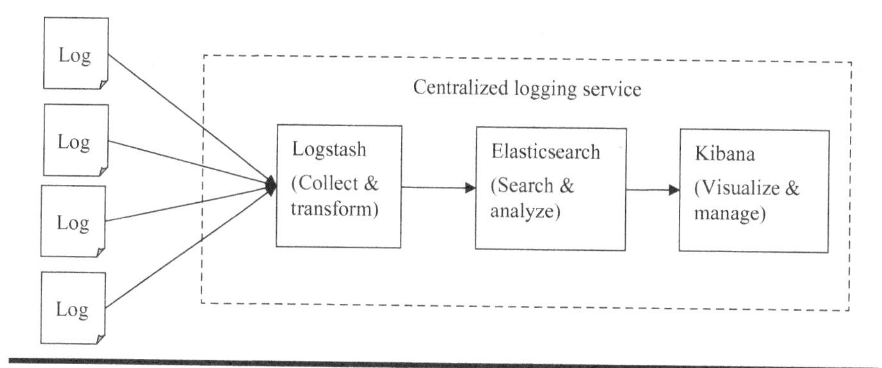


**Figure 8.15 Implementing a centralized logging service using an Elasticsearch, Logstash, and Kibana (ELK) open source stack.**

For example, there are log aggregation solutions that collect logs from each software and hardware component. The logs need to be stored in a central location as it is impossible to analyze the logs from the individual instances of each service. Open source tools and technologies can be used to implement a centralized logging service. For example, one of the open source technology stacks, ELK, which is the acronym for three open source projects: *Elasticsearch, Logstash, and Kibana* can be used. Elasticsearch is a highly scalable open source full-text search and analytics engine. It can store, search, and analyze big volumes of data quickly and in near real-time. Logstash is an open source tool for collecting, parsing, and storing logs for future use. Kibana helps in the visualization of data with charts and graphs. Thus, Logstash is used in combination with Elasticsearch and Kibana to realize the function of the centralized logging service. This is shown in Figure 8.15.

**(ii) Application performance metrics pattern**

**Problem**—How to collect metrics to monitor application performance?

**Context**—After monitoring different metrics from individual microservices, there is a need to convert the collected metrics into business meaning or values, i.e., one has to collect those metrics which really convey meaningful insights. So, it is a real challenge to find the metrics which map the application performance? In this situation, the Application performance metrics pattern is used.

**Solution—Application performance metrics pattern**—The purpose of APM is to detect and diagnose complex application performance problems to maintain an expected level of service. APM is the translation of IT metrics into business meaning or value. There are performance-associated metrics and automated solutions to capture all kinds of metrics. Further on, there are analytical platforms and products to derive actionable insights out of performance data in order to set right any kind of performance degradation.

Typically, the following metrics are meticulously collected and subjected to a variety of investigations for enhancing application performance. APM can help do several key things like:

- Measure and monitor application performance.
- Find the root causes of application problems.
- Identify ways to optimize application performance.

APM is one or more software (and/or hardware) components that facilitate monitoring to meet the following functional dimensions.

- **End-user experience monitoring**—This captures the user-based performance data to gauge how well the application is performing and identify potential performance problems.
- **Application topology discovery and visualization**—This supplies the visual expression of the application in a flow-map to establish all the different components of the application and how they interact with each other.
- **User-defined transaction profiling**—This examines the specific interactions to recreate conditions that lead to performance problems for testing purposes.
- **IT operations analytics**—This helps to discover the usage patterns, identification of performance problems, and anticipation of potential problems before they happen.

The key application performance metrics are:

- User satisfaction/Apdex scores (the Apdex score is a ratio value of the number of satisfied and tolerating requests to the total requests made)
- Average response time
- Error rates
- Count of application instances
- Request rate
- Application and server CPU
- Application availability

**(iii) Distributed tracing pattern**

**Problem**—How to trace a request end-to-end to troubleshoot the problem?

**Context**—In MSA, client requests often go to several services. Each service typically handles a request by performing one or more operations across multiple services. It is extremely common to have multiple versions of a single service running in production at the same time. This is prominent in A/B testing scenario or when we roll out a new release following the Canary release technique. When there are hundreds of microservices, it's almost impossible to map the interdependencies and understand the path of a business transaction across services and their multiple versions. The challenge here is how to trace a request end-to-end to troubleshoot the problem?

It is essential to have a service which:

- Assigns each external request a unique external request id.
- Passes the external request id to all services.
- Includes the external request id in all log messages.
- Records information (e.g., start time, end time) about the requests and operations performed when handling an external request in a centralized service.

**Solution—Distributed tracing pattern**—This pattern (alternatively the Distributed request tracing pattern), is used to profile and monitor applications, especially those built using a Microservices Architecture. Distributed tracing helps pinpoint where failures occur and what causes poor performance. Tracing gives insight into code executing across services.

**(iv) Health check pattern**

**Problem**—Whether a microservice is functioning normally?

**Context**—An evident cost of using microservices is an increase in complexity. With more dynamic parts in a microservices-centric system, the recurring challenge is to fully understand and troubleshoot performance problems. Deeper and decisive monitoring of the health of microservices helps to understand the overall performance of the system and detect individual points of failure.

**Solution—Health check pattern**—Microservices expose a *health endpoint* with information about the status of the service. A *monitor application* keeps track of this data, aggregates it, and presents the results in a dashboard. It is advised to create multiple specific health checks per service. This results in several noteworthy benefits.

1. Specific health checks allow the user to pinpoint the malfunction.
2. Latency measurements on specific health checks can be used to predict outages.
3. Health checks can have different severities.
   - Critical: the service does not react to any requests.
   - High priority: a downstream service is not available.
   - Low priority: a downstream service is not available; a cached version can be served.

### 8.2.5 Cross-Cutting Concern Patterns

Some of the Cross-cutting concern patterns used in MSA include:

(i) External configuration store pattern
(ii) Service registry pattern
(iii) Circuit breaker pattern
(iv) Blue-green deployment

**(i) External configuration store pattern**

**Problem**—How to avoid code-modification for all kinds of configuration changes?

**Context**—A service typically calls other services and databases as well. For each environment such as development, quality assurance (QA), user acceptance testing (UAT) or production, the endpoint URL, or some configuration properties might change. For configuration, a developer usually uses a configuration file (*.properties*, *.xml*, or another) inside the application. However, this method couples the package of the application with the underlying environment, and the developer needs to generate a separate package for each environment. Any change in any of those properties automatically insists on a re-build and redeploy of the service. The persistent question here is how to avoid code-modification for all kinds of configuration changes?

**Solution—External configuration store pattern**—One solution is to have an external configuration store. This is an operational pattern that decouples the configuration details from the application. The external configuration is generally unaware of the value of the configuration properties and only knows the properties to be read from the configuration store. Applications with an external configuration store pattern are shown in Figure 8.16.

One of the primary benefits of this pattern includes updating the configuration values without rebuilding the application. Once the package is generated, it can run on any environment without any hitch or hurdle. Any team (infrastructure or middleware) can manage the configuration without the help of a developer as the application package doesn't need to be updated. Furthermore, it centralizes all configurations, and the various applications can read the configuration properties from the same location.

**(ii) Service registry pattern**

**Problem**—How to enable service consumers or API gateways to know all the available service instances and locations?

**Context**—Microservices and their instances have to be identified before their leverage. With containers emerging and evolving fast as the most efficient runtime for microservices, IP addresses are dynamically allocated to microservices. If there is any movement of microservices, then there is a change in the IP address. This

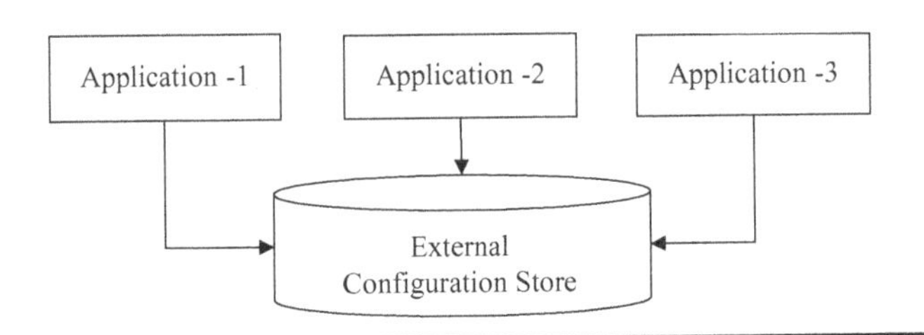


**Figure 8.16 External Configuration store pattern.**

makes it very difficult for service clients to locate microservices. So, the lingering question here is how to enable service consumers or API gateways to know all the available service instances and locations?

**Solution—Service registry pattern**—A service registry can store the metadata of every participating service. A service instance has to register itself in the registry when starting and has to de-register when shutting down or moving to a different location. The consumer or API gateway/router has to query the registry to find out the exact location of the service. In addition, there are two techniques, namely client-side discovery and server-side discovery, to discover the location of the desired service from the registry. They are:

- **Client-side discovery**—Service consumers keep all locations of providers and load-balance the requests across locations. The need is to implement a discovery process for different languages/frameworks which are supported by the application. Client-side discovery is shown in Figure 8.17. Typically, there are two steps. In Step-1, the client interacts with the service registry and requests the registry for the location of the desired service. The service registry returns the location and other metadata to the client. In Step-2, the client either sends the request directly to the service endpoint (if there is no API gateway in the application design) or it will submit the request to the API gateway.
- **Server-side discovery**—The consumer sends requests to the API gateway, which in turn queries the registry and decides which location of providers to send to. This is shown in Figure 8.18.

**(iii) Circuit breaker pattern**

**Problem**—How do we avoid cascading service failures and handle failures gracefully?

**Context**—A service generally calls other services to retrieve data, and there is the chance that the downstream service may be down. There are two problems with this: first, the request will keep going to the down service, exhausting network resources and slowing performance. Second, the user experience will be bad and unpredictable. The challenge is: How do we avoid cascading service failures and handle failures gracefully?

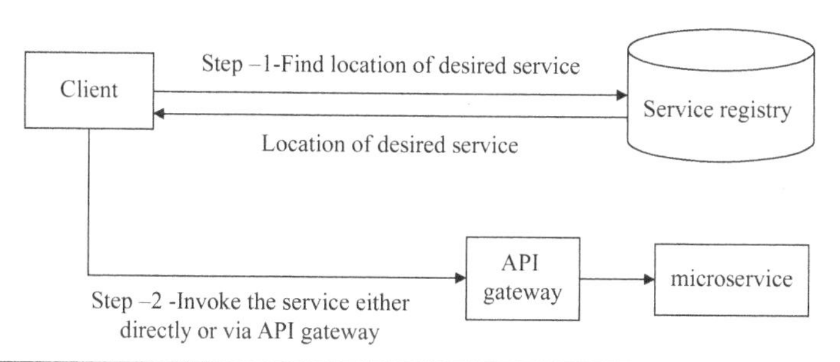


**Figure 8.17 Client-side discovery.**

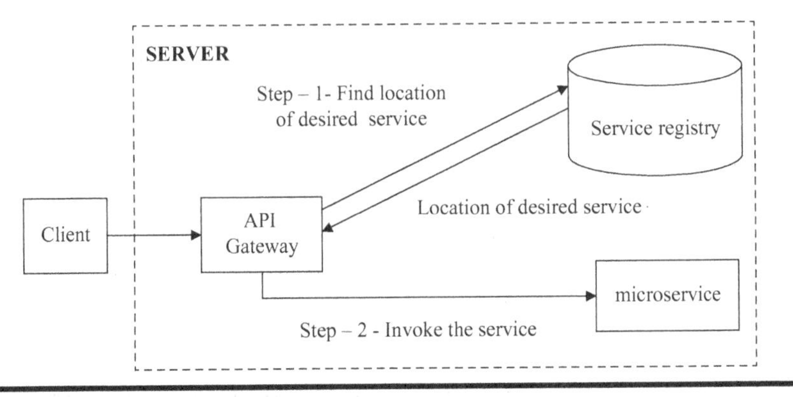


**Figure 8.18 Server-side discovery.**

**Solution—Circuit breaker pattern**—The consumer should invoke a remote service via a proxy that behaves in a similar fashion to an electrical circuit breaker. When the number of consecutive failures crosses a threshold, the circuit breaker trips (see Figure 8.19), and for the duration of a timeout period, all attempts to invoke the remote service will fail immediately.

The Circuit breaker pattern is a mechanism for the fast fail of requests toward unhealthy services and hence prevents unnecessary traffic and cascading fails. After the timeout expires the circuit breaker allows a limited number of test requests to pass through. If those requests succeed, the circuit breaker resumes normal operation. Otherwise, if there is a failure, the timeout period begins again.

Netflix Hystrix is a good implementation of the Circuit breaker pattern. It also helps to define a fallback mechanism which can be used when the circuit breaker trips. That provides a better user experience.

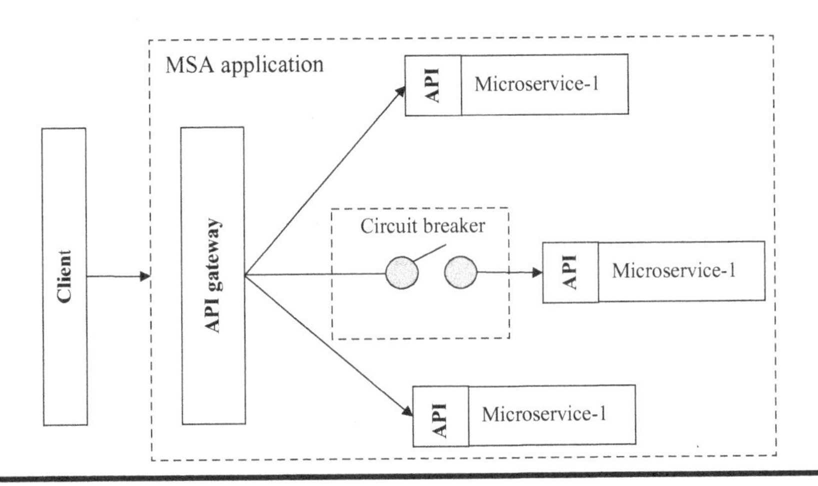


**Figure 8.19 Circuit breaker pattern.**

**(iv) Blue-green deployment pattern**

**Problem**—How do we avoid or reduce downtime of the services during deployment?

**Context**—With microservice architecture, one application can have many microservices. When there is a need to redeploy an enhanced/new version of a microservice, if we stop all the services for the redeployment of one service, the downtime will be huge and can impact the business. The challenge is: How do we avoid or reduce downtime of the services during deployment?

**Solution—Blue-green deployment pattern**—This deployment strategy can be implemented to reduce or remove downtime. This deployment strategy reduces downtime and risk by running two identical production environments, referred to as Blue and Green. Assume that Green is the existing live instance, and Blue is the new version of the application. At any time, only one of the environments is live, with the live environment serving all production traffic. All cloud platforms provide options for implementing a blue-green deployment. This is shown in Figure 8.20.

## *8.2.6 Additional Database Architecture Patterns*

Some of the additional database architecture patterns for MSA include:

(i) Database Integration pattern
(ii) Synchronous API calls pattern
(iii) Asynchronous messaging pattern

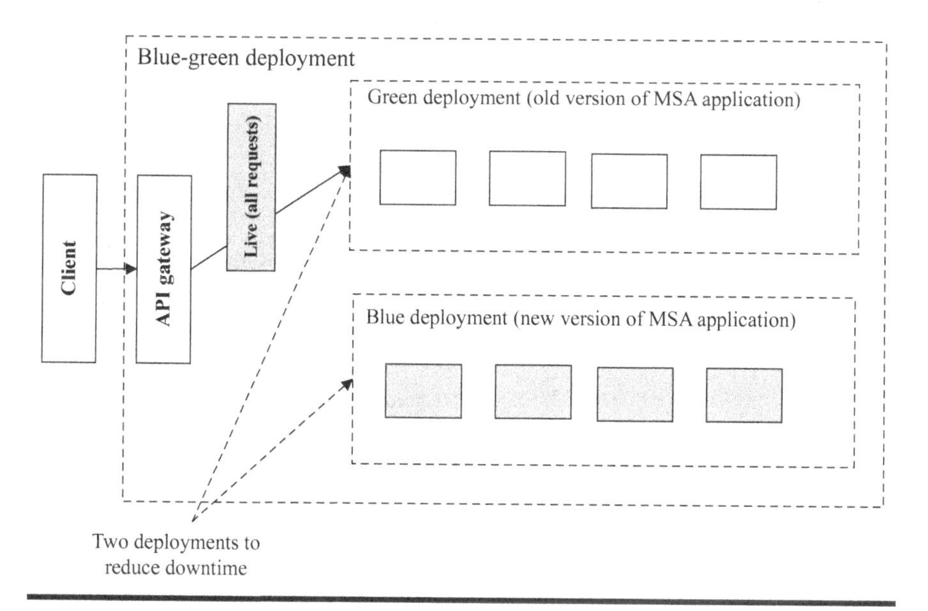


**Figure 8.20 Blue-green deployment.**

**(i) Database integration pattern**

**Problem**—How can two or more services perform read/write operations on the same database?

**Context**—There may be situations where many services need to access data from a central store. For example, consider that data about the user's login, user's profile, user's credit score, and user's transactions may be used by different services. If all data are related to the user's information, how can different services share user's data?

**Solution—Database integration pattern**—In this pattern, two or more services read and write data out of one central data store. All of the services go to this central data store as in Figure 8.21.

One of the significant advantages of database integration is simplicity. Transaction management is more straightforward as compared to other patterns. This is perhaps the most widely-used pattern of integration.

This pattern couples services together, making the Microservices Architecture more difficult to manage and maintain. Defining data ownership and updating the schema can become a bit difficult. Every change to a single service requires re-compiling and deploying all of the services. This supports scale up/vertical scalability. More hardware resources are needed to scale the database capacity.

**(ii) Synchronous API calls pattern**

**Problem**—How can a microservice query or access the data which is available with other microservices?

**Context**—In MSA, each service has its own data. Since atomic services offer only limited function, to deliver useful function, it is always required to access or query the data associated with a service, i.e., microservices need to access the data associated with other services. *Since direct sharing of data by more than one service is not permitted in MSA*, how to query or access the data which is available with other services?

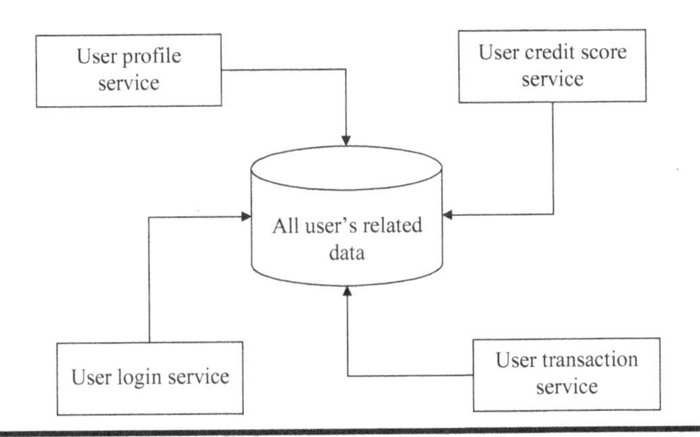


**Figure 8.21 Database integration pattern.**

**Solution—Synchronous API calls pattern**—In this pattern, the services communicate synchronously through an API. All the access to each other's data is coordinated through an API in a request–response fashion, and the service waits for data from the API to perform its action. Consider, for example, two services, namely a *user profile service*, and *user credit score service*. The user credit score service needs to read the user profile data. So, it invokes the user profile service through its API and gets what it needs. This is shown in Figure 8.22.

This provides the benefit of hiding many implementation details: The abstraction gives freedom to developers to implement the required changes as well as technologies without affecting each other and clients. For example, the user profile service could use Java and MySQL, while the user credit score service could use SQL server and .NET, and they can still easily speak to each other through the API.

**(iii) Asynchronous messaging patterns**

**Problem**—How to share database related events which are likely to trigger actions in other services without blocking or affecting the independent nature of services?

**Context**—In any applications, events are used to convey what notable changes have happened in the application. These events also trigger actions in other services. How do services keep informed about the events? How can it look for its interested events? How to share database related events which are likely to trigger actions in other services without blocking or affecting the independent nature of services?

**Solution—Asynchronous messaging patterns**—In this pattern, services exchange meaningful messages with each other through what are called commands or integration events. They are sent over asynchronous message brokers such as RabbitMQ, etc. Asynchronous communication between services using an asynchronous message broker is shown in Figure 8.23.

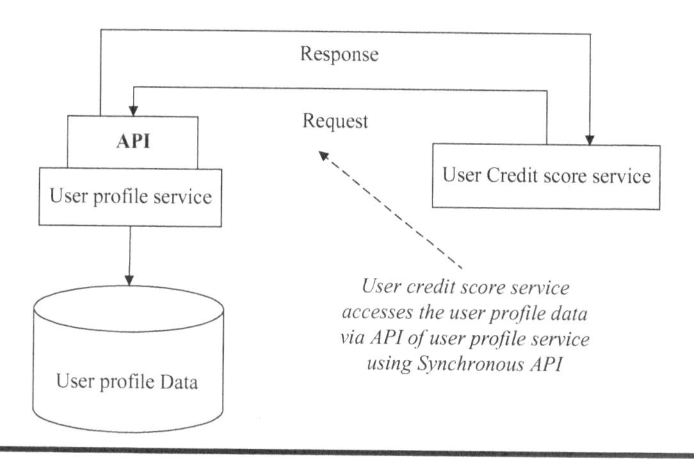


**Figure 8.22 Synchronous API call pattern.**

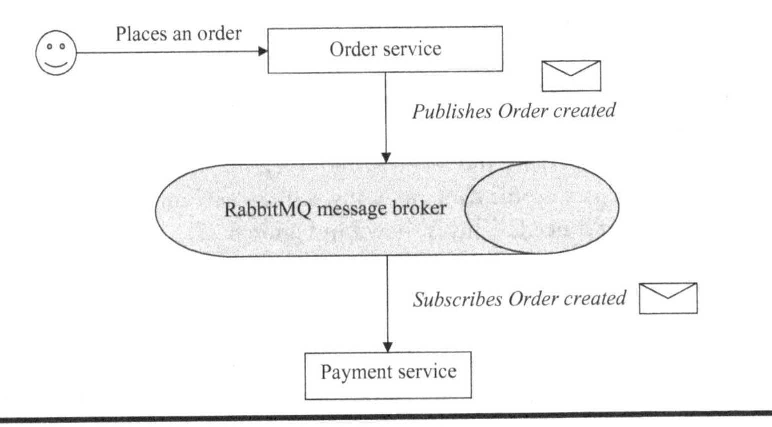


**Figure 8.23 Asynchronous message pattern via a message broker.**

Once a customer places an order with an order service, the order service creates an order and publishes the change of state, i.e., it publishes the *order created message* with asynchronous message broker RabbitMQ. The message broker sends the message to those services which have subscribed to this message. Say, for example, the payment service subscribes to the message, and once it receives the message, it starts the action of receiving payment from the customer.

**Two categories of messaging**—Typical messaging solutions are built on top of the properties of the transport. At a high-level, these transports could be divided into two categories: message queuing and message streaming.

- The *queuing solution* involves dealing with live data. Once a message is processed successfully, it is off the queue. As long as the processing can keep up, the queues won't build up and won't require too much space. However, the message order can't be guaranteed in cases of scaled-out subscribers.
- In the *streaming solution*, the messages are stored on a stream as they come in order. That happens on the message transport itself. The subscriber's position on a stream is maintained on the transport. It can reverse forward on the stream as necessary. This is very advantageous for failure and new subscription scenarios. However, this depends on how long the stream is. It requires a lot more configuration from storage perspectives, necessitating the archiving of streams.

## 8.2.7 Deployment Patterns

**Problem**—How to deploy a microservice with all its dependencies quickly?

**Context**—In the monolithic era, deploying or scaling a software system is just running multiple identical copies of the software into physical servers or virtual server. In the case of microservices application, there are many services and the services can be written in a variety of languages. Each microservice owns a specific resource, data, and monitoring and deployment strategy, and network configuration. So, the challenge is: How to deploy a microservice with all its dependencies and requirements?

Some of the deployment patterns for microservices include:

- Multiple services instances per host pattern
- Service instance per host pattern
  - Service instance per Virtual Machine pattern
  - Service instance per Container pattern
- Serverless deployment

**(i) Multiple service instances per host pattern**

In this pattern, multiple instances of the same service are deployed in a single (or same) host. The host may be a physical or virtual one. This is shown in Figure 8.24.

The Multiple service instances per host pattern has both benefits and drawbacks. One major benefit is its resource usage is relatively efficient. Multiple service instances share the server and its operating system. Another benefit of this pattern is that deploying a service instance is relatively fast. One simply copies the service to a host and starts it [6].

One major drawback is that there is little or no isolation of the service instances unless each service instance is a separate process. While you can accurately monitor each service instance's resource utilization, one cannot limit the resources each instance uses. It's possible for a misbehaving service instance to consume all of the memory or CPU of the host.

**(ii) Service instance per host pattern**

Another way to deploy microservices is by using a *Service instance per host pattern*. In this pattern, each service instance runs in isolation on its own host. There are two different specializations of this pattern, namely, (i) *Service instance per Virtual Machine* and (ii) *Service instance per container.*

**Service instance per Virtual Machine pattern**—This pattern is shown in Figure 8.25.

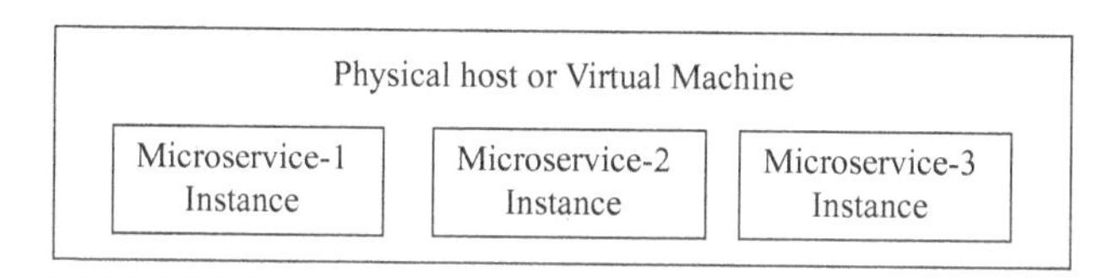


**Figure 8.24 Multiple service instances per host pattern.**

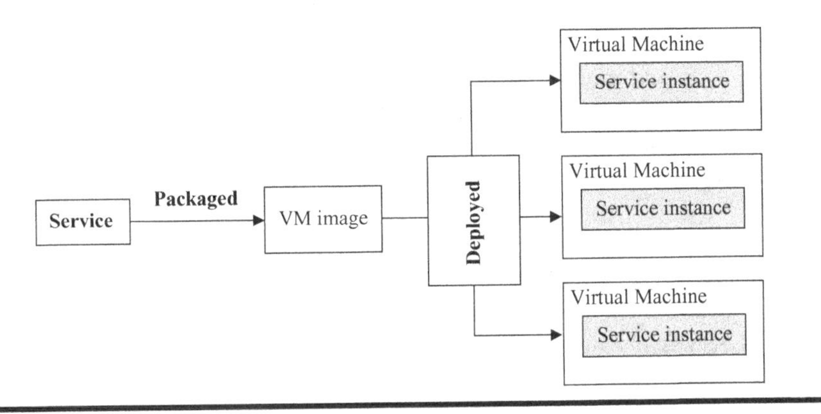


**Figure 8.25 Single instance per Virtual Machine.**

In this pattern, the service is packaged as a Virtual Machine image (VM image). This means that each service instance is deployed as VM that is launched using that VM image [7].

**Solution—Service instance per container pattern**—When using this pattern, each service instance runs in a separate container. Containers are positioned as the optimal runtime environment for microservices. Containers bring forth the much-required isolation. Containers can run everywhere. This kind of deployment is shown in Figure 8.26.

**Serverless deployment**—Serverless deployment hides the underlying infrastructure, and it will take a microservice's code to just run it. It is charged according to usage such as (i) how many requests it processed and (ii) how much resources are utilized for processing each request. To use this pattern, developers need to package their code and select the desired performance level. Various public cloud providers offer this service, where they use containers or Virtual

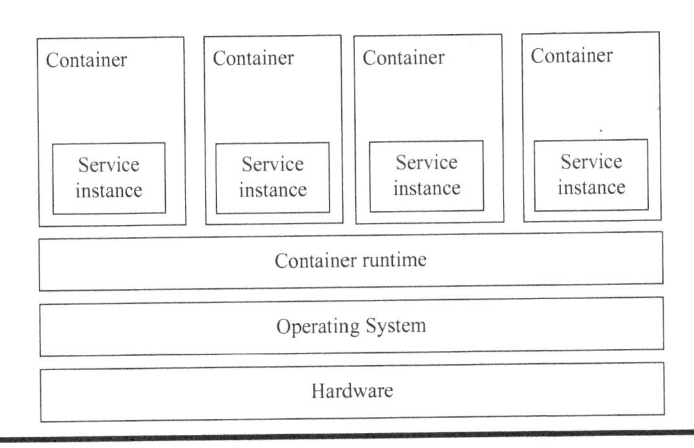


**Figure 8.26 Service instance per container pattern.**

Machines to isolate the services. In this system, users are not authorized to manage any low-level infrastructure such as servers, operating system, Virtual Machines, or containers.

Examples for serverless deployment environment include:

- AWS Lambda
- Google cloud functions
- Azure functions

One can call a serverless function directly using a service request or in response to an event or via an API gateway, or you can run them periodically according to cron-like schedule. Some of the benefits of serverless deployments are:

- Cloud consumers can focus on their code and application and need not to be worried about the underlying infrastructure.
- Cloud consumers need not worry about scaling as it will automatically scale in case of load.
- Cloud consumers need to pay only for what they use and not for the resources provisioned for them.

Some of the drawbacks of serverless deployments are:

- Many constraints and limitations, like limited languages support, better suits stateless services.
- Can only respond to requests from a limited set of input sources.
- Only suited for applications that can start quickly.
- Chance of high latency in case of a sudden spike in load.

***Summary***

Microservices architecture is definitely a positive development for software engineering. Existing applications are being modernized to be microservices-centric. Fresh applications are being built directly on MSA. However, there are a few crucial challenges and concerns. By leveraging design, integration, composition, decomposition, and deployment patterns, these difficulties can be overcome to a major extent. This document listed all the major microservices patterns in order to empower software architects and engineers to design highly flexible and futuristic applications.

***Exercises***

1. Describe in detail the need for design patterns for microservices-based applications.
2. List the different categories of design patterns for MSA.

3. Explain how design patterns help in a decomposing a monolithic application.
4. Assume that you are an application architect. There is a requirement to refactor a legacy application into a MSA-based application. Explain which design pattern you will use?
5. Assume that, as a developer, you are developing microservices that have highly sensitive functions. How do you hide the direct exposure of such a service from the client?
6. Explain in detail the different design patterns for database design.
7. When would you use blue-green deployment?
8. Which kind of service discovery is preferred when applications have a large number of microservices? Why?
9. Which messaging patterns facilitate you to design your services with maximum independence? Explain with examples.
10. Write a note on observability patterns.

## References

1. Kasun Indrasiri. Microservices, APIs and Integration. Medium. 2017. Available at: https://medium.com/@kasunindrasiri/microservices-apis-and-integration-7661448e8a86.
2. Software Design Patterns. Geeks for Geeks. Available at: https://www.geeksforgeeks.org/software-design-patterns/.
3. James Maioriello. What Are Design Patterns and Do I Need Them? Developer. 2002. Available at: https://www.developer.com/design/article.php/1474561/What-Are-Design-Patterns-and-Do-I- Need-Them.htm.
4. Karthick Thoppe. Microservices Design Patterns. TechBurst. 2017. Available at: https://techburst.io/microservices-design-patterns-a9a03be3aa5e.
5. Rajesh Bhojwani. Design Patterns for Microservices. DZone. 2018. Available at: https://dzone.com/articles/design-patterns-for-microservices.
6. Chris Richardson. Choosing a Microservices Deployment Strategy Part 6. DZone. 2016. Available at: https://dzone.com/articles/deploying-microservices.
7. Chris Richardson. Choosing a Microservices Deployment Strategy. NGINX. 2016. Available at: https://www.nginx.com/blog/deploying-microservices/.

# Chapter 9

# MSA Security and Migration

***Objective***

The objective of this chapter is to handle two complementary concepts, MSA security and MSA migration. By the end of the chapter, the reader will understand how security in MSA differs from that of conventional systems and how different security mechanisms are implemented in a MSA application using reference architecture. The will reader also understand the basic concepts of MSA migration, the motivating factors for MSA migration, issues associated with MSA migration, the migration process, and candidate applications for MSA migration.

***Preface***

When a business application grows in size, the development team also grows bigger, and companies end up with serious management and cooperation issues. In addition, modern business applications tend to go for collaboration-based product development to handle technological challenges. Microservices serves as an appropriate architecture style for the development of modern applications by decomposing the applications as independent services which are developed and deployed with small teams without any interdependencies. The migration to microservices architecture enables companies to develop their products more easily and flexibly. Migration to microservices is also challenging, though it is worth the effort in the long run. In the context of migration, one tends to have security-related questions in mind. According to this, this chapter discusses two important aspects, security in MSA and MSA migration.

In the first part, the chapter discusses the basic security requirements of any application, how the architecture of MSA applications differ from that of a conventional application, and how security mechanisms can be implemented in a MSA application. In the second part, the chapter discusses the basic needs of MSA migration, motivating factors for MSA migration, issues associated with MSA migration, the migration process, and candidate applications for MSA migration.

This chapter answers the following questions:

1. How does security get preserved in an MSA-based application?
2. How does MSA security differ from that of monolithic applications?
3. Do all businesses need to go for a MSA migration? What kinds of applications are appropriate for microservices?
4. What are the techniques required for MSA migration?
5. How does security get preserved in MSA?

This chapter provides the key to the above questions.

## 9.1 Basic Security Requirements

There are three security requirements for data security of any application, whether it is monolithic or microservices-based. They are confidentiality, integrity, and availability. These three requirements are basic building blocks of data security (Figure 9.1).

**Confidentiality**

Confidentiality ensures that the data is disclosed to only those users for whom the data is intended for, i.e., confidentiality ensures that sensitive information is accessed only by an authorized person and kept away from those who are not authorized to possess it. Examples of sensitive data include bank account details, personal information, health records, etc. If confidentiality is compromised, the data can be accessed by unauthorized persons, and it can lead to the loss of data privacy (privacy refers to the right of an individual to keep his or her health information private. Privacy deals with the ability of an individual to determine what data in a computer system can be shared with third parties).

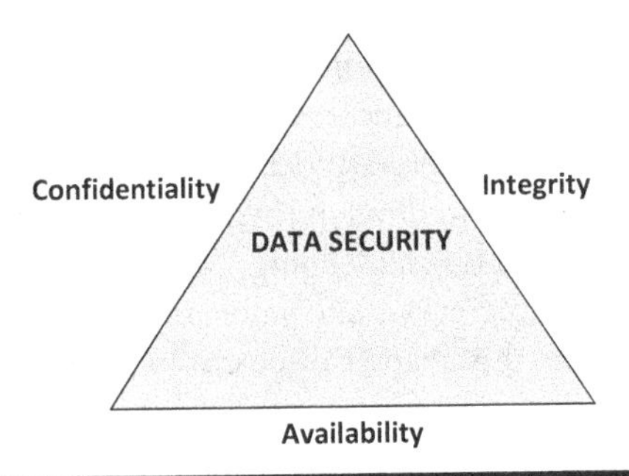


**Figure 9.1 Requirements/building blocks of data security.**

There are different attacks such as the following that can affect confidentiality:

- Packet sniffing—This refers to tapping networks and capturing data packets.
- Password cracking—This refers to various methods that recover passwords from data stores to attempt to gain unauthorized access to data.
- Eavesdropping—This is the unauthorized real-time interception of a private communication.
- Phishing—Phishing is the fraudulent attempt to obtain sensitive information such as usernames, passwords, and credit card details by being disguised as a trustworthy entity in a communication.
- Keylogging—Key logging or keystroke logging, is the action of recording the keys struck on a keyboard secretly, so that person using the keyboard is unaware that their actions are being monitored.

Security mechanisms for implementing confidentiality:

- Usernames and passwords.
- Two-factor authentication—Two-factor authentication (2FA), sometimes referred to as two-step verification or dual factor authentication, is a security process in which the user provides two different authentication factors to verify themselves to better protect both the user's credentials and the resources the user can access. In single-factor authentication (SFA), a user provides only one factor, typically a password. Two-factor authentication methods rely on users providing a password as well as a second factor, usually either a security token or a biometric factor like a fingerprint or facial scan.
- Biometric verification—Biometric authentication is a security process that relies on the unique biological characteristics of an individual to verify that he is authorized.
- Security tokens or key fobs—A security token is a physical device used to gain access to an electronically restricted resource.
- Data encryption—Data encryption is the process of converting data from plain text into another ciphertext using a secret key so that only people with access to a secret key can read it.

**Integrity**

Data integrity is the assurance that data can be accessed only by authorized people. Data integrity refers to the overall completeness, accuracy, and consistency of data stored in a database.

Integrity can be implemented by:

- Access control mechanisms.
- Checksums.
- Cryptographic checksums.

- Network administration should implement:
  - Proper documentation of system administration procedures, parameters, and maintenance activities.
  - Disaster recovery plans for occurrences such as power outages, server failures, or security attacks.
  - Redundancies during a disaster or failure.
- Measures must also be taken to ensure integrity by controlling the physical environment of networked terminals and servers from environmental hazards such as heat, dust, or electrical problems.

**Availability**

Availability implies that information is available to the authorized parties whenever required. Unavailability of data and systems can have serious consequences.

- It is essential to have plans and procedures in place to prevent or mitigate data loss as a result of a disaster.
- A disaster recovery plan must include unpredictable events such as natural disasters and fire.
- A routine backup job is advised in order to prevent or minimize total data loss from such occurrences.
- Extra security equipment or software such as firewalls and proxy servers can guard against downtime and unreachable data due to malicious actions such as denial-of-service (DoS) attacks and network intrusions.

Example attacks that affect availability are:

- DoS and DDoS attacks
- SYN flood attacks
- Physical attacks on the server infrastructure

## 9.2 Pragmatic Architecture for Secure MSA

In MSA, the application is broken into independent services, and each service has its own data. The application is typically accessed via the API gateway. In addition, clients can interact with the API gateway using a variety of client devices such as laptops and smartphones with Apple iOS, Google Android, etc. From a security point of view, an MSA application is perceived to contain three layers, namely a client layer, an API gateway layer, and a microservices layer [1]. Hence, implementing confidentiality, integrity, and availability is shared between these layers.

A pragmatic architecture for a secure MSA is demonstrated in references [1, 2], as shown in Figure 9.2.

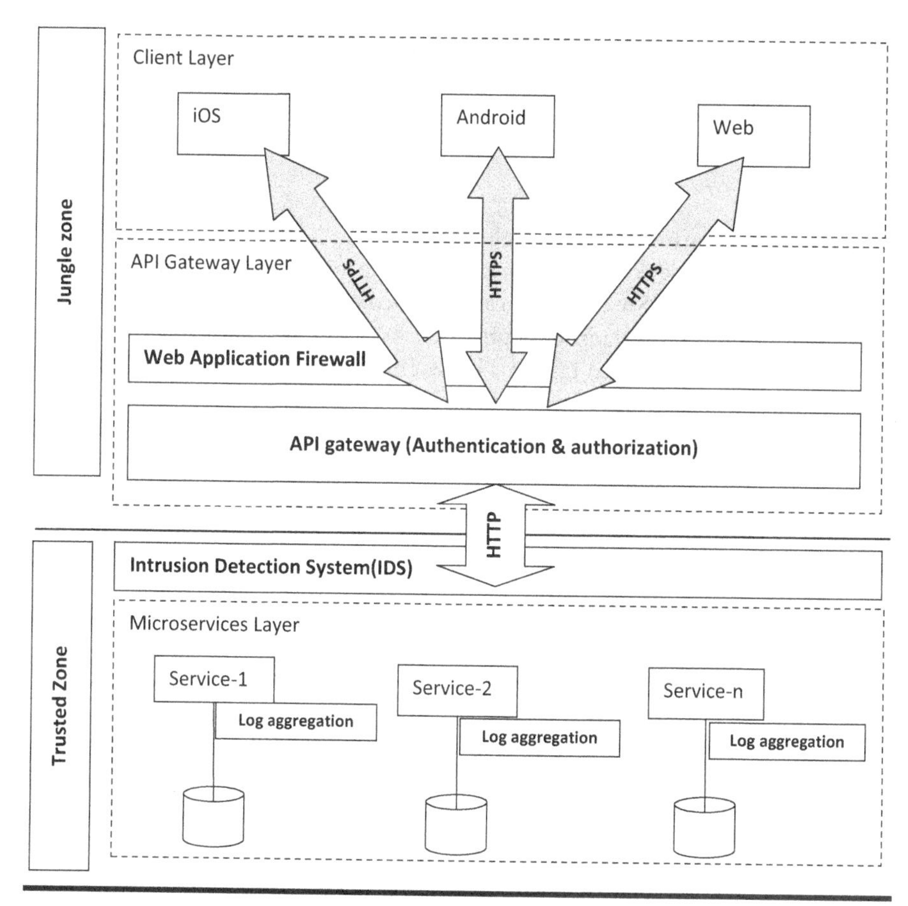


**Figure 9.2 Pragmatic architecture for secure MSA application.**

There is responsibility segregation through the different layers. The front layers, i.e., client layer and API gateway, take care of *confidentiality*; meanwhile, microservices handle *integrity*. *Availability* is shared between all the layers and if they are not accessible the platform is not working.

In addition to three layers, there are two security zones, the *jungle zone*, and *trusted zone*. The trusted zone is the zone inside the API gateway where exchanges can be done in a relatively easier manner. The jungle zone is the zone outside the API gateway where clients interact with the API gateway using a variety of devices and software. In this jungle zone, it is very much essential to take more security mechanisms in exchanges between gateway and client. The API gateway is the edge of an MSA-based application that is exposed to the client via the internet.

## 9.3 Security Mechanisms for MSA Applications

Different kinds of security mechanisms (see Figure 9.3) have to be incorporated to achieve the basic needs of data security, namely confidentiality, integrity, and availability.

**(i) Security mechanisms in the jungle layer**

Clients with various devices interact with the API gateway in the jungle layer. This layer is external to the MSA application and exposed to public networks. Any security vulnerability in this layer leads to security attacks. More and more security mechanisms have to be incorporated into this layer. Three mechanisms, namely perimeter security, the implementation of secure HTTP (HTTPS) and the implementation of web application firewall mechanisms are used as standard security mechanisms [2]

*Perimeter security*

Perimeter security refers to the implementation of proper security mechanisms at the perimeter so as to guard the company network and its resources. Common perimeter security mechanisms include:

- The company has to ensure that the network segmentation is properly implemented.
- The firewalls to external networks are properly configured.
- Only clients from within the system's network should be able to directly access individual microservices.

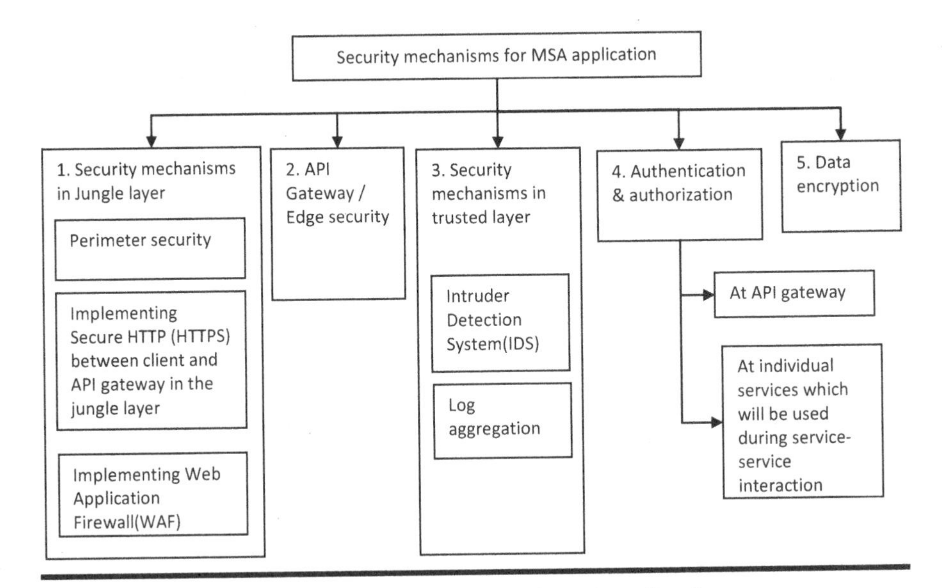


**Figure 9.3 Security mechanisms for an MSA-based application.**

- Only those components that must be accessible from outside the network should be exposed to other networks.
- Outside access to third-party systems like middleware should be limited to specific networks or hosts.

*Implementing secure HTTP(HTTPS) in the jungle zone*
Secure Socket Layer (SSL) certificates are small data files that digitally bind a cryptographic key to an organization's details. When installed on a web server, it activates the padlock and the HTTPS protocol and allows secure connections from a web server to a browser.

SSL certificates bind together:

- A domain name, server name, or hostname
- An organizational identity (i.e., company name) and location

An organization needs to install the SSL certificate onto its web server to initiate a secure session with the browser. Once a secure connection is established, all web traffic between the web server and the web browser will be secure. With an SSL certificate, HTTP becomes HTTPS, as shown in Figure 9.4.

All the exchanges over HTTPS are encrypted.

*Implementing web application firewall*
A web application firewall (WAF) has to be implemented as is shown in Figure 9.2, which can inspect all incoming requests for attempts to exploit common or specific web application vulnerabilities (such as SQL or Cross-Site Scripting injection attempts) and prevent suspicious requests from being sent to the API gateway. The scope of the WAF could also be expanded to cover third-party systems if they provide web services to external clients.

**(ii) API gateway/edge security**
In MSA, as mentioned earlier, the API gateway is the only component that is exposed to the internet, and it is the only component that can be accessed from the outside world and other networks. Client requests or calls to the API gateway can be made secure by:

- Hardening the API gateway
- Hardening the host operating system and platform on which the API gateway runs

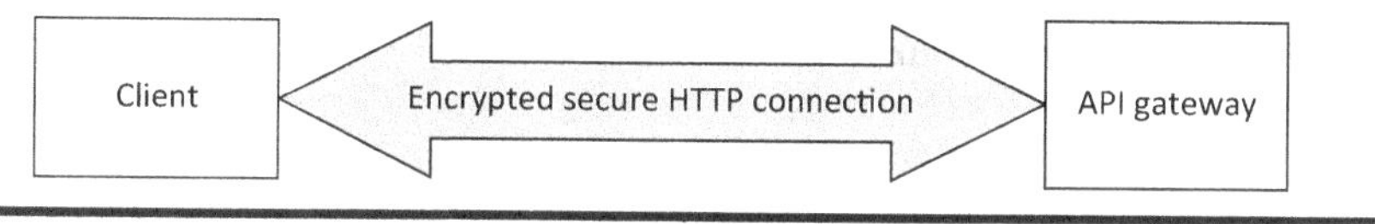


**Figure 9.4 Implementing Secure HTTP with SSL/TLS in the jungle zone.**

From the security point of view, API gateways usually handle the authentication and authorization from the external clients to the microservice level. Typically, an API gateway implements authentication and authorization using OAuth and JSON Web Tokens (JWT) as OAuth provides high scalability (please refer to Chapter 5).

**(iii) Security mechanisms in the trusted zone**

Implementing security mechanisms become important as the API gateway layer is likely to be compromised by its security. Standard mechanisms for implementing security in a trusted zone include:

- Implementing intrusion detection/prevention systems
- Log file aggregation
- Data encryption

*Implementing intrusion detection/prevention system*

An intrusion detection and/or prevention system (IDS/IPS) could be used to monitor the network traffic between the API gateway and the microservices; the microservices and the external systems and in-between the microservices themselves.

*Log file aggregation*

Typically, a large e-commerce application consists of multiple services and service instances that are running on multiple machines. Requests often span multiple service instances. Each service instance generates and writes information about what it is doing to a log file in a standardized format. *The log file contains errors, warnings, information, and debug messages.* The implementation of log file aggregation and correlation should be considered as log files help in understanding and retracing runtime behavior and request paths over multiple services. It is an important tool to reconstruct what happened during a security incident and to follow an attacker's actions after the fact.

*Data encryption*

In the database layer, one should consider encrypting the data stores of services that keep sensitive data. In a microservice environment, the separation of data into service-specific stores would enable us to be very selective in what we consider encrypting.

**(iv) Authentication and authorization**

*At the API gateway*

Authentication—Authentication is the process of verifying one's identity, genuineness, and credibility. In information systems, a user has to prove that he is an authenticated user with his unique identity features.

Authorization determines what permissions an authenticated user has in accessing different resources. It controls a person's access to the resources according to the privileges allowed for him. Typically the permissions are set by the owner of a resource. For example, an owner of a file can set different permissions such as *read permission*, *write permission*, and *execute permission* while he is creating a file. Privileges are set using various techniques such as *Access Control Lists* (*ACL*), *access controls for URLs*, *Role Based Access Control* (*RBAC*), etc.

In a MSA-based application, how to authenticate and authorize users to access the application is a big concern. The obvious place to implement first-level authentication and authorization are at the API gateway. In this model, the API gateway handles the authentication and the access controls to the individual microservices and their functions. The API gateway commonly employs an OAuth 2.0 protocol/open standard for secure authorization. But this kind of API gateway-based authentication and authorization becomes insufficient when an application handles sensitive functions and data. So, after API gateway authentication, the gateway has to forward the authentication tokens to the microservice, so that the services can implement more advanced verification measures according to the needs of individual services.

*During service-to-service interactions*
Since microservices are likely to offer limited functionality, they always interact with one another by sending messages according to the APIs of the services. Implementing service-to-service authentication while services interact with one another adds another level of security to applications. There are various approaches for implementing service-to-service authentication which include:

- HTTP basic authentication with username and password
- Single sign-on approach using standards such as Security Assertion Markup Language (SAML) and tools such as OpenID Connect
- Directory services such as active directory
- Client certificates
- Hash-based message authentication codes to ensure requests were not altered during transport
- API keys—authenticating services using simple shared secrets

## 9.4 MSA Migration

In the early 2000s, e-commerce applications were implemented with monolith architecture. Over time, customer and market demands became more complex and delivery expectations became more urgent. When the monolithic application grows in size with new features and functionalities, more and more developers need to work with the applications. This results in high interdependencies among the teams. Huge application sizes as well as the interdependencies among the team members prohibit the frequent deployment and continuous delivery of applications. The monolithic platform has the following issues [3, 4]:

*Tight coupling between front end and back end*—Monolithic platforms operate on a tightly coupled front end and back end. Any personalization or customization request involves editing the database, code, and front-end platform, which is extremely time-intensive.

*Software complexity*—As the size of the monolithic application grows with new features and functions, it becomes more difficult to maintain and more challenging to understand by the developers working with it.

*Lack of agility*—With monolithic commerce solutions, teams are usually structured according to their individual functions, such as front end, back end, or database. When a request is made that affects all of these functions, tasks have to be shared across multiple team members. As a result, rolling out new features or entering new markets takes too long and leads to missed business opportunities.

*Fragility*—In a centralized architecture, the individual parts are highly coupled and dependent on each other. This results in a single point of failure. This prevents individual developers from taking responsibility for the system.

*Inefficient testing*—In monolithic applications, even if a small part of the application is changed, the entire application needs to be tested in its entirety. In addition, because of the internal dependencies, the effort involved in automatic testing and quality assurance rises exponentially.

*Scaling issues*—Instead of adding power to the existing platform, with most monolithic applications, adding more servers—or scaling horizontally—is the only option. This in turn creates many other issues.

### 9.4.1 The Advantages of MSA

Unlike heavy and slow monolithic architectures, microservices are small services that are individually developed and deployed. Communicating via APIs, microservices reduce software complexity, scale vertically, and provide increased flexibility, speed, and resiliency. Microservices enable enterprise agility. Customer demands can be met in days or weeks versus weeks or months, which ultimately puts enterprises in a better position than their competitors.

MSA architecture provides the following benefits:

*Decoupling between front end and back end*—In MSA, front ends and back ends are decoupled. Changes can be incorporated in either layer individually and independently without affecting the other.

*Individual scaling*—The front end and back end can scale independently as they are decoupled. Traffic on one side, say front-end traffic, does not impact the back end. Developers can extend services to new touch points without needing to rely on the entire system.

*Increased speed and resiliency*—Without having to maintain full stack software, new user interfaces can be implemented rapidly. Development is more efficient because teams can work in parallel, and due to decoupling, changes can be made to the UI without having to test the core back-end logic.

*Experimental freedom*—Development experiments are not dependent on modifications to both the front-end and back-end code, and are therefore less risky. Developers can perform individual A/B tests for specific parts of a commerce site or build new Progressive Web Apps (PWA) without requiring the back end.

*More customization options*—Multiple front ends can be provided to cater to a wide variety of clients who access the application typically using smartphones or laptops on any pervasive device. All the client interfaces will ultimately connect to one API and one underlying system.

## 9.4.2 Motivating Drivers for MSA Migration

From [5], the important or primary motivating drivers for MSA migration include software maintenance, scalability, delegation of responsibilities to independent teams, easy support for DevOps, and frequent deployment/continuous delivery and agility. This is shown in Figure 9.5.

*Maintainability*—In MSA, a large application is divided into small-sized, independent microservices with each service having its own database. Since each service is capable of individual design, development, and deployment, developers can change their code without any dependencies. They can go for immediate

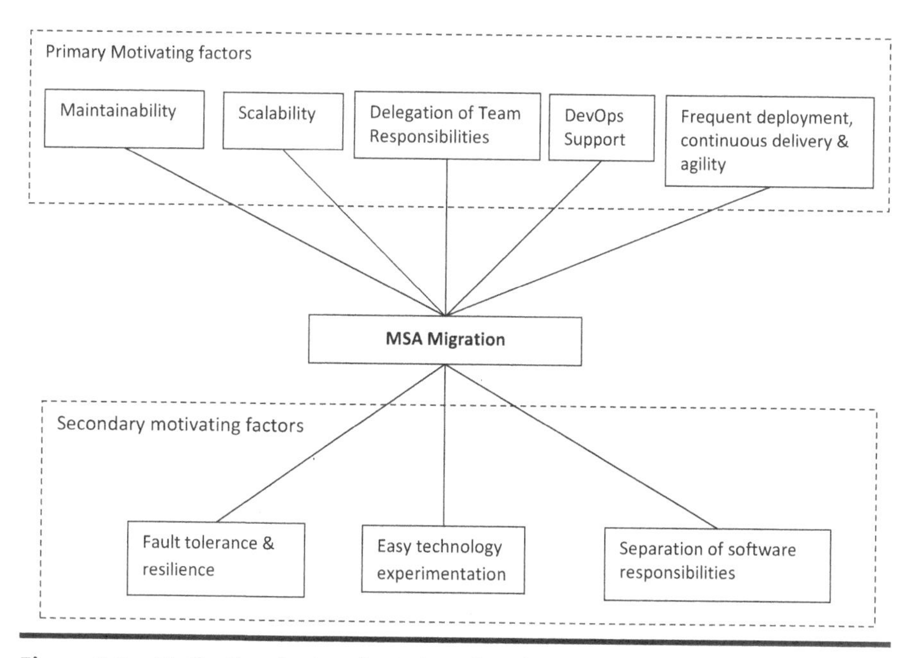


**Figure 9.5 Motivating factors for MSA migration.**

deployment without waiting for any other team to complete their work. Moreover, the small size of each microservice contributes to increasing code understandability, and thus to improve the maintainability of the code.

*Scalability*—In a monolithic application, the required scalability has to be implemented over the entire application. Consider an e-commerce application. Assume that the website needs to cater for around 3000 customers per second. But assume that there are only a very limited number of database operations/updates. Now to provide the required scalability, the entire application will be typically horizontally scaled, and load is balanced to evenly distribute the incoming requests. This is shown in Figure 9.6.

As shown in Figure 9.6, in a monolithic application, the entire application has to be scaled to provide the required scalability even to a small portion of the application. So, scaling monolithic systems requires a huge investment in terms of hardware and software.

In contrast, in MSA, the services can scale independently. The required number of instances can be deployed according to need, as shown in Figure 9.7.

As shown in Figure 9.7, three instances of microservice-1 are deployed for scalability, whereas only one instance of microservice-2 is deployed. Each microservice can be deployed on a different server, with different levels of performance, and can be written in the most appropriate development language. If there is a bottleneck in one microservice, the specific microservice can be containerized and executed

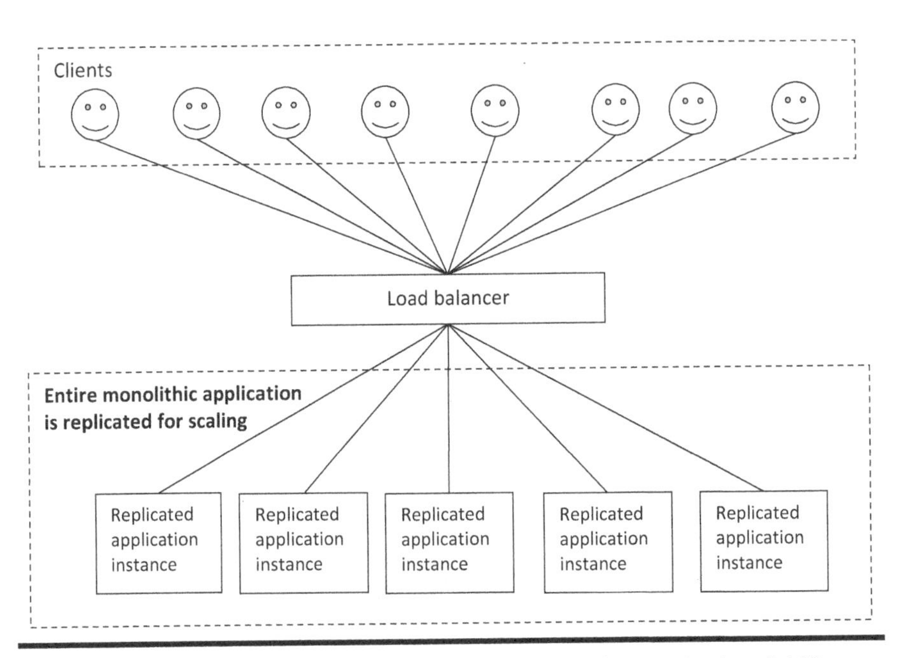


**Figure 9.6 Scaling the entire monolithic application (for required scalability, say in front end).**

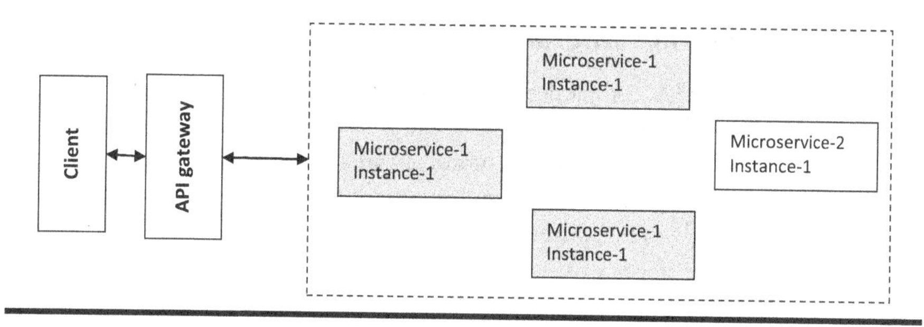


**Figure 9.7 Independent scaling of individual microservices.**

across multiple hosts in parallel, without the need to deploy the whole system to a more powerful machine.

*Delegation of team responsibilities*—In MSA, each small team owns the code base and can be responsible for the development of each service. Each team can maintain independent revisions and build environments based on its requirements. The distribution of clear and independent responsibilities among teams allows splitting large project teams into several small and more efficient teams. Moreover, since microservices can be developed with different technologies and with a totally different internal structure, only high-level and technical decisions need to be coordinated among teams, while other technical decisions can be made by the teams themselves.

*DevOps support*—The adoption of a DevOps toolchain is supported by microservices. Since each service can be developed and deployed independently, each team can easily develop, test, and deploy their services independent of other teams

*Frequent deployment, continuous delivery, and agility*—Since the teams of MSA applications work independently, new features and functionalities can be easily added. In addition, since there are no interdependencies among the teams, the new features or updates or revised versions of services can go for immediate deployment without waiting for other parts of the applications. Also, the application can be delivered continuously. In a nutshell, the application is delivered very fast so as to meet the business agility.

*Fault tolerance and resilience*—The failure of a single microservice does not commonly impact the whole system. Moreover, faulty microservices can be quickly restarted. Faulty microservices can be quickly replaced with alternate versions of the same service to deliver the correct output without the need to restart the whole application.

*Easy technology experimentation*—Microservices are small, and hence easier and faster to develop and experiment with new technologies, new languages, and features. These kind of heterogeneous languages or technologies are not supported by monolithic applications.

*Separation of software responsibilities*—Microservices are responsible for one single task within well-defined boundaries and are self-contained; therefore, development is greatly simplified.

### 9.4.3 Issues in MSA Migration

While migrating to MSA, companies face the following issues, as shown in Figure 9.8.

*Decoupling from the monolithic system*—The general behavior of our participants was to start the development of new non-critical features with a microservices-based architectural style. *Database migration and data splitting*—The migration of legacy databases needs to be addressed carefully. It is very difficult to split existing data according to the needs of microservices. On the other hand, the consultants recommended splitting the data in existing databases such that each microservice accesses its own private database.

*Communication among services*—Every microservice needs to communicate. They have to communicate on the network, which adds complexity and increases network-related issues.

*Effort estimation and overhead*—Estimating the development time of a microservices-based system is considered less accurate than estimating a monolithic system. Despite our initial thoughts—that the effort overhead should be higher at the beginning of the project, but lower once the initial setup of the system is done—they reported that the benefits of increased maintainability and scalability highly compensate for the extra effort.

*Effort required for the DevOps infrastructure*—For all participants, the adoption of microservices required adopting a DevOps infrastructure which requires a lot of effort.

*Effort required for library conversion*—Existing libraries require more effort for conversion. They cannot be simply reused, but rather need to be converted into one or more microservices, which again requires additional effort.

*Service orchestration issues*—Microservices-based architectural styles require an orchestration layer, which adds complexity to the system and needs to be developed reliably.

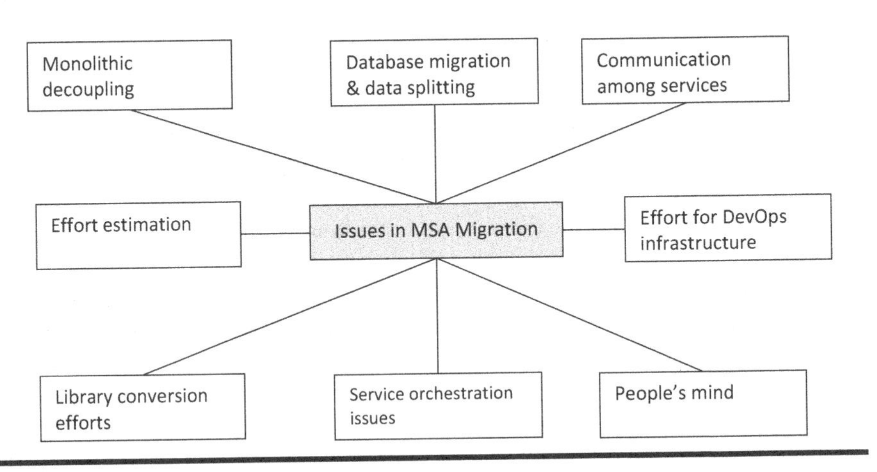


**Figure 9.8 Issues in MSA migration.**

*People's minds*—Changes in existing architectures are generally an issue for several developers. Developers are reluctant to accept such an important change to the software they wrote.

### 9.4.4 Migration Process Using Strangler Pattern

Rewriting a large monolithic application from scratch is associated with the following difficulties[6]:

- Rewriting a large application mandatorily requires a very good understanding of the legacy system.
- Rewriting a large application using MSA requires a huge effort.
- When a company follows rewriting the monolith from scratch, it cannot start using the new system until it is complete.
- There will be uncertainty until the new system is developed and functioning as expected.

Thus, instead of rewriting the entire application, the Strangler pattern suggests replacing the functionality of the monolithic application step by step.

The Strangler pattern is a popular design pattern for incrementally transforming a monolithic application into microservices by replacing a particular functionality with a new service. Once the new functionality is ready, the old component is strangled, the new service is put into use, and the old component is decommissioned altogether.

To implement MSA migration using Strangler pattern, three steps are followed. They are (i) transform, (ii) coexist, and (iii) eliminate.

- In the transform step, a new component is developed using MSA (transform).
- In the coexist step, both the old component and new service are deployed, and they both coexist for a period of time.
- When the new service is fully tested without any issues, the legacy component is eliminated.

These steps are shown in Figure 9.9.

The newly developed microservices are deployed as individual and independent units with relevant data and other dependencies.

### 9.4.5 Disadvantages of MSA Migration

- MSA migration involves a huge upfront cost.
- Implementing MSA is expensive and time-consuming.
- MSA migration involves huge resources.
- MSA applications are associated with complexities of distributed systems.
- MSA applications use high memory.

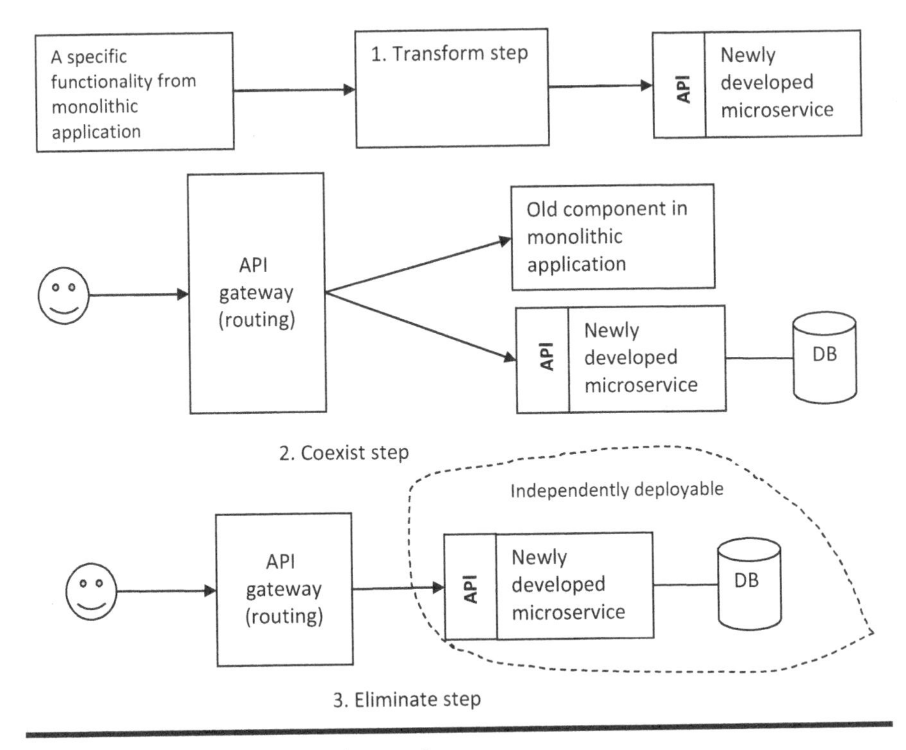


**Figure 9.9 The three steps of Strangler pattern.**

- Managing a large number of services is complex.
- Testing over the distributed deployment is complex.
- MSA involves multiple databases. With multiples databases, it is difficult to manage transactions.
- MSA requires skilled developers.
- Making remote calls is complex.

## 9.4.6 Candidate Applications for MSA Migration

The following are examples of candidate applications for MSA migration:

- Business applications committed to continuous innovation.
- Business applications which are committed to addressing market demands and continuously innovating to stay competitive at a more rapid pace.
- The monolithic platform requires a hard and laborious upgrade.
- Monolithic applications which are in need of a mandatory upgrade, but upgrading such applications is very hard and laborious.
- Applications which need to enhance customer experience.
- Applications which require connectivity, advanced personalization, and consistency.

***Summary***
This chapter discussed two important aspects, security in MSA and MSA migration. Every company tends to worry about security when migrating its resources to new technology or architecture. In this context, the chapter first discussed the core data security requirements, namely data confidentiality, integrity, and availability. How these three can be achieved in MSA was described with the help of reference architecture. In the second part, the chapter discussed the need for MSA migration, motivating factors for migration, issues associated with migration, migration process, and candidate applications for MSA migration.

***Exercises***

1. How does security in MSA differ from security in monolithic applications?
2. Explain the basic data security requirements for any application.
3. Explain the different security mechanisms for an MSA-based application.
4. List the motivating factors for MSA migration.
5. List the advantages and drawbacks of MSA migration.
6. Do you think all enterprise applications need MSA migration?
7. List the candidate applications for MSA migration.
8. Explain the issues associated with MSA migration.
9. How do we preserve privacy of data?
10. If containers and a cloud environment is preferred to MSA, do we have the same vendor-lock-in problems as in the cloud?

# References

1. Maxime Thomas. Secure a Microservices Architecture. Medium. 2017. Available at: https://medium.com/@maximethomas_46287/secure-a-microservices-architecture-9f148c4f3b5e.
2. Julian Hanhart. Building Secure Microservice Architectures. 2017. Available at: http://www.awesomo.ch/docs/term-paper/secure-microservices.pdf.
3. Mariia Robak. Successful Migration to Microservices: Why, When, and How. DZone. Available at: https://dzone.com/articles/successful-migration-to-microserv ices-why-when-and.
4. From Monolith to Microservices. ZAELAB. Available at: https://cdn2.hubspot.net/hubfs/4784080/Images/others/Whitepaper%20-%20From%20Monolith%20to %20Microservices_Full.pdf.
5. Davide Taibi, Valentina Lenarduzzi, and Claus Pahl. Processes, Motivations, and Issues for Migrating to Microservices Architectures: An Empirical Investigation. IEEE Cloud Computing, 4(5), 2017. Available at: http://www.valentinalenarduzzi.it/papers/Paper_id2.pdf.
6. Samir Behara. Monolith to Microservices Using the Strangler Pattern. DZone. 2018. Available at: https://dzone.com/articles/monolith-to-microservices-using-the-strangl er-patt.

# Chapter 10

# Platform Solutions for Microservices Architecture

***Objective***

The objective of this chapter is to describe how different standardized platform solutions are useful in the design, development, and deployment of microservices-centric applications. By the end of the chapter, the reader will understand how different kinds of platforms such as development platforms, deployment platforms, middleware platforms, and resiliency platforms facilitate the quick adoption of MSA.

***Preface***

It is an indisputable truth that standardized platform solutions consistently contribute to the growing adoption of microservices architecture in speedily and smartly produced enterprise-grade software applications. Predominantly there are cloud-enabled and native applications being carved out of microservices. In the recent past, a number of different kinds of platforms have appeared for simplifying and streamlining microservices-centric application design, development, and deployment. There are integrated development environments (IDEs) for a variety of programming languages. Further, there are powerful platform solutions for easing up continuous integration, delivery and deployment, logging, monitoring, governance, health-checking, security, composition, etc. Then, there are API gateways and management suites geared toward the leverage of MSA in a highly simplified manner. There are container-enablement platforms (Docker is the clear-cut leader) and container orchestration and management platforms (Kubernetes is the market leader) for packaging and running microservices at scale everywhere. Thus, to make MSA penetrative, pervasive, and persuasive, the role and responsibility of platform solutions are acquiring a special significance in the MSA era. This chapter is specially prepared for explaining the various platforms and how they conveniently contribute for the easier, risk-free, and quicker adoption of MSA for releasing business-critical and adaptive applications across multiple verticals.

## Introduction

Designing a scalable and fault-tolerant application is the need of the hour. Enterprise applications are becoming very complicated. An application can be scaled easily when the application services are stateless and loosely coupled. Having multiple instances of microservices and distributing them across geographically distributed servers are being touted as the way forward for producing highly scalable and available applications. An application's stability and reliability are being ensured through these techniques. As applications become web-scale, software applications and the underlying IT infrastructure have to be reliable in order to ensure business continuity. Traditional applications run on a single process, and hence even if there is a problem in a component, the whole application is bound to go down. Also, the scalability of a particular application component cannot be achieved due to the tight coupling of the application components. Updating and upgrading a legacy application is not an easy task and consumes a lot of time. An application's reliability is squarely dependent on the reliability of all the participating and contributing application components. MSA has the strength to overcome the deficiencies of conventional applications and to produce futuristic and flexible applications that can fulfill the growing expectations of businesses and application users.

MSA is an application architecture pattern that structures the application as a dynamic collection of loosely coupled and lightweight services. Microservices are not only logically separated but can also be physically segregated in order to produce and sustain distributed applications. The distributed and decentralized nature of microservices bring a number of distinct features that are not just logically separated but are also physically separated at runtime. Microservices enable continuous integration, delivery, and deployment. Microservices support horizontal scalability. The single point of failure of traditional applications is being eliminated through the leverage of microservices architecture.

## 10.1 Challenges in a MSA Approach/The Need for Microservices Platforms

MSA solves most of the operational issues associated with traditional application deployment. However, there are a few fresh concerns being raised by MSA. Most importantly, the number of microservices representing an application is on the higher side, and hence operational and management complexities are bound to rise further. There are several automated tools, accelerators, special engines, and other platform solutions to embrace MSA in a big way. Besides development teams, highly skilled release engineers and cloud operations team are required to tackle these challenges. Monolithic applications get modernized as microservices-centric applications. Enterprise applications get modified accordingly and are migrated to cloud environments to reap all the originally expressed benefits of the cloud idea.

Microservices are small in size, and hence for an enterprise and cloud IT environment, the number of service components goes up significantly. The connectivity complexity is bound to rise. It becomes a dense environment.

- Development teams come out with frequent changes and expect the updated microservices to be deployed quickly in production environments toward continuous innovation.
- Cloud infrastructure components (Virtual Machines [VMs], containers, application delivery controllers [ADCs], API gateways, etc.) are programmable and growing in number.
- Auto-scaling, self-healing, etc., are empowering cloud environments to be dynamic and adaptive.
- Endpoints and secrets are manually configured for each service. The manual configuration works well only for a limited number of microservices. When applications are being stuffed with a large number of fine-grained services, the manual configuration becomes very complex. Hence, automation is the way forward. Also, microservices are innately dynamic, and hence service endpoints become dynamic. If the service configuration is done wrong, then the stability of cloud environments is riddled with questions.

There are other noteworthy challenges extensively being associated with MSA. IT professionals and practitioners constantly unearth and articulate viable approaches to surmount them. Powerful and promising technologies, tools, and tips are being heavily demanded in order to overcome the concerns of MSA. Specifically speaking, experts are of the view that multifaceted platforms are the strategic answer for the accentuated MSA challenges.

## 10.2 Foundational Capabilities of Microservices Platforms

A microservices platform consists of a number of foundational capabilities that allow the efficient developing, building, deploying, and managing of such microservices, as vividly illustrated in Figure 10.1. Having understood the strategic implications of MSA, enterprises are keen on leveraging its distinct advantages as a part of digital transformation initiatives. The digitization and digitalization aspects are demanding the unique contributions of MSA.

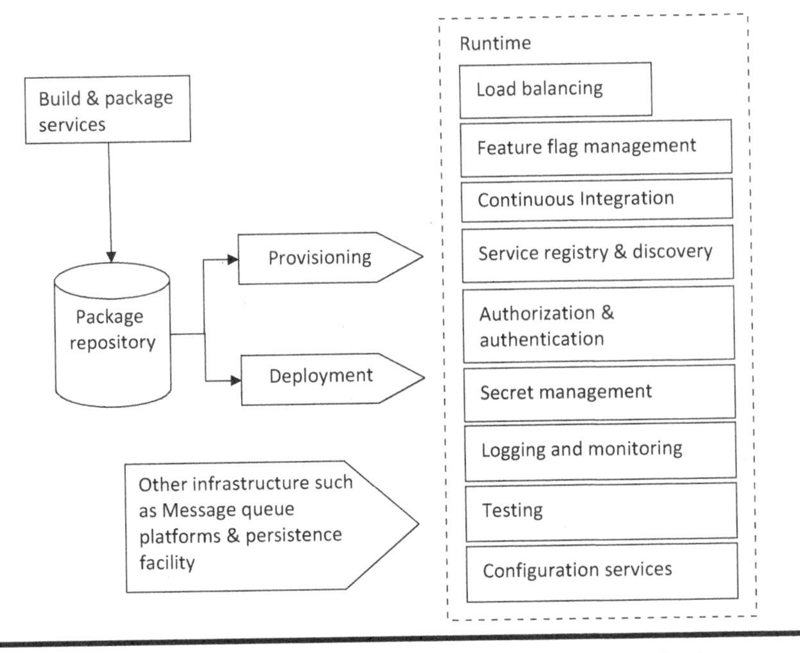


**Figure 10.1 The foundational capabilities of the microservices platform.**

As in Figure 10.1, after development is completed, the services are built and packaged. The packages are stored in a repository. Then, containers are provisioned to deploy the packaged services. In deployment, typically, each service is deployed in a container, and the containers are managed by orchestration platforms.

Once the services are deployed in containers, the operational or runtime environment is managed by different capabilities of the microservices platform. These capabilities include load-balancing, the dynamic addition of features to an MSA application, security-related secret management, dynamic service discovery, life cycle management of containers, logging, and monitoring, etc. [1]. These capabilities have become essential building blocks for microservices solutions.

**Load-balancing**—This, in the microservice era, happens on the client-side or on the server-side. There are load-balancing solutions in the form of hardware appliances, which guarantee higher performance/throughput, and the failure rate is very small. In the recent past, load-balancing was provided as a service through the virtualization concept. Load balancers are shared across multiple tenants. Software load balancers are also becoming popular, and they are being deployed on commoditized servers. Software load balancers are easily configurable and customizable. Typically, the load-balancing feature is being attached to the service locator module.

**Feature flag management**—The feature flag management capability refers to the facility to dynamically add new features to an MSA application package and deploy the new features. In addition, this feature has to maintain different versions of service instances of an application.

**Continuous integration/delivery (CI/CD)**—Microservices architecture (MSA) facilitates agile application design. There are proven frameworks, platforms, programming models, and methods for accelerated software development. Now, with the widespread adoption of the DevOps concept and culture, the goal of agile software deployment gets a strong boost. There are continuous integration, delivery and deployment tools, and technologies emerging and evolving fast for fulfilling the DevOps objectives. These tools bring the required automation for software testing, building, integration, and delivery. Without the tooling in place, there is no way that producing new microservices is easy.

**Service registry and discovery**—It is important for client devices and applications to find and access microservices. As the number and diversity of microservices continue to grow, there is a need for a service registry/repository and service locator. Microservices have to register their latest location address with service registry in order to be found and leveraged. A service locator plays a very vital role in enabling this requirement. Microservices are extremely dynamic, and hence it is essential that the exact location of the microservices and their instances are updated with the registry. Discovery tools such as Consul.io or etcd are popular in locating the desired services.

**Secret system**—Public and private keys are generated and used in order to enhance microservices security. Keys cannot be kept in the traditional configuration management systems. For the dynamic microservices era, there has to be a separate key management system in place in order to manage the key lifecycle, availability, and security. The microservices platform has to provide this feature.

**Authentication and authorization**—Every system has its own users (internal as well as external). Every user has to be accordingly identified, authenticated, and authorized to access IT services and business applications. The authorization has to be handled at the individual microservice level.

**Logging**—This is an important feature for capturing and stocking the log data of microservices. The log analytics is a vital function for extracting a lot of actionable and timely insights out of the log data. The log's intelligence comes in handy when automating several manual tasks. It gives the required knowledge to the microservices operations team to pursue counteractive measures in time. The format of the messages and configuration of forwarders are demanded. Format specifications typically include identification of the microservice, time, and severity. There should also be very specific security logging requirements, including formatting. Every microservice call (both inbound and outbound) must be recorded. A platform solution can do this, and if direct connections are established between microservices, then the logging logic has to be etched into each of the participating microservice.

**Monitoring**—This is another activity that is required to run software and hardware systems in a predictable manner. There are business rules and policies exclusively formed and firmed up for effective monitoring. Business workloads, IT platforms, and infrastructures ought to be minutely monitored for their proper functioning and delivery of their obligations. Monitoring systems are being built and deployed for different cloud resources (bare metal (BM) servers, VMs, and containers). A core requirement for monitoring includes the traceability of service requests. Any healthy microservices-centric application has to consider monitoring as the crucial data point in order to be successful in their operations, offerings, and outputs.

**Testing**—Microservices are often upgraded and updated for accommodating business and technology changes. These updated microservices have to pass through unity and integration testing gates. Once they cross through those hurdles successfully, they are ready to be delivered. IT teams do not want to push faulty code into production, and the microservices platform has to facilitate developers and DevOps professionals in pushing verified and validated code into production.

**Configuration services**—Increasingly, configuration services are used as a part of platform solutions. The idea is to stop different teams from setting up their own configuration services.

**Persistence**—Microservices require isolated data persistence models to maintain its state. SQL, in-memory, and NoSQL databases besides file systems are the technologies of choice.

**Messaging infrastructure**—Messaging has become the dominant facet for enabling microservices to interact with one another on a need basis. Messages are being passed in a synchronous manner (request and response) and in an asynchronous manner (publish-and-subscribe). Messaging platforms abstract the messaging-related capabilities of microservices. This would enable teams to use messaging easily without having to set up their own infrastructure. This might not preclude a team from setting up and using their own if the need arises. In short, queuing, publish–subscribe, and other fundamental message exchange patterns have to be employed for microservices to collaborate. Technologies like RabbitMQ or Kafka are popular options.

## 10.3 Classification of Microservices Platforms

Different kinds of microservices platforms (see Figure 10.2) include (i) microservices deployment platforms, (ii) microservices security and service resiliency platforms, (iii) API platforms, and (iv) microservices development platforms.

Platforms play a very crucial role in shaping up the microservices era. There are integrated development platforms for producing microservices. There are middleware platforms for enabling clients connecting with microservices and for streamlining microservices to talk to one another, and finally deployment platforms are emerging and evolving fast to speed up microservices-centric applications.

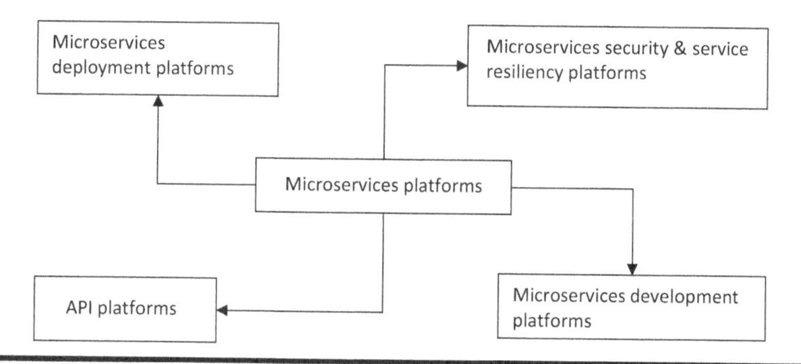


**Figure 10.2 The different kinds of microservices platforms.**

### *10.3.1 Microservices Deployment Platforms*

Microservices are fine-grained and designed, developed, and deployed by distributed teams. The respective teams take care of their microservices and their lifecycle. This means microservices are continuously updated and upgraded based on customer feedback, technology changes, and business sentiments. This means, there will be frequent deployments of microservices. That is, continuous integration, delivery, deployment, and response have become the new normal in the MSA era. There are pioneering platform solutions to automate these tasks. In addition, the deployment platform solutions provide the following benefits.

- Every microservice, when fully developed and debugged, has to be deployed in a production environment. For the sake of high availability, multiple instances of the same microservice can be deployed in distributed servers. With the multi-cloud strategy gaining momentum, microservices are being deposited in geographically distributed cloud environments. A microservice can be wrapped into a container with all its dependencies and can be deployed anywhere (edge devices, laptops, enterprise servers, public cloud servers, etc.). Since the microservices contain all the runtime dependencies packaged together in a standardized format, microservices run everywhere without a hitch or hurdle. The frictions between development, testing, staging, and production environments get eliminated through the flourishing containerization paradigm.
- The software portability goal, which has been hanging too long, is being fulfilled through the containerization. The Docker platform enables software developers and assemblers to quickly produce containerized applications and run them everywhere. Now, enterprise and cloud IT environments are being stuffed with a large number of containers hosting and running microservices, which, when composed, result in mission-critical, enterprise-grade, service-oriented, and event-driven applications.
- The lifecycle activities of containers are accomplished through container orchestration platforms such as Kubernetes.

### 10.3.1.1 Overview of Kubernetes

Kubernetes is an open source container orchestration and management platform that automates and manages the deployment of containers, resource allocation of the containers, health check and monitoring, replication and auto-scaling of containers, the abstraction of containers to expose it as a service and load-balancing, service discovery, etc. Different components of the Kubernetes platform [2] are shown in Figure 10.3

On a conceptual level, Kubernetes is made up of a bunch of nodes with different roles. The control plane on the master node(s) consists of the API server, the controller manager, and scheduler(s). The API server is the central management entity and the only component that talks directly with the distributed storage component etcd. It provides the following core functions [3]:

- Serves the Kubernetes API which is used by the worker nodes.
- Proxies cluster components such as the Kubernetes UI.
- Allows for the manipulation of the state of objects, for example, pods and services.
- Persists the state of objects in a distributed storage (etcd).

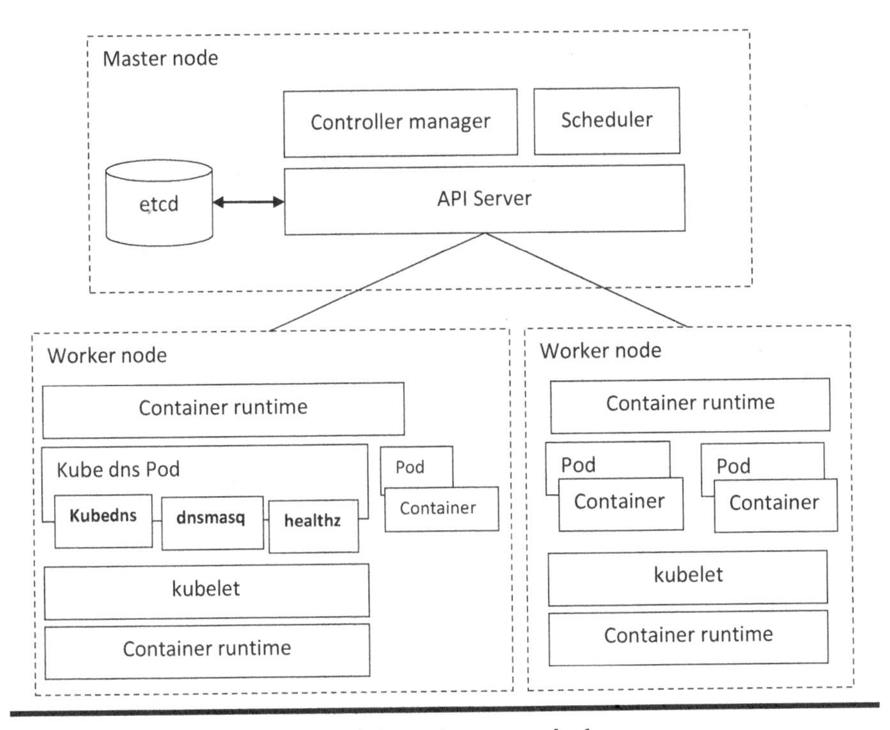


**Figure 10.3 The components of the Kubernetes platform.**

**API server**—The API server exposes APIs to perform CRUD operations on cluster resources. It validates the requests, executes business logic residing in different components, and persists the resulting state in *etcd*. The API server is accessible outside of the cluster for clients to perform administrative tasks.

The etcd is a distributed key-value persistent store where all cluster states are persisted.

**Scheduler**—The scheduler is responsible for watching unscheduled pods and binds them to run on specific nodes. It automatically schedules containers to run on specific nodes depending on resource and replication requirements. Scheduler knows the resources available on the nodes and selects a node to run pods depending on the resource availability and resources required by the pod.

**Controller manager**—The controller manager is responsible for running various types of controllers. Controllers watch the current state of the cluster and take corrective action to bring the cluster to the desired state. Some examples of controllers are a node controller and replication controller. A node controller is responsible for monitoring the node and takes corrective action if a node goes down. Similarly, a replication controller monitors the number of pods running and schedules new pods to be created if some of them go down to achieve the defined replication state.

**Kubelet** is the agent running on every node of the cluster and implements the pod and node APIs for the execution of containers. It is responsible for monitoring the containers and makes sure that they are running. It takes the pod specs and executes containers as per the specs.

**Kube-proxy** is a component that enables service abstraction. It proxies the client requests and routes it to pods within the node to load balance the requests.

**A pod** is a basic unit of Kubernetes which is created and deployed. It wraps the application containers and runs them on a node. Pods are mutable objects which are created and destroyed. One pod represents a single instance of an application. It can be replicated across nodes to provide high availability and elastic scalability. When defining a pod, the allocation of computing resources can be specified for the containers.

**Services**—As pods can be created and destroyed, there needs to be a mechanism to access the application through one endpoint. A service is an abstraction that defines a logical set of pods and routes client traffic to them. Pods can be created, destroyed, and replicated to multiple nodes, but clients can still access the backend pods through services.

**Kube DNS** is a built-in service that is scheduled to run as a pod in the cluster. Every service in the cluster is a given a DNS name. Services can be discovered by their DNS names. A Kube DNS pod runs three containers within it—*kubedns*, *dnsmasq*, and *healthz*. *Kubedns* keeps watching the Kubernetes master for changes to services and maintains the in-memory lookup to service DNS requests. *Dnsmasq* adds caching to improve performance, while *healthz* monitors the health of *kubedns* and *dnsmasq*.

## 10.3.2 Microservices Security Platform and Service Resiliency Platform

### Microservices Security Platform

Microservices-centric applications are distributed in nature, and hence networks play a crucial role in the success of microservices architecture. Microservices ought to be found and accessed over networks (internal as well as external). This means there may be many opened ports, which gradually increases the attack surface. We have to proxy microservices via a reverse proxy or use an API gateway layer. This way, we can shield and secure microservices from being exposed to the public network, and they can safely stay behind the enterprise firewall.

### Service Meshes for Service Resiliency

A service mesh is an inter-service communication infrastructure [4]. *Linkerd* and *Istio* are two popular open source service mesh implementations. With a service mesh:

- A given microservice does not directly communicate with the other microservices.
- Rather all service-to-service communications will take places on top of a software component called a service mesh or side-car proxy, as shown in Figure 10.4.
- A service mesh provides built-in support for some network functions such as resiliency, service discovery, etc. Therefore, service developers can focus more on business logic, while most of the work related to network communication

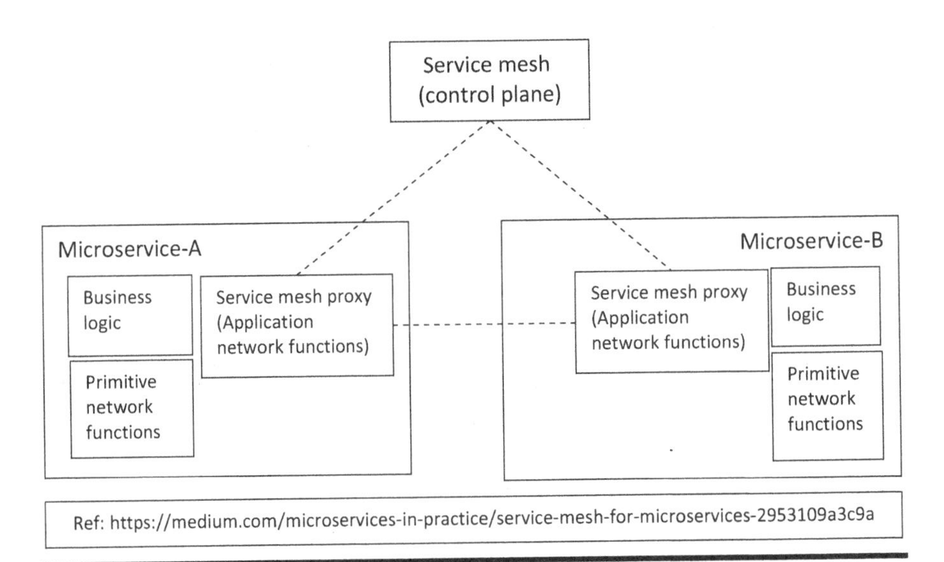


**Figure 10.4 Inter-service communication using a service mesh.**

is offloaded to the service mesh. Developers need not worry about circuit breaking when a microservice calls another service.

- A service mesh is language agnostic: Since the microservice to service mesh, proxy communication is always on top to standard protocols such as HTTP1.x/2.x, gRPC, etc., one can develop microservices using any technology.

**Business Logic**

The service implementation should contain the realization of the business functionalities of a given service. This includes logic related to its business functions, computations, integration with other services/systems(including legacy, proprietary, and SaaS) or service compositions, complex routing logics, mapping logic between different message types, etc.

**Primitive Network Functions**

Although most of the network functions are offloaded to a service mesh, a given service must contain the basic high-level network interactions to connect with the service mesh/side-car proxy. Typically, a given service uses network library functions to initiate network calls to service mesh.

**Application Network Functions**

There are application functionalities which are tightly coupled to the network, such as circuit breaking, timeouts, service discovery, etc. Those are explicitly separated from the service code/business logic, and service mesh facilitates those functionalities out of the box.

**Service Mesh Control Plane**

All service mesh proxies are centrally managed by a control panel. This is quite useful when supporting service mesh capabilities such as access control, observability, service discovery, etc.

### *10.3.3 API Platforms*

API platforms are the appropriate tool for building microservices. An API gateway is a single-entry point for all clients. It handles requests in one of two ways. Some requests are simply proxied or routed to the appropriate service. It handles other requests by fanning out to multiple services. With the wider adoption of microservices as the building block and deployment unit of cloud-enabled and native applications, there are open source as well as commercial-grade API gateway software solutions. The leading public cloud service providers (AWS, Azure, Google Cloud, IBM Cloud, etc.) use API gateway solutions for managing microservices APIs.

The Kong API gateway [5], a popular one in the open source category, acts as the middleware between service clients and API-attached and microservice-centric applications. It is extremely fast, RESTful, and platform-agnostic. Kong supports plug and play architecture, and hence it is possible to add additional capabilities (authentication, traffic control, rate limiting, logging, monitoring, analytics, etc.) through plugins. A typical Kong setup comprises two main components:

- Kong's server uses the widely adopted NGINX HTTP server, which is a reverse proxy that processes clients' requests to upstream services.
- Kong's data store is configured to allow the horizontal scaling of Kong nodes. Apache Cassandra and PostgreSQL can be used to fulfill this role.

Kong needs both of these components to be functional. Kong supports CLI and the admin API for managing Kong instances. The Kong dashboard provides a GUI for managing Kong instances. The Kong admin API can be accessed by Port 8001. Typically, services are created, and routes are added to them to access them through the Kong API gateway. Services have to be registered with the API gateway, which will create an upstream server in NGINX, the configuration of which is maintained in a data store. A single service can have many routes.

Further on, one can perform multiple actions to add, update, list and delete services, routes, and consumers. It is also possible to do active and passive health checks against service endpoints. One can also do load-balancing and proxy the requests to different upstream servers. Each node in Kong is stateless and is independent of others while handling requests from microservices clients. It is equally important to ensure the availability of a data store as it is the backbone of the API gateway. For production deployments, it is better to use Cassandra as a data store. There are other API gateway solutions on the market.

### *10.3.4 Microservices Development Platforms*

There are a few popular platforms such as Spring Boot emerging for building microservices.

**Spring Boot Platform**

Spring Boot is a project built on the top of the Spring framework. It provides a simpler and faster way to set up, configure, and run both simple and web-based applications when compared to the Spring core framework where one has to declare and manage many configuration files (XML descriptors) which is a tedious affair. This is the main reason why Spring Boot is acquiring a special significance in the development community.

Spring Boot smartly chooses all the articulated dependencies, and auto-configures all the features that are needed. It is possible to start the application with just a single click. Furthermore, it also simplifies the application deployment process. It does a number of things in the background, thereby the developers' workloads come down significantly.

The noteworthy features of the Spring Boot platform are:

- Spring Boot does the automatic configuration of an application by intelligently using the default information encoded in the class path and the application context. Also, it uses the various hints provided by the developers to configure an application. It takes the contextual information, and accordingly it does the whole thing. If we add a dependency in the *pom.xml* file and if it relates to a database, then Spring Boot assumes that the developer probably intends to leverage a database. Then, it auto-configures the application with database access. In short, when creating a Spring Boot Starter project, we select the features that our application needs and Spring Boot will manage the dependencies for us.
- It helps to realize standalone, enterprise-scale, and Spring-based applications. Thereby, the applications can run everywhere without any tweaking and twisting. With just a click, it can run on any web server.
- It provides production-ready features such as metrics, health checks, and other non-functional features such as security. It supports the externalized configuration.
- It reduces development time and increases productivity substantially.
- It provides a flexible way to configure Java Beans, XML configurations, and database transactions.
- It offers an annotation-based Spring application.
- It includes an embedded servlet container.

Spring Boot automatically configures an application based on the dependencies the developer has added to the project by using *@EnableAutoConfiguration* annotation. The entry point of the Spring Boot application is the class contains *@SpringBootApplication* annotation and the main method. Spring Boot automatically scans all the components included in the project by using *@ComponentScan* annotation. Not only enterprise-scale web applications but also business microservices are easily built by Spring Boot.

The reader can find out how to develop microservices using Spring Boot from the link [6]. In the above mentioned, there are three services, namely the Eureka service, item catalog service, and edge service. We have implemented all three microservices and shown how are registered with the Eureka service, and supplied a pictorial demonstration through a few screenshots. The first screenshot is the output of the Eureka service, which is a service registry. Other services have to register themselves with this Eureka service in order to be found and used. The above services have been developed using the following software:

1. Java version is Java SE Development Kit 8u202.
2. Eclipse IDE 2019-03.
3. Spring Boot 4.

The same outputs as in [6] have been obtained using the latest software versions. The output of the first service (Eureka service) is given in Figure 10.5.

The second service is the item catalog service. This is registered with the Eureka service and implemented and run. The result is shown in Figure 10.6.

Finally, the third and last service implemented is the edge service, and the result is given in Figure 10.7.

(*Note: The Source code for the above services can be obtained by email.*)

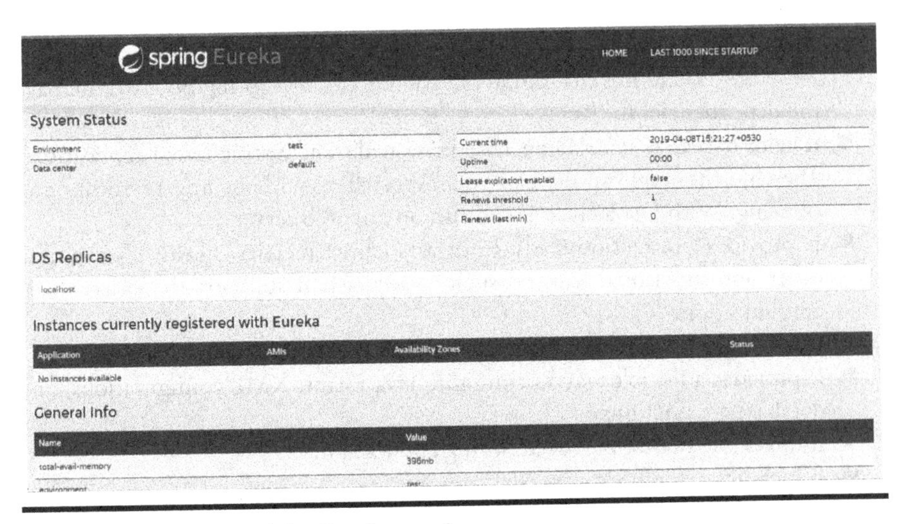


**Figure 10.5 Output of the Eureka service.**

**Figure 10.6 The item catalog service added to the Eureka service.**

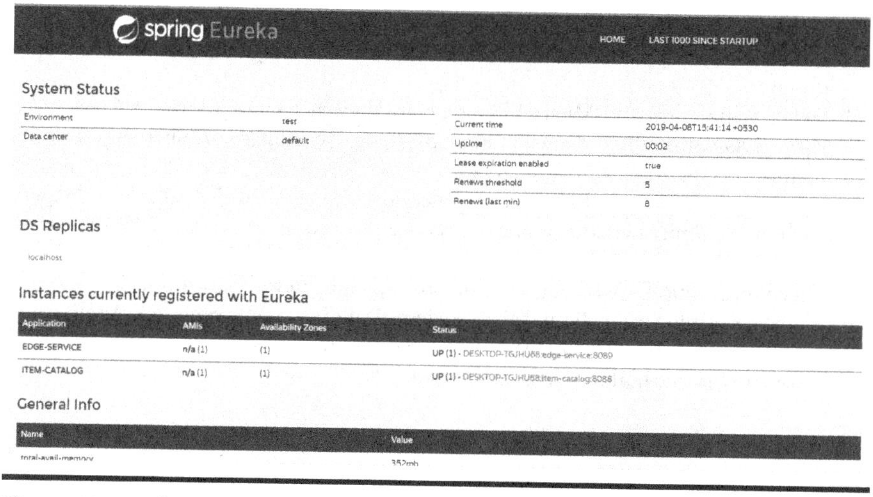

**Figure 10.7 The Edge service added to the Eureka service.**

### *Summary*

Microservices have emerged as the most efficient building block for next-generation applications across business verticals. MSA tends to design, develop, and deploy microservices-centric applications in an agile manner. However, there is a need for a few platform solutions in order to leverage the various benefits of MSA in an effective fashion. There are several regular and repetitive tasks while building microservices. These tasks are meticulously accomplished through versatile platform solutions. This chapter has listed the various MSA platforms and also described how these platforms come in handy with the beneficial usage of the unique MSA style.

### *Exercises*

1. Why do we need microservices platforms?
2. Explain in detail the different kinds of microservices platforms.
3. How does Kubernetes facilitate the deployment of microservices.
4. List the different features of Spring Boot.
5. Write some notes on service mesh.
6. Explain in detail the different capabilities of microservices platforms.

## References

1. Max Martynov. Why You Need a Microservices Management Platform and How to Build It. Grid Dynamics. Available at: https://blog.griddynamics.com/build-a-microservices-platform-for-replatforming/.

2. Vishwa Ranjan. Microservices and Traditional Middleware Platforms. DZone. 2018. Available at: https://dzone.com/articles/microservices-amp-traditional-middlware-platforms.
3. Stefan Schimanski and Michael Hausenblas. Kubernetes Deep Dive: API Server—Part 1. OpenShift. 2017. Available at: https://blog.openshift.com/kubernetes-deep-dive-api-server-part-1/.
4. Kasun Indrasiri. Service Mesh for Microservices. *Medium*. 2017. Available at: https://medium.com/microservices-in-practice/service-mesh-for-microservices-2953109a3c9a.
5. Faren. KONG—The Microservice API Gateway. Medium. 2018. Available at: https://medium.com/@far3ns/kong-the-microservice-api-gateway-526c4ca0cfa6.
6. Samarpit Tuli. Spring Boot Microservices: Building a Microservices Application Using Spring Boot. DZone. 2018. Available at: https://dzone.com/articles/spring-boot-microservices-building-microservices-a.

# Index

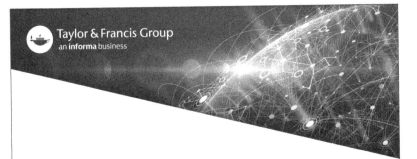